# Melting Pot Soldiers

THE UNION'S ETHNIC REGIMENTS

# THE NORTH'S CIVIL WAR

1. Anita Palladino, ed., *Diary of a Yankee Engineer: The Civil War Story of John H. Westervelt, First New York Volunteer Engineer Corps*

2. Herman Belz, *Abraham Lincoln, Constitutionalism, and Equal Rights in the Civil War Era*

3. Earl Hess, *Liberty, Virtue, and Progress: Northerners and Their War for the Union*

# Melting Pot Soldiers

## THE UNION'S ETHNIC REGIMENTS

SECOND EDITION

## William L. Burton

Fordham University Press
New York
1998

Copyright © 1998 by FORDHAM UNIVERSITY PRESS
All rights reserved.
LC 97–50163
ISBN 0-8232-1827-9 (*hardcover*)
ISBN 0-8232-1828-7 (*paperback*)
ISSN 1089-8719
The North's Civil War, No. 4

Library of Congress Cataloging-in-Publication Data

Burton, William L., 1928–
    Melting pot soldiers : the Union's ethnic regiments / by William
L. Burton.
      p.  cm.—(North's Civil War ; no. 4)
    Originally published: Ames : Iowa State University Press, 1988.
    Includes bibliographical references (p.   ) and index.
    ISBN 0-8232-1827-9 (hardcover).—ISBN 0-8232-1828-7 (pbk.)
    1. United States—History—Civil War, 1861–1865—Participation,
Immigrant.  2. United States—History—Civil War, 1861–1865—
Regimental histories.  3. United States.  Army—Minorities—
History—19th century.  4. United States.  Army—History—Civil
War, 1861–1865.  5. Immigrants—United States—History—19th
century.  I. Title.  II. Series.
E540.F6B87   1998
973.7′4—dc21                         97-50163
                                              CIP

Printed in the United States of America

For Ruthann

# Contents

*Preface to the Second Edition*    *ix*
*Preface*    *xiii*

1   PROLOGUE    *3*

2   ETHNIC POLITICS    *15*

3   "THE WAR IS COMMENCED"    *33*

4   RECRUITING THE ETHNICS    *46*

5   THE GERMAN REGIMENTS    *72*

6   THE IRISH REGIMENTS    *112*

7   THE OTHERS    *161*

8   SONG AND STORY    *176*

9   THE ETHNIC FACTOR    *199*

10   "WHAT THEN IS THE AMERICAN, THIS NEW MAN?"    *213*

*Notes*    *235*
*Selected Bibliography*    *257*
*Index*    *275*

# Preface to the Second Edition

A NEW EDITION of a book offers the author an opportunity to re-visit the subject, sometimes after the passage of several years. It is a chance for reflection, for pondering anew the original approach, for acknowledging errors, and for recognizing the contributions that readers make to the author's work. This volume corrects a few typographical slips in the first edition, and one or two factual errors caught by reviewers.

One of the real pleasures flowing from the initial publication of *Melting Pot Soldiers* was the response from readers. I heard, sometimes in voluminous correspondence, from readers in both this and other countries. The American Civil War has its addicts in other nations as well as our own. Most of these correspondents wanted to share their own research, or to request additional information or bibliography on their special interests. I am grateful to all who those who reacted in this fashion. Many Americans have an intense interest in ancestors who fought in the Civil War, and they devour books that offer a new perspective on their ancestors' experiences.

Some readers and some reviewers vigorously challenged this or that interpretation found in *Melting Pot Soldiers*. It is a mug's game to argue with reviewers; those most critical wanted a different sort of book altogether, while the friendly commentators (by far the majority) had the wisdom to recognize what the book attempted to do. And what the book attempted to do was offer a new frame of reference on ethnicity and the Civil War soldier.

Soon after the book appeared a friend who read it commented that I managed to "trash the Irish." But the comment was offered tongue-in-cheek because she realized that *Melting Pot Soldiers* did not "trash" any ethnic group; it simply argued that for most foreign-born soldiers ethnicity was just one aspect of their character, not the burning core of their very being. Today's romantic, who tailors the past to promote a favorite cause, abandons late nineteenth-century and early twentieth-century imagery with great reluctance. The very language commonly employed in descriptions of foreign-born soldiers in the Civil War singles them out as a race apart, men (and a few women) who differed fundamentally from their fellows either as heroes or as victims.

Reading the letters and accounts of the lives of individuals makes it clear that the ethnic soldier for the most part shared the motivations of his native-born counterparts. This does not denigrate the ethnic or detract from his contribution to the war effort; it makes him a complete human being. Recent scholarship more and more supports this view.

Individuals then and now act out of complex motivation. The typical Union volunteer (it was the same for the Confederate counterpart) did not rush to the colors solely from a sense of patriotism. To note, for example, that money was a factor in the decision to enter the military for many—perhaps most—volunteers is not to trash their motivations; it acknowledges the reality of their lives. Niels Peter Stilling and Anne Lisbeth Olsen, in their new study of Danish immigration to the United States, note that more than 500 young men left Denmark to enlist in the Union army, attracted by what from their perspective was the excellent pay for the soldier.[1] When German immigrant Marcus M. Spiegel made the decision in 1861 to volunteer for a Union regiment, he acted in part out of financial desperation: "This is the only time," he wrote to his wife, "that I can see a clear way of getting enough money to keep us comfortable."[2] Neither those young Danes, nor the Germans, nor the other foreign-born volunteers, differed in this respect from their American-born contemporaries.

The American Civil War was a thoroughly politicized war, especially so in the matter of creating armies North and South. Just as immigrants were by 1861 deeply involved in the North's political system, so were they deeply involved in the politics of forming Union regiments. Ethnic political leaders, like their native-born counterparts, enthusiastically plunged into regimental politics as a path to post-war careers. Some did not make it; they died in battle. But many survivors parlayed their military service into a political career, at the local, state, or national level. This is a feature of every American war, and so it is no surprise to find immigrants playing this familiar game. It does not diminish their contribution to the war effort to recall this fact.

The ethnic regiments in the Civil War, those units formed early in the war to appeal specifically to certain immigrants, were a paradox. On the one hand, they were a unique feature of this war, the only American war making a significant use of such units, and thus evidence that immigrants were "different" from other Americans. On the other hand, their appeal was only to a minority of those immigrants, most of whom joined "regular" regiments. Moreover, foreign-born soldiers joining an ethnic regiment often did so to demonstrate their 100% Americanism!

A central argument of *Melting Pot Soldiers* is that the Civil War acceler-

---

[1] See *A New Life: Danish Emigration to North America as Described by the Emigrants Themselves, 1842–1946* [Aalborg, Denmark: Danish Worldwide Archives, 1994], p. 13.

[2] See Jean Powers Soman and Frank L. Byrnes, eds., *A Jewish Colonel in the Civil War: Marcus M. Spiegel of the Ohio Volunteers* [Lincoln and London: University of Nebraska Press, 1994], p. 32.

ated the assimilation process for European immigrants. As Jacob R. Marcus of the American Jewish Archives recently put it, "For immigrants, for Jews, the war was an Americanizing forcing house."[3] Since so many immigrant volunteers themselves saw it this way, the only surprise is that it took posterity so long to recognize this facet of American history.

I welcome this opportunity, in a new edition, to have *Melting Pot Soldiers* reach a new and wider audience.

January 1997       W.L.B.

---

[3] In ibid., p. viii.

# Preface

It is a truism that historians tend to ask
questions about the past that are of direct
concern to the societies in which they live.

—LAWRENCE STONE, *Past and Present*

AMERICA is a nation of immigrants. This fundamental fact makes ethnicity one of the major themes in American history. Powerful and conflicting images appear and reappear in the enormous literature which tries to explain the nation's character. On the one hand, America is the haven of the oppressed, the refuge sought by millions of fearful, hopeful, and ambitious people from around the globe. This is the America symbolized by the Statue of Liberty, rags-to-riches success literature, and the conceit of many Americans that theirs is basically a good society. Opposed to this is the image of America as a land of bigotry and oppression, a land where immigrants encountered a harsh and prejudiced old-stock population, a land where ethnic minorities faced and still face exploitation and even violence. Historians regularly portray this image as one of the darker sides of the American character. According to this image, the record of ethnicity in America is part of the betrayal of the American Dream.

There are two ways to cope with these conflicting images, to reconcile them without doing violence to reason and logic. First, there is the reality of another fundamental fact: America is far from unique in being a nation of immigrants and an arena for contending ethnic groups. From India to Indonesia, Algeria to Argentina, or France to Formosa, ethnic conflict is the norm not the exception. Far from being unique in its history of ethnicity, the United States shares something that is part of the human condition. What is the record of ethnic conflict in other countries? Most of the world, for hundreds or even thousands of years, has been all too familiar with bloody confrontations between majorities and minorities, and ethnic minority fighting ethnic minority. So inured is the world to this spectacle that when hundreds of thousands of people died in genocidal fighting in Rwanda and Burundi in the 1960s and 1970s, neither the United Nations nor the Organization of African Unity took particular notice of the slaughter. The tragic spectacle of the ethnic Chinese fleeing Vietnam a decade ago was a grim reminder of the carnage in Indonesia ten years earlier when perhaps half a million Chinese died under the attacks of the old-stock Indonesians. The world accepts virtually as routine the deaths of thousands of people in ethnic conflicts in Sri Lanka, India, Syria, Bangladesh, Indonesia, Zimbabwe, and dozens of other countries. Seen in this context, the American image, even at its darkest, brightens considerably.

A second way to grapple with the conflicting images is to take a fresh look at the ethnic experience in America. Edmund Burke, writing his *Reflections on the Revolution in France,* complained that people have a tendency to draw the wrong moral lessons from history. History, he continued, was a vast storehouse of wisdom and error, and people rummaged around in it looking for materials they could use to attack political enemies and promote civil dissension. As jaundiced as Burke's view was, there is a certain element of realism in it. Add to it the attitude expressed in the everyday saying, "Familiarity breeds contempt," and the result can be pure cynicism. Cynicism is skepticism run rampant. The darker image of the ethnic experience in America includes much cynicism, along with ignorance about the rest of the world, and a disillusionment over the failure of the United States to live up to its own ideals. A common perception of pre–Civil War America is that of a society in which a bigoted Anglo-Saxon majority debased and exploited ethnic minorities, and immigrants arrived only to find themselves the victims of a system more vicious than that from which they fled. This is the perception found in such influential studies as Ray Allen Billington's *The Protestant Crusade, 1800–1860.* But there is another side to that coin. That other side shows America as a society in which immigrants quickly acquired political skills and political power. Within a remarkably short time after their arrival in the United States in large numbers, ethnic groups elected candidates to public office and compelled the existing major political parties to bargain with them. They formed their own militia units and controlled increasing numbers of city governments. The remarkable thing about the Know-Nothing phenomenon, after all, was not that it occurred but that it was doomed before it began. The power of the ethnics was already greater than that of the xenophobes, while the majority of "old-stock" Americans rejected xenophobia.

When I began research on ethnic regiments in the Union armies it was in the context of Ella Lonn's *Foreigners in the Union Army and Navy.* Lonn's large-scale work, the standard reference on the subject, was, as I quickly realized, both monumental in scope and extraordinarily dated and old-fashioned in its language and interpretation. Lonn accepted nineteenth-century views of "race," and her descriptions were stereotypical and as filiopietistic as the most ardent champions of ethnic separation. While her work remains invaluable as a source of information—despite its errors and omissions—its lack of critical analysis reduces its value for a real understanding of the subject. My initial assumption was that the subject of ethnic regiments offered an opportunity for colorful stories that would give substance and background to the contemporary debate over assimilation versus pluralism. That assumption was short lived.

In her wise and informative book, _Medieval People,_ Eileen Power wrote:

> Almost all that is worth knowing has to be mined like precious metals out of a rock; and for one nugget the miner often has to grub for days underground in a mass of dullness; and when he has got it he has to grub in his own heart, or else he will not understand it.

Power's admonition to the research historian beautifully fits the student of ethnicity in the Civil War. The nuggets are buried in the archives and libraries of the northern states, from Missouri to New England. Where they survive, the files of the individual regiments contain the ore that is the historian's raw material. Almost as valuable are the collected papers of governors and other state officials involved in both party politics and military recruitment and organization. As I went through the correspondence and other documents related to the ethnic regiments, I quickly realized that the subject was both different from and more significant than I originally envisioned.

Like the other volunteer regiments, the ethnic regiments were a direct outgrowth of state and local politics. Their formation, their relationships with the larger society, and their evolution tell us much about the mechanisms and attitudes of Civil War society. A vital concern of the historian is _change over time._ Almost no attention is given to this critical matter in previous studies of ethnic regiments. One of the most important things to learn about Civil War ethnic units is that they did change over time, and the changes tell us much about the role of ethnics in America.

Widely accepted canons of scholarship in the Western world demand objectivity, adherence to the evidence, and the use of critical analysis. We take for granted the application of such standards in most historical writing, but we accept without question a departure from them in certain kinds of history. Many states have laws requiring teachers to teach their students about the "contributions" of politically potent ethnic groups. No laws call for the application of conventional critical analysis to that history. The time is long past when America can afford a double standard in scholarship, with critical analysis reserved for some kinds of history and conveniently ignored for others.

_Melting Pot Soldiers_ is an effort to apply traditional historical analysis and a critical use of evidence to a highly emotional subject. An understanding of that subject relates directly to a major debate about the nature and character of American society. One of the most significant conclusions drawn in this study is that ethnicity, in the Civil War generation as today, is a fertile field of political exploitation. There are always people ready and eager to use it for their personal advantage. Equally important is the conclusion that the vast majority of both ethnics and nonethnics recognized the opportunists for what they were, and that whatever else they symbolized, the ethnic regiments represented the basic loyalty and patriotism of immigrants as well as their skill in manipulating political practices and institutions to their advantage.

I owe many debts, only some of which can be acknowledged here. The University Research Council of Western Illinois University provided financial support for some of the research. Dedicated and helpful archivists and librarians in city and state libraries and agencies gave access to regimental and other document collections absolutely essential to the study. Interlibrary loan personnel at my own university and others responded cheerfully to years of requests. Professor Ronald Rayman, formerly of the Western Illinois University Library, deserves special thanks. Dr. David Overy of the St. Cloud State University in Minnesota read the entire manuscript, made many helpful suggestions, and would certainly disown any responsibility for the results. Several generations of graduate assistants at Western, including John Allaman, Qi Wang, Jiwen Zhang, David Nolan, and David Faries, helped uncover obscure bits of information. My departmental colleagues and my wife suffered through years of my preoccupation and even obsession with the "ethnic regiments project." Whatever errors lurk in the finished product are my own.

# Melting Pot Soldiers

## THE UNION'S ETHNIC REGIMENTS

# Prologue

RIEDRICH KARL FRANZ HECKER found life on his southern Illinois farm a far cry from the romantic glories of revolutionary battlefields in Germany. "He presented a rather pitiable figure," Carl Schurz wrote to his wife after an 1854 visit. Hecker, the once dashing officer, " . . . now wore a gray woolen shirt, baggy and shabby trousers, and a pair of old carpet slippers." Once a handsome man, Hecker in 1854 was haggard, sallow, and weary. The Hecker farm was a humble log abode, its owner a tortured man, living in the past because his present life was not worth living. Happy to see his old friend, Schurz, Hecker cursed his illness (malaria). "Ah," he told Schurz, "you will see what will become of an old revolutionist when he has to live on quinine pills."[1] The two men parted, Schurz to continue his lengthy American tour on which he would hone his English and political skills, Hecker to remain behind, vegetating on his Belleville acres.

Less than six years earlier, Hecker had arrived in New York to a hero's welcome. One of the military leaders of the 1848 Revolution in Germany, he fled to Switzerland when the revolution failed. From his Swiss exile he emigrated to America; there he hoped to collect funds to support new assaults on the Prussian government. Hecker soon learned, however, that while many Americans cheered European rebels, they had little interest in financing them. Like millions of other immigrants, Hecker went to work.

A succession of jobs took the ex-soldier and lawyer to Philadelphia, Cincinnati, and St. Louis. During his stay in Cincinnati he founded the first Turner organization (gymnastic club) in the United States. From St. Louis, Hecker crossed the Mississippi River and purchased a farm near Belleville, thus becoming one of the famed "Latin Farmers," German-Americans noted and named for their educational and intellectual attainments.[2] Hecker's odyssey differed from that of thousands of other Forty-Eighter exiles only in its details.

Already settled in the Belleville area when Hecker arrived was the family of Heinrick (Henry) Kircher. Born in Beardstown, Illinois, in 1841, Henry Kircher and his family moved to Belleville in 1848. His father, Joseph Kircher, went into the hardware business in partnership with Henry Goedeking. Joseph Kircher, who had been a classmate of Gustave Koerner when the two studied law in Munich, migrated to America in 1833 and, after a marriage to a fellow German migrant, started raising a large family. His business partner was elected president of Belleville's first school board in 1848. Goedeking was more than a business acquaintance; he was also young Henry's godfather. Henry himself attended Oakfield Academy, a German-American school.[3] Hecker lived in the midst of a thriving, well-established German community. The Kirchers and Goedekings, in America for its economic opportunities, fit closely the profile of the typical German in the United States. There were only a few thousand Forty-Eighters like Hecker, but their influence and visibility outweighed their modest numbers.

Carl Schurz was among the most visible. Schurz was attending the University of Bonn when he was caught up in the revolutionary events of the day. First as a student leader in the university and later as a lieutenant in the rebel militia, Schurz's life changed forever as a result of his participation in the tumultuous events of 1848–1849. Like Hecker, Schurz fled first to Switzerland; from there he went to England and thence to Paris. Expelled from France as a dangerous foreigner, he returned to England and then made his way to America, arriving here in 1852.[4] Where Hecker never felt comfortable speaking English, and never lost his strong German accent, Schurz quickly mastered both spoken and written English. This skill, along with his interest in politics, encouraged Schurz's involvement in German-American public affairs.

When he visited Hecker, Schurz was on a lengthy tour of his new country. He liked what he saw and was excited by the prospects. In 1856 he bought a small farm in Watertown, Wisconsin. That same year he threw in his lot with the new Republican party in that state. His first major political enterprise was supporting the Frémont campaign before German-American audiences. In 1857 Wisconsin Republicans nominated him for lieutenant governor even though he was not yet a citizen. Schurz lost that race, but his skill as an orator and his ability to sway partisan audiences was established. By 1858 he was campaigning for Abraham Lincoln. Henry Goedeking's modest role in local politics was a commonplace for immigrants in mid-nineteenth-century America. Schurz's ambitions were national.

Hard work and ability won Schurz a national reputation. The revolutionary exile became a fixture on the American political scene. In 1858 he struck a blow against the rapidly fading nativist sentiment in the East. "True Americanism," an address delivered in Boston, helped defeat a proposal in Massachusetts to deny the ballot to foreign-born voters for two years after their naturalization. This confirmed his credentials as a spokesman for the immigrant population, but Schurz was far more than this; he was a political leader in his own right, for the native American as well as for the immigrant. In 1860 he led the Wisconsin delegation to the Republican national convention.

When Hecker and Schurz fought in Baden in 1848, at their side was a former Prussian officer, Augustus Willich. Willich had an unlikely background for a rebel. His father was an army officer, and he himself had a military education before entering the service. While in the Prussian army, however, Willich took the lead of a group of officers interested in reading and discussing forbidden books. His republican political ideas caught the eye of his superior officers, and Willich faced a court martial. He resigned his commission, took up the carpenter's trade (to demonstrate his commitment to the proletariat), and in 1848 Willich joined the revolution in Germany. Like Hecker and Schurz, he sought exile first in Switzerland, and then began a period of wandering that eventually took him to America.

By then Willich was a confirmed Marxist, an ideology that remained with him for the rest of his life. Far from a dogmatist, he carried on a war of words with Karl Marx; in a veritable duel of books the two men hurled charges and countercharges at each other. Following his 1853 migration to the United States, Willich held a variety of jobs in the East, where a chance encounter brought him into contact with another remarkable German-American — Johann Bernhard Stallo. That encounter led Willich in 1858 to Cincinnati.[5]

Only a novelist with a vivid imagination might set such a scene. Here, on the banks of the Ohio, an ardent socialist, a middle-aged revolutionary exile from Germany, an ex-Prussian officer and carpenter, was taken in hand by a pillar of the local establishment. Willich started still another career under Stallo's tutelage, this time as the editor of the *Republikaner,* a German-language newspaper. Schurz visited Cincinnati on his 1854 tour, and he found the "Queen City of the West" at that time a lively, growing municipality with a large German population. "The Germans live together in one part of the city — at least most of them," he reported to his wife, "and their streets are easily recognized by the conspicuous but not very advantageous old-country customs."[6] Cincinnati in the middle of the pre–Civil War decade still had a strong German character. Most of the foreigners living in the city were Germans, and two city wards were 50 percent German. These wards together carried the nickname "Over-the-Rhine," and their beer gardens and other cultural institutions gave that part of Cincinnati a distinctly European atmosphere.[7] Undaunted by the middle-class respectability of the German community, Willich used his newspaper editorials to promote socialism, denounce Catholicism, and criticize all organized religion. In its general political stance, however, the *Republikaner* backed Republican candidates and policies in Ohio, first Frémont and then Lincoln.

Who was the J. B. Stallo who enticed Willich to Cincinnati? He was not a Forty-Eighter and definitely not a revolutionary. Born in Sierhausen, Germany, in 1823, Stallo learned to read before he was four. In addition to Dutch, English, and French, he mastered the classical languages. At the age of sixteen, Stallo emigrated to America in search of economic opportunity. He lived first in the home of an uncle in Cincinnati, and then taught at St. John's College in Fordham, New York. He returned to Cincinnati to practice law, and he was there to give the welcoming address to Friedrich Hecker when the revolutionary hero paused in the Queen City in 1849.

Stallo was a polymath. Master of languages, a teacher, and a lawyer, he studied chemistry and physics and published significant work in philosophy. His *General Principles of the Philosophy of Nature* (1848) publicized Hegelian and evolutionary ideas in America.[8] Although raised a Catholic, Stallo renounced his religion, married a Protestant, and as a judge in Cincinnati raised his children in a thoroughly middle-class home. A leading figure in the German-American community, Stallo was a popular speaker and helped found the Republican party in Ohio. He recognized in Augustus Willich another extraordinary mind and lured him to Cincinnati. The judge tried to wean the ex-Prussian officer away from his Marxism, but had no success. Stallo was a Frémont elector in 1856 and supported Lincoln in 1860.

Stallo's career and the Kirchers and Goedekings in Belleville remind us that only a small part of the German population in America in the mid–nineteenth century were Forty-Eighter exiles. Most emigrated to the United States for economic opportunity. George Engelmann, for example, after a medical education at the University of Berlin and the University of Würzburg, came to America in 1832 with a commission from an uncle to look for profitable investments in land. He visited the Latin Farmers near Belleville, traveled to the Southwest, and then settled down to the development of a lucrative medical practice in St. Louis. One reason his medical career prospered was his skill with language; he was at home in English and French as well as in German.[9] Other Engelmanns were a part of the Latin Farmer settlement in Illinois. Not far from Hecker's little farm near Belleville, Adolphus Engelmann, the son of Friederich Engelmann, labored with his family to reproduce on the Illinois prairie the vineyards of Germany. In section 20, township 1 south, range 6 west, the Engelmann farm, "Looking Glass Vineyard," perched on a gently sloping hillside with a magnificent view of the Kaskaskia River valley. Beneath the house an arched brick wine cellar stored the bottled products of Scuppernong and Muscadine grape arbors.[10]

Adolphus Engelmann, born in 1825, served his adopted country in the Mexican War and suffered a severe wound. In 1848, while visiting Germany, he fought for Prussia in the war against Denmark. Although a staunch Republican, Engelmann was more interested in wine and his crops and flowers than in politics. He and his fellow Latin Farmers often provided hospitality to German visitors, and they shared practical knowledge about Illinois farming with newcomers like Friedrich Hecker. On the Illinois prairie as on the streets of Cincinnati, German-Americans recreated the culture of Germany.

Even more successful at such cultural replication were the Germans of Pennsylvania. Schurz was amazed at what he found there on his American circuit:

> What an astonishing spectacle these Pennsylvania Germans presented! Honest, pious, hardworking, prosperous people; good, law-abiding, patriot American citizens; great-great-grandchildren of my own old Fatherland, who had for several generations tilled these acres and lived in these modest and comfortable houses and built these majestic barns, and preserved the German speech of their forefathers, only mixing in some words and phrases of English origin. They called all English-speaking people "the Irish," and kept alive many of their old German domestic customs and habits, though they had lost all memory of old Germany.[11]

Like Cincinnati, Philadelphia had a large and thriving German population, complete with a Turner society. Unlike their rural counterparts, the Philadelphia Germans faced direct challenges to the preservation of their Old Country culture. At midcentury, they still persevered.

What seems clear about the America of the 1850s is that German-Americans, in addition to having a secure and comfortable cultural identity, played the game of American politics at several different levels. Both within their ethnic enclaves and as citizens of the larger polity, they held elective office and understood and participated in broker state politics. Both as members of an ethnic bloc and as Americans they worked party machinery. While most German-Americans, like the majority of all Americans, were politically anonymous—holding views shared by other Democrats and Republicans—their most visible and influential leaders came from the Forty-Eighters or the earlier generation of revolutionary activity in Germany.

In New York City, for example, the leadership of the German community and the interface between the Germans and the larger society was in the hands of men like Friedrich Kapp. A Westphalian by birth, Kapp earned a law degree at the University of Berlin. His first role in the 1848 Revolution was that of a newspaper correspondent, but a year later he was a rebel soldier. Exiled to Switzerland, he made his way to America and arrived in New York in 1850 with total financial resources of two dollars. He entered law practice, but his first love remained politics and journalism. Kapp wrote for the *Nation* and other periodicals, and in less than a year after setting foot in New York he was editor of the *New Yorker-Abendzeitung.* He backed the new Republican party when it appeared and skillfully used oratory as well as the printed word to turn the city's German-American voters into a powerful voting bloc.[12]

In Chicago a fellow Westphalian acted a similar role. Casper Butz wrote revolutionary tracts in support of the 1848 rebellion, fled to America in 1849, and arrived in Chicago in 1854. An ardent abolitionist, Butz wrote for the *Staatszeitung* and threw himself into city and state politics. He eulogized John Brown in an 1859 poem and used his pen to attack nativism and Know-Nothingism. Butz won election to the Illinois General Assembly in 1859, and the deepening sectional crisis found him a radical Republican leader in a pivotal state, a spokesman for the largest bloc of ethnic voters in Illinois.[13]

In downstate Illinois another refugee from an earlier revolution wove another thread in the web of German-American politics. Related by marriage to the Engelmann family (he married Sophia Engelmann in 1836, and he came to America with the Engelmann family in 1833 after the failure of the Frankfurt Revolt), Gustave Koerner tried several different sites in the United States before settling among the congenial Latin Farmers in the Belleville area. Koerner found politics more to his liking than farming and before long he was the most prominent German-American in the state. Elected lieutenant governor in 1852, Koerner joined the new Republican party in 1856 and worked for Lincoln in 1860.[14]

Francis A. Hoffman worked alongside Koerner in Illinois Republican politics. Born in Prussia, Hoffman emigrated to the United States in 1839. He taught school, entered the Lutheran ministry, then studied law and moved to Chicago. Like Koerner, Hoffman felt drawn to politics and in short order found himself elected to the Chicago City Council. Again, like Koerner, Hoffman ran for the post of lieutenant governor in 1860; he attracted German-American voters to a ticket headed by Richard Yates. The Yates-Hoffman ticket triumphed, and Hoffman opened an office in Chicago where he served as the new governor's liaison with the large German community in that city.[15]

When Carl Schurz fought in the revolutionary army in the Palatinate, he fought in the company of Franz Sigel, Louis Blenker, and Alexander Schimmelfennig. All these men fled to America. Franz Sigel became a school teacher and in 1857 was in St. Louis teaching at the German-American Institute. Before the decade ended, he was director of schools for the whole city. Louis Blenker farmed in New York and then tried his hand at business in the city. Schimmelfennig, after working in Philadelphia, moved to Washington, D.C., and took an engineering position in the War Department. Of all the Forty-Eighter exiles, Schimmelfennig came closest to a continuing association with a military life.[16]

This cursory survey of German-America in the mid–nineteenth century both reveals and obscures some facts of life. It reveals some of the extraordinary individuals caught up in the intellectual and political life of the times. It suggests the close ties of background, friendship, and even family relationships that bound Germans living in St. Louis, Chicago, Belleville, Cincinnati, and New York (and many other cities as well). It notes the activist role played by so many revolutionary exiles in journalism and politics. These men formed a close-knit and exciting intellectual community. Another member of this community was Gustave Struve. Struve fought with Hecker in Germany, joined the trek of exiles to America, and edited a socialist newspaper in New York. The background, the ties, the careers in America—it all seems a virtual model.

Such a model is deceiving. Much more typical are the thousands of immigrants like Nikolas Greusel. Greusel's name is not the household word that is the case with Schurz or Koerner or Hecker. Born in Bavaria in 1817, Greusel emigrated to the United States in 1834, along with his family. The teenager promptly found himself on his own in a strange city, and he survived in large measure because he got shelter and help from an American family—the family of Hamilton Fish. Greusel lived a wandering life for years, following jobs in the Midwest and taking time to serve in the Mexican War in a Michigan regiment. As the Union approached the moment of crisis in 1860, Greusel lived in Aurora, Illinois, and worked for the Chicago, Burlington, and Quincy Railroad.[17]

The Greusels, not the Schurzes or Kapps, made up the bulk of "German America" in 1860.[18] The few thousand Forty-Eighters and the exiles from the Frankfurt revolt contributed an inordinate proportion of their numbers to positions of intellectual and political leadership. It was coincidence, not cause and effect, that so many Germans emigrated after the 1848 revolution; the great mass of emigrants left Germany for economic, not political, reasons.[19] By the thousands and hundreds of thousands the migrants left Germany, and most did not leave from areas of political unrest. It was the hope of economic opportunity, not fear of prosecution at home, not radical political ideas, that brought them to America. Once here, the typical German-American was most likely to find a political home in one of the two major parties, to work within the system. Temporarily gathering together in ethnic neighborhoods in cities like Cincinnati, the Germans gradually adopted the geographic mobility so characteristic of American society. Those most politically active in Europe were most politically active in America.

Thomas Francis Meagher was a glutton, drank too much, and was not to be trusted. At least that was the impression "Meagher of the Sword" made on Fenian courier James Stephens. Stephens, who was in the United States in 1858 on a fund-raising expedition for the cause of Irish nationalism, met Meagher in New York, and the two men discussed Fenian activities and Irish independence. Stephens was in a sour mood; his fund-raising fared poorly. He eagerly sought dollars for his own cause, but he was disdainful of Irish-Americans doing the same thing for themselves.[20] The two men met with other Irish nationalists in New York, traveled together to Washington to meet with Fenian sympathizers, and when he returned to Ireland, Stephens carried with him a written statement of support from Meagher. But Stephens was skeptical; he thought Meagher's support was lukewarm at best.

Stephens was wise to be skeptical. Shortly after his return to Ireland, he received a letter from Meagher. "My dear Stephens," began Meagher with just a touch of the superior communicating with an inferior. The rest of the letter was flowery and a bit vague, but one thing was clear. "Meagher of the Sword" wanted his name removed from the letter of support for the Fenian movement. He did not want to jeopardize his chances for a political career in the United States by an association with a revolutionary movement in Ireland.[21]

Thomas Francis Meagher, born orator, prince of a fellow, witty, an altogether superior gentleman, was in the late 1850s struggling for place and position in his adopted country.[22] A Democrat, like most of his fellow Irish-Americans, his political sympathies in the deepening sectional crisis were with the South.

Meagher's credentials as an Irish patriot were impeccable. From his birth in Waterford, Ireland, in 1823, to the dramatic events of the 1848 rebellion against English rule, his life was dominated by romantic visions of an independent Ireland. In that summer rising of 1848, Meagher was captured with arms in his hand (hence the "Meagher of the Sword" appellation). Tried for high treason, he was convicted and sentenced to be hanged, drawn, and quartered.[23] Meagher escaped this dismal end when his sentence was commuted to exile in Tasmania. He sailed to Tasmania, escaped from that island in 1852, and made his way to New York. There he studied law, became a popular lecturer and writer, ingratiated himself with the American as well as the Irish society, and failed in an effort to publish an Irish newspaper. Always on the fringes of New York's upper classes, and constantly worried about money and "appropriate" employment for what he regarded as a man of his stature, Meagher in 1860 was too concerned about his own future to commit himself enthusiastically and publicly to the Fenians.[24]

Michael Corcoran had no such worries. This Irish-born New Yorker gloried in his role as the city's most ardent Irish nationalist. The son of a British army officer and once a member of the Irish Constabulary, Corcoran joined a militia unit in New York when he emigrated to America in

1849. Along with many other Irish-Americans, he saw militia activities as a gateway to the higher levels of Irish society. His early employment was in the city's Hibernian Hall, and his life followed an almost classic pattern of ethnic politics in New York when he entered public employment. As *Harper's Weekly* put it in a sly dig at the municipal patronage system, Corcoran "occupied a desk" at the post office on the eve of the Civil War.[25]

Corcoran's military career prospered. He entered the Sixty-ninth New York State Militia Regiment as a private and by 1860 he was its colonel. Then his Irish nationalism and his status as a militia officer in an American regiment clashed, clashed publicly and with great fanfare. Britain's Prince of Wales paid a visit to New York, a visit that was a direct challenge to Irish nationalists in the United States. Corcoran's Sixty-ninth Militia Regiment received orders to parade in the prince's honor. Corcoran refused to obey the order. His refusal put New York City and state officials in a quandary. Corcoran's popularity and political clout made the situation a delicate one. A court martial would acerbate ethnic relations, but on the other hand, an order is an order. In the event, charges were brought, and as 1860 neared an end Colonel Corcoran of New York's Sixty-ninth Militia Regiment awaited court-martial, charged with wilful disobedience of orders.

Corcoran's counterpart in Chicago was James A. Mulligan. Mulligan never saw Ireland, but he was a flaming Irish nationalist nonetheless. He was born in Utica, New York, in 1829, and after his widowed mother moved the family to Chicago and remarried, Mulligan read law and began its practice in that city. Raised in a strict Catholic family environment, he had an excellent public reputation. "A purer, better man does not live in the State of Illinois," gushed one contemporary sketch.[26] Mulligan drew from his family a love of Ireland and devoted much of his public life to the cause of Irish nationalism. His wife Marion Nugent, whom he married in 1859, came from a prominent Irish-American family. Mulligan read avidly in Irish history, and he joined a militia company—Shield's Guards—known in Chicago as a badge of respectability for young Irish-Americans. The popular young Chicago lawyer had in 1860 a status that seemed both to fit the American success myth and at the same time defy the stereotype of the persecuted Irish Catholic.

Privately, Mulligan strayed a bit from this image. Although a prominent Irish nationalist, he seemingly remained aloof from the Fenians. "He never lent himself to any of the secret and foolish schemes and plottings which so often have compromised the real interest of Ireland . . . ," claimed one biographer.[27] "James A. Mulligan ain't no *Fenian,*" proudly boasted a priest who was Mulligan's personal friend, "nor will he touch any Secret Society with a nine foot pole."[28] Father Thaddeus J. Butler of Chicago's Church of the Immaculate Conception defended Mulligan during an

1864 feud within the Chicago Catholic community, and at the very time Mulligan enjoyed this defense and the warm support of the city's Catholic hierarchy, he was a secret Fenian supporter.

"I want to thank you . . . from the bottom of my heart . . . for your donation and handsome letter to the 'Fenian Brotherhood' of Chicago," ran one letter of appreciation to Mulligan from a Fenian. "*Long, long* may you live. And may you soon have the opportunity of showing to the world in general and Mankind in particular *Priests particularized* what it is to fight for Irish independence and Irish rights," continued his admirer.[29] Only a master politician, which Mulligan clearly was, could maintain a public image as friend and supporter of the Catholic church and an ardent Irish nationalist who was *not* a Fenian, but who privately gave financial and moral support to the Fenians who regarded Mulligan as one of their own. Like Meagher in New York, Mulligan was too concerned with his personal career to allow public Fenian connections to jeopardize it.

If extraction and family traditions could make an Irishman out of a native-born American like Mulligan, then a life of nine months in the Emerald Isle itself is more than enough to create an Irish nationalist. Thomas Cass, born in Queen's County, Ireland, in 1821, emigrated to America with his family when he was just nine months old. The Cass family, like thousands of other Irish immigrants, chose Boston for its destination. Boston, the home of Cabots and cod, was also the home of some of the strongest nativist sentiment in America in the nineteenth century. Thomas Cass encountered some of that nativism as an adult in Boston.[30]

Company B of the Fifth Regiment of the Massachusetts Militia had an old and honorable history. An artillery company, its lineage went back as far as 1789. In the nineteenth century, like many another militia company, it evolved into a social organization, a kind of club for young men of the upper-class society. At midcentury Company B suffered from lax discipline and financial mismanagement. Membership in the company lost some of the glitter and attraction. This opened its ranks to those whose social standing left something to be desired.

Young men of Irish families got invitations to join Company B, and one of those young men was Thomas Cass. By 1854 the young Irish-American was commander of the unit, known as the Columbia Artillery. The very next year newly elected Gov. Henry J. Gardner proposed a bill in the state legislature to ban all military companies composed of persons of foreign birth. Since the Columbia Artillery was now almost entirely Irish, the bill seemed aimed directly at it. Governor Gardner's inaugural address made clear his intention to limit service in the state militia to persons born in the United States, and the Massachusetts legislature soon passed a bill that followed these nativist sentiments. In protest, the men of Company B resigned their militia positions and formed their own quasi-military organization called the Columbia Association. This association kept intact the basic format of the old militia unit, but without state support or recognition.[31]

Thomas Cass, unlike Chicago's James Mulligan, had to find a way to continue his militia connection outside the law. The results for the two men in practical terms were actually quite similar, despite the legal differences between Massachusetts and Illinois. Each remained in the public eye in a military role and in a post with glamour and social standing. The matter is even more complicated and the parallel more apt when we learn that Cass was a very successful business man (he was a shipowner and a shareholder in the Boston Tow-Boat Company). Beyond that, Cass was active in the Democratic party, regularly served in ward offices, and at the end of 1860 was a member of the board of the School Committee for the city of Boston. This was a position of considerable power and influence for an Irishman in a city supposedly in the grip of Know-Nothingism and nativism.[32]

What happened in Boston was not unique. Connecticut experienced a similar revulsion against foreigners in state militia units. Like Massachusetts, the Nutmeg State for a brief period came under the influence of Know-Nothingism in the mid-1850s, and, like Massachusetts, suffered minimal consequences from this flirtation with nativism. A Connecticut law ordered the dissolution of all militia units whose members were foreign born. Thomas W. Cahill commanded one such unit. Cahill, born in Charleston, Massachusetts, in 1826, was one of the founders of the Washington Guards of New Haven. The group later changed its name to the Emmet Guard, a name more befitting its Irish character. That the Know-Nothing influence in New Haven was ephemeral can be seen in the fact that in 1859 Cahill won election as a New Haven alderman. He was reelected in 1860 and 1861.[33] Although born in the United States, Cahill, like Mulligan, was a leader in the Irish-American community and an Irish nationalist.

This sampling of Irish-Americans on the eve of the Civil War reflects the diversity of that ethnic group. For the Corcorans in big cities, content to pursue a career within the ethnic fold, open and enthusiastic Irish nationalism was invaluable. For the Meaghers and Mulligans, whose aspirations required acceptance and support from the larger society as well as the Irish, such sentiments were more cautious and hedged. Where a Cass or a Cahill found his military role modified by nativist reactions, a Corcoran or a Mulligan deliberately exploited militia connections for social and political advantage.

Election to public office, a share of political patronage, and growing influence within the two major parties were key features of the American political scene for both German-Americans and Irish-Americans as the nation moved past the midcentury mark. While a Carl Schurz with national fame and influence was rare, a Casper Butz or a Thomas Cass at the state or local level was common. The political leader whose role was that of imposing demands from an ethnic group on a major party, or rounding up support from an ethnic group for the party, was an established player in the political drama.

The ethnic scene in America was extraordinarily complex. Men like the Koerners, Engelmanns, Stallos, and Willichs constituted a lively, interconnected world of letters and politics; they had no real counterparts among the Irish-Americans. Both immigrant groups housed significant numbers of practicing politicians, people like Francis Hoffman, Friedrich Kapp, Thomas Cass, and Michael Corcoran. Whether in their urban centers, or scattered through the countryside and mingled with the larger population, the sheer number of immigrants forced other Americans to reckon with them.

# CHAPTER 2

# Ethnic Politics

*Alien,* n. An American sovereign in his probationary state.

—AMBROSE BIERCE, *The Devil's Dictionary*

ILLIAM A. ALLEN, working hard to establish a medical practice in downstate Illinois, used blunt language when he touched upon politics in letters to his wife, Millie:

> As to the party question I want to say, that *my* party contains a great many illiterate and unchristian members I am willing to admit, but that it contains anymore that any others I deny, it is also true that it is blessed with the drunken Irish but that class is not any greater than the filthy, ignorant superstitious Dutch that hangs to the tail of the Rep. party.[1]

Although a Democrat himself, Dr. Allen was clearly not happy with the large numbers of Irishmen associated with his party, and he looked with equal disdain upon the Germans, whom he automatically associated with the Republican party. His fellow Americans of 1860 widely shared the rural physician's prejudices, but the intolerance of language did not translate into action when it came to party politics.

Allen did *not* propose to Millie that her party expel its German members, and he certainly did not suggest that Democrats abandon their Irish supporters. Neither did he so much as hint that the two of them turn away from the major parties and join a nativist political party. Nativism by 1860 had little influence in serious political activity.

Numbers and geography explain the failure of nativism and reveal much of the story of ethnic politics in 1860 America.

The 1860 census counted 34,513,000 persons residing in the United States. Thirteen percent of these, well over four million people, were foreign born.[2] Almost half the foreign-born residents lived in the New England and Middle Atlantic states, while most of the remainder were in the states of the Old Northwest. Less than 10 percent of the nation's immigrant population lived in the South.

While climate, historical patterns of migration, the institution of slavery, the trans-Atlantic fare structure, and other factors helped shape the distribution pattern of immigrants, economic forces were the most potent determinants. America's immigrants came largely from northwestern Europe, and they crossed the Atlantic in search of economic opportunity. Nativist sentiment in some measure existed in every part of the nation, but nativism did little to influence the destination of the typical immigrant. Despite the outbreak of strong nativist sentiment in New England in the 1850s, for example, both Irish and French-Canadian settlers continued to pour into the region's cities. Southern blacks regarded immigrants with contempt, looking upon them as "white niggers." But it was lack of economic opportunity that kept most migrants out of the South, not the sentiments of the inhabitants. Demand for white labor in the South was low, and European peasant farmers led a miserable existence there.[3]

Four European sources supplied the bulk of America's aliens. Ireland, the many German states, Britain (a classification that included English, Scots, and Welsh), and Scandinavia sent their sons and daughters to North America in a human tide. Oftentimes the migrants had a choice of destinations. Canada and the other British dominions, Latin America, and even other European countries attracted a share of the migrants, but most chose the United States.

Dramatic rhetoric associated with the Know-Nothing movement of the 1850s obscures its short life and failure. Democrats and Republicans for the most part refused to pander to nativist political demands. Indeed, the Know-Nothing party itself, short lived as it was, came into being in large measure because neither the Whigs (and later the Republicans) nor the Democrats catered to those Americans who wanted antiforeign action. The two major parties instead *courted* the immigrant, seeking to recruit him both as voter and as party activist. Democrats and Republicans in Congress consistently spurned Know-Nothing overtures, and in the national government the sole achievement of Know-Nothingism consisted of a few speeches. That the Know-Nothings failed even to get immigration restriction is additional evidence that nativism in 1860 was a spent force. More Americans saw the immigrant as a valuable factor in economic development than saw him as threat. The William Allens in the Democratic party and their counterparts in the Whig and Republican parties grumbled and complained and fumed at foreigners, but their party organizations and leadership wooed and welcomed the newcomers.[4]

Dr. Allen's sentiments, as widely shared as they were, tend to distort our perception of the political scene in another way. Not all the Irish were Democrats, and certainly not all Germans were Republicans. Ethnic voters (except in a few localities) seldom voted simply *as* ethnics. Religion was more important than ethnicity in shaping voter behavior, and ethnics often split over local issues. Like their fellow Americans of native birth, immigrants disagreed with each other and could not be counted on to follow ethnic leaders slavishly. Despite his public claims about the influence he exercised over German voters, Carl Schurz privately admitted to an old friend that "I am more popular with the Americans than with the Germans, for some of them are envious." Even so, in 1860 Schurz became head of the "foreign department" of the National Central Committee of the Republican party. In this post he laid elaborate plans for influencing German, Dutch, Norwegian, and other ethnic groups through the use of mailing lists, teams of speakers, and his own personal contacts. After Lincoln's victory in 1860, Schurz and other ethnic leaders claimed that the election results reflected ethnic support for the Republicans, but that claim vanishes under close scrutiny.[5]

Who elected Lincoln? In his own famous answer to that question, Wisconsin historian Joseph Schafer insisted that the influence of the foreign born was not a critical factor. Lincoln's victory, he asserted, came primarily from native-born voters. Other scholars not blinded by ethnic pride or prejudice tend to agree with Schafer. Despite the efforts of leaders like Schurz, the mass of foreign-born voters followed their own counsel. Like the native American, the foreign-born voter cast his ballot on the basis of complex motivation, with local issues like temperance and ethnic rivalries, along with state and national issues of many kinds, influencing his decision. For the ethnic as well as the nonethnic voter, habit and inertia might also be significant in a given election.[6]

All of this does not mean that there was no "ethnic vote" on the American political scene. There was, but it was local in nature, and religion was more important than ethnicity in the creation of the ethnic bloc. The familiar Irish vote in many cities was really the Irish-Catholic vote (which was, of course, one thing that alarmed the nativist), and in big cities that bloc vote in 1860 went to the Democratic party. "Ward-heeling, bloc voting, boss leadership—in short, the city machine—sooner or later gave the Irish and their political serfs, the new immigrants, local control in many places in the Northeast and about Chicago," concluded Oliver MacDonagh.[7]

Apart from the municipal Irish-Catholic machines, however, there was no monolithic immigrant vote. Typical voters were more interested in issues that directly affected them than in abstract appeals to nativity. Immigrants varied quite widely in voting behavior, a fact that Schurz learned repeatedly—as did other ethnic politicians. Where patterns are discerned among immigrant population, they show the influence of religion rather than nativity. Even this pattern is an unreliable guide to the political scene in 1860. Geography broke up any possible large-scale uniformity based

upon religion. The Irish-Catholic in New Orleans had views not compatible
with the Irish-Catholic in New York. German Protestants in North Carolina
did not share all the political positions of the German Protestants in Wisconsin. The only safe generalization about the ethnic political scene in 1860
is that it was complicated and lively. A visit to several different sites in
1860–1861 reveals both the complexities and the practices of America's
ethnic politics.[8]

How did an ethnic group get involved in politics? This question finds
its clearest and most definitive answer for the Germans of Milwaukee.
Milwaukee was the "most conspicuously German" of all the cities of the
Great Lakes region in the nineteenth century; the city was often referred to
as the *Deutsch-Athens* of America, and German community was the most
salient feature of the city's culture. At midcentury 64 percent of the total
population was foreign born, and two-thirds of these came from Germany.[9]
A visitor to Milwaukee found German signs and house names, German
domestic architecture, German restaurants, German newspapers, and the
German language spoken on the streets. Many residents never learned English; they spent their lives within a familiar ethnic enclave.

Those ethnic neighborhoods were not the sordid ghettos so familiar to
subsequent generations of immigrants. The German experience in Milwaukee was a far cry from the later conventional wisdom about immigrant
groups, a wisdom that stresses the pitiable economic situation of the immigrant, his personal and social disorganization, and tragic conditions of
slum life. That same wisdom usually tells of the immigrant excluded from
the larger society by nativist prejudice. All this is contrary to the German
experience in Milwaukee.[10] Far from a suffering minority cowering under
Anglo-Saxon domination, Milwaukee Germans were a prospering, vigorous, self-confident people, so sure of their place in America and in their
city that on the eve of the Civil War there already were political divisions
within the German community comparable to those within the native population there and in other cities.

Milwaukee Germans did begin their political activity as a bloc, as an
identifiable interest group pursing a common goal. That was in 1843, when
they (and the city's Irish residents) petitioned the territorial legislature for
the right of noncitizens to vote for delegates to a proposed state constitu-
tional convention. This initial political venture occurred not because native
politicians tried to control and manipulate their votes, but because their
own leaders stimulated participation in the political process. Once involved, the Germans remained involved. By the 1850s Germans held ward
and minor city offices, and the regular election of Germans was taken as a
matter of course by city residents. Indeed, by this time, Germans competed
with each other for political office; their ethnic unity broke down as their
political power and political maturity grew. The reason for this change was

simple enough; there were only two issues on which all Germans could agree. The first was opposition to nativism; that issue kept most Germans in the Democratic party even after the Republican party attracted German leaders into its ranks. The second issue was temperance; any proposal to pass a temperance law was sure to encounter a united German front. In most respects, then, German political activity in Milwaukee on the eve of the war was nonethnic.[11]

Disagreements among Germans could be bitter and profound. Protestants, for example, sounded as prejudiced as any traditional WASP on the subject of religion. "The Irish are our natural enemies," announced one German Republican in 1854, "not because they are Irishmen, but because they are the truest guards of Popery."[12] German Catholics, on the other hand, stood firmly within the Democratic fold, and denounced the Republicans as "haters of foreigners, despoilers of churches, and Catholic killers. . . ."[13] The German population also split politically in a sort of generation gap. The Forty-Eighters, whose liberal politics and hostility toward organized religion irritated the earlier immigrant generation, had little in common with either older settlers or those whose Catholicism or Lutheranism remained firmly fixed as a key part of their lives. Carl Schurz made strenuous efforts to entice more Milwaukee Germans into Republican party ranks with little success. Loyalty to the Democratic party was based on their memory of Whig nativism and the fact that the Forty-Eighters were Republicans. At the same time, virtually all Germans agreed that it would be a mistake to form their own party, or a party of foreigners against the natives. The latter move, argued the *Wisconsin Demokrat,* "would drive us into a union with Irishmen, those American Croats."[14]

Both major parties sought German support, but the Germans behaved so much like native Americans that no appeal attracted all Germans *as* Germans. The Republican party backed Carl Schurz for lieutenant governor in 1857; he lost that race, with most Germans remaining loyal to the Democrats. In 1859 Schurz sought his party's nomination for governor and lost that race, too. All the while, most Germans stood firmly with the Democratic party, a party that denounced Schurz as a Prussian spy![15] In short, Milwaukee and Wisconsin Germans were far from a monolithic voting bloc and as likely to compete with each other as they were to support a common cause or candidate. So thoroughly assimilated were they into the American political scene that the Germans, unlike the Irish, paid almost no attention to German nationalism as a political issue.

More dispersed around the state than the Germans, the Wisconsin Irish were more unified politically. In large measure, this reflected the greater religious unity of the Irish. While some Germans went into the Republican party, the Irish remained Democrats almost to a man. As a conscious political bloc, the Irish began their activities at the same time and under the same circumstances as the Germans. After that similar beginning, however, the two ethnic groups followed quite different paths. Committing themselves completely to the Democrats, the Wisconsin Irish acquired an influence that belied their relatively small numbers in the state. By midcentury the Irish got almost twice the amount of state school funds that their share of the population warranted.[16] The Wisconsin Irish vote was a bloc vote, but one that Democratic leaders had to retain with patronage and spoils. To a degree the Wisconsin Democracy, as was the case in other northern states, was *hostage* to the Irish. In 1852 the state legislature had a Democratic majority, and in a dramatic episode that year the Irish demonstrated their hold on the party.

In a highly partisan vote, the state legislature passed a resolution expressing sympathy for imprisoned Irish patriots, including John Mitchell, Smith O'Brien, and Thomas Francis Meagher. The resolution urged the president of the United States to force Britain to release the prisoners and allow them to emigrate to American. Wisconsin Gov. Leonard J. Farwell was a Whig, and he vetoed the resolution. Legislative leaders then could not agree on an alternative resolution that might escape the governor's vote, and the controversy erupted into the state's newspapers, with Wisconsin citizens hotly debating an issue that had nothing to do with Wisconsin. Thus Irish nationalism was a potent force in the Irish wing of the Democratic party.[17] Like the Germans, the Irish opposed temperance laws and nativism. Unlike the Germans, the Wisconsin Irish exercised an influence disproportionate to their members because of their skillful exploitation of their position inside a single party.

One other ethnic group played a significant role in Wisconsin politics. Almost half of the Norwegians in America lived in the Badger State. Clannish, isolated from the larger society by a language barrier, scattered across the state in farming communities instead of congregating in large cities, the Norwegians were staunch Free-Soilers and later transferred their allegiance to the Republican party.

Linguistic skills were critical to political leadership among the Norwegians. More inclined to read Norwegian language newspapers like *Emigranten* and *Faedrelandet* than the American press, the Norwegians relied heavily upon a small number of men who developed English fluency while retaining the Norwegian language and cultural ties. One such leader was Hans Christian Heg.

Born in Lier, Norway, in 1825, Heg migrated to American with his parents at age eleven. His father, Even Heg, published the first Norwegian newspaper in America, the *Nordlyset*. Young Hans rapidly acquired a knowledge of English, and acquired, too, a taste for politics. He served on town and county boards, and the Heg farm was a political and cultural center for Muskego area Norwegians. Heg threw himself wholeheartedly into Republican politics after that party appeared, and served as a delegate to the state convention in 1857. Vastly outnumbered by the Germans and Irish (there were about 21,000 Norwegians in Wisconsin in 1860, compared to 60,000 Irish and 124,000 Germans), the Norwegians controlled a few local offices, but their chances of becoming a major force in state politics were slim. Heg's growing influence in the Republican party was due as much to his own skills as to his role as ethnic leader. In 1859 Heg ran as the Republican candidate for state prison commissioner, and when he won he became the first Norwegian to hold a state elective office in Wisconsin.[18] In 1860 Wisconsin's Norwegians clustered in ethnic islands, played a largely defensive role in politics, and watched the Germans closely. Like the Swedes and Danes, the Norwegians brought to American as a part of their cultural baggage an attitude of suspicion if not hostility toward Germans.

Who elected Lincoln? In Wisconsin the Republican triumph in the 1860 election was due largely to the votes of its Yankee population.[19] Many of these Yankees were themselves internal migrants, coming to Wisconsin from New England. The Republican victory left the state with a volatile political situation. Almost all of the Irish and a large majority of the Germans opposed abolition, while the state's Republican governor, Alexander Randall, was an ardent abolitionist. The state's most prominent Republican, Carl Schurz, worked hard for Lincoln's election and made extravagant claims about the contribution of German votes to Lincoln's success. After a rest from the rigors of the campaign, Schurz joined other Republican leaders in Springfield, Illinois, where the president-elect in early 1861 was learning what his own election meant in terms of party politics and patronage.

Lincoln thought highly of Schurz and assumed that the Forty-Eighters had indeed made a critical contribution to his victory. He gave Schurz an entire afternoon out of a busy schedule and much of a evening as well. Lincoln confided his plans to Schurz and the two held a frank talk about the future. "As I was leaving . . .," Schurz later told his wife, "I told him that I should ask his administration for a few offices for my friends."[20] Ethnic politicians played the patronage game like their native counterparts.

In 1860 the largest Irish city in the world was New York City. Almost half of the eight hundred thousand people living there were foreign born, and the largest number of those by far came from the Emerald Isle. New York's mayor, and the head of a political machine centered on Mozart Hall, was Fernando Wood. Although born in Philadelphia, when he moved to New York he became adept at the art of ethnic politics. As seen by one journalist in the early 1860s,

> Wood was always calm, cool, and collected. His hair and mustache
> were dyed black, and his thin, spare face, elegant manners, and precise
> method of speech, gave him the appearance of a refined and scholarly
> man. He never lost his temper, was always agreeable, polite, and even
> courtly.[21]

Agreeable, polite, and courtly, Mayor Wood was also the most infamous of
New York's mayors, a distinction for which there is keen competition. Once
a Know-Nothing, he became a Democrat and a leading pillar of Tammany
Hall. When he fell out with the Tammany organization in the fifties, Wood
set up a rival organization, Mozart Hall, and in 1859 he ran first in a three-
way race for mayor. Wood's political machine rested upon the support of
the foreign born, most particularly the Irish. Perhaps the most notorious of
machine politicians in New York's history, William Marcy Tweed, paid
Wood the ultimate compliment in later years: "I never yet went to get a
corner lot that I didn't find Wood had got in ahead of me." On the eve of
the Civil War, however, the Tweed Ring was still little more than a gleam in
its master's eye; Fernando Wood was New York's most successful practi-
tioner of corrupt politics.[22]

Wood's flirtation with the Know-Nothings seemed like a wise move at
the time. New York's older residents, shocked by the behavior of immigrants, wanted help from their government. Gangs of young Irishmen
roamed the streets, looking for excitement and making trouble; Irish
toughs perverted the electoral process by roughing up the opponents of the
Democratic machine on election day. Neither the police nor the militia had
much success in controlling these ruffians. It was the perception of the
native population, too, that aliens monopolized patronage positions. The
perception was inaccurate, but inaccurate perceptions can be as influential
as accurate ones. While the Irish held more customs house positions than
other immigrants, for example, they still held in 1860 a smaller number of
such positions than their portion of the population suggested they might
hold.[23]

New York's Irish population, in contrast with other immigrant groups,
was by 1860 thoroughly immersed in politics based upon ethnic appeals.
Even the most friendly observers of the Irish political scene admit the
crudity of these Irish ethnic politics. Joseph F. O'Grady, for example, tells
us:

> Constant harangues of politicians urging the Irish to think, act, and
> vote as Irishmen and the arguments of the Young Ireland political refu-
> gees that the ex-peasant should neither ignore the old country nor
> forget his hatred of England combined to create strong feelings of
> cohesiveness.[24]

Both church leaders and Irish politicians deliberately fostered the image of
the Irish as a victimized, threatened group, beset by a hostile native popula-

tion. Irish voters to a considerable extent were hostage to their European heritage, even when this was clearly contrary to their self-interest in the United States. New York's Irish politicians ran on platforms and slogans supporting Irish nationalism—an appeal that was purely emotional and obscured the real issues confronting most people. Irish-American politicians were masters of political vulgarity, at whipping up ethnic prejudice. In late October, 1860, for example, a monster torchlight parade occurred; most of the marchers were Irish. The parade theme was a crude exhibition of antiblack sentiment. Posters and banners carried by the marchers included coarse representations of blacks and raised the bugaboo of racial amalgamation if the Republicans won. It was the kind of political circus associated in later years with the Deep South. The two Democratic organizations, Mozart and Tammany, never addressed the real problems of the immigrant population. In their ruthless exploitation of the ethnic vote, they ignored housing, education, and poverty, choosing instead to stress ethnic cohesion, Irish nationalism, and the need for alien Americans to stand together against antagonistic native-born Americans.[25]

New York's numerous German population in 1860 supported no political machine. In part, this was due to the absence of serious nativist sentiment toward Germans. Native Americans usually saw the Germans, despite language differences, as industrious, kindly, hard-working, and quiet—models of good citizenship compared to the Irish. While leaders like Frederick Kapp wielded considerable influence, Germans were immune to blatant appeals to European nationalism. A German-American politician could win little attention by denouncing foreign enemies of a nonexistent German nation. Many prominent Irish Democrats in 1860 and early 1861 gave powerful support to the South; no prominent Germans did so. No prominent Irish-American in New York was an abolitionist. The most influential ethnic newspaper, the *Irish-American,* was proslavery and antiblack. Germans landing in New York City came under the benevolent protection of aid societies supported by previous arrivals and second generation German-Americans. Irishmen landing in New York often fell victim to vicious exploitation by New York Irishmen who were skilled con artists.[26]

New York's Irish voters saw the election of Lincoln as a disaster. A great "Union Meeting" at Cooper Institute on 28 January 1861 was virtually a mockery of unionist sentiment. The meeting grew out of an appeal to all men of all parties who were *against* Lincoln. James T. Brady, the principal speaker, was a prominent "responsible" Irishman, an attorney and future judge. Brady, saying that he did not believe in coercion, urged the South to be patient and generous while the North sorted out its problems.[27] Lincoln had an enemy in the Irish population of New York as he prepared to assume the burdens of office.

President-elect Lincoln was thoroughly familiar with ethnic politics long before he ran for the White House. That was a game one had to play in Illinois. During his unsuccessful run for the Senate in 1858, he eagerly curried German voters and criticized the Irish. He leaned heavily upon the expertise of Gustave Koerner, and tried to attract German voters with popular speakers like Friedrich Hecker. As a Republican candidate, Lincoln feared the use of "imported" aliens as well as the Illinois Irish. He described his worries in a letter to a fellow Illinois politician:

> On alighting from the cars and walking three squares at Naples on Monday, I met about fifteen Celtic gentlemen, with black carpet sacks in their hands. They dropped in about the doggeries, and were still hanging about when I left.[28]

Lincoln voiced his concern about imported voters in a speech at Merodosia, Illinois, and quite predictably angered those persons who saw this as evidence the Republicans were still nativists. To counter such charges, Lincoln, the following year, secretly purchased a German newspaper published in Springfield and used the *Staats Anzeiger* to bolster his image as a friend of the immigrant.

Lincoln's Illinois held a large foreign-born population in 1860. Of the 324,643 immigrants the census recorded there that year, 130,804 were German. Over 87,000 Irish made up the next largest group, with less than half that number of English origin. About 10,000 Scandinavians, mostly Swedes and Norwegians, were the only others of political significance. Chicago had more foreign-born than native Americans, while the counties opposite St. Louis held large numbers of Germans. The "foreign vote" was a formidable one in the Prairie State.[29] Blocs of foreign voters could be decisive in local elections, although neither major party strictly controlled a foreign vote. Irish Catholics tended to support the Democrats, while Jews were evenly divided between the two parties. Germans were independent voters despite the efforts of the Koerners and Heckers. Like their Wisconsin counterparts, they were politically mature, sure of their place in society, and as apt to compete with each other as support a common candidate.

In sharp contrast to the New York Irish, the Germans of Illinois in 1861 were solidly pro-Union. When a general preparedness meeting in Chicago attracted a crowd of thousands in early January, the city's German leaders called a preparedness meeting for Germans on 8 January. Among other speakers, Casper Butz addressed the throng at German House that evening, and the occasion provided an interesting contrast with the meeting held the same month by the New York Irish.[30]

"I have just taken a survey of the State of Indiana," wrote Carl Schurz in the spring of 1860, "a hard state, but I think we can carry it if proper exertions are used." Schurz was right; Indiana was indeed a "hard" state. In 1860 it was the most proslavery of all the northern states. Feelings against blacks were intense. Most Indiana settlers arrived there from the South, and the Hoosier State included a smaller proportion of foreign born among its residents than any other northern state. In outlook and sympathies, Indiana residents were southern. Almost as regular as clockwork, the state gave its votes to Democratic candidates. Lincoln and the Republican party found little support there in 1860.[31]

Most of the state's German and Irish residents (and these two ethnic groups made up the bulk of the foreign-born population) were Catholics. Most were Democrats. Over half the immigrant population was German, and their largest concentration was around Indianapolis. German schools, German churches, a German press, and Turnvereines flourished in the state's capital city.[32] Like the Germans, the Irish were Democrats. Unlike the Germans, the Indiana Irish backed the emotional cause of nationalism for the old country. Many Irish residents came to Indiana after prior settlement in New York, Boston, or Canada, and they committed themselves as thoroughly to Irish nationalism as their eastern countrymen. German Protestants, a minority, supported Lincoln. Germans were in a quandary in 1860; usually Democrats when they thought about issues like temperance and nativism, they leaned toward the Republicans on the subject of abolition.

Harry S. Lane, the Republican candidate for governor in 1860, won an election that offered no clear choice between proslavery and antislavery adherents. Lane's campaign position was to leave slavery alone where it was and oppose its extension. That was not as far as most Germans wanted to go and much further than most Irish wanted to go. Lane's term as governor was brief; he went to the U.S. Senate and his running mate, Lt. Gov. Oliver P. Morton, became the state's chief executive officer. Morton was a temporizing man, anxious to test trends and political winds before committing himself. The state he led had strong economic ties with the South; those ties coupled with popular sentiment gave Indiana an uneasy and volatile political climate in early 1861.

"Our Proclamation for 1861! Our Union—It must be Preserved." With this ringing declaration the *Boston Pilot* greeted the new year following Lincoln's election. But in less than a month the *Pilot,* the organ of Irish Catholic opinion in Massachusetts and one of the nation's most influential shapers of Catholic opinion, shifted its position. Men of Massachusetts, cautioned the *Pilot* in early February, should refuse to march off to a fratricidal war. In just two weeks, the "Union must be preserved" gave way to "Massachusetts vs. the Union." Patrick Donahoe's weekly newspaper accurately mirrored both the confused political situation inside the Bay

State and the mixed emotions of the nation's Irish Catholics.[33]

Most Massachusetts Irishmen, with fresh memories of the nativism of the previous decades and remembering, too, the anti-Irish elements of Know-Nothingism there in 1854, favored the Democratic party. Ironically enough, nativists in the state were in the Irish Catholic political camp in the face of the sectional crisis. Both groups regarded the Republicans as a threat to the Union, because they feared that Republicans put the question of the immorality of slavery above the defense of the United States constitution.[34] Always complex, Massachusetts politics turned more Byzantine than usual in 1860–1861.

The election of 1860 gave Massachusetts a new governor, John Albion Andrew. His very name shouted WASP. Born in Maine, Andrew attended Bowdoin College, entered law practice in 1840, and helped organize the Free-Soil party and the Republican party. His 1860 election included the largest popular majority in state history. He was an ardent abolitionist in a state whose largest ethnic group—the Irish—and the only politically significant ethnic group, adamantly opposed abolition. Boston's large Irish enclave viewed the new governor with suspicion. Here, after all, was a city with a long and sometimes violent history of abolitionist sentiment. The Boston "slave riot" and the local confrontations between abolitionists and the law were as fresh in the Bostonian memory as the xenophobia of the recent past. The 100,000 readers of the *Pilot* got a steady diet of defensive, abrasive, and sometimes indignant rhetoric aimed at unifying Irish sentiment against an antagonistic larger society. Would John Albion Andrew be "perfidious Albion," and would his large electoral majority be translated into a revival of nativism? An intensifying national crisis did not erase local concerns from Boston politics.

Congregationalists still dominated the political life of New Haven, Connecticut, in 1860, and New Haven, like Boston, carried a heritage of bitterness and mistrust between natives and aliens. A potent political brew bubbled in the old Puritan community. Here, as in the other principal cities of the state, a classic rural-urban conflict complicated the religious discord between Protestant and Catholic. Residents were increasingly irritated at what they saw as undue and growing influence in Connecticut affairs on the part of Boston and New York. Close ties and regular public contacts between Irish Catholics in Connecticut and those in Boston and New York rubbed salt into this festering wound. Like Boston, New Haven in the heyday of Know-Nothing power saw the dissolution of Irish militia units. As recently as 1850 Connecticut still had one of the most homogeneous populations in the Union. Ten years later, a rapid influx of Irish Catholics (along with smaller numbers of other ethnic groups) gave the state a population in which one out of every six residents was foreign born. New

Haven's population in 1860 was 27 percent foreign born, most of whom were Irish.[35]

There was a large enough German population in the city to attract notice. German-language newspapers enjoyed a large circulation, and local resentment toward Germans was less a matter of politics than it was an irritation at their sometimes use of their native tongue.[36] The relative absence of enmity toward Germans compared with the Irish was due in large measure to the fact that there was no German bloc vote. New Haven had a German Democratic Club, and it had a German Republican Club. The much smaller number of Germans, too, made them appear less threatening to the natives.

New Haven shared a striking characteristic with Boston in addition to the tension between Irish and non-Irish. The city had a long history of strong abolitionist sentiment and activity. People still remembered the *Amistad* trial of 1842, a trial involving a slave mutiny and the most famous U.S. Supreme Court decision related to slavery prior to the Dred Scott case. As in Boston, the local Irish population harbored intense antiblack prejudice, another factor that disturbed the larger society. Finally, strong temperance feelings among many native Americans acerbated relations with the city's Irish population.

Candidates Abraham Lincoln and Stephen Douglas both spoke in New Haven during the 1860 campaign. Lincoln's theme was that of mutual forbearance between North and South, and despite the local Democratic majority in the city, he won a majority of the votes cast in the fall election.

One other ingredient in the New Haven brew should be noted. While in this state as elsewhere the Irish tended to cluster at the bottom of the economic ladder, there were enough prosperous Irish families to arouse the animosity of the less well-off natives. Massive concentrations of urban Irish obscure the presence of some Irish who were skilled city workers, climbing the ladder of success. One observer in a small town northwest of New Haven noted that the Irish there were regarded by the natives as industrious and ambitious, ready to buy up any land that came on the market. "As fast our American families fall into decay and are obliged to sell their property," he remarked, "the Irish catch it up."[37] Prosperity and land acquisition aroused animosity as readily as poverty in urban ghettos.

Brotherly love was conspicuous by its absence in Philadelphia in the middle of the nineteenth century. As recently as the late 1850s as many as six different political parties vied for popular support. There was a Know-Nothing party and an Anti-Know-Nothing party. Dying Whig sentiment was split among Regular Whigs, Clay Whigs, Whigs, and American Whigs. A Peoples' Reform party competed with a Citizens' Reform party. Philadelphia during the peak of nativism in the middle fifties had a splendid row over the composition of its police force, with a nativist mayor taking great pride that one qualification for a Philadelphia cop was that he be native born. (The rule was impossible to enforce as the city's Irish and German population mushroomed.)

It was Philadelphia that witnessed the death throes of the Native American party when its national convention occurred there in June 1855. Party deliberations were secret, but it was no secret that the party disintegrated when northern and southern delegates proved unable to reconcile their sectional differences.[38] The irony of the spectacle is compounded by the fact that sectionalism served as an instrument of destruction for nativism. The same year that the Native American party died in Philadelphia, the Republican party was born there.

In 1860, when the country seemed on the verge of self-destruction, when great debates raged in the hustings, what issues inflamed the voters of Philadelphia? As much as anything else, it was the streetcar. Citizens contended mightily over the question of whether streetcars should run on Sunday. Running the cars on Sunday, claimed opponents, would "disturb the worship of God, would impair the morals of the public, would cause much additional labor, would create a great demand for intoxicating liquor, would tempt the laboring classes to squander their money, and would expose the suburbs of the city to plunderers."[39] Excited citizens threatened to tear up the tracks to keep the cars in their place on Sunday. As quickly as it arose the streetcar issue faded away. Here, as elsewhere, ephemeral matters could and did loom larger in politics than weightier questions.

Abolitionists existed in Philadelphia, but with little popular support. This vociferous minority aroused opposition in every quarter. Irish citizens especially hated the abolitionists. When abolitionists attempted to hold public meetings, they could do so only with police protection. Yet Republicans (under the name of the Peoples' party) won the 1860 election. Union sentiment prevailed. The year ended in a flurry of mass meetings held to demonstrate loyalty to the Union. The Philadelphia Democrats Union meeting at year's end was really a show of support for the national government, unlike its New York counterpart.

Cincinnati treated abolitionists at least as shabbily as the City of Brotherly Love. Lincoln was hissed and booed when he spoke against slavery there in 1859. Slavery was a physical reality to the city's residents; they could look across the river into Kentucky and see slaves at work in the fields.[40] Cincinnati's large German and Irish communities tended to see free blacks as economic rivals, and their prejudice was blatant. As in many other cities, the Queen City's police force included many Irishmen, and their brutal treatment of the residents of the black "Bucktown" was notorious. The Irish cops were generous with their nightsticks; they were known to enjoy bashing the heads of the "damned Dutch" when the occasion offered itself. As with Philadelphia, there were strong economic ties between the city and the South.

President-elect Lincoln made a stop in Cincinnati on his slow and tortuous journey to Washington. His earlier comments about alien voters returned to haunt him; Cincinnati's ethnic communities carried political clout. The audience for Lincoln's speech included many Germans, and Lincoln chose his words carefully. His focus was the working man. In America, he noted, working men are the most numerous portion of society and are thus the foundation of the government. "In regard to the Germans and other foreigners," he concluded his remarks, "I esteem them no better than other people, nor any worse."[41]

Nativism in Cincinnati by 1860 was victim to demographic and political realities. The power of the German population was considerable, and the two major parties tried to attract the foreign born, not alienate them. Like Milwaukee, Cincinnati had a firmly established German population with differences between the Forty-Eighters and the more conservative residents. Germans joined both major parties. The Irish, clustered in neighborhoods near the waterfront where they sought work as unskilled labor, were firmly in the Democratic camp; they were energetic in opposition to abolition. The Cincinnati economic ties to the South and the sentiments of the ethnic communities put the city in a delicate and tense mood on the eve of Lincoln's inauguration.

Before we visit the last city on this brief journey around the North, let us identify the elements of commonality at each stop. From Wisconsin to Connecticut, from Chicago to New York, a pattern emerges. Everywhere, communities of ethnic Americans exercised major political influence. For Irish-Americans this involved an often decisive voice in Democratic party affairs. Germans and other groups of the foreign born participated in both major parties. Far from reviled and ridiculed, the foreign born were ardently wooed by the two parties. Foreign-born Americans served in elected office; held positions of authority in the party system; and, where their numbers permitted, dominated urban political machines. Nativism existed within the population, and so did interethnic rivalries. Irish Catholics, for a variety of reasons, strongly opposed abolition, held contrary views about the nature of the Union, and frequently gave Irish nationalism a higher political priority than defending a threatened national government headed by Republicans. Throughout the North, ethnic communities supported ethnic political leaders who had by 1860 a well-developed sense of party machinery and knew how to exploit the patronage system. Partly as a heritage of the nativist activity of the fifties, and partly as deliberate "out-

sider as victim" behavior, members of ethnic communities used several social institutions, from the church to drinking societies, as symbols and
instruments of cultural cohesion. Where these social institutions were most
visible and powerful, and where the ethnic political power was most narrowly partisan, native Americans had the strongest fear and distrust of the
foreign born. Finally, whatever hindsight tells us about the approach of the
Civil War in 1861, no one in America at the end of 1860 knew that America
stood on the brink of its greatest national tragedy. People did have other
concerns, and the rest of life went on while leaders North and South sorted
through their options.

Missouri, to the dismay of Carl Schurz, was an insoluble problem of
ethnic politics. The "Show-me" state in 1860 had a total population of
1,200,000; 100,000 of those were slaves. The state's foreign-born population was 160,514; well over half of these were Germans. Missouri was a
Democratic state in 1860, but St. Louis, its largest metropolitan center, was
Republican. St. Louis was in addition the center of the state's foreign-born
population.[42] While Germans farmed and lived in small towns like Hermann, where they re-created so thoroughly the atmosphere of the old country that Hermann bore the nickname "Little Germany," the largest concentration of Germans was in and around St. Louis.

The river city was a "must-stop" for Germans visiting America, and
German immigrants often came to St. Louis before they made a final decision about a home in their new country. The first Turner society was organized in May 1850, and it was followed shortly by another familiar German institution, a rifle club. The St. Louis Turners provided a thermometer
for rising sectional temperatures in 1860–1861. Their increasing stress on
marksmanship, drill, and even bayonet practice recorded the intensifying
political crisis. The society increased its purchases of powder, and the regular meetings and drill of the Turners were a prominent feature of German
life in the city. More than 60,000 Germans lived in St. Louis. Friedrich
Hecker visited the city; Franz Sigel lectured to the Turners in early 1860.
Prominent local citizens included Peter J. Osterhaus, a Forty-Eighter who
became a bookkeeper and merchant; Henry Boernstein, who owned and
edited the St. Louis *Anzeiger des Westens;* and Theodore Rombauer, who
had directed an arms factory in Hungary before leading his large family to
St. Louis. Germans of St. Louis, like those of Milwaukee and Cincinnati,
were not a monolithic political bloc. Sharp divisions separated the generations and set apart the politically active Forty-Eighters from their more
conservative predecessors. But unlike Milwaukee, St. Louis in 1860–1861
harbored tenacious anti-German prejudice within the native population.
This originated in several quite different perceptions of the Germans. Politically conservative Americans objected to the liberalism of the Forty-

Eighters; proslavery whites objected to abolitionist Germans, and middle-class Americans objected to the behavior of German riverfront workmen. There was something about the Germans for everyone to hate.

During the 1860 presidential campaign Carl Schurz hit hard at the St. Louis electorate; his appeal was to Germans and non-Germans alike. In the city's Verandah Hall, the evening of 1 August 1860, Schurz delivered a speech entitled "The Doom of Slavery," clearly a desperate gamble in a slave state! The Wisconsinite tried to convince Missouri slave owners that abolition and the Republican party were in their own long-term interests. Slaveholders, he argued, are the slaves of slaves. Historical tides move against slavery in the nineteenth century, he insisted, just as they moved against serfdom and feudalism in Europe.

> Slaveholders of America, I appeal to you. Are you really in earnest
> when you speak of perpetuating slavery? Shall it never cease? never?
> Stop and consider where you are and in what day you live.

In the climatic moment of his oration, Schurz pulled out all the emotional stops. "Hear me, slaveholders of America!" he cried. "If you have no sense for the right of the black, no appreciation of your own interests, I entreat, I implore you, have at least pity on your children!"[43]

Schurz's "Doom of Slavery" effort fell on deaf ears in Missouri. In a campaign characterized locally by vicious political infighting, Lincoln came in a dismal fourth in a field of four candidates. On 6 February 1861 another meeting occurred in Verandah Hall. This time Francis P. Blair, Jr., congressman and Republican party stalwart, presided over an effort representing one of many such mass Union meetings to restore unity to Missouri Republicanism. This time the audience in Verandah Hall heard appeals for party and national unity. This time the city and the state were in the midst of a visible and shattering crisis.[44] Missouri threatened to leave the Union altogether or tear itself apart. Blair, already a popular figure with many Germans, invoked images of country above party, unity above partisanship, and the need for Germans and non-Germans to join hands in the larger goal of saving the Union.

St. Louis Germans in early 1861 responded to such pleas. Germans in the event provided virtually the only organized opposition to secession within the city. When the Missouri General Assembly met in Jefferson City in December 1860, its members debated the issue of secession. Incoming Gov. Claiborne F. Jackson persistently pushed prosouthern arguments in his inaugural address; he called upon Missouri to stand by the South. The assembly decided that a special convention should consider secession, and when the call for the convention went out, Blair went to work in St. Louis to promote the cause of the Union. Secessionists harassed his meeting. Blair then organized gangs of "Wide Awakes," but they lacked arms. There were plenty of arms in the federal arsenal in St. Louis, but official state forces had the inside track on access to those arms—and those forces favored secession.

Frank Blair considered his options. The city was a tinder box. Union supporters lacked arms. Any open importation of muskets for the "Wide Awakes" would likely set the city ablaze. An art exhibit offered a solution. Boxes of "plaster casts" brought into the city for the exhibit actually carried arms, and as southern states began leaving the Union, Blair and his followers prepared for confrontation with secessionists in Missouri. To the dismay and surprise of Governor Jackson and his backers, Missouri voted more than three to one to stick with the Union. Now the St. Louis arsenal took on an increasingly vital role. Whoever got the key to its arms would control the city and probably the state. The Turners continued their drilling with a new sense of urgency. Governor Jackson ordered the state militia into camp at St. Louis.

# CHAPTER 3

# "The War Is Commenced"

"Our country calls; away! away!"

—WILLIAM CULLEN BRYANT

HAT the country needs now, mused New England poet James Russell Lowell, is a Fugitive Law for runaway republics. The first runaway was South Carolina; the Palmetto State seceded 20 December 1860. Other southern states followed quickly. Not all northerners regarded secession as a bad development. In Philadelphia a mass meeting of citizens heard an Irish speaker urge his listeners to let the southern states go in peace. "Pity, forgive," argued poet-abolitionist John Greenleaf Whittier, "but urge them back no more."[1] Confusion was a more common sentiment in the North than bellicosity. The situation was fraught with uncertainties. What did southern senators and congressmen now represent in Washington? What would happen to trade between the sections? What should the states and the federal government do? The new governor of Pennsylvania, Andrew G. Curtin, was the son of Irish immigrants. His inaugural address in early January voiced the uncertainty of many Americans. Curtin expressed friendship for the seceding states but insisted that the national laws and the constitution must be enforced. That was the crux of the problem facing President-elect Lincoln.

Lincoln arrived in Harrisburg 22 February 1861, still on his long journey to Washington. Pennsylvania's capital was his last stop before going on to the nation's capital. State militia units paraded in his honor. It was a dubious honor:

> The dull and lustreless muskets, the varied and grotesque uniforms, the feathers and tinsel of officers . . . all demonstrated a lack of readiness for war. The patriotism of the men was evident, but neither spirit nor equipment was ready.[2]

Lincoln raised an American flag at a ceremony in Independence Hall earlier that day, and his own words mirrored a sense of doubt and a forlorn hope that sectional conflict could be averted.

Violence was feared from southern sympathizers even in the North and in Washington. Lincoln made a secretive trip from Harrisburg to Washington, and reached the capital at 6:30 the next morning. There was no great welcoming ceremony. Instead, visitors and residents alike saw groups of armed men drilling in public areas. Lincoln was quite right to be cautious. The drilling soldiers were not all friendly. "They were strongly tinctured with secessionism," remarked one observer, "in fact, passed resolutions to the effect, and looked for a favorable opportunity to strike a blow at the government."[3] One thing the new chief executive did not lack was advice. Oliver Wendell Holmes wanted a firm hand in Washington:

> If Mr. Lincoln says he will execute the laws and collect the revenue, though the heavens cave in, the backs of the Republicans stiffen again and they will take down the old Revolutionary king's arms, and begin to ask whether they can be altered to carry minie bullets.[4]

*Though the heavens cave in. . . .* Such apocalyptic language was more than hyperbole.

As soon as secession began, many ordinary Americans, both native and foreign born, expected war as an inevitable next step. In late December a former officer in the Swiss army volunteered his services to the governor of Wisconsin. J. F. Hauser was typical of the countless other Americans writing to every northern governor. "In times of danger & trouble of the native or adopted country," he wrote, "the Patriots will join to the common banner." Good patriot Hauser also hoped that his gesture would be awarded with a commission. Members of militia units throughout the North inspected their arms (usually with dismay), listened to pep talks, and drilled with more serious demeanor than usual. Not all the union meetings were like those of Philadelphia and New York. More typical was the 4 February 1861 gathering in Milwaukee, where 1,800 people heard Republican and Democratic speakers alike call for an end to partisan bickering and demand national unity. Even here, however, there was bitter disagreement among the people over proper wording of resolutions to be forwarded to appropriate officials.[5]

Meanwhile, Connecticut arms factories continued their booming business, filling orders received from southern states. The Colt, Sharps, and Whitney firms shipped weapons south as fast as they manufactured them. Hundreds of tons of gun powder left the state for southern destinations.[6]

At 4:30 A.M. on 12 April Edmund Ruffin, who left Washington after the election carrying a John Brown pike, supposedly pulled the lanyard on a columbiad aimed at Fort Sumter in Charleston harbor. Ruffin, for whom the sobriquet "fire-eater" might have been invented, fired a cannon charged with powder only recently delivered from a Connecticut factory. The assault on Sumter electrified the North and ended all doubts about appropriate action. "The war is commenced," began a telegram received by Governor Curtin that same morning. Similar telegrams reached every corner of the North as the day wore on, and popular reaction was prompt and spontaneous.[7]

In New Haven, the Grays hurried to their Chapel Street armory and hoisted the Stars and Stripes. The *New Haven Palladium* had an "extra" edition on the streets by noon. Flags appeared on businesses and homes all over the city and Jeff Davis was hanged in effigy.[8] Identical scenes expressed overwhelming popular emotion in towns and cities from Maine to Minnesota. Swept away with doubts in the next few days were feelings of accommodation and compromise. Americans expected universal support of the moral struggle against the South. Offers of military service and political advice flooded into every state capital. A veritable orgy of patriotism swept the North, and ethnic Americans, for the most part, shared in the excitement. Passions intensified when word of Maj. Robert Anderson's surrender of Fort Sumter on 14 April followed the news of the first attack.

Flags blossomed around Cincinnati streets until the city gave the appearance of a Fourth of July celebration. Two hundred ladies in Lafayette, Indiana, manned fifty sewing machines, making shirts for militia volunteers. College students held patriotic rallies, and at Athens, Ohio, students raised a big flag above the dome of the main college building. A group of armed workmen left Philadelphia to repair sabotaged bridges on the Baltimore railroad. Military bands played and paraded and school children went to work making flags and banners. Crowds gathered daily before newspaper offices to read the latest bulletins posted in windows; newspapers sold out as soon as they hit the streets. Ministers and priests gave patriotic sermons to their flocks. Literary societies listened to fervent oratory and passed stirring resolutions of support for the federal government. Businessmen and local governments offered to pay extra money to those local residents who volunteered for military service; recruiting offices for state militia units were swamped with eager customers. Mass meetings were a daily ritual. Home guard units drilled, and vacant lots and city parks turned into parade grounds. In Milwaukee, saloons and cigar stores buzzed with excitement as men gathered to discuss the latest bulletins. Local militia units grappled with confused and conflicting orders, and everywhere special trains carried soldiers off to state capitals or to existing militia camps. Everywhere, the war fever included strong political and ethnic overtones.

While Fort Sumter agitation peaked, an appeal went out to Cincinnati Irish-Americans. "The country which has made you its citizens calls on you to support the Constitution that has made you free . . . ," ran the entreaty in local newspapers. Irish-Americans were urged to attend public meetings held to express Irish support for the Union. Crowds gathered at both the Catholic Institute and later at the Union Hall, elected officers, gave loud approval to patriotic speakers, and managed to connect American loyalty to Irish nationalism. Irish-American speakers gave similar orations to huge audiences in other cities. In New York, for example, the earlier charade of a "Union" meeting gave way now to a genuine gathering; leading Irish-American politicians — including Fernando Wood — told a cheering throng the time had come to give unstinting support to the Union. Crowds in Boston heard the same message, as did those of Chicago. At first glance, it appeared that Irish-Americans, their political leaders, and the general population all agreed the war wiped away previous Irish sympathy for the South, and there was a united front between all Irish and native Americans in the new common cause. Even the English-Americans of Philadelphia, ignoring the Irish charges of past and present English tyranny, joined in the growing chorus of national unity.[9]

Wherever German communities flourished in the North, similar scenes of ethnic enthusiasm prevailed. In Cincinnati, Judge Johann B. Stallo spoke to a large gathering of German-Americans in the city's Turner Hall. "So long as the naturalized citizen has the same privileges as the native born, so, too, must he conduct himself like a man and fight and protect the Union and the Star Spangled Banner." Stallo's words hit home. His aim was at what he called "freedom-loving Germans," and the gap between the Forty-Eighters and the more conservative Germans closed. In Newark, New Jersey, Chicago, Philadelphia, Milwaukee — everywhere almost identical scenes occurred. German-American political leaders, like their Irish counterparts, encouraged their constituents to show enthusiasm for national unity, to join with native Americans in the war against the South.[10]

Privately, many an individual German-American repeated the public displays of loyalty and support. I was a military man in my native country, wrote George H. Walter to Wisconsin's Governor Randall, and now that I have enjoyed America's liberal society I want to use my skills in her defense. "I deem it my duty and the duty of all foreign born Citizens of this Republic," he told the governor, "to bear a large share in the maintenance of the same."[11] So deluged were some governors by such mail from Germans that they hired extra German-speaking secretaries to translate and answer the correspondence. Many Germans, both individually and in their organizations, known for opposition to abolition and sympathy for the South, repeatedly and publicly declared support for the Union.

While most of this change of heart by both Germans and Irishmen was genuine and reflected a reaction to southern aggression at Charleston, some of it was self-defense. Angry mobs in northern cities had little patience with either native-born Americans or immigrants whose loyalty was in doubt. On 20 April in Pittsburgh, for example, an Irishman was beaten by an infuriated mob on the strength of a rumor that he had rebel sympathies. Newspaper offices of both native-American and immigrant newspapers suffered destruction at the hands of superpatriots. Rabble roamed the streets of Philadelphia, seeking ethnic and nonethnic victims suspected of disloyalty. Individual informants charged immigrants with traitorous views in private communications to public officials. Germans and Irishmen with memories of nativism especially feared such charges and worried that wartime hysteria would revive xenophobia in the North.[12]

Despite all the mass meetings, resolutions, and speeches proclaiming loyalty, native Americans had what could be seen as contrary evidence about immigrant loyalty. Philadelphia's official organ of the city's Catholic bishop, the *Catholic Herald,* before the war began consistently echoed prosouthern, anti-Republican views. Its editor, John Duffy, published racist material that fit the antiblack attitudes of the largely Irish-Catholic readership. Duffy was always quick to react to what he regarded as insults to Irish-Americans. He proved a staunch defender, for example, of New York's Colonel Corcoran when Corcoran refused to parade the Sixty-ninth Militia Regiment in honor of the Prince of Wales. The *Catholic Herald* was high on the list of Philadelphia's mobs in April 1861, and the paper quickly displayed an American flag to prove its patriotism.[13] By late 1861 the paper toned down its anti-Lincoln language, but even in 1863 it still mounted a vigorous defense of the Irish engaged in the antidraft riots in New York. In the hothouse atmosphere of April 1861, the record of the *Catholic Herald* was easy to interpret as unpatriotic — as was any criticism of the administration in Washington.

The *Boston Pilot,* the most prominent organ of Irish Catholics in the Northeast, for years defended immigrants against real and perceived slights, and sectional crisis did not change its feisty attitude. As the year began the *Pilot* continued its own campaign for the vindication of Colonel Corcoran, whom it saw as a victim of blatant anti-Irish officialdom.[14] To at least some readers, the *Pilot's* first loyalty was to Ireland and the Catholic church, and not to the United States.

Ethnic Americans themselves in April 1861 were often confused about their loyalties. For years their own political leaders urged them to regard themselves as a people apart from the larger population. Whether it was a clarion call to Irish nationalism or a frequent reminder that non-Irish Americans were hostile, the persistent message aimed at the Irish-American community in many cities was that the Irish were different — they were not like other Americans. Beneath the initial excitement and enthusiasm exhibited by natives and immigrants alike in early 1861, there were tensions. Like the Irish Catholics, German ritualists (Catholics and Lutherans) displayed the most uncertainty about their proper role in the war. The first surge of public support for the war in ethnic communities was oftentimes short lived. The rate of volunteering for military service slowed (as it did in nonethnic communities as well) as winter approached and the scale of the war became more apparent. That the initial enthusiasm in many instances was shallow and not deeply felt can be seen in the increasing opposition to the war found among both Germans and Irishmen. By 1862 in Wisconsin when the state began a draft to meet its federal troop quota, the new governor, German-born Edward S. Salomon, was embarrassed by the small number of his countrymen willing to join the army. Growing numbers of aliens sought exemption from service on the basis of their legal status as foreigners. In April 1861, however, these developments still lay months in the future. What they suggest is that public enthusiasm for the war among Irish and German political leaders overlay a considerable amount of uncertainty among the immigrant population. Nowhere in America were the uncertainties, the tensions, the shifting ethnic political loyalties and the animosities between different ethnic groups as well as between immigrants and native Americans more apparent than in one of the most foreign of all American cities, St. Louis, Missouri.[15]

"The Hessians! The Hessians!" The cry of alarm sprang from a rider on a swift horse. Galloping Paul Revere–like along St. Louis streets, he preceded row upon row of silent marching soldiers. As one spectator recalled:

> These troops did not march so much as shuffle along; and I can see them now, for never since that time have I seen troops in any part of the world at all like them. I was instantly struck by the look of detachment of their faces, the machine-like movements of their bodies, the long, shuffling, dogged step. . . . I received an impression as of a quick impact of something silently fatal, bewildering, crushed, ghastly.

The grim automatons young Francis Grierson (a cousin of Benjamin Grierson) saw plodding through St. Louis streets were actually nervous and fearful German volunteers, and they marched toward a bloody confrontation with the cream of the St. Louis aristocracy. Grierson's recollection was that of "stupid looking" people, the riffraff of the city, setting out to pick a fight with dashing southern aristocrats, dazzling dragoons in brilliant uniforms, playing at soldiering and living in tents equipped with every delicacy by their wealthy families. It seemed inconceivable that battle could occur, that the Washington Guards, the Laclede Guards, and other upper-crust soldiers involved in what was an exciting and colorful pageant might actually engage in combat with "weak-kneed Hessians and Negro-worshippers." Grierson was wrong on at least two counts; the Hessians were not weak-kneed, and they were quite definitely not Negro-worshippers. One assumption was correct; there was no combat between the Germans and the Missouri militia that day.[16]

Ethnic politics in St. Louis were unique.[17] Over half of the city's population was foreign born. Germans, by far the largest group of foreigners, in 1860 voted for Lincoln and a Republican congressman, and staunchly supported the Republican party. Only a few years earlier, the Germans, like the Irish (who were the second largest group of foreign-born residents) stood firmly in the Democratic camp. No nativist stigma tainted Republicanism in the river city, and in the early 1850s most of the Irish-Americans there were Republicans! In contrast to the rest of the state, settled principally by migrants from the South, the native white population of St. Louis came largely from New York, Pennsylvania, Ohio, and Illinois. Local issues and influences, coupled with local demography, combined to give the city a character quite unlike that of the rest of the state; they gave ethnic politics there a history different from most of the rest of the North.

St. Louis German-Americans championed abolitionism, but they were also racists. Their abolitionism rested on self-interest, a belief that white working men enjoyed greater prosperity and freedom in a state without slavery. Since the Republican party there evolved out of the Democratic party, it included few temperance crusaders. There was no reason, then, for Germans, who stood together in defending the Union and promoting abolition, not to flock into the Republican party. By the late 1850s, when the Irish switched *their* allegiance to the Democrats, religious prejudice encouraged some of them to do so. Irish-Catholics were Democrats; German Protestants and freethinkers saw this as an additional inducement to switch their partisan loyalties. Both major German-language newspapers in St. Louis in 1860 implored readers to vote for Lincoln and stand firm for the Union.[18] Thoroughly assimilated into the American political system by 1860 (a trait shared with Milwaukee Germans), St. Louis Germans listened to arguments couched more in the language of American political history and traditional American ideologies than in ethnic pleas and voted and acted accordingly. Other St. Louis residents, of course, tended to see a bloc of foreigners pursuing ideals alien to those of most white state residents.

St. Louis was home to the largest federal arsenal west of the Mississippi. Control of its contents became increasingly critical as the sectional crisis worsened and secession began. In early 1861, as Governor Jackson ordered militia units to St. Louis as part of a plan to hold the state for the South and win control of the arsenal, the stage was set for a dramatic struggle involving champions of state's rights, southern sympathizers, opponents of abolition, and nativists against Unionists, abolitionists, and German-Americans. Colorful militia units settled down at "Camp Jackson," paraded, postured, and partied; the Turners fortified their hall, and an internal power struggle developed among the U.S. Army officers at the arsenal. Out of the Camp Jackson affair emerged one of the great ethnic sagas of the Civil War, but a saga firmly grounded in reality.

Stored in the St. Louis arsenal at the beginning of 1861 were 30,000 muskets, 1,000 rifles, and a huge quantity of ammunition. In the federal subtreasury building in the city was $400,000 in gold. Together, these caches constituted a rich prize for whichever group possessed them. On 1 January 1861 Washington sent a detachment of forty men to guard the arsenal. Indignantly, Missouri authorities demanded to know why it was necessary for federal soldiers to guard property in St. Louis. There was, of course, no good answer to such a question.

In February Nathaniel Lyon of the regular army arrived in St. Louis on assignment to help guard the arsenal. Lyon, an old Free-Soiler, contacted Frank Blair, and the two men and other Union stalwarts held long discussions on the best plan for securing the arsenal and its contents against seizure either by state forces or irregular armed groups then drilling within the city. Together, Lyon and Blair persuaded Washington to recall the arsenal commander, a notorious southern sympathizer. An American was assigned to the regiments of Germans drilling in German neighborhoods so that the men learned to understand commands in English. On 13 March these volunteer regiments made a surprise march to the arsenal, where they took an oath of loyalty to the federal government and took arms issued by Lyon, who by then managed to have sole command of the facility.

Then came the 12 April attack on Fort Sumter. What was a tense waiting game took on a new sense of urgency. Lyon knew that his small force of regulars, even with the assistance of the poorly trained volunteers, had little chance of withstanding a determined assault by the Missouri militia units. The captain sent a message to Gov. Richard Yates in Springfield, Illinois, suggesting that Illinois request federal arms to equip the Illinois state forces. Yates complied, and in a secret, dead-of-night operation, the bulk of the arms remaining in the arsenal crossed the Mississippi safely into Illinois. Lyon and his local supporters now were free to move against the Missouri militia units at Camp Jackson. To get firsthand knowledge of what faced him there, Captain Lyon disguised himself as a blind woman and drove through the camp in a carriage.

So it was on 10 May that four regiments of grim men tramped through the St. Louis streets, frightening young Francis Grierson and many other residents. While many of the men were German-Americans, the ranks included Union supporters of Yankee stock as well. Blair himself led one regiment; Henry Boernstein, Franz Sigel, and Nicholas Schuttner—all Forty-Eighters—led the other three. By ten o'clock that morning Camp Jackson was surrounded. Governor Jackson's troops surrendered without a shot being fired. With 1,100 prisoners in tow, the Germans began the long march back to the arsenal.

Just who fired the first shot that May day in St. Louis remains a matter of dispute. As the long column filed through the city streets, irate citizens pelted the soldiers with insults and stones. Some witnesses claimed the German soldiers — nervous and poorly disciplined, and taunted beyond endurance — wheeled around and fired toward the bystanders; they hit some of their own rear rank comrades as well as innocent bystanders. Other witnesses insisted that a German officer deliberately ordered to his men to fire at their tormentors. Still other accounts say that a hidden assassin fired a pistol at the soldiers, and they returned fire in self-defense. Whatever the truth of the matter, when the shooting ended between eighteen and twenty-five men, women, and children lay dead on the streets and walks, some dying in their own yards and homes. Who was guilty and who was innocent in the carnage on St. Louis streets in the reports that flashed around the country that day depended in large measure on the politics of the newspaper reporting the incident.[19] When order was restored, the guards and their prisoners resumed their march. In the event, it was the aftermath of what came to be known as the "Camp Jackson Affair" that was more important than individual guilt or innocence.

First, while Missouri became the scene of bloody battlefields during the Civil War, the state stayed within the Union; St. Louis, with its resources and strategic location, remained safely in Union hands. St. Louis Germans deserved much of the credit for this. A year after the event, one of Frank Blair's bitter political opponents admitted as much. "Enough, for shame," cried future U.S. Senator Charles D. Drake, "that Americans by birth were false to their country and its flag; enough, for rejoicing and pride, that Americans by adoption were true to both."[20] Drake went on to bemoan the fact that his native-born fellow Americans were his enemies, while his "alien brothers" were his friends. All honor to the volunteers who took Camp Jackson, he concluded. The Germans saved St. Louis. That was the conclusion drawn by German-Americans and their leaders around the country; while somewhat overdrawn, that was the conclusion accepted in other states and by later historians. The Camp Jackson Affair gave a great boost to ethnic pride, and the St. Louis volunteer regiments, short lived though they were, were among the first foreign military units in the Union armies.

One of the casualties in St. Louis street fighting that day in May was the master-at-arms of the St. Louis Turnverein, Constantin Blandowski. Almost immediately, despite his obviously Slavic name, he entered the German-American hall of fame. Blandowski, proclaimed ethnic political leaders, was both a German-American martyr and the first officer to die for the Union. (The famous Elmer Ellsworth died 24 May almost two weeks later.) Konstantin(e) Blandowski (or Blandowsky) was actually a Polish soldier-of-fortune.[21] Born in Upper Silesia, just inside the German side of the border with Russia, he was trained in Germany, served in the French Foreign Legion, fought in the Hungarian rebel forces in 1848, and afterwards came to America. That Blandowski became a German hero is testimony to the eagerness of the major ethnic groups to exploit every opportunity for a claim on the national conscience. In the months and years ahead there would be many Blandowski cases, and some would be Irish as well as German.

Many St. Louis citizens, horrified and outraged by what they saw as inexcusable slaughter by alien barbarians run amok and incensed by the seizure of public property and the imprisonment of Missouri citizens by foreigners, sent family members to safety outside the city (some fled themselves) and made preparations to defend themselves and their city against rumored attacks by the "lop-eared Dutch." The affray convinced many southerners—who needed little convincing anyway—that their suspicions about the treacherous character of foreigners were now confirmed. Most of the men captured at Camp Jackson and released a short time later fought in the Confederate army, and their legacy of the May days in St. Louis was a bitter hatred of the Germans.

For better or worse, the Camp Jackson incident and the national notoriety accorded the role of the Germans in St. Louis was perfectly timed to increase public awareness of the ethnic element in the Civil War. It offered striking evidence, if any were needed, that ethnic politics were a significant factor in the wartime posture in the North. Colonel Michael Corcoran, the fiery Irish nationalist awaiting court-martial in New York when sectional hostilities began, is additional evidence. "Looking back at the Civil War," notes historian Robert C. Nesbit, "one is struck by the pervasiveness of politics in the volunteer army from top to bottom. . . . "[22] The Civil War, that most political of all American wars, was fought with military forces that accurately reflected the political situation in America at the time. Ethnic politics were very much a part of the political scene.

"Military organizations reflect the societies they serve."[23] The same kind of man goes into military forces in America, whether in the Revolution, World War I, the Civil War, or even the peacetime army. Patriotism, love of adventure, the pursuit of glory, and other motives drive the volunteer, but two motives dominate: the search for manhood and economic opportunity. Native-born and immigrant Americans acted out of similar motivations. Civil War armies mirrored Civil War society.

American armed forces in 1861 had several decades of their own history, decades in which practices and traditions were firmly entrenched. One such tradition was the use of political influence as a method of personal advancement.[24] Military men often appealed to political friends on matters involving their own careers; appeals to the public through the press also occurred. While there was a custom that the American military stayed out of the political process, the principle did not apply to individual officers pursuing their own careers. That military practice continued with a vengeance through the Civil War years.

Another familiar part of the social-military tradition of America was the volunteer militia company and regiment. Such organizations often reflected the class structure of the city in which the company was located. Large cities like Chicago and New York had old militia units whose primary purpose in peacetime (at least in unofficial terms) was to provide status and entertainment for members and families. In New York, for example, the famed Seventh Infantry was known as the "Silk Stocking Regiment"; its roster was a cross section of the city's aristocracy. When immigrants found their membership in such militia units barred by discrimination or law, they formed their own units. Membership in ethnic military organizations (and in the nonethnic units) was a common path to social climbing, a way to get the attention of the local power structure and rub shoulders with the influential. New York's Sixty-ninth Infantry Regiment, the Irish regiment commanded by Colonel Corcoran, was just the most famous of similar units in other cities. In the early days of the war, it was regiments of this kind that set off promptly for Washington to defend the capital against the threat of Confederate attack.

In some cities these military companies of foreign-born soldiers actually existed before any native American units. In Milwaukee, during the 1850s when Know-Nothing sentiment was strong, Germans formed an artillery company. The thought of self-defense was clearly involved. The Irish of the city put together their own volunteer militia, and finally an American military company was organized.[25] The American-born James A. Mulligan, when his family moved from New York to Chicago, deliberately cast his lot with the local Irish-American establishment in that city and enlisted in an Irish company. This was what the ambitious young Irish-American was expected to do. Irish companies ordinarily identified themselves with the name of an Irish patriot, while German companies selected names reminiscent of traditional German military organizations. Already in place, then, in American society, in addition to the ethnic component in local and national politics, was a tradition of ethnic military organizations.

Immigrants also were deeply involved in America's military life in other ways. Well before the war broke out, the rank and file of the small regular army was dominated by immigrants. So small was the army (about 16,000 men in April 1861), however, that it was clear from the beginning of hostilities that the state militias would bear the major responsibility for waging the war. Immigrants loomed large there, too. For example, Robert Patterson, born in Ireland in 1792, emigrated to America with his father at the turn of the century. Patterson built up the largest textile business in the country, fought in the Mexican War, was active in politics, and at the outbreak of the Civil War he was in command of the Pennsylvania volunteer militia with the rank of general.[26] Patterson's combination of business interests, political activities, and participation in the state militia was not at all uncommon, either for ethnic or nonethnic leaders.

After the attack on Fort Sumter, when President Lincoln issued the first call for volunteers, the federal government turned to the states for the military manpower required to wage war. From the beginning the basic building block of the Union army was the regiment. Before the war ended, the North organized over 2,000 regiments of infantry, cavalry, and artillery.[27] In the early days of the war many regiments were recruited for only three months' service. The normal period of enlistment after these early days was for three years, and about 1,600 regiments and artillery batteries were three-year units. The three-year infantry or cavalry regiment was the most characteristic military organization of the Civil War. The regiment was the center of the soldier's life; he identified with it, and recruiting focused on the regiment. It is the Union regiment that is the subject of this study, and, in particular, the regiments that most vividly record the ethnic experience in the war.

Regiments were organized in different ways and around a variety of foci. Geographically, regiments came out of city neighborhoods, congressional districts, counties, regions, and other areas. Recruiters often appealed to a very limited population. There was a Teachers' Regiment, a Lead Miners' Regiment, a Temperance Regiment, and a valiant effort was even made to organize a Christian Regiment. One admirer of Frederick the Great tried to recruit an outfit of men over six-feet tall. New York's Tammany Hall sponsored a volunteer group. Of all the special interest or exotic regiments, however, by far the most numerous and most significant historically were the ethnic units.

An ethnic regiment in the Union army was one with the following three characteristics. (1) At the time of its organization, a large majority of its members were foreign born, or sons of foreign-born fathers. With few exceptions, this means the soldiers were members of the same ethnic group. This includes as well evidence that the men were deliberately recruited as ethnics. (2) Members of the regiment identified themselves and their regiment as an ethnic organization. (3) The larger society regarded the regiment as an ethnic organization. This definition excludes some regiments often cited in the general literature as "German" or "Irish," but where substantial evidence suggests that a majority of the members were *not* members of a given ethnic group. It excludes, possibly, a small number of regiments whose membership was largely made up of a single ethnic group, but where there is no evidence that either the men themselves or the larger society identified the unit as ethnic. Finally, the focus here is limited to regiments; the multitude of companies, batteries, and naval units touched with some tint of ethnicity is ignored.

Foreigners visited the United States in large numbers during the Civil War, and military men observing the process by which the North raised an army the size of the French army in a matter of months were amused, startled, horrified, and in the end unbelieving that a modern army could be raised in such a way. One of the most discerning of such visitors was Camille Ferri Pisani, who accompanied the Prince Napoleon to America in the summer of 1861. Ferri Pisani found recruiting fascinating. "I would be tempted to dismiss it as comedy," he told a correspondent, "except we know amid all the vulgar fantasy a huge army is being organized and transported to the field of battle." He had a good understanding of how the system worked:

> As soon as the act of Congress was made public, thousands of citizens, with no mandate but their own more or less justified confidence in themselves and their notoriety, took over the huge program of recruiting and the formation of staffs and units for their own benefit. Meanwhile, the government quietly watched the singular spectacle of an army organizing itself, and waited patiently for this army to be placed in its hands. . . . One man would call for all those who accepted him as a captain, and raise a company. Another, appointing himself colonel, raised a regiment. A few declared right away that they would organize whole brigades. A free and boundless competition — the very spirit of all American enterprises — was at the basis of these singular operations. Each military contractor naturally tried to ruin his competition. Such a person, who had begun his operations as a general, would successively lower his rank for lack of customers and would eventually settle for command of a platoon. Another, exalted by the popular response, increased his company to a regiment and then to a brigade. . . . In the United States the military and moral credit . . . of a certain number of citizens acted as an intermediary between the State and the mass of the population. They were the levers which gave birth, almost suddenly, to a mediocre army perhaps, but still an army. Furthermore, it is quite a large army, and with time it should become quite good.[28]

Ferri Pisani's keen eye caught the very essence of the way in which the North raised its host. It was a system based on the entrepreneur, individual initiative, competition, and political patronage. It was a system tailor-made for ethnic politics.

# CHAPTER 4

# Recruiting the Ethnics

War is not merely a political act, but a political instrument, a continuation of political relations, a carrying out of the same by other means.

—KARL VON CLAUSEWITZ, *On War*

N a hot, muggy Saturday in late July 1861, the Illinois congressional delegation in Washington gave its attention to one of the more critical aspects of the war against the Confederacy. The senators and congressmen argued questions of patronage. It was a particular kind of patronage that day. Who would get the nod for the state's quota of brigadier generals in the growing Union army? State governors appointed colonels to head the volunteer regiments then being raised in each state, but only President Lincoln could name the generals. The president, however, acceded to state political leaders a certain power of nomination.[1] Like all other states, Illinois wanted its share of such appointments—and as many more as it could wheedle out of the White House. Patronage was the lifeblood of American politics; the Civil War, far from changing that fundamental fact, increased its importance. Whatever else it meant, the war vastly increased the amount of patronage at every level of government. Back in Illinois, Gov. Richard Yates received a steady stream of requests, pleas, and complaints about patronage and military appointments. From the raising of regiments to the selection of their officers, partisan politics were omnipresent. Chicago and downstate political leaders sought favors and appointments for themselves and their friends, relatives, and supporters. County officials kept the governor apprised of the ratio of Democrats and Republicans enlisting in the military. So tense was the situation in some parts of the state that several observers feared that if too many Republicans volunteered, treasonable Democrats remaining at home might win control of the government. People took their politics seriously in Illinois, and they carried partisanship along with them into uniform. The major of the Twenty-ninth Illinois Infantry put it this way:

Many of [our officers] are Democrats and Every whear theay can, theay Recommend to you for promotion, men of theire own Claise, and by this meanes the Democracy (purverted as it is) proposes to insirt its insidious coils around the Hearts of the People for the purpose of gaining the controls of the Government, and let me say to you that wheare Ever I have found a Republican, I have found an unconditional American Man. . . .[2]

Governor Yates might ignore the decidedly paranoid fears of some correspondents, but neither he nor any other governor could ignore the pressures of party politics in the process of accepting volunteer regiments for federal service and appointing the officers in those regiments. Wartime patronage attracted applicants like moths to a flame. There were wagon masters, drivers, sutlers, contractors, suppliers, and any number of other possibilities. Political maneuvering occurred at every level from inside the regiments to the corridors of the state capitol. Many Republicans asserted the claim that since the Democratic party was the party of treason and rebellion, *all* spoils must go to deserving Republicans. Northern governors proved surprisingly stubborn in resisting the more outrageous partisan demands.

Indiana's Gov. Oliver P. Morton, completely lacking in military knowledge and experience, found himself appointing officers he never met. As with peacetime patronage appointments, he had to rely upon the advice of others. He had to weigh rival claims, listen to invective and accusations, soothe the disappointed, and urge the victors to be magnanimous. Morton, who was not noted for determination and strength of character before the war, made a serious effort to involve both political parties in the state's military effort. Whatever his inner qualms, Morton did approach his political opponents and got their help in raising troops. As late as April 1861, for example, the *Indianapolis Sentinel* — a Democratic paper that bitterly opposed the use of force against the South and opposed the war when it began — along with one of its editors, John C. Walker, denounced the war as a profit-making enterprise for New England. Morton appealed to Walker to raise a regiment among the state's Irish-American citizens. Walker agreed.[3]

As the nation's recruiting effort began, officials in Washington made a basic decision that both enlarged the patronage possibilities in the states and strengthened the role of partisan politics in the war. Casualties, illness, desertion, and resignations brought an inevitable shrinkage. The logical and efficient way to cope with this situation was to form either pools of replacement companies or organize three-battalion regiments, with one battalion kept in reserve for training and recruitment. In July 1861 Congress passed a law to mandate ten company volunteer regiments, with no provision for replacements. This encouraged every northern state to organize new regiments — every new regiment meant additional patronage — instead of replenishing the strength of existing regiments. Even in 1864, with understrength regiments a serious problem, states resisted the belated efforts of Washington to fill up old units rather than create new ones. Politics overrode military and economic efficiency. Most field officers in the Union forces were ordinary politicians whose primary qualifications were party influence. It followed, then, that the same persons and organizations involved in peacetime political activity took the lead in recruiting Union armies. Those ethnic politicians already involved in party affairs turned their attention and energies to the military patronage system.[4]

Carl Schurz, the most visible and perhaps the most influential ethnic politician at the national level, promptly put his acknowledged skills to work after Fort Sumter. He contacted President Lincoln, U.S. senators, and state officials in an effort to establish an ethnic presence in the army. He sought a general's commission for himself, urged Lincoln to create a German brigade, and even won Lincoln's early agreement to create such a brigade. An embarrassed Lincoln had to withdraw that permission when he realized that he had accepted too many eager volunteers in the early weeks of the war.[5] Unabashed, Schurz continued to bombard him with suggestions on how to run the war and what to do for German-Americans. Schurz eventually accepted an appointment as ambassador to Spain, and when a German brigade was created another German-American led it.

Old pro Gustave Koerner kept track of the appointment of general officers and knew from week to week how many Democrats got these plums and how many went to Republicans. Koerner used his influence with the Yates administration in Illinois to promote plans for German-American regiments and sought commissions in newly formed regiments for deserving Republicans and fellow German-Americans. At the same time, Koerner recognized the foolishness of creating an infinite number of regimental fragments, and he urged Yates to control such appointments. The best control, of course, would be to limit new appointments until his own regiment was filled. Koerner even competed with his fellow German-American politicians in this respect. When Koerner decided that the Democrats had their share of military appointments, he encouraged Yates to give a larger share to Republicans.[6]

Old soldier Hecker immediately left his Illinois farm when the war began and enlisted as a private in a three-month–German-American regiment in St. Louis. He was over fifty at the time. Koerner visited St. Louis, saw Hecker, and found him thoroughly committed to the Union cause. What Hecker did not know was that events in Chicago would quickly end his romantic gesture of serving as a common soldier.

Prominent German-American leaders in Chicago (as elsewhere in the North) promoted the idea of an all-German regiment. Those involved in the enterprise included Caspar Butz; George Schneider, who was the editor of the *Illinois Staats Zeitung;* Anton C. Hesing, Cook County sheriff; and Lorenz Brentano, who was active in German-American affairs in the city and who would be a presidential elector in 1864. This group approached Charles Knobelsdorf (a veteran of the armed forces of Schleswig-Holstein) and Julian Kuné (who fought in the 1848 revolution in Hungary) with a proposal for an ethnic regiment. Kuné and Knobelsdorf agreed and began recruiting volunteers. Sheriff Hesing organized a company himself, and Kuné went off to Washington to seek permission to get a regiment accepted outside the Illinois quota. Meanwhile, Hecker's friends went to work. They summoned him to Chicago to command the "Hecker Regiment," the very unit Kuné and Knobelsdorf were organizing! Hecker, for his part, arrived in Chicago to find that the "Hecker Regiment" existed primarily in the fertile imagination of its initiators. It was a humbug, he told Koerner. "I found officers in great numbers, but few privates. Like a condottiero, I had to begin recruiting and found a good deal of opposition." Kuné returned from Washington and discovered to his chagrin that in his absence Hecker had won the position of colonel of the regiment and Géza Mihalotzy, another Hungarian exile, was lieutenant colonel. As was so often the case, Mihalotzy's bargaining chip was a company he had organized and offered to bring into the regiment. Knobelsdorf was out completely; Kuné accepted the post of major as a consolation prize. Sheriff Hesing and other Chicago entrepreneurs thereupon sent a petition to Governor Yates, urging him to give Knobelsdorf a commission as captain in another regiment, citing as justification Knobelsdorf's efforts in organizing the Hecker Regiment.[7] Hecker himself, after laboring diligently to organize his unit, found that the Twenty-fourth Illinois Infantry was impossible to command.[8] He also complained bitterly that the administration in Springfield discriminated against his regiment because it was German, but his complaints were unfounded.

The story of the organization of the Illinois Twenty-fourth Infantry was not unusual. From its inception as an idea, through the double-dealing and intragroup and individual rivalry, the German-American regiment followed a pattern similar to scores of others around the North. What happened was not unique to the ethnic experience; it happened with other kinds of regiments as well. If anything, the chicanery connected to the origin of the Twenty-fourth Infantry was mild — although the subsequent history of the regiment more than made up for this modest beginning. The political origin of the regiment does not distinguish it from nonethnic units; only the ethnic appeals and arguments employed by the organizers set it apart from any other regiment. When he cooperated with German-American leaders in such matters (as he did with any other power brokers in the process), Governor Yates expected favors in return. Patronage was a complex business. Once the Twenty-fourth Infantry entered government service, Yates appealed to its colonel (as he would to any other officer under similar circumstances) for a return favor. He asked Hecker to appoint a deserving German from Jacksonville as regimental sutler.[9]

Governor Yates received so many pleas and demands from German constituents and German political leaders that he hired a German-speaking secretary to handle the volume of correspondence. Caspar Butz, Sheriff Hesing, George Schneider, Lieutenant Governor Hoffman, and other spokesmen for the state's German population kept steady private and public pressure on the governor to get a fair share of the spoils of war for their ethnic community. Senator Browning in Washington found it expedient to lobby for the acceptance of the Twenty-fourth Infantry into federal service (the state oversubscribed its quota, a common problem in the early days of the war). Individual Germans from around the state bombarded Yates with offers of help, often claiming special expertise because of prior service in German armies. Chicago leaders watched national developments as well as those within the state, and they were quick to react to any perceived slight to Germans or German champions.

Irish-Americans took the same path in April 1861. The major differences in the behavior of the two groups lay in the violence of the Irish rhetoric and in the complications stemming from Irish nationalism. Other ethnic groups in Illinois, such as the Scots, worked the same political levers, but their smaller numbers meant that their impact was minor. Only the Germans and the Irish in Illinois organized ethnic regiments. When a Chicago businessman tried to organize a Scottish regiment, Yates gave him the same friendly response he gave to the Germans and Irish, but the Scottish effort failed.[10]

The Illinois story was repeated in every northern state where ethnic numbers and leaders supported such efforts. In Cincinnati Judge Stallo led a drive for a German regiment. The Cincinnati Germans, worried about a reaction from the larger society about *too* much German visibility, borrowed a tactic from St. Louis Germans and selected a non-German as the colonel of the first German regiment in Ohio.[11] It was no coincidence that the colonel was Stallo's law partner, Robert L. McCook. August Willich was the real military brain behind the regimental organization, and the core of early volunteers for the Ninth Ohio Infantry came from the Turnverein. In New York Frederick Kapp and other political and business leaders from the very beginning of the war agitated for German regiments. And so it went in Philadelphia, St. Louis, Milwaukee, Indianapolis, and other cities and regions with significant concentrations of Germans. Even if an all-German regiment were not the immediate goal, ethnic politics demanded a proportionate share of wartime patronage. As one writer to Wisconsin's Governor Randall put it:

> As there has been no German appointments made yet to the proposed Redgiment, it is thought by many of my Friends in Milwaukee that some prominent German should receive some position in the Military department at Madison. . . .[12]

This familiar kind of communication attained a generic quality, familiar to anyone involved in military patronage.

To a large extent, recruiting appeals to ethnics were exactly the same as those for all Americans. Whether the appeal come from an existing militia unit, a state government, or the national government, the techniques and arguments were the same. The Union was threatened and patriots should join up and fight to defend that Union. It was an effective argument, and one that scarcely needed to be made in the early months of the war. There was no shortage of men willing and anxious to fight for their country. Most ethnic Americans joined nonethnic units, and so the appeal and sentiment were common to both kinds of recruits. There were, however, some techniques and arguments used to attract ethnic volunteers that differed from those employed for other young men.

That Americans generally recognized a need for different appeals to the foreign born is evident in the work of the Loyal Publication Society. The society, formed in New York in 1863 when enlistments were down and opposition to the war flourished, included both foreign-born and native Americans among its leaders. The president was Francis Lieber, a well-known German-born philosopher and political theorist. Other officers of the society included such pillars of the American establishment as James A. Roosevelt, William E. Dodge, Jr., Charles Butler, and Charles Astor Bristed. In its first year of existence the society published and distributed 500,000 tracts, all intended to strengthen patriotism and counter the defeatism and discouragement spreading through the North.[13] Some of these tracts appeared in a variety of foreign languages, and their purpose was to persuade the foreign born to support the war. Such tracts, however, for the most part repeated arguments used since 1861 by ethnic American politicians.

Cultural chauvinism was perhaps the most common appeal used to recruit ethnics. Whatever the ethnic group, speakers and posters and newspapers worked ceaselessly to convince its members that their ethnic background made them superior military material — and probably morally superior to the native born as well. "Swedes!" cried one Scandinavian spokesman, "have you forgotten that in the course of mankind's progress, enlightenment, and freedom the Swedish people were always found among the most zealous defenders?" An Irishman, according to the typical refrain repeated endlessly at rallies of Irish-Americans, just by virtue of being Irish was better than other people. That an Irishman's heritage made him a natural-born fighter was an argument used with such frequency that both the Irish and the non-Irish came to accept it as fact. So firmly fixed was this racial stereotype that it is still used by historians ruminating about the role of the Irish in the Civil War. Scholars outraged at the very thought of racial or ethnic stereotyping have no qualms about affixing this characteristic on the Irish. Germans heard from every side the claim that theirs was a superior race and culture; Germans were "natural lovers of freedom and fighters for good causes." Since most immigrants enlisted in "American" outfits, these ethnic appeals had only limited influence.[14]

Language was important. Much recruiting of ethnics was undertaken in languages other than English. Recruiting posters in German plastered store fronts, fences, and any convenient surface in German neighborhoods. Speakers at rallies put their appeals in the language native to the audience. But there was more to it than simply making the contact. The foreign-born young man who lacked skill in English felt more comfortable with the thought that his introduction to military life might be in his own tongue. Swedes gravitated toward companies led by Swedish officers. Potential officers and noncommissioned officers had a great advantage if they were bilingual. For the non-English-speaking immigrant, language was most critical at the company level. Even within nonethnic regiments, a company of Swedes or Germans or Italians was common. It was with the corporal or sergeant or lieutenant of his own company that the recruit had the most regular and important contact, and the entrepreneur raising a company in an immigrant neighborhood enjoyed better success when he spoke the local vernacular.

Unabhängiges
Deutsches Regiment
für Illinois


Recruting posters in German—our example above is for the Gustave Koerner effort in Illinois—offered assurance to the young German that the strangeness of military life would be eased partially by the use of a familiar language.[15]

One appeal was viturally unique to the Irish. Irish nationalism played a major role in recruiting members of that group. Perhaps the most effective of all recruiters among Irish-Americans was New York's Michael Corcoran. His name conjured up in the public imagination the very image of the quintessential Irishman. He was in constant demand as a speaker at patriotic rallies, and other recruiters used his name on their recruiting posters to gain instant attention and recognition. Much of Corcoran's appeal lay in his fiery nationalism—Irish nationalism. In the late summer of 1862 Corcoran made a triumphal visit to Philadelphia, where he encouraged the enlistment of more Irish-Americans. At a rally in the city Corcoran couched much of his entreaty in words already familiar to his audience. He bragged about his famous refusal to let his regiment parade in honor of the visiting Prince of Wales in New York, reminded his listeners that he was an ardent Fenian, and asserted that Irishmen had a special reason to join the army and get military training. "When this unhappy civil war is at a close," thundered Corcoran, "and the Union restored, there will be tens of thousands of Ireland's noblest sons left to redeem their native land from the oppression of old England."[16] The Civil War as training ground for a postwar army of liberation for Ireland—many an Irish nationalist used the argument. Thomas Francis Meagher made the identical plea in Boston. Mulligan did it in Chicago. Irishmen were constantly exhorted to fight for the honor of the old country, fight in the memory of ancient Irish heroes, fight as the "Wild Geese" fought in the armies of France and other enemies of Britain. It took a wild leap of imagination, of course, to made a connection between enlisting in the Union army and adding to the luster of Ireland, but speakers had no trouble making that leap.

Common to all ethnic groups was the argument that the immigrant owed a duty to his adopted homeland. The typical newspaper announcement used a familiar set of arguments. The Irishman was told that he enjoyed the fruits of living in a free country and thus bore the responsibility for defending it against its enemies. In similar manner, a poem petitioned Welshmen to support their adopted homeland:

> The sons of ancient Britons come
> with wild hurrahs;
> They join the host that guard our home,
> And crush the foes who madly roam
> To rob our fields and change our sheltering laws.

(Not *every* Welshman is a natural poet!) A meeting of Irish-Americans in Philadelphia in August 1861 passed a series of resolutions (a favorite outdoor sport all across America that summer), including one that reminded Irishmen that they owed a duty to the land that gave them work and shelter when they fled the old country.[17]

While Germans were immune to the kind of strident nationalism so prevalent in Irish recruiting, some Germans, especially Forty-Eighters, were susceptible to a different kind of persuasion. At a huge rally in New York's Union Square in April 1861, German-Americans heard repeated reminders of why many of them fled Europe. Germans with Republican beliefs unable to attain those ideals in Europe found them in the United States and now must defend them. Liberty, argued Frederick Kapp in his peroration that evening, is indivisible; Germans should defend it wherever they find it.[18] Disunion, ran a related argument for Germans, was a curse of the German peoples in Europe. Now that the South threatened to divide America it must be opposed; Germans did not want the miseries of Europe reproduced in the New World. Those Germans who were abolitionists responded to entreaties to fight the evils of slavery.

Ethnic rivalries and suspicions made any ethnic group and any individual foreign-born American vulnerable to a particular appeal almost absent from native-American recruiting. Irish-Americans worried that Germans might out-do them in patriotism and thus win more sympathy from the larger population. Scandinavians feared the growing influence of the Germans and felt compelled to demonstrate their own attachment to America. Germans, particularly those sensitive to insults and discrimination at the hands of either native Americans or other ethnics, especially the Irish, wanted to set all doubts about their own enthusiasm and love of country to rest by volunteering for military duty. When a call went out in the Midwest for the formation of a Scandinavian regiment, part of the justification for the regiment was a comparison between the vigor of the Irish and German activity and the inactivity of the Scandinavians. Hans Christian Heg, who issued the call, warned his countrymen that they not only needed to be concerned about how they compared to the Germans and Irish, but also how the Americans would regard them. The radical German-language press in Missouri compared the Irish unfavorably with Germans, although religious prejudice as well as ethnic competition was involved there.[19]

Sheer competition for bodies to fill company and regimental quotas drove recruiters to desperate measures. In his determined efforts to get a commission in either an ethnic or a nonethnic regiment, young John R. Winterbotham—he ended up in the 155th New York Infantry, a regiment known as the "Wild Irish Regiment"—prowled through prisons in New York City, offering criminals bounties above the legal maximum to enroll in his company. Similar questionable tactics were employed by many if not most ethnic recruiters. Swedish officers promised special favors and commissions to Scandinavians as an inducement to join the ethnic unit. Recruiting "agents" received a head fee of as much as five dollars for every person delivered to an office, and inside the offices might be found whisky or beer as an additional tool for the recruiter.[20] Recruiting agents tended to be rogues, claimed the Princess Agnes Salm-Salm (not always a reliable or unbiased reporter), and her husband tried to convince President Lincoln that Union recruiting of foreigners should be put on an efficient basis by going directly to the source—the Old Country.

> There were thousands of young men who would have liked to emigrate if they could only find the means to pay their passage, and being compelled to serve in the armies of their native country for a very low pay, and no bounty at all, they would most willingly serve in that of the United States, on receiving free passage, a round sum of money, four-

teen dollars a month, and after the expiration of their time a grant of a considerable number of acres from the Government.[21]

The Princess Salm-Salm claimed that an effort to bribe a high official with $20,000 to win Lincoln's approval for the scheme failed. She did, however, manage to use her own personal charm and wiles to win a commission for her inept German husband. The use of bribes, agents' fees, and an imaginative circus atmosphere was certainly not unique to ethnic recruiting; it simply acquired its own distinctive flavor there.

Charismatic leaders undoubtedly played a significant role in attracting ethnic volunteers. A Michael Corcoran or a Thomas Meagher, skilled in the flamboyant oratorical techniques of the time, aroused genuine enthusiasm in large audiences. In the early days of the war that enthusiasm readily translated into enlistments. Corcoran turned away five volunteers for every one accepted in early 1861. As the war dragged on, charisma counted for less and cash counted more. In April and May 1861, ethnic recruiting posters used huge type and screaming headlines to attract eyes to leaders' names and ethnic ties. This gradually changed in the months and years that followed, until the most prominent feature of a recruiting poster was likely to be the bounty money and pay. Huge type in a late 1863 poster for Mulligan's Brigade, for example, announced a total of $402 in bounty money for each volunteer. This trend was evident, too, in nonethnic recruiting, but there is evidence that the monetary appeal was especially effective with the ethnics, who realized that army pay plus the bounty money resulted in higher income than farm work or unskilled labor—if indeed jobs were available. Ferri Pisani offers a vignette observed shortly after his arrival in New York in 1861:

> I saw poor, famished Irishmen devour these seductive posters with their eyes, fascinated as they were by the devilish hands pointing to the complacent listing of the soldiers' rations: bread, wine, meat, vegetables, and beer.

Such financial inducements were important elements in the ethnic recruiting done as immigrants stepped off the boat in New York or Boston and gave credence to the irate charge by Confederates that the North hired "foreign mercenaries."

When immigrants chose an ethnic regiment instead of an "American" regiment, they did so for specific reasons.[22]

Foreign languages played a role for the non-English speaker. Foreign language organizations often enlisted in a body in the ethnic regiment.[23] Swedish rifle clubs, German Turnvereine, and choral societies assured their members of a unit with cultural affinity and of instruction and command in their own language. Even though most Irishmen spoke English, they sought out an Irish regiment when having a priest for a chaplain was important.

They knew most regiments had Protestant ministers for a chaplain. Authorities quickly learned that one way to discipline an Irish regiment was to threaten to replace the priest with a Protestant.

Much ethnic color and ceremony were associated with the ethnic regiments. In Pennsylvania, Col. Alexander Schimmelfennig's German regiment gathered in July at a farm owned by one of Schimmelfennig's friends for entertainment prior to its departure to the seat of war. The soldiers heard singing by a Young Maennerchor, and by the Germania, Orion, and Orpheus singing societies. The men themselves sang and enjoyed theatrical performances in German and even had a kind of busmen's holiday with traditional military exercises.[24] Every ethnic regiment had a unique flag (often used instead of the state flag carried by regular regiments), adopted unit mottoes such as "For Gud og vort Land" for the Fifteenth Wisconsin Infantry, and "Kaempft tapfer fuer Freiheit" for the Ninth Ohio Infantry. Members of ethnic units might wear distinctive uniforms, enjoyed regimental doctors who knew their language, and celebrated holidays (St. Patrick's Day a notorious example) in their distinctive manner.

Geography was another factor in the formation of ethnic regiments. A common practice of the time was that of recruiting an entire regiment in a small area—a city neighborhood, a county, or a congressional district. If the local area was already populated heavily with members of a single ethnic group (such as several St. Louis neighborhoods in 1861), an ethnic regiment had a natural attraction. From the very beginning of the war, local ethnic organizations adopted the practice of mounting ceremonies for regiments of their countrymen. Such ceremonies included feasts of familiar food on special occasions, as the first formal parade for the departure from training camp. Swords with inscriptions were gifts to popular officers, and every unit got its flags in formula ceremonies with formula speeches.

Still another advantage of the ethnic regiment was its greater visibility. This was important to some individuals, but it was critical to ethnic politicians. It was one thing to publish dry statistics about how many Germans from this or that city volunteered (and to make invidious comparisons with the Irish), and it was something quite different to point with pride to the living presence of an entire regiment of Germans. After that, everything the regiment did, from initial organization to flag ceremony to emotional departure, to battles and campaigns brought additional good publicity for the ethnic group. There was, of course, some risk in this, too. A riot in camp or poor performance on the battlefield brought ethnic slurs as quickly as praise accompanied good deeds. Ethnic regimental identity made it easier to solicit contributions from businessmen and organizations to support the unit, to organize charitable activities, and to involve families and churches in the life of the regiment.

Of all the factors behind the formation of ethnic regiments, however, the most critical by far was the entrepreneurship of a charismatic leader. Some individual had to take the initiative, and that initiative usually came from an ethnic politician or a person with military experience in the Old Country or someone with a high profile in the ethnic community. It was the name of such men that appeared in large block letters on the recruiting posters early in the war. Join MULLIGAN'S BRIGADE! Join MRS. MEAGHER'S OWN regiment! Such leaders either had familiarity themselves with the ethnic political system as well as state and national politics, or had the support of people who did. In all the hustle and competition of 1861 and early 1862 there simply had to be a skilled entrepreneur to round up the necessary political and financial resources essential for the birth of a regiment of volunteers. There had to be, for example, a Louis Blenker to push, push, push for the money and authority, who knew what levers to press in Albany or Washington to get a regiment accepted for federal service. Blenker, as even his detractors admitted, was good at this. Blenker knew how to use federal officials to pressure state officials and how to use state officials to influence the right people in Washington. He knew enough to be aggressive in promoting his own cause and position. In the hectic summer days of 1861, Blenker offered Washington an obvious way out of the problem of too many ambitious colonels trying to organize too many understrength regiments. Let me take over, he suggested to General McClellan, and I'll see that viable regiments are brought up to strength and put into a brigade commanded by me.[25] No doubt with tongue in cheek, Blenker even promised to do the job free of all political influence! He got the necessary grant of authority. What Blenker did in New York (and Washington) Koerner did in Illinois and others did elsewhere.

Proportionate to their numbers in the population, more English-Americans served in the Union armies than any other ethnic group. But despite several efforts in the early months of the war to organize British regiments, none succeeded. Two elements were lacking. English-Americans lacked a sense of ethnic identity, and their political leaders made virtually no effort to create one. Here and there efforts were made to raise a British company, but English-Americans, like Canadian-Americans and most Scots, simply blended into the larger society. They were the "invisible ethnics."

Ethnic regiments emerged from one other source. In New York City on the eve of the war the vast majority of men enrolled in militia units were foreign born.[26] Like the Sixty-ninth Regiment led by Corcoran, these men and their regiments and companies simply entered federal service in a body. Many of the three-month regiments created after the Fort Sumter attack had this origin. In cities like Chicago, several separate Irish companies merged to form a regiment. The process was simply the continuation of an old tradition, one that since the 1830s saw military organizations based upon ethnic origin.

The Civil War is the great American epic. Nothing in the nation's history did so much to create myth, manufacture legend, challenge the character of the people, and shape the destiny of the nation for so many generations. Dominating town and city parks in thousands of communities, North *and* South is the statue of the soldier. In the North, it is the standard issue version of the Boy in Blue, clutching a musket and standing above a memorial to a local regiment or to the honored dead from the area. In the South the uniform differs, but the stance, the message, and the meaning are all the same. It requires an effort of will to look coldly at that titanic conflict and recognize that like any war of such monumental proportions it involved participants who saw it simply as an adventure, a path to easy wealth and notoriety, or just one more stop in a lifetime of soldiering. The polite label for these men is soldier of fortune. There are several less polite terms applied to them. When war clouds gathered over America, thousands of adventurers poured into the country, most of them in the North but some in the South as well. The Civil War was the opportunity of a lifetime if the opportunity sought was a quick commission and prospects of rapid promotion. From every country of Europe they came, Swedes, Italians, Hungarians, Poles, Frenchmen, Englishmen, Swiss, Luxembourgers, Spaniards, and Russians. They came across the Canadian border as well. Many were propelled by idealism, a determination to fight for a free society against a slave society, but many came seeking more mundane goals, and not a few were rascals and frauds. Part of the story of the ethnic regiments and of the role of the foreign born in the Civil War is the story of these soldiers of fortune.

European history is filled with countless tales of military adventurers, and their role in American history goes back at least to the Revolution.[27] Indeed, ethnic leaders in 1861 frequently recalled the stirring tales of Revolutionary ethnic heroes as they urged their compatriots to enlist. Swarms of mercenaries came to North America uninvited and pestered the Continental Congress for appointments. Congressmen grew weary of the barons, counts, marquises, and ordinary generals and lesser officers touting their skills and experience and soliciting military posts. A handful of these place seekers performed valuable service; they made real contributions to the ultimate victory. Washington, D.C. and the several state capitals in 1861 witnessed the same events all over again. Even President Lincoln devoted much of his limited time to meetings with the adventurers.

William Howard Russell, the acid-tongued correspondent of the *London Times,* met enough frauds and miscreants when he covered the Crimean War to be wary of them when he came to the United States to report on the Civil War. On 3 December 1861 he attended a dinner where he was introduced to a Col. George Frederic D'Utassy. The colonel had a strange tale to tell. He was born in Hungary, he informed Russell, served in the Austrian army, and then joined in the 1848 Revolution. Wounded and taken prisoner at Temesvar, he escaped; a series of incredible adventures led him finally to Constantinople, where he undertook the training of the Turkish cavalry. From Turkey he went to Greece and worked for British officials as a sort of general factotum and interpreter. Greece, it turned out, was just a stop on the way to the United States, where the colonel fell on hard times; he was even reduced to teaching fencing lessons and foreign languages to earn a living. Fortunately the war came along to rescue him from the tedium of this existence, and in a mere seventeen days he personally organized a crack regiment of foreigners to serve the Union.[28] Russell knew a tall tale when he heard one. His instinct told him D'Utassy was a rascal. His Garibaldi Guard was an incredible collection of nationalities and uniforms and quarreling factions. Russell's instincts that December night were on target; he, and the nation, would hear more about the Hungarian colonel.

Frederich Otto Baron von Fritsch also found the war a blessing. Born in Weimar in 1834, he served as a cavalry officer in the Saxony army. He came to America in 1856 and promptly fell on hard times. In 1860 he went to Mexico, and although his purpose was to study Spanish he managed to join in a brief revolutionary war in 1862. Taken prisoner by rebels and about to be executed, Fritsch was rescued by a French colonel and, expelled from Mexico, he sailed to Cuba. It was in Cuba that he first learned about the American Civil War, and so he rushed to Washington in search of a commission in the Union army. In the capital Fritsch made the usual rounds. He haunted the hotels and bars, striking up conversations with likely individuals. The Prussian minister in Washington refused to make an appointment for him with Lincoln, but the British minister did. The president referred him to Stanton, Stanton told him to try a state governor, and Fritsch went off to the Willard Hotel, where all aspiring officers, politicians, and promoters stayed. At the Willard he met New York's Governor Morgan, who told him to find a colonel. Following this tip, Fritsch went to the hotel popular with a certain class of Germans, looked in the bar, and there found an inebriated colonel. He had the good fortune, of all the colonels in Washington, to encounter Gotthilf Bourray d'Ivernois, an Austrian soldier of fortune, who served in the Austrian and Papal armies before coming to the States. Fritsch and Bourray went to the Willard, sought out Governor Morgan, and the governor upon Bourray's tipsy recommendation, gave Fritsch a commission in the Sixty-eighth New York Infantry. This regiment, named the "Cameron Rifles" after the then secretary of war, was an ethnic hodgepodge but with more Germans than anything else. Bourray and the Sixty-eighth already had a checkered record. When the colonel and his regiment marched to city hall in New York three months earlier, a deputy sheriff arrested Bourray because the regiment had failed to pay its debts—clearly a sour note to sound when the men were waiting to receive their battle flag.

> Now equipped with a commission, Fritsch prepared to join his regiment: I paid my bill at Willard's Hotel [he wrote] and checked my trunk, packed with the citizen's outfit. By advice, I also secured a large, fine canteen, and had it filled with the best rye whiskey, bought a box of good cigars, and had a big luncheon wrapped up; then I spent the balance of the night talking to officers and ex-officers, and, while treating them, getting a good deal of information.

The baron was off to war.[29]

It was an odd sort of war he encountered. At the camp of the Sixty-eighth he learned (1) that Bourray never drew a sober breath, and (2) that his commission meant nothing because the regiment had no vacancy. The latter difficulty Bourray managed to resolve. He so abused and berated one of the other officers that the man resigned and Fritsch got the spot. Fritsch thus found himself in a regiment filled with animosity, led by a drunken ne'er-do-well, and with dim prospects. Things took a turn for the worse at this point. He went on a march, got sore feet, and realized that life in the Sixty-eighth was not for him. And then Dame Fortune smiled on him. As Fritsch nursed his sore feet, Gen. Alexander Schimmelfennig walked by. Taking pity on his countryman, Schimmelfennig offered Fritsch a position on his own staff. Colonel Bourray took the news with bad grace, but Fritsch happily escaped from the Sixty-eighth. Bourray was later dismissed from the army for drunkenness, and Fritsch found his new position a dead end for his military career.

While the motives of the soldiers of fortune and adventurers were unmistakable, those of other volunteers were more complex.

Early volunteers were, first and foremost, patriots. That was the postwar recollection of Col. Alexander C. McClurg, one of the distinguished staff officers in the western army. Most authorities agree with McClurg's assessment. There can be little doubt that a sense of duty and love of country prompted most of the early enlistments. "I am not the one to stay at home when danger threatens my beloved country . . .," wrote Joseph Griner to his mother after he joined a Pennsylvania regiment. Nineteen-year-old Rice C. Bull, in upstate New York, joined the 123d New York Infantry in the summer of 1862 for exactly the same reason. That sense of duty and love of country remained a powerful motive well into the second year of the war for most Americans.[30]

Part of the nostalgia associated with the war is the assumption that

THE GLORIOUS 9TH! The Ninth Massachusetts Infantry was that state's first Irish regiment. This recruiting poster, printed after the unit's first leader, Colonel Thomas Cass, fell at the Battle of Malvern Hill, appeals to Irish nationalism and promises a priest as a regimental chaplain. (*Massachusetts Historical Society*)

# The Glorious 9th!

## IRISHMEN

## To the Rescue!

### Irish Americans of Massachusetts!

The indomitable valor and bravery which distinguished your ancestors on many a bloody battle-field in past ages, have descended to you untarnished. Your fellow countrymen of the 9th Massachusetts Regiment have proved at "Hanover Court House," at "Mechanicsville," at "Gaines' Mill," and at "Newtonville," that it has not degenerated. They are worthy inheritors of the courage and prowess of the heroes who fought at "Clontarf," at "Beal-an-ath-Buidhe," at "Limerick," at "Landen," at "Cremona" and "Fontenoy."

The Union and future glory of this great sanctuary of freedom is in danger. A host of Southern traitors seek to destroy our free democratic government, and erect upon its ruins a contemptible and Despotic Aristocracy.

Irish valor and bravery, have, to a great extent, thus far, impeded the march of these native Vandals, and driven back their superior numbers in dismay. Wherever the "chivalry" of the South have dared to encounter. on an open field, our Irish braves, they have found to their cost that Irishmen, as of old, are still invincible.

No Regiment in the service of the United States, has earned more imperishable glory than the 9th Regiment Massachusetts Volunteers, and its late gallant and heroic Colonel. The fortunes of war have thinned its ranks; it must not be allowed to perish for want of brave men to fill up its numbers.— The honors it has earned you can share. The living heroes of the 9th are still "eager for the fray." They pant to be led once more against the enemy—the enemy of human freedom—the enemy of mankind. They long to avenge their brave compatriots.

"We swear to revenge them!—no joy shall be tasted. The harp shall be silent, the maiden unwed,
Our halls shall be mute, and our fields shall be wasted, Till vengeance is wreaked on the liberticides' head."

They call upon you from the banks of the James to fill up their ranks, to share with them the laurels of the past and the glory of the future. Will you not respond to their call?

"Our green flag flutters o'er us, The friends we've tried are by our side, And the foe we hate, before us !"

## The City of Boston has voted a

## Bounty of $100!

In addition to thirty-eight dollars allowed by the United States, for every volunteer who joins the 9th Regiment. to defend the best and freest government ever vouchsafed to man. In joining the Ninth, you join your own gallant kith and kin. You will be led to the battle-field by officers of your own ancient race. who have proved themselves inferior to no others of our grand army. Here, too, the

### FLAG OF IRELAND!

Is carried side by side with the Starry Banner, and Irish bravery will obtain the credit it deserves. The laurels you win will deck your own brows—others will not obtain the credit which belongs to you. And while your prowess and invincible valor shed aditional lustre on

## The Stars and Stripes!

They will cast a bright ray of glory on the

## GREEN FLAG!

and the unconquerable nationality it represents.

In this Regiment you will have

## A CHAPLAIN OF THE OLD FAITH

To minister to your spiritual wants and dispense the priceless blessings of religion.

Your families will be provided for by the BOUNTY OF THE STATE, and you will receive in Pay, Rations and Clothing, an allowance more than that for which many of you toil at laborious drudgery, equally, if not more dangerous, than the field of honor and glory.

The nation provides also a handsome pension for you if disabled, and for your wives and little ones if you fall at the post of duty. What employer, let us ask, does the like ?

Our brave countrymen, hitherto, have rushed to the battle-field without bounty, with little hope of reward. Can YOU hesitate NOW, when such ample provision is made for you and yours?

Let the ranks of the glorious 9th be at once manned by heroes, worthy successors of those who have fallen, and fit companions of the veterans still eager for the fight. This Regiment is yours. Its history—its glory—its past—its future, are yours, and shed a lustre not on you only, but on the Irish race. The only power in Europe which supports the South is your ancient enemy, the Government of England.

"Then onward your green banners rearing, Go flesh every sword to the hilt;
On outside is virtue and Erin, On this is the Saxon and guilt."

## ☞ The Sum of $188,00! ☜

Will be paid to each volunteer as soon as mustered into service. Pay and Rations from enlistment.

Transportation for volunteers, over any of the railroads to Boston, furnished to those wishing to join.

The undersigned has received full power from the City Government of Boston to recruit the ranks of the 9th REGIMENT to its full quota.

☞ All applications for enlistment to be made at the

## Headquarters, 112 Washington Street, Boston,

### Over Little & Brown's Bookstore, to

## Capt. B. S. TREANOR,

### OR HIS AUTHORIZED AGENTS.

J. E. Farwell & Co., Steam Job Printers, 37 Congress Street, Boston.

# THIRD IRISH

## REGIMENT

From Massachusetts, and First Irish Regiment for Nine Months' Service.

## 25 ABLE-BODIED MEN

Wanted to fill up the Company to be commanded by

### CAPTAIN WILLIAMS,

Formerly of the MASS. 24th; now of the 55TH (IRISH) MASS. REG'T.

Come with us and our IRISH HERO,

# CORCORAN

Let us carry the American Eagle over the Potomac, down like an avalanche through the land of Dixie, emulating

### THE GLORY of the other IRISH REGIMENTS.

# $150 Bounty

And all who Enlist will receive the STATE AID.

All Recruits to this Regiment, on signing the Muster Roll, will go at once into comfortable quarters, and receive full rations of the best the market affords. Apply immediately to

## Captain WILLIAMS, or, Lieut. LEONARD!
### No. 109 CAMBRIDGE STREET, BOSTON.

Herald Job Office, No. 1 W illiams Court, Boston.

THIRD IRISH REGIMENT. Appealing to the famous name of Colonel Corcoran as well as the harp of Ireland, this recruiting poster for a third Irish regiment for Massachusetts appeared during the tumultuous days when Irish ambitions in the Bay State exceeded reality. *(Library of Congress)*

# Unabhängiges
# Deutsches Regiment
## für Illinois.

### Der Gouverneur hat den Unterzeichneten beauftragt, ein
## unabhäng. deutsches Regiment für Illinois

zu organisiren. Alle, die geneigt sind, der Union ihre Dienste in der Stunde der Gefahr zu weihen, und vorziehen, unter gedienten deutschen Offizieren zu fechten, haben nun eine Gelegenheit. Das Regiment ist als „deutsches Regiment" acceptirt, und sowie eine Compagnie gebildet ist, kann sie sogleich nach „Camp Butler," bei Springfield, abgehen, wo sie Lager bezieht und verpflegt wird. Nur kräftige Leute sollen sich melden, da die Musterung streng ist. Das Regiment kann sich seine Offiziere selbst wählen, vorbehalten der vorgeschriebenen Bestätigung von Seiten des Gouverneurs.

Die folgenden Herren haben einstweilen die Bildung von Compagnien übernommen:

**Julius Raith, Ad. Engelmann, Wilhelm Ehrhard, Chr. Drockenbrodt.**

**August 14, 1861.**

## Gustav Körner.

UNABHÄNGIGES DEUTSCHES REGIMENT. Quite restrained compared to the symbolism and language of Irish recruiting posters, this German-language broadside announces the formation of what would become the Forty-third Illinois Infantry. *(Illinois State Historical Society)*

# Rekrutirungs-Bureau

## für das
# 5. WISCONSIN REGIMENT.

### Gesucht!

Gesunde

kräftige

## Männer

### Zur Anwerbung auf drei Jahre, oder die Dauer des Krieges.

Jeder erhält gute Kost und Kleidung und 13 Dollars monatlich nebst ärztlicher Pflege. Außerdem erhält jeder 100 Dollars Bounty Geld oder 160 Acker Land und Anfang im Dienstgen und ehrenvoller Entlassung aus dem Dienste. Sobald 6 bis 8 Mann angeworben sind, werden sie durch einen Dolmetscher beim Regimente eingeführt. Weitere Aufschlüsse werden ertheilt, wenn man sich an den Unterzeichneten wendet.

**Port Washington, 28. Nov. 1861.**

## J. C. Schröling, Rekrutirungs-Officier.

REKRUTIRUNGS-BUREAU FÜR DAS 5. WISCONSIN REGIMENT. By late November 1861, as this poster for the Fifth Wisconsin Infantry indicates, volunteers were sought for three years or the duration of the war. *(State Historical Society of Wisconsin)*

# Rekruten Verlangt

für das

# 26. Regiment
## Wisc. Volunteers!!

**Ver. Staaten Bounty : $402 für ehrenhaft aus dem Dienst entlassene Veteranen !**

**$302 für Neue Rekruten !**

27 Dollars und eine Monats-Löhnung im Voraus werden bezahlt, wenn die Mannschaft in den Dienst gemustert wird. Löhnung und Beköstigung beginnt vom Tage der Anwerbung.

Jeder Deutscher sollte sich diesem Regimente anschließen.

Rekrutirungs-Office : Vier Thüren oberhalb der Stadt-Halle, an Ostwasserstraße, 7. Ward, Milwaukee.

Druck des „See-Boten."

REKRUTEN VERLANGT FÜR DAS 26. REGIMENT WISCONSIN VOLUN-TEERS!! As the war dragged on, both ethnic and nonethnic recruiting posters changed their appeals in the direction of increased financial incentives, as the announcements for the Twenty-sixth Wisconsin Infantry and the Twenty-third Illinois Infantry reveal. *(State Historical Society of Wisconsin)*

# MULLIGAN'S BRIGADE!

## LAST CHANCE TO AVOID THE DRAFT!

# $402 BOUNTY!
## TO VETERANS!

## $302 to all other VOLUNTEERS!

All Able-bodied Men, between the ages of 18 and 45 Years, who have heretofore served not less than nine months, who shall re-enlist for Regiments in the field, will be deemed Veterans, and will receive one month's pay in advance, and a bounty and premium of $402. To all other recruits, one month's pay in advance, and a bounty and premium of $302 will be paid.

All who wish to join Mulligan's Irish Brigade, now in the field, and to receive the munificent bounties offered by the Government, can have the opportunity by calling at the headquarters of

# CAPT. J. J. FITZGERALD

Of the Irish Brigade, 23d Regiment Illinois Volunteers, Recruiting Officer, Chicago, Illinois.

Each Recruit, Veteran or otherwise, will receive

## Seventy-five Dollars Before Leaving General Rendezvous,

and the remainder of the bounty in regular instalments till all is paid. The pay, bounty and premium for three years will average $24 per month, for Veterans; and $21.30 per month for all others.

If the Government shall not require these troops for the full period of Three Years, and they shall be mustered honor out of the service before the expiration of their term of enlistment, they shall receive, UPON BEING MUSTERED O the whole amount of BOUNTY remaining unpaid, the same as if the full term been served.

### J. J. FITZGERALD.

Chicago, December, 1863.

Recruiting Officer, corner North Clark & Kenzie Stre

MULLIGAN'S BRIGADE. "Mulligan's Irish Brigade" was actually the Twenty-third Illinois Infantry. Mulligan won War Department permission to call his regiment a "brigade." *(Chicago Historical Society)*

# THE SCOTCH REGIMENT.

A REGIMENT OF INFANTRY, to be denominated the "*Scotch Regiment*," has been accepted by the Governor of the State of Illinois, for the service of the United States Government, to serve for three years, unless sooner discharged.

It will be composed chiefly of Scotchmen and the descendants of Scotchmen, although good men or other nationalities will not be excluded from entering its ranks.

## The Regiment will be Armed with the Most Effective Weapons
### USED IN MODERN WARFARE,

and placed at once in the Camp of Instruction, at Chicago, Ill., where comfortable barracks, good rations and necessary clothing will be supplied to all who enlist.

The Regiment in its

## COSTUME AND ORGANIZATION,

will be different in some respects, from any other regiment in the service. The Sutler's Office, of which so many complaints have been made, has been placed in charge of a Regimental committee, thus securing the best articles at the lowest prices, while the profits of the office go to the Regimental fund, out of which many comforts will be obtained for the soldier without cost.

The pay of Privates in the United States service is $13.00 per month, in addition to Clothing and Subsistence; and

## A BOUNTY OF ONE HUNDRED DOLLARS

will be paid to each soldier at the end of the war. Should Congress vote 160 ACRES OF LAND to each Volunteer, the soldiers serving in this Regiment will receive it. But as no action has as yet been taken on this subject, and as no authority has been given to any officer or regiment to offer it, those having the organization of the Scotch Regiment in charge, refrain from presenting inducements which are unauthorized, and which may lead to trouble and disappointment in the future.

Parties raising companies or parts of companies will be appointed officers of such companies or parts of companies; and any one desiring to enlist, will be supplied with all needful information by applying to the Head Quarters of the Regiment, 101 Washington St., Room No. 8, Chicago    P. O. Box 3380.

**DANIEL CAMERON, Jr.,**
ACTING COLONEL.

THE SCOTCH REGIMENT. The Sixty-fifth Illinois Infantry carried the name of the "Scotch Regiment," but its ethnic identity was diluted from its inception. *(Chicago Historical Society)* abolitionist sentiment motivated Union soldiers. Writing near the end of the century, and near the end of his own life, Gen. Jacob D. Cox recalled that he and others, who were "antislavery men bred in the bone," went into the fight after Sumter to fight slavery.[31] Men like Cox were the exception. The reaction to the Emancipation Proclamation by Union soldiers laid to rest any notion that antislavery sentiment was a strong motive for the typical volunteer. So strong was their feeling on the subject that many vowed not to reenlist when they heard the news of the Proclamation.[32]

Close behind patriotism as a motive was a sense of adventure. "It would be useless," confessed a soldier in the Fifteenth Massachusetts Infantry, "for me to claim that I have enlisted from purely patriotic motives, as no one would believe it. . . ." It was love of adventure, he continued, that lured him into uniform. The younger the soldier, the more likely that the excitement inherent in leaving home and taking a train to a distant part of his country was behind the move. John A. Page, who ended the war as a general, was a student at Northwestern University when the war started. Page was from an army family, and when the intense excitement following the Sumter assault and surrender gripped Evanston, he and his friends walked all the way into Chicago to share the bustle and ferment in the city. That was Saturday. On Monday, teenager Page enrolled in an artillery battery.[33]

Along with the sense of adventure went peer pressure and the desire to go along with friends. Recruiting officials grew familiar with the sight of two or more close friends stepping into the office, each one determined to stick with the group. Young men who grew up together, who lived in the same neighborhood, went into uniform together.[34]

Michael Griner and his wife, Sophia, had six children. Griner was sixty-two years old in August 1862 when he enlisted in the Twelfth New Jersey Infantry. It certainly was not youthful excitement or peer pressure that moved Griner to enlist. To him, the army simply offered a desperate unemployed man a job. Even a recruit in the Civil War earned a wage equal to that of a farm hand, and a common laborer found the military financially attractive. Officer's salaries were much more generous, and they provided a real stimulus for enlistment. Once a volunteer learned the ropes and the possibilities, he often tried to improve his prospects. "Money, Money is the god of some men," complained a private in an Illinois regiment to Governor Yates. He appealed to Yates for a commission so that he, too, could worship the same god. Local employment conditions frequently influenced individual decisions to enlist. A downturn in building, for example, encouraged unemployed laborers to volunteer.[35]

Every individual operated from a unique combination of motives. For the most part, there was little difference between the ethnic and the non-ethnic volunteer.

Titus Crawshaw, who enlisted in the Third New Jersey Infantry, was an English immigrant. His father, still in England, asked his son why he joined the American army. He did it, he told his father, to keep the Union safe. If the Union were not preserved, he explained, then America would become as bad as the German states. It was simply his duty to fight for it. Norwegian-American Hans Heg gave his wife the same explanation in more than one letter home, and he wanted his children to develop the same sense of duty. Ella Lonn's exhaustive study of foreigners in the Union army concludes that the preservation of the Union was the fundamental drive behind foreign-born enlistments. In short, the patriotism of the foreign born, translated into a belief that the Union and the Constitution had to be preserved, motivated them in much the same fashion as native Americans.[36]

Valentin Bechler, born in Karlsruhe in 1820, brought his wife and children to America in 1853. In August 1861 Bechler enlisted in the Eighth New Jersey Infantry. What motivated a middle-aged family man to take such a drastic step? An inability to pay the rent and get a job forced his hand. To put food on the table and keep the family together encouraged many an immigrant to volunteer. In addition to the army pay, the family also received a modest stipend from the local ethnic aid society. Immigrants like Bechler, at the bottom of the economic ladder, had no use for abolition. "I wish all abolitionists were in hell . . .," he told his wife in November 1862. The *Boston Pilot* frequently made the same point in its column, accurately reflecting the Irish-American opposition to abolition. Freeing the slaves was simply not a significant motive among the ethnics. George Augustus Sala, the cynical correspondent of the *London Daily Telegraph,* insisted that aliens in the Union army were mercenaries pure and simple. Sala contemptuously dismissed the notion that foreign-born Americans felt any patriotism toward the United States. Pure selfishness put them into the military. Sala's assessment was far too prejudiced. That an economic motive lay behind many ethnic enlistments, however, was apparent. One student of the subject put it quite bluntly, "Faced with the choice of hunger or military service . . . the Irish in New York responded to the initial call to arms more readily than other groups in the population." French visitor Ferri Pisani agreed. The high pay of the army was an irresistible attraction to the more wretched of the immigrants.[37]

Like their native-born compatriots, immigrant Americans often enlisted in search of adventure. Irish-American Thomas Francis Galway was just fifteen when he joined the Eighth Ohio Infantry. Before he settled on that unit he visited another; he wanted a regiment where he felt at home and where the members fit his romantic image of what soldiers were like. Officers in the Fifty-fifth New York Infantry, a largely French regiment, referred deprecatingly to themselves as the Gardes Lafourchettes — the

Knife and Fork Guards. Hans Heg found, somewhat to his surprise, that he took to military life quite readily and that it was an exciting life.[38]

In virtually every respect, then, the ethnic and the native-born soldier shared the same motivations in joining the Union forces. Yet there were some important differences.

At least some volunteers felt that this was a way to demonstrate to native Americans that they were loyal to their adopted country. Hans Mattson of Red Wing, Minnesota, in a long and moving letter to his wife in October 1861, explained why he, a Swedish-American, joined the American army. The honor of "our nation" (Sweden) was at stake, he explained, and the Americans made it clear that they expected us to help in the great struggle. In other words, Mattson believed that he had to show native Americans that Swedish-Americans were just as patriotic as they were — and after the war the Americans would remember this and think more kindly toward the Swedes. Irish-Americans often shared this feeling. Knowing that they still faced actual or potential prejudice, they believed that military service would convince nativist Americans that Irish immigrants were loyal to their new homeland, and that valor on the battlefield would erase prejudice at home. Ethnics fought, not to free the slaves, but to free themselves from prejudice. A Private Casey put it baldly in a letter to his Irish captain:

> Perhaps when it is all over they will turn their attention to the burning of convents and Chinese as they have done before. . . . The Irish Catholic so bravely fighting for the Country will get no thanks when peace will be proclaimed. . . . Take the Irish for instance from the army of this union and this war perhaps will last for fifty years to come. . . . Let the Irish then do the fighting and we want all the credit.

Implicit in Casey's logic was the assumption, that, however grudgingly, Americans would have to give credit where it was due if the Irish won the war for them. This was a motive utterly lacking in native-American soldiers; they did not have to worry about earning the gratitude and loyalty of the immigrants.[39]

While a native-American soldier, especially one with some education, might see the war as an abstract struggle for liberty, this was a common feeling among the educated foreign born. A German, especially a Forty-Eighter, in explaining his reasons for joining the army, was quite likely to include in that explanation a reference to the cause of liberty in the wider world. What was happening in America was one chapter in a larger, older struggle of people for political freedom. The editor of the *Mississippi Blätter* (St. Louis) published a long, thoughtful analysis of the national crisis on 21 April 1861. The struggle, he wrote, was the second American Revolution, it was a continuation of the long history of a fight for freedom, a fight that the Gracchi fought in Rome, that Cromwell fought in England.[40] Some volunteers who flocked to the United States in the early months of the war, genuinely believed that the war was a struggle for freedom in abstract, worldwide terms, and they wanted to help.

One ethnic group had a unique set of motives. Irish nationalism, so frequently used as an appeal by ethnic leaders, prompted many an Irishman to enlist. "Irishmen," wrote Ella Lonn, "never ceased to try to use America to forward Irish independence." Irishmen tended to follow the old adage that the enemy of my enemy is my friend. They regarded Britain as hostile to the North, and so that provided an incentive to support the North. "Many Irish soldiers in the northern army were ardently hoping to humiliate Britain by humbling her protegé, the south, and to aid their emerald fatherland. . . ." The Irish-born Gen. James Shields saw the American Civil War as an excellent opportunity for Irishmen to acquire military training to use against England. Fenians organized "circles" in Union regiments to whip up enthusiasm for the Irish cause and recruit volunteers for a postwar attack on English forces in Ireland. This kind of activity thoroughly characterized rank-and-file Irishmen as well as their leaders. "A great many Irishmen, in fact," noted the French visitor, the Comte de Paris, "looked upon the war as nothing more that a favorable opportunity for preparing to crush England." It was common practice for Irish volunteers to publicize their intention to join their compatriots and strike a blow against England as soon as possible after peace in America.[41]

Irish nationalism had a pathetic quality about it in the context of an American war. Every motive used to justify support for the Union in the North was used by Irishmen in the South to justify support for the Confederacy. This led Irishmen not only to fight enthusiastically against each other on Civil War battlefields, but sometimes to care little about which side they fought on so long as it meant fighting with fellow Irishmen. Many believed that this somehow promoted Irish independence. David T. Maul tells the tale of Irish-American Confederate prisoners who joined Mulligan's "Irish Brigade."[42] These "Galvanized Yankees" had a more basic loyalty to Ireland than to the South; almost forty members of Mulligan's regiment at one time fought in Confederate units. Southern Irishmen compared the South's struggle for independence with Ireland's struggle for independence, while northern Irishmen equated Ireland's dream of national unity and independence with that of the North. Irish nationalism had no real counterpart among members of other ethnic groups, and it was a unique motive for that group of ethnic soldiers.

Chicago, 18 June 1861: Hundreds of Germans assembled at a solemn but gala occasion to listen to Friedrich Hecker. The old soldier and revolutionary was now Colonel Hecker, the commanding officer of the "First Hecker Jaeger Regiment." The occasion was the flag presentation ceremony marking the eminent departure of the Twenty-fourth Illinois Infantry — the first German regiment recruited in Illinois. The fifty-year-old Hecker borrowed the language of Napoleon as he addressed his men:

> Soldiers! Comrades! It is now twelve years ago that I stood opposed in strife to the despotisms of Europe, and took up arms against them in behalf of freedom and independence. . . . I am now old and gray, the last hours of my life not far off. Are you ready to follow this flag?[43]

The question, intended as rhetorical, the sort of flowery language appropriate for a showy occasion, in the event was a quite legitimate one.

Popular enthusiasm and patriotic rhetoric carried foreign-born and native Americans alike through the exciting business of creating a people's army. The excitement of leaving home, joining hundreds and thousands of other young men in training camps, experiencing both the monotony of drill and the color of military pageantry — all of this included a momentum that hid, for the moment, the reality of the political controversy inherent in this citizen's army. The controversy soon appeared, and Hecker was an early victim.

# The German Regiments

The hurrahs for popular favorites, the fury of rous'd mobs. . . .

— WALT WHITMAN, *Song of Myself*

AR initially was good for Colonel Hecker. Several years earlier, when Carl Schurz saw him on his farm, he was demoralized and defeated, almost slovenly. Now he was off to the field of battle, and the change was remarkable. A small man physically, his blue eyes glittered in his fine-boned face. His mustache and pointed beard, shot through with gray, betrayed the fifty years his long, dark hair and erect bearing denied. Something of a young dandy as a lawyer in Baden, he possessed a degree of self-confidence that others saw as conceit. The colonel's vocabulary of profanity, expressed in a mixture of German and English, was legendary. Slackers and incompetents in the Twenty-fourth Illinois Infantry got the full force of his vituperative tongue. He saw himself as a strict disciplinarian; his men saw him as a martinet. From the moment their mutual life began in Illinois, the regiment and its commander suffered strained relations.

Major Julian Kuné, the Hungarian revolutionary who helped organize the Twenty-fourth Illinois, swallowed bitter disappointment when the German became its colonel. Kuné tried to transfer out of the regiment even before it left Illinois. In a personal letter to Governor Yates, he claimed that while he got along well with all the other officers of the Twenty-fourth, Colonel Hecker simply lacked the essential qualities of leadership.[1] Hecker had a vile and uncontrollable temper, the major charged, and the result was increasing dissension and distrust among the men. Kuné told Yates that he actually feared the prospect of going into battle under the circumstances, and he asked for permission to leave the Twenty-fourth and raise a new regiment. His request was denied; he accompanied the regiment when it left Illinois and entrained for Kentucky.

Colonel Hecker knew there was trouble in the ranks. He attributed the

72

problem to a conspiracy, a cabal of disgruntled officers that plotted his ruin.[2] He even demanded a court of inquiry, which he thought would expose the conspirators and strengthen his position. He was convinced that he had a set of rascals for his staff and that the ranks were full of drunkards and worse. A particular target of his outrage was 2d Lt. Jacob Poull, who ran a brothel in Chicago before joining the army. Poull's civilian career violated Hecker's sense of propriety, and his name was among those whom Hecker wanted dismissed from the regiment. The colonel was frustrated by his lack of authority to hire and fire as he pleased, and so he cast about for a way to achieve his goal within the maze of army regulations. At last, when the regiment arrived in Kentucky, he thought he had found a way. At his request, Maj. Gen. John C. Frémont gave permission to "reorganize" the regiment, dismiss "unfit" officers, and rid the unit of insubordinates. Hecker promptly cashiered several officers, including Major Kuné, who had claimed to be on good terms with his commander.[3] Brigadier General Benjamin M. Prentiss approved Hecker's actions, and the colonel read the notices of dismissal to the regiment. His triumph was short lived. He had managed, in a sense, to shoot himself in the foot. His actions ignited a political firestorm in Illinois.

The army was already unhappy with the first German regiment from Illinois. Don Carlos Buell, the newly appointed commander of the Department of the Ohio, discovered soon after he assumed his post that there was a sticky situation, perhaps even an incipient mutiny, in the Twenty-fourth Illinois Infantry. Brigadier General O. M. Mitchel inspected the camp of the Hecker regiment, and his account made grim reading. "I regret to report," wrote Mitchel, "the 24th Ill. Volunteers in a very demoralized condition."[4] Mitchel visited the regiment's camp near Louisville, found thirty to forty soldiers AWOL, and when he looked in on the saloons lining the waterfront he found them packed with the men of the Twenty-fourth Illinois Infantry. He managed to get them back to camp at the point of the bayonet. He described the officers as engaged in an acrimonious struggle for supremacy within the regiment.

When Hecker accepted the regimental flag in happier days five months earlier, he asked rhetorically if the soldiers would follow the flag. He should have asked if the men would follow *him*. In Kentucky he got the answer to that question. His strict discipline, autocratic manner, and inability to cope with a citizen's army soon alienated him from the group. He reprimanded officers in front of the men and struck the men in a rage when they failed to obey his orders.[5] His effort to reorganize the regiment brought matters to a head.

Officers dismissed by Hecker immediately appealed their case to the secretary of war, Simon Cameron. Cameron had no choice under the regulations; he reinstated the officers to their former assignments. Hecker thereupon approached Governor Yates, who thoughtfully did nothing. With that avenue closed, Hecker turned to his old friend Gustave Koerner. Koerner could do nothing; the dismissals were illegal. Hecker's control of his own regiment slipped out of his hands. As he complained in a plaintive letter to the governor, he no longer knew who held commissions in his regiment and who did not. With his battle for control of the regiment lost, Hecker took sick leave and returned to his Illinois farm. There he brooded over what seemed a rank injustice. *He* had created the Hecker Jaeger Regiment, and now his enemies controlled it.[6]

The War Department, anxious to put the regiment's troubles behind it, gave command of the Hecker regiment to its lieutenant colonel, Hungarian refugee Géza Mihalotzy. Be firm, Mihalotzy was told, restore discipline to the regiment and thus remove a source of annoyance to the army. That same day, Hecker and the dissident officers got orders to report to Springfield, Illinois.[7]

The political situation was tense in the Illinois state capital as the officers of the Twenty-fourth Infantry returned to that city. Hecker sought political support, and his friends responded.

Governor Yates had nothing to win and everything to lose by any role he might play, either as governor or as commander of the state militia. Friends urged him to stay completely out of the affair, and let the U.S. Army handle it. Caspar Butz rushed down from Chicago to defend Hecker; as one of the German-American power brokers he made clear his intentions of seeing justice done to Hecker. Unable to see the governor immediately upon his arrival, he put in writing his advice on what should be done. "I am acting in this whole matter," he informed the governor, "out of a sense of duty to an old and tried friend, who bears one of the most resplendent names in the annals of the German Nation." He reminded Yates that Hecker was a Republican party stalwart and had worked hard in Yates's behalf in the last election. While Hecker may have made some mistakes, Butz acknowledged, there is no doubting the purity of his motives and the nobility of his character. In case such arguments might not convince Yates to side with Hecker, Butz issued a warning. The German press, he claimed, sided unanimously with the old soldier in his current troubles. Butz went to Hecker's farm to console and counsel the colonel. Together, the two men carried out a campaign whose aim was the defense of Hecker through German-American political leverage.[8]

Butz directed his opening arguments to Thomas Mather, the state's assistant adjutant general. (Hecker had already approached Allen Fuller, the adjutant general.) Hecker is in the right, Butz asserted. "Now my dear Sir," he warned, "if this fine Regiment shall be sacrificed, because a few dissatisfied inefficient officers manage by hook or by crook to make Mr. Cameron reinstate them, *the Germans want to Know at whose door they have to lay the blame.*" And just in case that message was not clear enough, Butz told Mather that he should advise the governor that if they did not get satisfaction in the matter, they might well question their continued loyalty to the Union cause. For his part, Hecker addressed Yates directly and outlined both a new story of conspiracy and a way for the governor to settle the matter gracefully. The whole business, claimed Hecker, was the work of a disloyal clerk in Yates's office; the clerk conspired with the dissident officers to manipulate regimental affairs. The beauty of this analysis was that it identified a villain who had no vested interest in the matter or any pressure group to stir up trouble.[9]

Moving in its own mysterious ways, the War Department in mid-November abruptly restored command of the Twenty-fourth Illinois Infantry to Hecker. Lieutenant Colonel Mihalotzy got orders to go to Chicago and round up AWOL soldiers. Butz returned to Chicago, resumed his duties as court clerk, and continued his campaign for the vindication of Hecker. He singled out new villains; now the plot was laid at the door of unidentified "malicious persons and correspondents of the Chicago *Tribune.*"[10]

Caspar Butz was only one German-American politician to intervene in the Hecker affair. Other power centers got involved and proposed different solutions. The lieutenant governor, after all, was the unofficial Yates ambassador to the Illinois German community, with an office in Chicago where part of his duties was to tend to such matters. By the end of November, with Hecker back in titular command of the Hecker Jaegers, Hoffman proposed another way out of the situation. Hecker's formidable temper, Hoffman acknowledged, was at fault, but intriguing officers also bore a share of the blame. The best thing to do, Hoffman advised, was to fall back on army regulations. Replace Hecker at the head, and then follow the usual musical chairs procedure, with officers moving up in rank on the basis of seniority. Hoffman later had second thoughts on the recommendation and urged Yates to put an American officer in charge of the regiment to reduce ethnic political intrigue and restore public confidence in the regiment and the Yates administration.[11]

Hecker's best friend in the regiment was the surgeon, William Wagner. Together with Hoffman he worked out a compromise solution to the discord in the state's first German regiment. First, even though Hoffman objected, knowing it would affront a strong segment of the Germans, Hecker should resign. (Hoffman's objection may have been a pro forma one; in the early stages of the discussions he did admit that Hecker should resign.) Then, most of the dissident officers would resign and get posts in other regiments, except for the most outspoken Hecker partisan, the Jewish officer Edward Salomon. The leader of the anti-Hecker faction, Capt. August Mauss, would be restored to his position in the Twenty-fourth. (It was Mauss who earlier insisted that Salomon had to go.) Governor Yates went along with the Wagner-Hoffman scheme. He sought and obtained from Secretary Cameron permission from the army to waive its rule about the reappointment of resigned officers (a rule intended to cope with ambitious officers regiment hopping to advance personal careers) and find posts elsewhere for the "worthy men and good soldiers" who left the Twenty-fourth for the good of the service. Cameron went along, and in late December, Hecker resigned.[12] For a brief few days, Hoffman thought the crisis was passed.

Colonel Hecker, to put it mildly, did not think the compromise much of a compromise. He took his case to the columns of the *Illinois Staats-Zeitung*. Caspar Butz, complaining that the regiment still harbored unrest, criticized the arrangements and Hoffman's role in them. Now, Butz told Yates indignantly, the Germans have *two* resignations flung in their faces; first it was Sigel, and now Hecker. German tempers were rising.[13] One way to sooth those tempers, he advised the governor, would be to appoint a friend of Sigel's as the new colonel of the Twenty-fourth Illinois Infantry. For its part, the *Illinois Staats-Zeitung* reacted with fury to Hecker's departure. The newspaper blamed Yates and Hoffman for the whole business.

> At the heart of the State of Illinois are two men, one of whom as Governor has brought little honor, the other as the Lt. Gov. much dishonor upon the State. The former (the Governor) *completely ruined by the immoderate use of whiskey and near the gate of that psychical state, called delirium tremens.*[14]

The *Illinois Staats-Zeitung* called for the ouster of the governor and his "Stump-tailed" colleague. Hecker himself concluded by 1862 that Hoffman was the cause of all his troubles.

In accordance with the compromise plan, the Twenty-fourth's lieutenant colonel became its new colonel. Géza Mihalotzy and the reorganized regiment continued to suffer for some months from internal bickering, but the worst was passed. The regiment and its commander (despite his being found guilty of a minor charge in a court-martial the following summer) went on to a distinguished career in the Union army. At Chickamauga, Mihalotzy suffered a wound in his sword hand, and in February 1864 he suffered a fatal wound at Buzzard Roost Gap. The Twenty-fourth Illinois Infantry recovered completely from its unfortunate early history, and when mustered out in July 1864, its members were justly proud of their service to the Union. At a fiftieth-anniversary reunion of the regiment in 1911 the survivors heard a memorialist tell them that in 1861 the first thought of the German volunteers of the Hecker Jaeger was that of saving the Union.[15] For the rank-and-file soldiers, that was indeed a fair assessment.

Friedrich Hecker brooded through only a brief retirement on his Illinois farm. German-Americans in Illinois raised a second regiment, the

Eighty-second Illinois Infantry, and the command was offered to Hecker. A bit wary after his experience with the first German unit, he insisted on guarantees against intrigue and internal turmoil before accepting. Caspar Butz continued to work for Hecker. He kept before Governor Yates the specter of German discontent and reminded him that Germans expected Hecker to command another German unit. The governor listened, and he resisted the suggestion of Maj. Gen. Franz Sigel that Sigel name the officers in the new regiment. Yates gave the second German regiment to Hecker, and Edward Salomon of the Twenty-fourth was appointed lieutenant colonel.[16]

The wrenching political battle centered on the first German regiment was not repeated in the record of the second. Mustered into federal service in October 1862, the Eighty-second compiled a good record on many battlefields. Hecker's finest hour in the war probably came at Chancellorsville. Mixing German and English in his excited commands, Hecker got his troops in formation before the advancing Confederates, and then, just as the southerners rushed out of the woods behind fleeing wildlife, the Eighty-second's color bearer was killed. Grabbing the flag himself, Hecker roared the commands to fix bayonets and fire, then charge, and was himself struck down by a bullet.[17] Fortunately, the missile struck his silver snuff case and so the wound was not fatal; a few months later he rejoined his regiment.

As casualties mounted in the many months of campaigning, the ranks of the Illinois Eighty-second thinned alarmingly. By midsummer 1863, Hecker was pleading for replacements. Ethnicity faded before the necessity of the situation. In his need for men, Hecker forgot the original plan for a German regiment. As he put it to Governor Yates, "fill up the 82nd Regiment of Ill Vols. with conscripts as soon as possible."[18] Discouraged by his failure to win a promotion to brigadier general, Hecker resigned his commission in early 1864 and retired to Illinois. Its ranks increasingly diluted by native-born replacements, the Eighty-second Illinois Infantry completed its Civil War service only a shadow of its original Germanic self.

Illinois fielded one more German regiment. While the Twenty-fourth and Eighty-second regiments drew their members largely from the metropolitan Chicago area, the third German unit was born in downstate Illinois. Outside of Chicago the largest concentration of Germans in Illinois was in the Belleville-East St. Louis area, and that area gave birth to the Forty-third Illinois Infantry known as the "Koerner Regiment."

In the early days of the war, many Germans from this region went to Missouri and joined one of the several German regiments formed in that state. This reduced the pool of potential recruits for a German regiment in downstate Illinois, and when the call went out for volunteers, it went to the sons of immigrants more than to the foreign born. Most Germans in the Forty-third, then, were American born, and the regiment contained two Swedish companies. It still qualifies as an ethnic regiment, however, because the appeal was made to Germans and their sons, the regiment regarded itself as German, and it was so regarded by others. Many of the American-born Germans spoke no English.

Three men recruited the Forty-third. Gustave Koerner, after whom the regiment was named, had the influence and name recognition needed for the task. Julius Raith, the second father of the regiment, was born in Germany in 1820, migrated to the United States in 1836, served in the Mexican War, and was active in Democratic politics. Adolphus Engelmann, Koerner's brother-in-law, was the third man in the enterprise. No partisan bickering marred the formation of the "Koerner Regiment," but its organization was painfully slow. When it was mustered into federal service in October 1861, it contained only eight companies instead of the regulation ten. Still lacking those companies, the regiment moved to Missouri in December. From there, Julius Raith, who had been elected colonel, appealed to Governor Yates to send another one and a half companies to the Forty-third. Ethnic origin now was not as important as body count; the colonel and all officers knew that any regiment whose enrollment dropped dangerously low risked having its commanding officer reduced in rank to lieutenant colonel, and the ripple effect of that reduction went down through the rest of the officers. Engelmann was the Forty-third's lieutenant colonel.[19]

"Koerner's Regiment" was bloodied first at Shiloh. In that encounter the regiment acquitted itself well, but Colonel Raith suffered a mortal wound, and Engelmann took command as the new colonel. He led the regiment for most of the rest of its history.

Engelmann, who was one of the famed "Latin Farmers" of Illinois, maintained a voluminous correspondence with his family during his time with the regiment, and those letters offer a window into the life of the regiment as well as Engelmann himself. Like any soldier, Engelmann had an almost obsessive interest in events at home while he was away; he always wanted to hear details of what the family did; how the crops prospered or did not; and what friends, neighbors, and relatives were doing. An ardent horticulturist, the colonel recorded impressions of plants, landscapes, and farming in the regions through which he traveled. Like Hans Christian Heg, he enjoyed army life for the most part. To the extent possible he kept up his familiar life-style while campaigning; good food, good wine, good cigars, and good companions were important to him. Like most Latin Farmers, he was an abolitionist, and he was appalled at what he saw of slavery in the South.[20] At his own farm in St. Clair County, Engelmann regularly experimented with new vines, flowers, shrubs, trees, and other plant life; he kept up this activity from a distance all through his military career, sending back to Illinois by Adams Express a stream of cuttings, trees, seeds, and the like. From the homestead in turn he was supplied with cases of his own wine and other good things from the land. Read in English, and with no knowledge of their author, it would be impossible to assign to him an ethnic identity.

When Engelmann in his personal correspondence or official letters did touch upon ethnic matters, it tended to be far from dramatic or of grave significance. A few days after taking command of the regiment, the colonel asked Gustave Koerner to find a physician for the Forty-third who could write English. At that time he had to write all the English correspondence for the regiment himself. When he entertained his officers, it was with German food, wine, and conversation. He records visits to the regiment from volunteer women from Illinois who brought such home comforts as sauerkraut, herring, onions, and wine to the men.[21] He encouraged his wife to write in English, but on her visits to his headquarters they spoke together in German—the language in which she was most at home. Adolphus Engelmann bears a striking resemblance to Yankee George F. Newhall of the Eleventh Massachusetts Infantry. Newhall had a profound interest in the world of nature. At every opportunity he scouted the local countryside, studied flora and fauna, sketched what he saw, and wrote all about it to his parents. Yankee Newhall and German-American Engelmann would have felt quite at home with each other. When the Forty-third Illinois Infantry's three-year enlistment period expired, the colonel appealed to his troops to reenlist. Addressing the soldiers at Little Rock, Arkansas, 4 January 1865, Engelmann stressed duty, patriotism, bounty money, and the optimistic outlook for an early end to the war. His speech contains no hint of ethnicity, no appeal to German culture, no mention of history. It could have been the speech of any colonel to any regiment in similar circumstances. Engelmann himself had already been officially discharged in mid-December 1864, and he returned home after his appeal to the regiment. Reorganized as a veteran regiment, and with drafted men added to its ranks to allow its continued existence, the Forty-third Illinois Infantry soldiered on until its final muster out in Illinois in November 1865.[22]

The three German regiments from Illinois had much in common. They fought hard and well for their adopted country. Their records, as do the records of so many Union regiments in the Civil War, inspire astonishment when read today; the hardships endured, the bloody fighting—often hand to hand—and the willingness of men to suffer much for their cause and their comrades, all of this is ample testimony to the loyalty of the ordinary German-American soldier. All of the partisan political energies of German-Americans in Illinois centered in the first German regiment. All of the bloc rivalries, the personal competition, the working out of appropriate relationships between the Germans and the rest of society—all of these matters were tested and resolved in the ordeals of the Hecker regiment. The Forty-third and Eighty-second regiments engendered no quarrels and aroused no political passions. Of the three original colonels, two died on the battlefield and the third suffered a wound. Of the three original colonels, only Hecker, his ambitions frustrated by his failure to win promotion, resigned from his regiment and returned to his Illinois farm.

Compared to its neighbors, Indiana in 1861 had a modest portion of foreign-born residents among its total population. Over half of the state's immigrants were German, and while the largest concentration of the Germans was in and around Indianapolis, most of the Hoosier State's larger towns and cities included some Germans. Indiana Judge William H. Otto worked with Carl Schurz and Gustave Koerner on the 1860 Republican party platform committee. Germans already had militia units in existence when the war began, with a "Steuben" artillery company in Evansville as an example. German-American politicians agitated for a German regiment with the outbreak of hostilities, and competing candidates to lead such a regiment made the selection of a colonel a delicate one for the state's governor. After a citizen's committee called upon Gov. Oliver P. Morton to organize a German regiment (the state's Irish-Americans pressured him for the same action), he hesitated briefly and then displayed a stroke of political genius. Knowing that there was no hope of satisfying the various blocs of German-Americans, Morton reached outside the state and offered the command of the Indiana German regiment to Augustus Willich of Ohio. His move neatly flanked all the would-be German colonels and their claques within the state and disarmed critics by the wisdom of his choice; Willich was too widely esteemed by Germans everywhere for Indiana ethnic politicians to grumble at the tactic. Moreover, Morton's maneuver brought to Indiana the man who became the most admired ethnic officer of the Civil War. Like German-Americans in other states, those of Indiana divided their political loyalties between the Republicans and the Democrats; the same gap between Forty-Eighters and earlier settlers characterized Indiana Germans as it did those elsewhere. The prestigious outsider avoided the Grays vs. Greens squabbles.[23]

Willich was already in an Ohio regiment when he got the invitation to head the Thirty-second Indiana Infantry. After the firing on Fort Sumter, he was one of more than a thousand Germans who crowded into Cincinnati recruiting offices. The ex-Prussian officer enlisted as a private in the Ninth Ohio Infantry, the first German regiment organized in that state. His action fit his ideals and symbolized his solidarity with the proletariat. He was also disgusted with the pushing and shoving for advantage and with the highly politicized atmosphere surrounding the formation of the regiments.[24] At the same time, given his experience and position in the Cincinnati German community, there was every expectation of his election to lead the regiment.

When Cincinnati's German-Americans met in April 1861 to discuss the leadership of the state's first German regiment, Judge Stallo—probably

Willich's closest friend—was on hand. During the debate, Gustav Tafel, who would himself later command a German regiment, presented a telling argument. Stallo's law partner, Robert McCook, had important connections in Washington, Tafel reasoned. This was important at a time when federal authorities had more requests to form regiments than the government needed. It made sense to elect as colonel a man whose influence made acceptance of the regiment a more likely possibility.[25] When the vote was taken, McCook got six votes and Willich four. McCook, who had no military experience, promptly began a program of self-education in military tactics while Willich went to work on the task of organizing and training the German volunteers. Willich's official post was that of adjutant, but before long he was the major of the Ninth Ohio and in that capacity went off to campaign with the regiment in West Virginia. It was there he got the invitation from Indiana Governor Morton to lead that state's German regiment. Willich promptly accepted. There was a bit of ambition in the Marxist idealist after all. Willich set up a recruiting headquarters in downtown Indianapolis, and by 24 August the Thirty-second Indiana Infantry was ready for federal service.

Colonel Willich enjoyed good relations with Governor Morton. Like any other commander he complained about equipment and wanted more support, but when the order came to lead the regiment to Kentucky, he obeyed immediately. On 28 September 1861, the Thirty-second Indiana Infantry made a ceremonious departure for the seat of war. The occasion was solemn and touching and reveals something about the character or Willich and his relations with his men. Unlike many of his compatriots in similar positions, Willich was a poor man. At that moment he lacked the funds to buy a horse. So it was when the Thirty-second Indiana Infantry made its last parade down Indianapolis streets toward the railroad, Colonel Willich led it on foot. The demeanor of the commander and the bearing of the volunteers made a favorable impression on the spectators.[26]

Indiana's Thirty-second Infantry won a reputation as one of the "fightingest" regiments in the Union army. It lost 171 men to battlefield deaths, while 97 died of other causes. In its first major battle, Rowlette Station in December 1861, the regiment won a national reputation when some 500 soldiers of the Thirty-second beat off an attack by 1,300 Confederates. National recognition came again, both for the regiment and its commander, at Shiloh. There, on the second day of bloody and confused battle, the Thirty-second Indiana Infantry came under heavy attack. The German-American volunteers wavered, and the line of battle threatened to crumble. Major General Lew Wallace saw what happened next. An officer rode swiftly around the left flank of the regiment, stopped in front of the troops, and turned his back to the enemy fire. The officer was Willich, and he proceeded to put the soldiers through the manual of arms, drilling them while men dropped from Confederate bullets. Lew Wallace said later that the episode was the most audacious thing he saw. "The effect was magical," he recorded. Other officers emulated Willich's feat on other battlefields, but none caught the popular attention given the Marxist immigrant. For his gallantry and courage under fire, he won promotion to brigadier general. That promotion was earned; it was also preceded by a typical campaign of military-civilian politics.[27]

As early as November 1861 Operation Willich was underway. Lieutenant Carl Schnitz, Willich's adjutant, in a letter marked "Confidential," wrote to the Indiana Adjutant General. It was the outline of a plan to get a brigade, a German brigade for the colonel. "It has been and is now the desire of all the intelligent Germans, that wish our country well, and are acquainted with my colonel, that he should be put in command of a German brigade," wrote Schnitz.[28] By the time Willich got his star, however, authorities in Washington were leery of ethnic brigades, and when he assumed his new command he was heading a nonethnic brigade.

"He is one of God's noblemen." Those words written to a Cincinnati newspaper reflected a widely held opinion of Augustus Willich. He was quite likely the most admired, respected, and attractive of the war's ethnic leaders. Balding at the front of his head, with an exhuberant black beard reaching down to his tie, Willich presented an appearance of dignity — with a twinkle. He shared every hardship with his men, led them where the fighting was most fierce, and treated privates as human beings. His devotion to his men won their affection. In camp, when the military situation permitted, Willich was not reluctant to lecture his soldiers on the virtues of socialism. We have no evidence on how his Germans reacted to his socialist messages, but at the least they probably received them in an attitude of tolerance and good humor. Willich introduced several new tactics in the training of his brigade. He used bugle calls as signals on the battlefield, where noise, confusion, and smoke made for chaos in communications. He drilled his troops in a system of "advance firing"; this involved alternate firing and loading in four ranks as troops advanced and permitted a continuous fire upon enemy formations.[29]

Willich never lost his heavy German accent, and he gave orders in simple words that mixed English words and German syntax. His brigade gave a reception in his honor near Nashville and, as the regiments paraded past him, the soldiers raised homemade banners bearing some of their favorite Willich orders. One banner read, "Boys, what for you spraddle out the road so wide for." Another bore the message, "Bugler, blow fight." At the hard-fought Battle of Chickamauga, the general's laconic orders to the Eighty-ninth Illinois Infantry were simply, "Now boys, one more try." Only a leader supremely confident of his own ability and equally confident in the willing support of the men under his command could exercise authority in such a homespun manner. In a biting contrast to other ethnic and nonethnic generals, Willich maintained a spartan personal existence; he had a single private soldier as his personal servant.[30]

Despite all this, the Thirty-second Indiana Infantry survivors in 1863 refused to reenlist. Only two hundred of the original volunteers still served in the ranks. The regiment's flag carried the names of sixty-one battles. During the first year of its history, Adj. Carl Schnitz tried hard to keep a flow of German replacements flowing to the regiment. Willich himself did everything possible to keep the men of the Thirty-second content while he remained colonel. Even though he did not tolerate intoxication, like most Germans of his generation, he regarded beer as one of life's necessities; when Gen. William Sherman ordered all alcoholic beverages cut off to the regiment, Willich personally rode to Sherman's headquarters and got the supply of six kegs of beer a day restored as a matter essential to the morale of his German troops. Another morale booster in the early days to the foreign-born soldiers was the regular use of German at the company level; even American officers—who had failed in their efforts to persuade the Germans to sign a temperance pledge—had access to company books with orders written out in both German and English. When Willich left the regiment to take over a brigade, the command of the regiment devolved on Lt. Col. Heinrich von Tebra, who had been the drillmaster in training days and who had, like his colonel, military experience in Prussia before coming to America. But like all the other ethnic regiments, attrition diluted whatever ethnic ties existed when the unit organized.[31]

With any ethnic regiment, even with the Thirty-second Indiana that had a clear and most distinguished record as one of the very best of its kind, it is difficult to grasp just how important ethnicity was to the average soldier. Once the beer and language are discounted, what was left? What did it mean to serve in the ranks of a German regiment? Years after the war ended, the regiment's historian recalled that "We were called Germans (Dutch by the enemy) but the majority of us were born or raised under the flag which we served—the stars and stripes. . . . We were all American citizens." By the time school teacher Michael Frash joined the Thirty-second in October 1864, the Indiana German regiment had lost its ethnic character. Earlier efforts in Indiana to raise a second German regiment failed. The few volunteers attracted to the enterprise ended up in an American regiment. Indiana's relatively small German population was no doubt a major factor in these developments. It is possible that an angry reaction to unfair accusations of German cowardice at Chancellorsville turned off enthusiasm in Indiana either for filling up the Thirty-second or forming a second regiment, but direct evidence for this is lacking.[32]

Augustus Willich survived a wound, four months in a Confederate prison, the rigors of years of active duty, and, rewarded with brevet promotion when he left the army, returned to Cincinnati where he was honored by election as country auditor. He returned to Germany for a brief visit and tried to volunteer for service in the Franco-Prussian War—an indication that his nationalism might well have been stronger than either his Marxism or his republicanism—but his offer was declined. Willich studied philosophy at the University of Berlin, but his heart was in his adopted country. He returned to America and settled down in the small town of St. Marys, Ohio, at the invitation of an old comrade-in-arms, Maj. Charles Hipp. Living alone in a boarding house, but enjoying a peaceful life in a community that regarded him with the same affection once demonstrated by his troops, General Willich lived out his days. Always active intellectually, he traded his Marxism and political debates for literature and organized among the St. Marys citizens a Shakespeare Club.

Augustus Willich stands far removed from Friedrich Hecker and from virtually all other ethnic military leaders of the Civil War. Always the idealist, he never exploited his war record for political or financial reward. Austere in his personal habits, his life bears little resemblance to the flamboyance surrounding the lives of so many commanders of ethnic regiments. In the judgment of Ella Lonn, Willich was among the most appealing personalities of the Civil War. His most devoted admirers, she concludes, were the American officers who served under him.[33]

Willich was sui generis, then, and little can be gained by comparisons between the Thirty-second Indiana Infantry and the German regiments of Illinois. Perhaps the most significant element of commonality is the gradual loss of ethnic identity for the regiments as the war progressed.

New York, with its huge immigrant population, fielded more ethnic regiments than any other state, and almost a dozen German regiments came from the Empire State.[34] Of all these units and their commanders, none stands in sharper contrast to Willich and the Thirty-second Indiana Infantry than does Louis Blenker and the Eighth New York Infantry.

Louis (Ludwig) Blenker, born in Germany in 1812, was a wine merchant in Worms and then a participant in the revolutionary events of 1848. One of the thousands of Forty-Eighter exiles to America, Blenker tried several occupations in his adopted homeland. He sold a weekly German-language magazine, the *Criminalzeitung,* farmed in upstate New York, and was struggling with a small business in New York City when North-South hostilities began. The war liberated Blenker from a monotonous and humdrum existence that was ill-suited to his personality and self-image. He threw himself enthusiastically into the task of raising a German regiment and soon commanded the Eighth New York Infantry, the "First German Rifles." Blenker and his German soldiers attracted much attention even in a city saturated with the noise and glitter of military mobilization.

Carl Schurz called on the new colonel of the Eighth. He found Blenker unchanged from the "personality of extraordinary picturesqueness" he had known in Germany in 1848. Blenker lived in style in a New York hotel, the Prescott House, and there he played host to his distinguished guest. He offered Schurz wine and a cigar and astonished the waiter with a command to "Bring me a case of Burgundy and a box of your best Havanas." Blenker invited Schurz and his wife to visit the regiment, which was in camp in Terrace Garden, East 58th Street. When the two arrived at the camp, a band started playing and the colonel, resplendent in a new uniform, escorted them to a special platform before which the regiment paraded in their honor. Carl Schurz got the full Blenker treatment, a flaunting of military pageantry designed to impress regimental guests with the importance of the "First German Rifles." As Schurz recalled the scene, after the troops paraded before the stand, "The officers were dismissed by Colonel Blenker with a wave of the hand that could not have been more imperial if Louis XIV himself performed it."[35]

When the "First German Rifles" left New York for Washington, it was to a wild demonstration of public enthusiasm. Blenker's soldiers were smartly turned out, and their officers wore a variety of colorful uniforms. German-Americans lined Broadway to cheer the departing troops, as did thousands of other New Yorkers, all cheering the marching men and enjoying the martial music. Blenker acknowledged the yells with gracious gestures, his mind already busy with plans for the impact he and his German soldiers would make on Washington society.

"Another Arrival of Troops" was the newspaper headline announcing the entrance of the Eighth New York Infantry in Washington, but Washington residents quickly realized this was *not* just one more Union regiment. This was something special. In contrast to the many understrength volunteer regiments, the "First German Rifles" not only had a full complement of a thousand men, it also had an artillery unit, a medical detachment complete with ambulances, and the men had two different sets of uniforms; in addition to the regular blue uniforms the Eighth New Yorkers had their own distinctive gray costumes for parade purposes. Special squads of sappers and miners paraded with leather aprons, carrying their axes, saws, picks, ropes, spades, and other tools of their martial trade. Washington society soon learned to recognize the dramatic picture of Colonel Blenker, riding about Washington streets with his red-lined cape flying behind him. Whispers of Blenker's lurid past circulated around the capital city and added to his allure. Descriptions of his lavish hospitality made an invitation to the camp of the "First German Rifles" a top priority of wartime Washington's social elite. The colonel attracted critics as well as admirers; not everyone appreciated his version of proper military style. Henry Villard thought his fellow German an embarrassment to his countrymen. The sight of Blenker posturing in Washington streets, arrayed in a gorgeous uniform, and accompanied by a large staff of mounted officers, struck him as pure humbug. Blenker, in Villard's estimation, was nothing but an adventurer, out to exploit the national emergency.[36]

Ordinary soldiers of the Eighth New York Infantry, when not engaged in some lavish spectacle at the behest of their commander, had the usual breaks in camp routine. In early June a band of drunken men of the "First German Rifles" acting on the belief that they had been fired upon, seized an innocent civilian and beat him. Not satisfied with one victim, they then thrashed a soldier in a New Jersey regiment. When arms were distributed to the regiment, members of one company refused to accept its muskets because they wanted rifles. Sixty-two men went to jail for disobedience of orders. Such stories were commonplace in any regiment, however, and they did not tarnish the image of the Eighth New York Infantry. Before long three additional German regiments joined with the Eighth in a German brigade, led by Blenker.[37]

From his knowledge of Blenker in Europe, Schurz knew that beneath the posturing and bravado the colonel was a man of courage and determination. Blenker and his men, originally held in reserve at the First Bull Run Battle, gave a good account of themselves in covering the chaotic retreat of the Union forces on 21 July 1861. Within days of that July battle Blenker got a star, and as a brigadier general set about the organization of a second German brigade. Secretary of War Simon Cameron, impressed by what he heard of Blenker at Bull Run, gave his support to the enterprise, as did General McClellan.[38] Blenker got his second brigade and became the only Civil War officer to command an ethnic division in the entire war. Late 1861 and early 1862 were his days of glory, and he enjoyed them to the fullest.

Blenker's German encampment near Washington excited interest and admiration throughout Washington and the Army of the Potomac. Spectators drove out to see what rapidly became a major tourist attraction. His camp was laid out in the fashion preferred by Europeans. Tents stood in neat and orderly rows, each regiment in the division separated from the others. Lanes were lined with ornamental trees, including fir and cedar. Blenker's own tent exuded luxury and ostentation. McClellan himself seized every opportunity to visit the German general and enjoy the bountiful table and martial displays provided by the Forty-Eighter. Almost any stray German adventurer looking for an appointment and unable to find an official regimental position took up residence in Blenker's "court." There gradually grew up a large body of officers, unpaid and lacking official commissions, who served in Blenker's entourage as unofficial aides-de-camp. Accompanied by this retinue, Blenker's tours of inspection around his domain were triumphal processions. Although alcoholic beverages were officially banned in army camps, Blenker's Germans got their regular rations of beer; and brandy, wine, and other potables appeared routinely on their leader's groaning dinner table, along with extravagant courses of German cooking. Blenker received distinguished visitors in his famous blue tent with unfailing courtesy. If McClellan or another high-ranking officer was a guest, General Blenker soon shouted his favorite order, "Ordinans numero eins!" That signalled the appearance of champagne. Foaming bottles settled on tables laden with fruit and cake, while a band played Italian music to entertain the company.[39] One can only imagine the reaction Augustus Willich would have, had he the opportunity to visit Blenker!

It was a long way from a small dairy farm in rural New York to the heady life of a general in the Army of the Potomac. Blenker took a special joy in ordering around the genuine and fake members of the German nobility who made up his volunteer staff. He appreciated the exquisite irony of a revolutionary exile instructing a prince to deliver an order, a count to inspect pickets, or a baron to trot along behind him when he toured the encampment. In the end, however, it was the ragtag collection of fawning adventurers that helped prove his undoing.

A modest social note appeared in Washington papers in early October 1861. "Prince Salm-Salm, of Prussia, is now attached to the staff of General Blenker. He was appointed Colonel of the Kentucky Cavalry, but this change was made at his own request."[40] Not mentioned in the note was Salm-Salm's long and desperate search for a military appointment, his inability to speak English, which made the search doubly difficult, and that the appearance of the Prussian prince prompted a bitter controversy among Blenker's German supporters. Prussian princes were anathema to many Forty-Eighters.

Gustav Struve was a captain in the Eighth New York Infantry. Fifty-six years old when he enlisted, he was too old to abandon his revolutionary and socialist principles just for the sake of holding a commission in Blenker's German regiment. Claiming that he spoke for the entire regiment, he lodged a protest against the Salm-Salm appointment. Blenker forced his resignation.[41] Getting rid of Struve did not settle the issue.

For months stories had circulated in New York and among the larger German-American community about the life-style in the Blenker encampment, and about the "orgies of foreign princes, counts and barons" on Blenker's staff.[42] Beyond the prurient curiosity about life-style lay the far more serious political differences between the liberal and radical Forty-Eighters and the Germans willing to accept the throngs of disreputable European aristocrats crowding around Blenker and the German division. There were other stories about the behavior of the German soldiers in Virginia. German soldiers, it was charged, looted the countryside and ravaged the farms of Virginia like medieval freebooters, despite their soldierly behavior in camp. Blenker, complained his critics, wrapped his scarlet cape around his shoulders and ignored the behavior of his troops while he tolerated and encouraged the dissolute behavior of the crowd of adventurers surrounding his headquarters. German newspapers, like the *New York Demokrat,* brought up older stories about alleged improprieties connected to the early days of the Eighth New York Infantry in New York. The outraged Struve published a pamphlet denouncing the Salm-Salm appointment. Washington newspapers printed rumors about financial irregularities in Blenker's command, while other stories vigorously denied those irregularities. It was plain to all concerned that the Salm-Salm episode was the tip of the iceberg; discontent and dissension were rife in the German division. General Blenker's swollen staff of eight personal aides, too many of whom were were "shipwrecked" officers from German and Austrian armies, was now a collective albatross around his neck.

Even while the rumors flourished, the German general had his defenders. The *Washington Evening Star,* all through the fall and early winter of 1861–1862, denounced his detractors, denied allegations of financial irregularities, insisted that Blenker would not resign, and tried to counter critical stories in Washington and New York newspapers. M. C. Gritzner published a booklet aimed at German-Americans that reviewed the charges made against Blenker. Gritzner argued that Blenker was a victim of anti-German prejudice, the same prejudice that existed from Missouri to the Atlantic coast.[43] Blenker's enemies in Europe, he charged, spread lies there that made their way across the Atlantic.

Karl Heinzen, a Forty-Eighter journalist in Boston, led the assault on General Blenker. From the early months of the war Heinzen regularly and sarcastically harangued overly ambitious German officers. Before the war, he raged, every German vagabond and adventurer wanted to be a newspaper editor; with the war that ambition changed to an appointment as colonel of a regiment. Heinzen gleefully and publicly identified the prewar occupations of officers he disliked and exposed fake titles of nobility sported by those Germans seeking fame and fortune by exploiting America's national agony. "The first theater of war for most of the German colonels," he wrote in the columns of his paper, *Der Deutsche Pionier,* "was the beer hall."[44] Heinzen allowed the pages of the *Pionier* to be used by people writing accusations against Sigel, Steinwehr, and other German officers. Increasingly disturbed by what he heard about Blenker, Heinzen decided after the Salm-Salm episode that he would drive Blenker out of the army.

It was a long and vindictive campaign. Heinzen reprinted charges made in the *New York Tribune* that officers in Blenker's division split illicit profits of a thousand dollars a month extorted from regimental sutlers. He charged Blenker with censoring newspapers (including the *Pionier*) and portrayed the general as a thoroughly corrupt swindler, jailbird, and fugitive from justice in Europe. He even hired a lawyer to investigate charges of criminal conduct by Blenker in Europe; the lawyer found the record murky and advised the New York journalist to be cautious in making allegations about Blenker. Undaunted by this advice, Heinzen published accusations of criminal misconduct against Blenker, and the charges became part of a congressional debate in Washington about Blenker. That debate centered on the senatorial confirmation hearings for his appointment as general. He was confirmed, but his military career languished thereafter. Mustered out of the service in March 1863, he retired to his New York farm where he died later that same year.

Was Blenker guilty of financial misconduct? He never replied publicly to the many charges made against him. His lavish life-style certainly seemed beyond the salary of a colonel or a general. If we can believe the testimony of a thorough scoundrel, Blenker was guilty as charged. In March 1862 Col. George D'Utassy testified that he met with General Blenker in September 1861, shortly after Blenker got his star. D'Utassy claimed that he had a witness with him, a Captain Brey, who heard the conversation with Blenker. The General asked D'Utassy how much one of the female concessionaires with his regiment was paying him each month, and D'Utassy replied nothing. Whereupon Blenker told him that he would have to pay fifty dollars a month for each woman with a concession in the regiment. (D'Utassy's regiment was in Blenker's brigade.) Blenker demanded a fifty-dollar payment on the spot, and D'Utassy handed over three twenty-dollar gold pieces. When he asked Blenker for ten dollars in change, Blenker laughed and told him the extra ten dollars would go toward that month's camp expenses. Any testimony by Colonel D'Utassy must be regarded with suspicion, however. Carl Wittke, after a careful evaluation of the evidence, concluded that the sale of beer in Blenker's camp gave net profits of six to eight thousand dollars a month to the sutlers holding the contract, but there is no evidence that Blenker himself profitted from the arrangement. Several of his quartermasters did go to prison. Perhaps the only verdict we can reach in this case is the traditional Scottish one of "Not Proven."[45]

Blenker's career tells us much about the political quarrels within the German-American community. For years after the war politicians and journalists fought over the Blenker case, and it was apparent both then and later that there was keen competition for generalships among German leaders.

Meanwhile, what befell the Eighth New York Infantry? Prince Felix Salm-Salm, whose appearance on Blenker's staff in 1861 prompted a political crisis, remained on Blenker's staff but found his position increasingly precarious. In August 1862 he married Agnes Leclerq, one of the most remarkable women of the Civil War era. By October 1862 Salm-Salm was the new colonel of the Eighth New York Infantry. Agnes engineered this shift in the family fortunes, and the prince remained colonel of the Eighth until its discharge.

Agnes Leclerq (if indeed that was her real name before her marriage to the prince) remains a mysterious figure with what can only be called a checkered past, a past with tantalizing glimpses of her life as revealed in the shifting mists of legend and deliberate obfuscation. Like many other tourists, Agnes visited the camp of the German regiments near Washington in late 1861. Never known for reticence, she observed Blenker under full sail and decided that he was "half a Prussian commanding general, half a Turkish pasha." Just who she was and what brought her to Washington remain questions with several different answers. One account says that she was a prominent Washington socialite, born in Canada to humble parents, that she worked as a young lady for neighbors near the family farm on Lake Champlain, and that she then became an actress with a traveling troup. From the profession she turned to that of a circus rider, billed as "Miss Leclerq." Another, and much more romantic story, has Agnes as an Indian princess, the product of a liaison between an English colonel (this may account for her later interest and skill in army politics) and the daughter of an Indian chief. Stolen by Indian warriors, she was sold to a circus manager who took her to South America. Trained as a bareback rider, she escaped the clutches of the circus entrepreneur when the troup played in Havana and made her way to Boston. There she encountered a wealthy relative who introduced her to polite society. It was sheer accident that on a visit to Washington she met Prince Felix, fell in love, and married him. "So the Indian Princess became a German Princess," concludes this tale, "and the wife of a man whose ancestral tree went way back to the Crusades, and who was the junior brother of a reigning Prince on the Rhine." Whatever the reality of her past, Agnes, now the Princess Felix, promptly took the inept prince in hand.[46]

To Agnes, despite her romantic attachment to him, Salm-Salm was simply a wastrel aristocrat, one example of the thousands cluttering the streets of big cities and clamoring for position in the military machine. The princess, schooled in the rough-and-tumble world of the adventuress, took immediate action when her new husband's staff position was threatened. The two of them went to Albany, New York; their goal was a regiment of his own for the prince. The competition was fierce, even for a Prussian prince. The princess, who understood the system of Civil War politics very well indeed, befriended a New York senator, who gave her access to Governor Morgan, who beguiled by the beauty, personality, and determination of Agnes, gave command of the Eighth New York Infantry to Prince Felix.[47] The princess strongly hinted in her memoirs that *other* females in Albany used more than wile to gain advantage for their husbands.

With a secure position and steady salary, life for the royal couple turned idyllic. Agnes had her own servant, and the colonel wrangled a captain's commission for an old friend who then became a sort of major domo for them, managing all the details of their lives and arranging for a steady round of entertainment. As the Princess Agnes later recalled the good old days of 1861–1862:

> As we had to do nothing but amuse ourselves, and kill the time agree-ably, scarcely a day passed without some excursion, pleasure party, dinner, or ball; and for the entertainment of the soldiers care was taken likewise.[48]

The princess found that the American way of war suited her immensely. The rich Americans did not care if a few hundred million dollars were squandered in the name of patriotism, and so she did her duty. The only cloud on her horizon was the occasional appearance of an Irish soldier. She detested the Irish.

New York's "First German Rifles" left federal service in April 1863, its term of enlistment expired. What, wondered *Harper's Weekly*, would Prince Felix do now? The prince and princess had a keen interest in the same question. It so happened that another New York regiment, the non-ethnic Sixty-eighth Infantry, ended its service about then, and part of the regiment reenlisted as a veteran regiment. In that regiment was Otto von Fritsch; the lieutenant colonel was a German named Steinhausen, who assumed that he would be appointed colonel of the reorganized regiment. But once again, Agnes triumphed. She wrangled the post for her husband. Because the veteran regiment was seriously understrength, she persuaded the governor of Illinois to assign a company of Illinois soldiers to the Sixty-eighth. More than that, Governor Yates gave the princess a captain's commission to help defray her expenses in caring for the wounded. Fritsch (not altogether a reliable witness since he hated the Salm-Salms) claims that when the Sixty-eighth New York Infantry left federal service at the end of the war, Salm-Salm was under arrest and under suspicion of financial mis-management but that he escaped trial by fleeing to Mexico. Fritsch raised the money to send Agnes to join her departed spouse. Later, Prince Felix almost lost his life in the expulsion of the French from that country, re-turned to Europe, and died in the Prussian army during the Franco-Prus-sian War. Agnes returned to America to write her memoirs.[49]

For both Blenker and Salm-Salm, ethnicity was a commodity for ex-ploitation. Salm-Salm, who never really committed himself to anything except survival and position, was much less successful at this exploitation than was Blenker. Both men used their ethnic ties and the war to promote lucrative military careers for themselves and their cronies. When his last regiment, the Sixty-eighth, teetered on the brink of dissolution from a shortage of men, Salm-Salm (and his wife) resorted to every possible tactic to get recruits. The Sixty-eighth New York Infantry (which Lonn labels "partly German") was a failed attempt at the formation of an ethnic regiment. Almost from the beginning its officers realized that getting enough Germans was impossible, and so they resorted to drafted men to fill the ranks. Once again, for the officers, ethnicity was less important than career advancement.

Ethnic politics and personal animosities play a large role in the history of the New York German regiments. Leopold von Gilsa, the former Prussian officer who led the "DeKalb Regiment," the Forty-first New York Infantry, distinguished himself in battle and actually commanded a brigade with the rank of colonel. There is evidence that his promotion to brigadier was blocked by the jealous machinations of the Princess Salm-Salm. When the organizers of the Sixty-eighth New York Infantry sought the help of Franz Sigel in filling up the companies, he refused. Blenker's first replacement as colonel of the Eighth New York was its original second in command, the Hungarian Julius Stahel; in the course of a remarkable career Stahel gained command of a corps and then yielded the command to Carl Schurz just to keep Blenker from getting a promotion to major general—according to the German supporters of Blenker. One finds in the New York German regiments the same overwhelming fascination and preoccupation with place and promotion that characterized the American military establishment in general. These German regiments had their fair share of rogues and mountebanks, and their members just as regularly as other veterans parlayed their war records into postwar offices. The regiments also had their share of heroes and martyrs. In a classic example of the connections between regular party politics and ethnic politics, the state's Republican party sponsored a German regiment, the "Frémont Rifles," the Forty-sixth New York Infantry commanded by Rudolph von Rosa, a move that, typically, aroused the jealousy of other ethnic commanders.[50]

Each year the adjutant general of every state publishes an annual report. As the chief administrative officer of the state militia forces, the adjutant general in each northern state held a position of great responsibility in the recruitment, organization, and administration of the volunteer regiments when the Civil War began. When the adjutant general of Ohio published his report for 1862, that report came in two editions. One edition was the familiar and traditional volume in English; the other edition was in German. That simple fact tells us much about the role of Ohio Germans in forming the state's military units.

As they did over the North as a whole, Germans in Ohio tended to enter "American" regiments, but the state created from six to twelve German regiments. Counting the German regiments from Ohio is something of an arcane art. The total depends upon the ethnic pride of the counter, the month and year of the count, how the marginal evidence is evaluated and, ultimately, the definition used for ethnic regiment. Bosse and Rosengarten, bursting with ethnic pride, credit the Buckeye State with an even dozen German regiments. Kaufmann counted four "pure" German regiments, but a total of eleven identified as German. Lonn concludes that six of the Ohio regiments were clearly German, while four others were more than half German.[51] There are good reasons for taking the most conservative number — six — as the number of German regiments from Ohio. The six include the 9th, 28th, 37th, 106th, 107th, and 108th Ohio Infantry regiments.

Both Bosse and Rosengarten identify the 3d Ohio Cavalry as a German regiment, while Lonn regards that unit as only partly German. The historian of the regiment not only makes no claim to ethnicity, but his account lacks any reference to ethnic identity for the regiment. A recent study of the regiment and its surviving records includes no ethnic references. Correspondence from a cavalry trooper to his family contains not a word about a German character for the regiment. The 74th Ohio Infantry, cited as German by Bosse and Rosengarten, fails the same test; letters from a soldier to his family include no ethnic references, and Lonn says that the best judgment is that the membership was over half German. As for the 47th Ohio Infantry, which both Bosse and Rosengarten claim was German and Lonn cites as over half German, the regiment's own historian vigorously asserts it was not a German regiment. "The regiment," he noted, "was composed of four companies of Germans and the balance of Yankees as they were called." The four German companies included many Americans as well as foreign-born volunteers, and the chronicler tells us that at least thirteen different nationalities made up the membership. And so, despite the organization of the regiment under the patronage of the German-American political leader Charles Wilstach and being known as the "Wilstach Regiment," as well as electing as its first colonel, Frederick Poschner — a native Hungarian — its German identity remains doubtful. A large collection of personal correspondence from a member of the regiment suggests that there was a recognized German element within the regiment but that Germans were a minority. Finally, the traditional nicknames for Ohio regiments include six German regiments, with the 9th Ohio Infantry as the First German Regiment and the 108th Ohio Infantry as the Sixth German Regiment. All of this attests again to the difficulties inherent in ethnic regiment definition and one more caution about reliance on filiopietistic literature.[52]

In every state fielding ethnic regiments there was a tendency for one regiment of each ethnic population to attract the most public attention, to be more associated in the popular imagination with that part of the population. That was usually, although not always, the first such regiment recruited. In Ohio, the Ninth Ohio Infantry, the first German regiment, remains today *the* German regiment from the state. For its members and for Ohio's people, the regiment was "Die Neuner." It was also the state's first three-year regiment.

15 April 1861: Cincinnati Germans, reacting to the Fort Sumter attack, met in the Turner Hall to hear condemnations of the South and speeches of support for the Union. "I know the Germans will fight!" declaimed one orator. "Our American boys of course mean well enough," he continued, "but they don't know how." The speaker was Robert L. McCook, the law partner of the judge and German-American political leader, Johann B. Stallo. McCook was the son of a Scotch-Irishman who moved from Pennsylvania into Ohio in the 1820s. Daniel McCook prospered in Ohio; he sired nine sons, while his brother, John, produced five. All fourteen sons served in the Union forces, and so did both fathers. Thirteen of the Mc-Cooks won officer's commissions. It was one of the most remarkable family sagas of the Civil War. When he addressed the Cincinnati Germans that April night, Robert McCook already had strong ties with that ethnic community, despite his own different ancestry. To some extent those ties emerged from his law partner, but they also reflected his own preferences and friendships. McCook knew his audience; he knew that many were Turners, and that the city's Turners prided themselves not only on their physical fitness and training, but also on their marksmanship and drill. Most Americans, in sharp contrast, had no background that would put them on a par with the Germans in this respect. McCook himself knew absolutely nothing about the military, and he did not speak German. He also knew that many of his listeners were Forty-Eighters and others with military experience gained in Europe. Out of that 15 April gathering came a call for a German regiment, a call that elicited an overwhelming outpouring of support from the city's German population.[53]

Recruits gathered at Camp Harrison, located at a race track just outside the city. When a newspaper reporter visited the camp, he found lots enthusiasm and lots of mud. "The recruits," he wrote, "looked for all the world like sick roosters on a rainy Sunday."[54] While the volunteers slogged through drill and picnicked with relatives on sunny weekends, serious questions about strategy emerged in the discussions held by the organizers. Might the foreign birth of the vast majority of the volunteers be a handicap to winning acceptance of the regiment in Columbus and Washington, especially in light of the anti-German sentiments emanating then from St. Louis? (Cincinnati newspapers gave almost daily accounts of what was happening in that Missouri river city.) What kind of leadership will most likely wield the most potent influence in official Washington? The debate ended, the men cast their votes, and Ohio's first German regiment had a Scotch-Irish-American colonel, Robert L. McCook. A second and unanimous vote, however, made Augustus Willich the "military father of the regiment" with the rank of adjutant. Willich, known affectionately as "Papa Willich" to the men, undertook the real work of whipping the volunteers into shape, while McCook studied military manuals and carried out the political maneuvering needed to win approval in Columbus and Washington for the Ninth Ohio Infantry as the first three-year regiment from Ohio. The hero of Fort Sumter, Maj. Robert Anderson, swore the men into federal service at Camp Dennison on 27 May 1861. In less than two months *Die Neuner* took its baptism of fire in West Virginia. By that time Willich was gone, raising his own German regiment in Indiana.

Everything about the Ninth Ohio reflected its ethnic background. Almost all the soldiers used German as their first language, the officers commanded in German, written orders were posted in that language, the favored beverage was beer — in large quantities — the songs sung were German, and the Willich drilling was straight out of Prussian army practices. The colonel took all of this with good grace, and in time developed a thorough knowledge of procedures and tactics through his self-study, from observing Willich and the other veterans, and as a quick learner from experience. For their part, the Germans respected their non-German commander. At the Battle of Holly Springs, Kentucky, in January 1862, Willich had the command of a brigade, and his distinguished service there won him a promotion to brigadier.[55]

*Die Neuner*, in well-defined contrast to Blenker's Eighth New York, and especially to the tribulations of the Illinois Twenty-four and Eighty-second Regiments, enjoyed extraordinary internal harmony and a noticeable lack of political animosity both within the ethnic community and between the Germans and non-Germans in Cincinnati. Two factors seem critical in accounting for this. One was Willich, the other McCook. Good leadership did make a difference.

The Ninth Ohio had broad community support from its very inception. Cincinnati newspapers gave regular, detailed coverage of the regiment's organization, training, and campaigns. No doubt the long tradition of "Over the Rhine" Cincinnati helped in this attitude. As the very first German regiment, the Ninth had a large pool of potential recruits and thus no cutthroat competition for bodies, a problem with later ethnic regiments. As the colonel, McCook had the advantage of long familiarity with German politicians, and *he* was sought out as the commander; he did not conspire and pressure to gain the position. Colonel McCook faced only a modest number of tensions and disciplinary problems with his German soldiers, and when problems did arise they were the kind found in any regiment; they did not stem from ethnicity. There is anecdotal evidence of McCook's warm relations with his men, of his ability to make playful use of their ethnic identity. At the Battle of Carnifax Ferry, West Virginia, in September 1861, when McCook was on his own after the departure of

Willich, the colonel fully exploited all this background. As one newspaper account described the battle:

> McCook dashing furiously along the lines, shouting as he went, in a tone that rang like a trumpet on the field, that he had tried them before, and he knew what they would do, that he and the Adjutant General would lead them up, and that they would carry those works if the ditch had to be filled with dead Dutchmen before they could get over, that the traitors would soon see what his Dutchmen could do, and thus working the enthusiastic fellows up, till in the patriotic frenzy of the moment they would have stormed anything; the "Dutchmen" yelling and waving their swords and clashing their muskets, flinging up their hats. . . .

Even after allowing for newspaper hyperbole, it is apparent that Colonel McCook's rhetoric, far from insulting, was taken in good spirit by his soldiers.[56]

In the same year that he won his star, McCook was murdered. In one of the many senseless and vicious tragedies of the war, McCook, who was ill and traveling in an ambulance at the time, was shot by bushwhackers in northern Alabama.[57] The Ninth Ohio, already with a new colonel because of McCook's promotion, heard the news and exploded in anger. The men rushed to the scene, burned all the houses in the neighborhood, and lynched several men thought to have been participants in the atrocity.

Die Neuner's new colonel was Gustav Kämmerling. It was under Kämmerling that the Ninth Ohio, along with the German regiment from Indiana (the Thirty-second), won a place as one of the most distinguished in the Union armies, most notably for action at Chickamauga. Kämmerling was a Forty-Eighter; he had been a friend and comrade-in-arms of Willich in Europe, and he joined with Willich in building the first German regiment in Ohio in early 1861. He was the heir apparent when the command fell vacant.[58]

Inscribed on the Ninth Ohio Infantry flag was the motto, "Kämpfet brav für Freiheit und Recht" (fight bravely for freedom and justice). During its three years of service the regiment won the nicknames of "Bloody Dutch" and "Dutch Devils" from its Confederate enemies.[59] Men of the Ninth fought hard and played hard. At a stop in Cincinnati after their stint in West Virginia and before going on to Kentucky, they went on a monumental but good natured binge with the enthusiastic support of the city's residents. At Chickamauga, half of the five hundred men who fought lay dead or wounded when the action ended. It suffered more casualties than any other regiment there, and covered itself with more glory.

If one could construct a "model" ethnic regiment, the Ninth Ohio might well fit that ideal as closely as any. Born and nurtured with the popular support of both ethnic and nonethnic populations, with an absence of the bitter squabbles so common in this experience, and with a brilliant battlefield record, Die Neuner returned to Cincinnati and an enthusiastic reception when it left federal service. Even the Ninth Ohio, however, experienced some problems.

Colonel Kämmerling, who was a competent if not charismatic officer, was given a dishonorable dismissal from the service. The charge against him centered on improper discharges given soldiers of the Ninth Ohio.[60] What happened seems to have been a common enough occurrence. When the regiment's term of enlistment expired, the men refused to reenlist as a veteran regiment, and so the colonel and the men returned to Ohio. Some of the soldiers in the Ninth were not yet eligible for discharge, but the colonel took them along with the rest. Members of the regiment forwarded protests to Gen. George Thomas. President Lincoln changed what had initially been a dishonorable discharge to a dishonorable dismissal, but not until after the war ended was Kämmerling's discharge changed to honorable. Perhaps his improper action in late 1864 stemmed from his failure to win promotion. In any event, the business added a somewhat sour note to the final days of the regiment.

A more serious matter, and one reflecting the universal tendency among ethnic regiments, was the gradual loss of support for the regiment among the ethnic community. Attrition, the ever-present enemy of the volunteer regiment, eroded the unit's strength; the decline began as early as the fall of 1862. By October of that year, Lt. Martin Brauer, in Cincinnati to keep men flowing to the regiment, complained that the only recruits he found were undesirable or ineligible. The able-bodied men, he told the adjutant, have got enough of soldiering. "Soldiers can be had for money," he morosely concluded, "but there must be great pile." This was not just the plaint of an ineffective or lazy recruiter; it was the universal problem of the ethnic regiments as the war continued, and one shared with nonethnic regiments.[61]

Starting with the Twenty-eighth Ohio Infantry, the Second German Regiment from Ohio, the political stresses and partisan quarrels surfaced. The Twenty-eighth Ohio Infantry grew out of the initiatives of John A. Gurley, a Republican congressman from Ohio. Governor William Dennison was incensed when he learned of the regiment's existence, since his office was left out of the arrangements, and an effort was made to select the officers before he could make any recommendations. Like the Ninth Regiment, the Twenty-eighth was raised in the Cincinnati area shortly after the First German Regiment. The imbroglio surrounding its origin and organization delayed the approval of a slate of officers, and so it was early July 1861 before the Second German Regiment entered into federal service at Camp Dennison. August Moor, who led the Twenty-eighth, was born in Leipzig in 1814 and emigrated to the United States in 1833. He served in both the Mexican and Seminole Wars. Moor was thus not a Forty-Eighter, but he was a participant in the revolutionary movement of 1831, which prompted his removal to America. Mexican War service for Moor consisted only of recruiting some companies which saw no active duty. He commanded a brigade at Second Bull Run, and the Twenty-eighth served in the brigade. Although breveted after the war, Moor had a modest record prior to his mustering out in 1864.[62]

Ethnicity was gradually diluted in the remaining Ohio German regiments. The Third German Regiment, the 37th Ohio Infantry, one of the workhorses of the Union armies, had a long career of arduous fighting and campaigning, while never achieving the luster of the 9th. There is no denying the ethnic character of the regiment, however; at its 1890 reunion, most of the commemorative speeches were in German. It was the major of the 37th who enticed Augustus Willich to spend his retirement years in St. Marys, Ohio. Slowness and difficulties encountered in recruiting the Sixth German Regiment, the 108th Ohio Infantry, showed that the well was running dry. Unable to get the number of volunteers needed to justify a colonel for commanding officer, the top officer of the Sixth German Regiment was Lt. Col. George T. Limberg. Perhaps the well was drying up in another sense, too. In October 1862 Limberg faced a court-martial on a charge of stealing horses. Found guilty, Limberg was cashiered and dismissed from the service.[63]

The Ohio experience with its German regiments, then, was positive on the whole. It was distinguished by a relative lack of political bickering so common in other states. It shared with all other states the gradual loss of support for such units as the war dragged on.

Alexander von Schimmelfennig and the Seventy-fourth Pennsylvania Infantry offer a glimpse of still another side of the ethnic regiment experience. Schimmelfennig, born in 1824 in what was then the Prussian province of Lithuania, attended a military school and entered the Prussian army at the age of sixteen. He fought in the Schleswig-Holstein War of 1848, but afterward served in the revolutionary army in the Palatinate, along with Louis Blenker, Franz Sigel, and Carl Schurz. The revolution aborted, he joined other political exiles in Switzerland and England, and finally the United States in 1853. Schimmelfennig brought to America much more experience and military training than the typical Forty-Eighter.[64] Within a year after reaching the United States he published a book on the Russo-Turkish War, and he worked as a military engineer for the War Department in Washington. Four days after President Lincoln's call for 75,000 volunteers in April 1861, Schimmelfennig issued a call for volunteers for a German regiment. The response was quick and enthusiastic. While he labored as a single entrepreneur, however, a group of influential German leaders in

Pittsburgh, with ample financial resources, was rapidly recruiting several companies of German volunteers and looking for an experienced military man to lead a German regiment. From their efforts, rather than his own, Schimmelfennig got his chance to command a German regiment.

When the Pittsburgh Germans gathered eight companies, they offered the command to Schimmelfennig, who promptly accepted. The organizers wanted a man who lacked political ambitions and was free of partisan ties. With Schimmelfennig they found such a man, a rarity among ethnic officers. Small of stature, slender, and with no concern for his personal appearance, he made a startling contrast with Blenker. Like Hecker, he had a sharp tongue and sour disposition. He did not suffer fools gladly, and he devoted himself single-mindedly to the task of raising enough additional recruits to get the German regiment accepted into the Union army. By late summer 1861 the ranks were full enough for the outfit to be mustered in as the Thirty-fifth Pennsylvania Infantry. Then it was on to Philadelphia and more training and recruitment, and there ethnic politics struck hard.

A panel of "tavernkeepers, beerbrewers, clothing store men" and others, united in a dislike of the Forty-Eighter, persuaded authorities in Washington to stop the organization of the Thirty-fifth Infantry.[65] Schimmelfennig himself, sick with the small pox, had his authority to raise a regiment revoked. While he languished in bed, his supporters rallied and mounted a strenuous campaign of lobbying and threats in his behalf. So fierce and effective was this campaign (his supporters warned Washington that they planned mass demonstrations in major eastern and midwestern cities) that his authority was restored. Backing down, Washington blamed the whole thing on "clerical error." Throughout the affair, the Forty-Eighter's partisans were more intent on preserving his position and the image of a German regiment than they were in adding a regiment to the Union army. They welcomed any kind of recruits from any state in order to save the idea of a German regiment from Pennsylvania.

By the time Schimmelfennig recovered his health and returned to the regiment, he found that it had been reorganized and was now the Seventy-fourth Pennsylvania Infantry. The Seventy-fourth was in the Army of the Potomac and assigned to a brigade led by Henry Bohlen. The brigade was in a division commanded by Carl Schurz and the division was in the First Corps under Franz Sigel. In Europe, Schimmelfennig commanded Schurz; now he was under his old subordinate's authority. The colonel of the Seventy-fourth Infantry observed Schurz as he drilled his division and complimented him. Where did you learn how to do this? he asked Schurz. "First from you," Schurz told him, "and then from the books you recommended to me to study, at Zurich, you remember." Even the reserved Schimmelfennig had to be pleased with that reply.[66]

Schimmelfennig and the Seventy-fourth Pennsylvania Infantry experienced their first combat at Freemen's Ford in August 1862. Henry Bohlen was killed in that battle, and Schimmelfennig took over command of the brigade. The Seventy-fourth continued under the direction of German officers, first Adolph van Hartung and then Gottlieb Hoburg, until it left federal service in August 1865. After laudable service at Second Bull Run, Schimmelfennig won Sigel's recommendation for a brigadier's star, but Washington took no action. Schurz, who knew how such things were done, interceded in Schimmelfennig's behalf. He contacted the Pennsylvania congressional delegation, whose members then lobbied Secretary of War Stanton. Pressure was put on Lincoln, who told Stanton to placate the Germans and make Schimmelfennig a general. The Forty-Eighter got his star, and fought as a brigadier at Chancellorsville. Chancellorsville brought ethnic rivalries and prejudices to the center of national attention.[67]

Following Hooker's defeat at Chancellorsville in May 1863, rumors and newspaper reports spread stories of panic and confusion among the German soldiers in the Union forces. The "cowardly Dutch" became the scapegoats for the Union debacle. Schimmelfennig and Schurz, outraged at what they regarded as ethnic insults and a surfacing of Know-Nothingism, did everything they could to counter the public perception of a German failure at Chancellorsville. German-American political leaders called protest meetings, but the damage was irreparable. Even within the military, where informed opinion should have negated charges against the Germans, antiforeign sentiment was strong. Otto von Fritsch encountered that sentiment even as the Union forces regrouped after the battle. When he asked an American colonel to move his regiment to a better position, the colonel's reply smarted. "We are comfortable enough here," the colonel snarled, "fill (the gap) with runaway Dutchmen." Faced with insults both in the military and at home, German morale plummeted. Many officers resigned their commissions. German recruitment lagged. Nothing that Schurz or Schimmelfennig or other leaders wrote or said made a dent in public opinion. Friedrich Kapp organized a large protest meeting in New York, but this time fiery speeches, ethnic pleas, and threats failed to move the larger society. After Chancellorsville, German enthusiasm for the war never recovered.[68]

Schimmelfennig himself continued in his command, but his worst fears about ethnic politics and prejudice had been realized. Long before Chancellorsville he believed that the Union army suffered from favoritism, jealousy, and poor leadership. On the rare occasions when he socialized with his men and loosened his tongue with a social drink, he complained about nepotism and the tendency of German-Americans to favor their countrymen even when they were incompetent.[69] Politics and the competition of ambitious officers, in his view, seriously hindered the northern war effort. While such views no doubt stemmed largely from his own sour attitude, the unseemly fight over his promotion, and ethnic prejudice uncovered at Chancellorsville, those perceptions were quite accurate. It was both the triumph and the tribulation of a citizen army raised in a democracy that politics and political bickering were an integral part of the military machine. When I. I. Siebuck, Joseph Abel, Joseph G. Siebuck, and Charles McKnight recruited the nucleus of a German regiment in Pittsburgh, and when Schimmelfennig completed the recruitment in Philadelphia, they stressed that they sought veterans, Germans who had served and fought in Europe. To the larger society, the German regiments were touted as something special, soldiers better than amateur native Americans might hope to produce. This made those same Germans a natural target of frustration and resentment when things went wrong at Chancellorsville. The very insistence upon ethnic notoriety and separate identity in the creation of ethnic regiments was thus a factor in the upsurge of ethnic prejudice in the wake of military defeat. Exaggerated claims of ethnic prowess led both to unfilled expectations and jealousy on the part of native-born Americans.

Schimmelfennig won national attention again for his role at Gettysburg. He did well in the early stages of the battle, but then narrowly escaped capture by hiding in a pigsty for three days. That escapade naturally won some notoriety in the aftermath of a battle that the North regarded as a victory. Schimmelfennig continued in military service until the end of the war. His health broken by hard campaigning, a wound, and tuberculosis, he died in September 1865.[70]

Pennsylvania contributed five German regiments to the northern forces. In addition to Schimmelfennig's Seventy-fourth Infantry, the Twenty-seventh, Seventy-third, Seventy-fifth, and Ninety-eighth Pennsylvania regiments met the criteria for ethnic regiments. Organized by Charles Angeroth and Max Einstein, the Twenty-seventh Regiment was originally a three-month militia unit but was reorganized as a three-year regiment with Einstein as its colonel. Recruited in Philadelphia, the Twenty-seventh included many non-Germans in its ranks, and for most of its period of service was under the command of Adolph Buschbeck. Einstein's early departure from the command of the Twenty-seventh occurred as a result of pressure applied by Louis Blenker—one more example of the political squabbles among German-Americans. Buschbeck and the Twenty-seventh Pennsylvania Infantry compiled a distinguished record before the regiment left federal service in June 1864. The Seventy-third Infantry also came from the Philadelphia area, and its formation was largely the work of German-born John A. Koltes. The ranks of the Seventy-third included many English and Irish names as well as those of native-born Americans. It qualifies only marginally as a German regiment. Like the Twenty-seventh, the Seventy-third produced a truly distinguished record at Chancellorsville, Gettysburg, Missionary Ridge, Resaca and Kenesaw Mountain battles, and with Sherman in the March to the Sea.

Henry (Heinrich) Bohlen, although born in Germany, was an American citizen. His father, Bohl Bohlen, a Philadelphia merchant and naturalized U.S. citizen, was vacationing in Bremen when Henry was born. Bohlen led a life that puts him in the category of soldier of fortune, but not on the level of so many rascals in that group. He decided while still a teenager that he wanted to be a soldier, and his father sent him to a military school in Germany. Bohlen left school before graduation and, after a visit to America, returned to Europe and served in the French army, assigned to a regiment in Belgium. When his father died, he returned to Philadelphia to take over the family business, but with the outbreak of the Mexican war he abandoned commerce for the military life again. When that war ended, Bohlen sailed to Europe and enlisted once again in the French army to fight in the Crimean War. He survived Crimea, settled briefly in Holland, and when he got word of the outbreak of the Civil War in the United States, sailed to Philadelphia and began raising his own regiment. Bohlen recruited the Seventy-fifth Pennsylvania largely among the Germans of Philadelphia, and he used his own money to cover organizational expenses. He started recruiting at the beginning of August 1861 and on 7 August he got his commission as colonel. By October 1861 Colonel Bohlen commanded the Third Brigade in Blenker's division. It was a remarkable performance, even by Civil War standards. Soldier of fortune he might have been, but Bohlen was certainly a soldier and a courageous one. His short Civil War career ended 22 August 1862 when he died at the head of the Eighth Virginia Infantry while leading an attack at Rappahannock. His death, as noted earlier, gave Schimmelfennig command of the brigade.[71] Bohlen's career suggests that the label of soldier of fortune did not always have a pejorative meaning. Bohlen was no champion of democracy or of Republican principles. He fought against republican revolutionaries in Belgium in 1831 and for the French empire in the Crimea, but when he threw in his lot with the Union in 1861, it was not as a mercenary seeking personal financial gain. A military adventurer, he served his country well before his death in Virginia.

A native Würtemberger, John F. Ballier, recruited the last of the Pennsylvania German regiments—the Ninety-eighth Pennsylvania Infantry. Gathering in most of his volunteers from the Philadelphia area, Ballier enlisted many European veterans into his regiment, and both he and the regiment ended the war with an excellent record. Colonel Ballier won a brevet appointment for his service in the 1864 Richmond campaign. Like most ethnic regiments, the Ninety-eighth gradually shrank in size as the war took its toll. Ballier left the regiment in July 1864, and when the regiment ended its career in June 1865, it was led by an American officer, Lt. Col.

Charles Reen. The Ninety-eighth included one Irish company, a mixture that often produced animosity and conflict in other units, but the meager records of the Ninety-eighth show no ethnic conflicts. The Fifth Pennsylvania Cavalry, however, composed largely of German and Irish troopers, but claimed by neither group as one of its own, built a reputation as the "most inept" regiment in the Civil War, with chronic brawling between its German and Irish troopers.[72]

When he made his official report to Missouri Governor Hamilton R. Gamble in early 1862, the state's adjutant general noted with considerable pride that the state's loyal citizens flocked into military units in numbers greater than the quota allowed Missouri. Virtually all of the response to the first call for volunteers came from St. Louis, Adj. Gen. Chester Harding, Jr., reported, and most of those volunteers in the spring of 1861 were Germans. Harding's estimate of the proportion of German volunteers was a bit high. While the contributions of St. Louis Germans to the Union cause in the early days of the war was significant, and while Germans certainly made up a majority of the volunteers in the first regiments, many other groups were also involved. Missouri's first volunteer regiment, for example, headed by Francis T. Blair, was slightly less than half German; its ranks included a company of Irish volunteers, and perhaps 42 percent of the recruits were American and French. By contrast, the Second Missouri Infantry volunteer regiment consisted almost exclusively of Germans. That Second Regiment had as its colonel one of the most controversial figures in the St. Louis German community—Henry (Heinrich) Boernstein.[73]

Born in Hamburg in 1805, Boernstein acquired both a Catholic education and a hatred of Catholicism in Lemburg, served a stint in the Austrian army, and developed a radical political philosophy before coming to America in 1849. By March 1850 he was in St. Louis as editor of the *Anzeiger des Westens*. In between his other activities, Boernstein wrote a scandalous anti-Jesuit novel and devoted his great energies to the task of bringing culture to St. Louis Germans. He was anti-Semitic as well as anti-Catholic and used the columns of the *Anzeiger des Westens* to assault all organized religion as well as to urge St. Louis Germans to abandon the Democratic party and join the new Republican party.[74] When war came Boernstein turned his formidable talents to the organization of a regiment of German volunteers.

The St. Louis correspondent of the *New York Times* was appalled at this development. The new colonel, reported the *Times,* was a "political charlatan, who knows nothing about military affairs" and who is "universally detested." The *Times* estimate no doubt reflected the opinion of Boernstein's political enemies in St. Louis. Always the center of controversy as a newspaper editor, there was no reason to expect his role to change when he donned a uniform. In the estimate of one student of Missouri history, the colonel of the Second Missouri Infantry was "part revolutionary, part bigot, part culture vulture and wholly sensationalist."[75] Still, despite the rather disreputable air surrounding him, Boernstein did throw himself wholeheartedly into the task of saving St. Louis and Missouri for the Union. The *Times* may have been correct in its assertion that soldiers of the Second Missouri refused to stay in the regiment under Boernstein when it was reorganized as a regular three-year regiment. Boernstein left the regiment to become an American consul in Bremen (Lincoln's appointment removed a political embarrassment because Boernstein was involved in the unseemly feud between Frémont and Blair over Frémont's military administration in Missouri). As a regular three-year regiment, the Second Missouri was commanded by Col. Friedrich Schaefer, who fell at the Battle of Murfreesboro the following year.

Not every St. Louis German who crowded the recruiting offices in the early days of the war did so with a burning sense of patriotism. John T. Buegel, an immigrant from Mecklenburgh, found himself in a city where war brought a quick halt to the construction business, which many new arrivals depended upon for employment. Jobless, young Buegel volunteered for the Third Missouri Infantry, an ethnic regiment led by the redoubtable Franz Sigel. Buegel later recalled another motive for his enlistment—a desire to confound those Americans who regarded Germans with disdain and contempt. Nondescript and odd in their appearance, the volunteers in the Third Missouri Infantry drilled diligently and soon presented a fine appearance. "The majority had a certain amount of education and culture," Buegel recalled. "The main thing, however, was that each one was eager to teach the German-haters a never-to-be-forgotten lesson." The Third Missouri Infantry took part in the "Battle of Camp Jackson," and Buegel and his friends took great satisfaction at the abject surrender of the previously contemptuous young native-born southern aristocrats. "When the rebels saw that there was no escape," he wrote, "and that the Dutch really meant business, they surrendered and laid down their arms."[76]

Franz Sigel, the colonel of the Third Missouri Infantry at the time of its organization, led the regiment only thirteen days before he accepted an appointment as a brigadier, only to become an inept general and a symbol of both glory and frustration to Germans all over the North. The first five Missouri regiments, all three-month organizations, were reorganized at the end of their enlistment period, and many of their members joined either nonethnic units or other German regiments. In this respect, the Missouri experience was a microcosm of the North as a whole. Enlistment for the Fifth Missouri Infantry, the last of these three-month German regiments, went very slowly and painfully as the spring of 1861 faded into summer. Not until May did the ranks of the Fifth fill, and in August the regiment disbanded.

The Fifteenth Missouri Infantry attracted both Germans and German-speaking Swiss. It was organized in the late summer and early fall of 1861. Francis J. Joliat, the colonel, was a thirty-six-year-old immigrant who spoke a mixture of German, French, and English. Known as the "Swiss Regiment" or the "Swiss Rifles," the Fifteenth Missouri drew its recruits from the St. Louis region; most who joined were freshly arrived artisans and farmers who, not having mastered English, sought the comfort of a familiar tongue. Even if the regiment included many Swiss-Americans at the time of its initial organization (its historian claims that two-thirds of the men were Swiss), there is little doubt that more and more Germans joined as the weeks and months passed. Illness forced the original colonel to resign in late 1862, and for most of the unit's subsequent career the commander was Joseph Conrad, claimed as one of their own by both Swiss and Germans. Whether Swiss or German, the regiment and Conrad both established a record as one of the best Missouri regiments. Troopers from the Fifteenth Missouri planted a Swiss flag at the top of Missionary Ridge in one of the high points of the regiment's history. Conrad himself regarded his command as a German regiment. Americans in the regiment assumed that they were in a German regiment, although that conclusion probably reflected language more than anything else. For its officers, the important thing was preserving the regiment as a unit, or preserving their own rank in it or another regiment. That was a higher priority than ethnicity. Ordinary soldiers in the ranks of the Fifteenth Missouri would no doubt be amused by twentieth-century arguments about the Swiss versus the German identity of their regiment.[77]

Of the Missouri regiments, the most quintessentially German organization was the Twelfth Infantry. Commanded initially by Col. Peter J. Osterhaus, the Twelfth Missouri incorporated in its ranks many of the Germans from the three-month regiments as well as large numbers of Germans from Illinois who joined a Missouri unit rather than wait for a German regiment to organize in their own state. Extremely ambitious, Osterhaus soon moved on to command a brigade and then a division. When Osterhaus in 1864 received a commission as a major general, Lincoln admitted that he made the appointment in large measure to placate German-Americans, a classic example of a political nomination. When Osterhaus left the Twelfth Missouri (he commanded the regiment only three days), the leadership devolved on Otto Schadt. Plagued by illness, Schadt lasted only a few months before he resigned and the regiment came under the officer most intimately associated with its history, Hugo von Wangelin, the Latin Farmer from Belleville. Wangelin's career in the army is strikingly similar to that of Willich. He fought in fifty battles, lost an arm at Ringgold, ultimately commanded a brigade—and began his saga by enlisting in the Twelfth Missouri as a private.[78]

A real immigrant outfit, the Twelfth Missouri's ranks were 92.3 percent immigrants, and 84 percent of those immigrants were Germans. Other immigrants came from France, Denmark, and Switzerland. There were only 61 native-born Americans among the 931 original volunteers, and some of those came from German immigrant families. Most of the recruits were from cities and towns, in contrast to the typical Union regiment with its farm boy plurality or majority. The Twelfth Missouri was a fighting regiment, and its 49 combat deaths, 36 fatal wounds, and 132 nonfatal wounds testify to this. The regiment was remarkable in another way. At least two companies of the Twelfth Missouri came from Illinois; they were largely young Latin Farmers from the Belleville area. Osterhaus himself lived for a time in that part of Illinois, and Hugo Wangelin was a Belleville Latin Farmer. Wangelin knew personally many of the Illinois soldiers, and the surviving documentary record provides an exceptional portrait of the operation of an ethnic regiment and its members.

Henry Kircher was in the Twelfth Missouri Infantry. A machinist when the war started, Henry joined a three-month Illinois militia unit, the Ninth Illinois Infantry. Henry and the other German-American recruits from the Belleville area volunteered from a sense of deep patriotism and loyalty to the Union; they were better educated than the native-born Americans they met in the Ninth Illinois, and that part of their background as well as their ethnicity gave them a sense of separate identity. Kircher was bilingual. His surviving letters are in both English and German, while his diary entries (which cover much of the same subject matter) were commonly made in English. A typical Civil War diary kept by an enlisted man consisted of brief, often scattered entries, pencilled scribbles, smeared and semiliterate, often repetitious references to food, the weather, distances marched, and word about news from home. In contrast, the Kircher diary provides a valuable picture of the life of an enlisted man in a German regiment. Henry found life in the Ninth Illinois quite unattractive; the army, he thought, was too political. After the regiment was organized at Springfield it moved to Cairo, and Henry decided to return to Belleville when his term of enlistment expired. Before he could do so, he received a letter from his godfather (who was his father's business partner), Henry Goedeking:

> We think (wrote Goedeking) that it does not look very patriotic, if you should quit the military service now, after having had the intention to serve your country in this war, and it might give causes of sneering remarks to some people here, who are hostile against you boys of superior education.[79]

Bowing to this social pressure, but hoping to escape the animosities and bickering encountered in the Ninth Illinois, Kircher enlisted in a German regiment in a neighboring state, the Twelfth Missouri Infantry. It was his home for the remainder of his military career. The intriguing aspect of that letter home is that the argument centered on a perceived class difference, not ethnicity. Henry Kircher's experience raises once again the question of just how important, and what were the forms, of ethnicity for the member of the ethnic regiment.

In his diary and letters home, Kircher recorded ordinary and very human feelings. He was concerned about family members, hometown news, and his own future. His own educational background and family heritage can be seen in literary references, in quotes from favorite poets, and in the advice he gave a younger brother about reading and learning to play a musical instrument. Certainly it was not the typical soldier who asked his family to send his mathematics and physiology textbooks so that he could study when his boring military duties permitted. Like officers (Kircher got a commission in the Twelfth) and enlisted men throughout the Union army, he complained about prices charged by the sutler, bragged about how much money he saved from his army pay, daydreamed about what he would do when the war ended, and described his friends and the routines of everyday life. Henry received similar letters from his German-American friends. Like many Union soldiers, including the German-Americans, Henry occasionally expressed anti-Negro sentiments, although his feelings were less rabid and more casual than most others on this subject. In most respects, the thoughts and behavior of Henry Kircher in an ethic regiment are much like that of a native-born American of good education in an American regiment.

Henry joined a German regiment in part to escape what he saw as political bickering and insults between Germans and non-Germans in the American regiment he first knew in Illinois. In the Missouri Twelfth Infantry he found that he had not escaped them. Rather, the German regiment had three cliques. First, there was the Belleville or Illinois clique, composed of the German-Americans like Kircher himself who came from that part of the Prairie State. Secondly, there were the Missouri or St. Louis Germans. Finally, those whom Kircher referred to as the "neutrals" consisted of everybody else.[80] Kircher believed the bickering and feuding between the cliques had its origin in envy; each group was jealous of the share of promotions won by the others. This experience of competing groups inside a regiment was a common Civil War phenomenon. It often was based upon the geographic origin of the soldiers, and, while usually good natured, it could turn nasty.

Henry Kircher saw himself as different from non-Germans. The language difference was most obvious and probably his most meaningful ethnic characteristic. Henry was bilingual, and most of his fellow Germans in the Missouri Twelfth spoke only German. The non-Germans ordinarily had only English (or French or other native tongue) as a means of communication. Henry Kircher came from a community and a family that placed considerable emphasis on literacy and learning in both languages. He was conscious of this situation and made occasional references in his diary and letters about language. Henry's own English quickly took on a contemporary coloration; he adopted such colloquialisms as "rebs" and "skeddadled." Kircher assumed that he and his fellow Germans were different in other ways. Germans were better. They enjoyed better health than non-Germans because they were cleaner, followed a better diet, took more care with the preparation of food, and in general practiced better personal hygiene. He looked down upon Jews, blacks, and Yankees, and expected a higher standard of conduct from Germans than from others. Henry was embarrassed if a fellow German behaved foolishly or drew unfavorable attention to Germans. His taste for wine and special foods set him apart from non-Germans. In most respects, however, Henry Kircher was very like his fellow soldiers. When his tastes, interests, and attitudes differed, the difference reflected class and education more than ethnicity.[81]

Colonel Hugo von Wangelin (who was a family friend of the Kirchers) lost an arm at the Battle of Ringgold, and so did Henry Kircher. Henry also lost a leg, and those wounds ended his Civil War. Sent home, he did what many another ethnic and nonethnic veteran did; he exploited his status in politics. A photograph taken at the time shows a handsome young man, standing straight despite a missing arm and leg; his face suggests wisdom and suffering beyond his years. This photograph, circulated in the Belleville area, won sympathy and votes and helped elect Kircher to the post of circuit clerk. He later became mayor of Belleville. His postwar political career was in keeping with the mainstream of American life in those years. Ethnic and nonethnic soldiers alike frequently turned to politics at the local, state, or national level. Soldiers like Henry Kircher were the strong core of the Union forces. Intelligent, staunchly patriotic, possessing a powerful sense of duty, loyal to family, friends, and state as well as the nation, Henry Kircher and the soldiers like him in ethnic and nonethnic regiments alike gave the North its victory in the Civil War.

Missouri fielded one German cavalry regiment, the Fourth Missouri. Its commander was an American, Col. George E. Waring, Jr. Waring was an employee of the New York City Park District when the war began, and his personal, zealous devotion to horses led him to Missouri and the command of a cavalry unit. Waring cared more for horses than for human beings. He was contemptuous of the troopers of his regiment, which, he thought, was a collection of a thousand ill-tempered Germans. Colonel Waring was vain, preoccupied with status and appearance, and his published history of the Fourth Missouri Cavalry chronicles the qualities of his horses instead of exploits of his soldiers. The regiment was fortunate to have as its lieutenant colonel Gustav von Helmrich, a twenty-eight-year veteran of military experience in Germany. Like other ethnic regiments, the

Fourth Missouri Cavalry gradually lost its ethnic character as replacements diluted the ranks. And like other ethnic regiments, the officers, along with appropriate state officials, had a greater concern for the preservation of the unit and the positions of the officers than with the continuation of a distinctive ethnic character.[82]

Wisconsin contributed one German militia regiment (the Fifth) and as many as nine regular three-year regiments that were largely German. Of the latter, the Wisconsin Ninth Infantry fits most closely the model of an ethnic regiment, and its origin, role in state politics, and history followed a familiar pattern. The Ninth Wisconsin Infantry was known as the "Salomon Guards," and the origin of the name provides a clue to the key element in the regiment's record. When Wisconsin governor A. W. Randall in August 1861 called for the formation of five additional regiments in the Badger State, he specified that one of those regiments would be German. Fredrich Sigel Salomon, a Forty-Eighter from Prussia and the brother of the state's lieutenant governor, Edward S. Salomon, raised that German regiment, the Ninth Wisconsin Infantry. A third Salomon brother, Charles, took over the Ninth Wisconsin Infantry in 1862 after Fredrich won promotion to the rank of brigadier. The "Salomon Guards" had strong popular support from the Milwaukee German community, and despite severe winter weather during its training in Camp Sigel on the shores of Lake Michigan, the regiment enjoyed a remarkable record of good health. The Twenty-seventh Wisconsin Infantry, which was perhaps half or more German in its membership, had another Forty-Eighter for its commander, Col. Conrad Krenz, while still another Wisconsin Forty-Eighter, Fritz Annede, led the Thirty-fourth Wisconsin Infantry, which was over half German. A third Forty-Eighter, Milwaukee lawyer Joseph Vandor, briefly commanded the Seventh Wisconsin Militia in 1861. The Fifth Wisconsin Militia and the Twenty-sixth Wisconsin Infantry, the latter commanded first by Wilhelm Jacobs and then by F. C. Winkler, appear on the Fox list of the fightingest regiments of the Union armies. Forty-Eighters also served in Wisconsin German regiments in the lower ranks; famed journalist Bernard Domschcke, a rabid abolitionist and ardent Republican party stalwart from Milwaukee, enlisted in the Twenty-sixth Wisconsin Infantry and rose to the rank of captain.[83]

A competition for status began in the early days of the Civil War, and that competition continues. Every major ethnic group—and some of the minor ones—competed in a battle of numbers. German-Americans, like the Irish and Scandinavians, wanted credit for every possible member of their ethnic group in Union military units. Ethnics serving in Confederate forces get little attention in this battle of numbers, because their numbers were much smaller and they served the losing side. Estimates of the numbers of Germans fighting in the land and naval forces of the Union range from 176,817 to 216,000.[84] The exact number can never be known. A reasonable figure is probably 200,000 men of German birth in the Union army and navy. Whether Germans contributed more than their "share" to the military is subject to endless partisan debate. Variable factors in that debate include the question of whether one includes Negro soldiers among the share of the native born, and the assumption that immigrant groups by their very nature tended to include a disproportionate number of men of military age, compared to the population as a whole.

Of the 200,000 Germans serving the North, one estimate is that 36,000 fought in ethnic regiments.[85] A strict definition of an ethnic regiment would likely reduce this figure. Whatever the precise numbers, there can be no doubt that the overwhelming majority of Germans served in nonethnic units. The significance of the German regiments is not in their numbers, but in their symbolism.

A close connection existed between the Forty-Eighters and the ethnic regiments. Given the political activism of the Forty-Eighter generation, the connection was natural enough. The colonels of German regiments were usually Forty-Eighters, and they played an initial role in the creation of those regiments. At least eighteen Forty-Eighter colonels commanded German regiments at one time or another, and many other regimental officers came from the politicized generation. Another six or seven Forty-Eighter colonels commanded nonethnic regiments. The number of Forty-Eighters in the United States in 1861 remains another unanswerable question. Recent estimates suggest that many of the so-called Forty-Eighters were actually ordinary immigrants rather than political refugees, but from a group of three to four thousand men a truly remarkable number served the Union cause in important military capacities.[86]

There is irony in this situation. Ethnic regiments gave Germans their highest visibility in the war years. German political activism and influence promoted such regiments. During and shortly after the war, Forty-Eighters lost their political radicalism and their identity as a subgroup within the body politic. They abandoned their dream of a united democratic Germany and tied their political fortunes firmly to their adopted homeland. The gradual loss of ethnic identity by the German regiments closely paralleled this political shift.

Six of the German regiments made the Fox list of the Union's fightingest regiments. This is a smaller number than one might expect, given the total number of such regiments, but numerical estimates tell us nothing concrete about the quality and contributions of ethnic regiments.

Wars have a tendency to add new words to a nation's vocabulary, and the Civil War was no exception. German regiments added a distinctive but short-lived verb to American English. A once-popular song preserves the word:

> I met him again, he was trudging along,
> His knapsack with chickens was swelling,
> He'd "Blenkered" these dainties, and thought it no wrong,
> From some secessionist's dwelling. . . .[87]

It was quite typical of American humor to use the name of the most extravagant of the German generals as a synonym for theft—or perhaps we should say, liberation. The few lines quoted above come from a poem and song based upon another and flattering image of the soldier in the ranks of the German regiments—"I Fights Mit Sigel!" Newspapers and magazines all over the North took up the phrase and endlessly repeated it to express admiration and respect for the German soldier doggedly following and fighting under the leadership of what was probably the most popular of all the German officers, Franz Sigel.

Long before the war ended the German regiments were reorganized out of existence. Individual Germans fighting in nonethnic regiments had most of the same motives and experiences as those in the ranks of the ethnic units. The pull of language, friendships and peer pressures, the accident of location, and above all, the persuasion of ethnic political leaders accounts for the enlistment of individuals in ethnic units. In a prescient letter written in 1864, Carl Schurz described America as a "melting pot." Schurz and other ethnic leaders during the Civil War labored strenuously to promote German identity in the North and the ethnic regiment personified those very successful efforts. Two years after the war ended, Schurz decided the melting pot was undoing all efforts to maintain a German identity in America. The German spirit fades away, he told his wife, and the American spirit triumphs.[88] German regiments called national attention to a German presence and contribution, at the very moment when that German identity began to fade. The Civil War marked the peak of a distinctive German political influence in America. It faded rapidly thereafter. During their brief existence, in the checkered careers of such regiments as the Twenty-fourth Illinois Infantry and the Eighth New York Infantry, the German regiments provided a mirror image of the ethnic political battles in the larger society and the overweening ambitions of individuals willing to put the pursuit of personal careers and pride above the common good. In this, there was little, if any, difference between the ethnics and the native born. With both groups, the record suggests that there were at least as many heroes as villains, and that the common soldier displayed a heartening love of country that shamed those who abused the system to personal advantage.

# The Irish Regiments

*E Pluribis Unum. Erin go Bragh*

Ye boys of the sod, to Columbia true,
Come up, lads, and fight for the Red, White and Blue!
Two countries we love, and two mottoes we'll share,
And we'll join them in one on the banner we bear:
Erin, mavourneen! Columbia, agra!
E Pluribis unum. Erin go bragh.

— JAMES DE MILLE, "Song of the Irish Legion"

A N Irish regiment already existed when the Civil War began. This was the Sixty-ninth New York Volunteer Militia, the best-known militia unit in the country. Hostilities at Fort Sumter found Michael Corcoran very much in the public eye, as the colonel of the Sixty-ninth awaited court-martial for his refusal to parade the regiment in honor of the visit to New York by the Prince of Wales. The episode itself illustrated the conflicting loyalties of many Irish-Americans. On the one hand there was the urge to demonstrate allegiance to their adopted homeland; on the other hand there was the fierce partisanship toward Ireland coupled with a hatred of England. Most Irish-Americans were Democrats, and that illustrates another element of ambiguity in Irish thinking. Many Irish-Americans in early 1861 sympathized with the South. Thomas Francis Meagher's hesitation in April 1861 exemplifies this feeling. While thousands of northern Irish-Americans crowded into recruiting offices, Meagher remained at home, troubled by conflicting loyalties, and reminded of his public professions of support for the South in the weeks prior to the rupture. Further divisions in the Irish community emerged during the momentous spring of 1861.

Corcoran himself showed no public indecision. He immediately offered New York his services and those of the Sixty-ninth Militia. The offer coincided with a torrent of news and rumors pouring through New York streets and into government offices in Albany. Governor Edwin Morgan was the target of frantic entreaties from Washington to send troops to protect the capital from enemy assault and internal subversion. The celebrated "Silk Stocking" New York Seventh Militia was the best equipped of the state's military organizations, and the governor promptly ordered it to Washington. His own status still uncertain, Colonel Corcoran issued a public call for volunteers and was swamped by the response of thousands of Irish-Americans anxious to enlist in an Irish organization.

"I hope you will quash at once the court martial on Col. Corcoran," read a telegram to Governor Morgan from wealthy New York business man James Bowen. Other influential New Yorkers showered Albany with similar messages. The Sixty-ninth Irish regiment is ready to go to war, Thurlow Weed informed the governor, and the only barrier to its prompt service was the charge against Corcoran.[1] And so Governor Morgan, as he dealt with shrill calls for blankets and underwear, with rumors that the Seventh New York Militia had been ambushed and needed help, with telegrams from the secretary of war Simon Cameron soliciting assistance from the Empire State, responded to the emergency and dismissed the charges against Colonel Corcoran. With this legal barrier removed, the North's first Irish regiment, the Sixty-ninth New York Militia, enlisted in the federal service for three months and gathered men and equipment for its progress to the seat of war.

Pleased with the response to his call for volunteers, Corcoran remained troubled by another aspect of his complicated situation. He was a staunch Fenian, a member of the organization's Central Council, and the very popularity of the war among the young Irishmen of New York gave him pause. Like other Fenians, Corcoran regarded militia training and actual combat as valuable experience for Irish nationalists who could then use their skills in a war against England. On the other hand if too many Fenians joined the Union army, the survival of the movement was in jeopardy. And so, in one of his last acts in New York as the Sixty-ninth prepared to leave, Michael Corcoran prepared an address to the city's Fenian Brotherhood. If you are not already in the army, Corcoran urged his supporters, stay out of it. Reserve your lives for the service of Ireland.[2] As one of the three original founders of the Fenian movement in America, Corcoran wielded considerable influence among Irish-American nationalists. Many, perhaps most, members of the Sixty-ninth were Fenians. Corcoran's advice added to the confusion of loyalties already plaguing the New York Irish. For the men of the Sixty-ninth, however, there was neither doubt nor hesitation as on 23 April 1861 New York's Irish militia began its journey toward Washington.

Colonel Michael Corcoran, his thin face quite handsome beneath unfashionably smooth and short hair, wore a uniform heavy with gold epaulets and topped with a dramatic sash. A large badge, which was one of his trademarks, was attached to his coat and repeated the regimental flag—an Irish harp on a pole with the stars and stripes. His mustache and beard were neatly trimmed. This 23 April was warm for a New York spring, and the crowd around Great James Street grew restless as the hours wore on and the men of the Sixty-ninth remained at ease. Finally, with the delivery of some equipment, the moment for departure arrived and Corcoran led the regiment off to the exuberant cheers of the largely Irish-American crowds. Every housetop and window along the line of march held cheering, waving Irish women. All along Broadway more thousands of well-wishers shouted enthusiastically as the soldiers marched past. Escorting the Sixty-ninth were six hundred men of the Phoenix Brigade whose members paused at frequent intervals to fire a brass cannon. Barking dogs, darting children, and throngs of happy friends and relatives filled the street alongside and behind the marching men. Ignoring orders to stay off Pier Four, where the regiment was to board a steamer, the spectators pushed and shoved their way toward the end of the pier where the ship waited. Some citizens were trampled in the melee. Every individual present was determined to say a personal farewell to every acquaintance and the result was a near riot. Men were kicked and bayonetted. Some soldiers lost their muskets and parts of their uniforms as they struggled to break through the mob and board the ship. Finally the tumult faded as the last troopers straggled aboard. Tired members of Irish civic organizations, who by the thousands accompanied the regiment to its embarkation, collected their bedraggled and torn banners and returned to their homes and the normal routine of life in New York. The steamer, *James Adger,* laden with tired and seasick soldiers, headed toward Annapolis. The Sixty-ninth New York Volunteer Militia was off to war.[3]

When the Sixty-ninth made its way ashore, Corcoran, newly equipped with his official commission as a colonel in the federal service, introduced his men to military routine with guard duty along the roads toward Washington, and then it was off to the capital. News of the regiment's impending arrival preceded it, and as the Irishmen marched into Washington they were greeted by enthusiastic crowds waving green flags. Brushing aside the complaints of the Jesuit president and some of the priests at Georgetown University, the Sixty-ninth set up its tents and kitchens on the university campus. Floating atop a flag pole was a new banner presented to the regiment, a large silk flag carrying the message, "Presented to the 69th Regiment in commemoration of the 11th October, 1860." This message, recalling the regiment's refusal to parade for the Prince of Wales, was surely a unique slogan for a Union regiment in the Civil War. Another green regimental flag bore a more traditional motto: "Gentle when stroked, fierce when provoked." This motto lay between two Irish wolfhounds, rampant. Two American flags also wafted above the tents of the Sixty-ninth.

In the weeks that followed, the Irish soldiers quickly settled into a daily round of drill, guard duty, and socializing with the natives. Morale was high, and as Pvt. James M. Rorty noted in a letter in late May, the only grief to befall the regiment in those heady days was that caused by a broken bottle of Jamieson's whiskey. For its part, the *Boston Pilot,* which in early April fervently supported both the war effort and Irish participation in it, began to have second thoughts on the subject. Even as the Sixty-ninth settled into its Washington encampment, the *Pilot* decided that the war was a mistake, at least for the Irish. The first enemies the Sixty-ninth will face, the *Pilot* gloomily predicted, would be other Irish soldiers, fighting on the side of the Confederacy. Irishmen will fight Irishmen instead of their real enemies—the nativists—concluded the *Pilot*'s editor.[4]

May gave way to June, June to July, and the end of the three-month enlistment of the first Irish regiment approached. There seemed to be a risk that the New York Irish might fold their tents and return home without seeing action.

In mid-July General Irvin McDowell began the campaign against Beauregard that history remembers as First Bull Run, and the Irish Sixty-ninth got its baptism of fire just as enlistments expired. Disgruntled with the situation and angry because of a belief that they had been trifled with, the men of the regiment agreed to fight even though their period of service ended on the eve of battle. The *Boston Pilot* proved a good prophet; the first Confederate troops encountered by the Irish Sixty-ninth were Irish longshoremen in the Louisiana Zouaves. Whatever contemporary critics and later armchair generals said about First Bull Run, for the Union's first Irish regiment it was a long, hot, and arduous day, a day that ended with Colonel Corcoran and many of his men prisoners. Most of the regiment's prisoners soon returned to Washington and thence home to New York, but Corcoran refused to give his parole and languished in Confederate prisons for over a year.

As a captive, Michael Corcoran became a national hero. All over the North recruiters exploited his fame and that of the "Gallant Sixty-ninth" to encourage young Irishmen to enlist in Irish regiments. The day after his capture, a Confederate privateer was captured, its crew tried for piracy, and convicted. Faced with the prospect of the execution of men they regarded as legal agents of the rebel government, the South selected by lot from among its Union captives a high-ranking officer to be a hostage for the safety of the Confederate officers in Union hands. That officer was Corcoran. Fortunately for the colonel, the courts held that the southern privateer was a legitimate man-of-war and not a pirate.

*Harper's,* the *Pilot,* daily newspapers, travelling orators, broadsides, and even song writers proclaimed the feats of Corcoran and the Sixty-ninth in the months after Bull Run.

> Though from Bull Run we retreated,
> Did they not fight ten to one
> But we will avenge the insult
> When we bring back Corcoran.[5]

Despite rumors that he had escaped, however, Corcoran remained incarcerated. It was not the last time in the war that a battlefield defeat and a prisoner of war caught the public imagination and were transmogrified into victory and a hero.

Archbishop John J. Hughes of New York urged President Lincoln to make Corcoran a general. Hughes based his plea not on Corcoran's merits or achievements, but on what was already a familiar and effective argument of ethnic politics: the promotion of Corcoran would soothe the injured feelings of Irish-Americans. Other voices took up the cry for Corcoran's elevation and Lincoln went along with the proposal. Bureaucratic glitches delayed the official appointment, but when Corcoran eventually won his release he found that he was not only a brigadier general, but that his appointment dated from the July day he was taken prisoner at First Bull Run. New York politics took another familiar turn in the Corcoran case. G. W. Bungary of the *New York Tribune* approached Governor Morgan with a plan to give Corcoran a patronage appointment as New York City's Harbor Master. The salary connected to the position would be paid to Mrs. Corcoran while her husband remained a captive. When Corcoran himself heard about the proposal he reacted indignantly, asked his wife to return the money, and said he would not dream of accepting money for work he did not perform. Efforts to use state funds to reward ethnic soldiers became an increasingly acrimonious issue in state politics as the war continued.[6]

Thirteen months after losing his freedom, Corcoran and many other prisoners were exchanged for comparable captives in northern hands in August 1862, and he journeyed north to a hero's welcome. First, there was dinner at the White House with the president and other distinguished guests. His picture graced the cover of *Harper's,* and he made a triumphant procession to several northern cities in each of which he gave patriotic addresses and urged the Irish-American community to support the war. His earlier doubts about the wisdom of this for the cause of the Fenians vanished. Between the speeches and recruiting the new brigadier general put together four Irish regiments from New York into the "Corcoran Legion," also known as "Corcoran's Irish Legion." The regiments were the 155th, 164th, 170th, and 182d New York Infantry. Assigned to the Seventh Corps of the Department of Virginia, Corcoran and his Legion were stationed near Washington by November 1862.

Despite Corcoran's notoriety and his personal skill as a stump speaker, raising Irish regiments by the fall of 1862 was not easy. While Corcoran was a captive, an Irish Brigade was created (see below) and that drew down the pool of available manpower. Even in New York recruiting Irish ethnic regiments became a tedious and highly competitive enterprise. Critical journalists complained that Irish regiments included more than their share of society's castoffs, and while much of this rhetoric reflected prejudice, there is some evidence that the "second generation" of Irish regiments did harbor a good number of less desirable soldiers. Recruiting methods by then encouraged such a situation. As volunteers grew scarce, regimental organizers resorted more and more to "agents" who collected a fee for each body delivered to an organizing company. Officers or would-be officers trying desperately to recruit enough men to assure themselves a commission in a new regiment often resorted to outright bribery and worse to attract their quota. Whiskey and money were the principal tools, once patriotism and sense of duty faded. The case of the 155th New York Infantry offers an example of the trend.

Young John R. Winterbotham, age nineteen, despite his disdain for the Irish, resolved to join in the formation of the "Wild Irish Regiment," the 155th New York Infantry, destined to be a part of Corcoran's Legion. Winterbotham, like many other ambitious young Americans with some education, sought a commission in any organization possible. He tried "Spinola's Brigade" and "Sickle's Brigade" and then settled on the task of organizing a company of his own that could be attached to the "Wild Irish Regiment." To get his company filled, Winterbotham toured New York's jails and prisons, offering bribes to criminals to entice them into his company.[7] While he struggled for a position in Corcoran's command, he praised the "immortal" Corcoran; if prospects dimmed, he spoke disparagingly of the general. When family influence won Winterbotham his coveted staff position with Corcoran, his criticism changed to praise, to be followed by scathing descriptions of the Irish enlisted men, whom Winterbotham saw as childlike, drunken, and poorly educated. Many of Winterbotham's fellow officers in the "Wild Irish Regiment" were American, not Irish, and they thoroughly enjoyed the perks of an officer in the Civil War army. Lieutenant Winterbotham was neither an exceptionally selfish nor unusually ambitious and prejudiced young Union officer; his counterpart existed by the hundreds in Union and Confederate units. He perfectly represented the society that produced the citizen army of 1861–1865. In his first skirmish, Winterbotham performed poorly and lost his sword in a sea of mud. By the time his military career ended he suffered three wounds and was a skilled and mature officer. The men and officers of Corcoran's Legion were very much like the men and officers in other regiments, driven by the same aspirations, subject to the same weaknesses, and in the end, winning the war for the North.

Colonel James P. McIvor, born in 1837 in Ireland, was thoroughly familiar with the Irish, and he had no illusions when he took command of the 170th New York Infantry. McIvor got his initial experience with an Irish regiment as a captain in the 69th New York Militia, and he became the lieutenant colonel of the 170th with the organization of that regiment as a part of Corcoran's Legion in late 1862. His new regiment was recruited in New York City and in Brooklyn, and McIvor found that, like many another Civil War regiments, the curse of the unit was alcohol. McIvor took over as colonel of the 170th in January 1863, and he had to fight to keep his Irish soldiers fit for duty. Here is how he phrased the problem in an official letter in December of that year:

> I beg leave most respectfully to request that you will not sell any more Whiskey to the officers of the 170th Regt N. Y. Vol unless on an order approved by and signed by a Field officer of the Regt. for if you do I assure you that before four weeks expire there will not be a Line officer for duty in the Regt.

McIvor's plea caused an uproar among his officers when its recipient posted it on his office wall for the world to see. McIvor believed in calling a spade a spade, and when one of his officers requested permission to resign from the regiment for "family reasons," the colonel quickly approved the request with the despairing comment, "Approved and recommended for the benefit of the service for the reason that Lieut Rodgers is a worthless drunken scamp."[8] Corcoran rejected McIvor's note as unmilitary. Whiskey, despite claims of stereotyping, was a particular bane of Irish regiments and ultimately it proved the undoing of General Corcoran.

Michael Corcoran was a popular officer and his fame gave him a degree of influence with President Lincoln. After organizing the Corcoran Legion he served as a division commander and was a popular speaker on the ethnic circuit. His name was used on recruiting posters and newspaper ads throughout the North, wherever Irish regiments formed. For many Irish-Americans, Michael Corcoran personified the role of Irish-Americans in the Civil War. For all this, he faced stiff competition for public attention as Thomas Meagher and other Irish leaders used his name as an attraction to their own recruiting efforts. Corcoran's career was curiously devoid of military achievement, despite his rank and succession of divisional commands. His fame rested largely on his rhetoric, his Fenian activities, and his initial role as a celebrated prisoner after Bull Run.

In April 1863 Corcoran's role in a shooting dulled the luster surrounding his name. The episode itself was common enough in the Civil War; it combined whiskey, confusion, conflicting testimony, and a fatality on a dark night. On 11 April Corcoran received orders to get his four regiments into the lines by three o'clock in the morning, and he had just thirty minutes to do the job. Corcoran mounted his horse and galloped off to spread the word to the several regiments, clustered in encampments near Suffolk,

Virginia. On the way he encountered Lt. Col. Edgar Kimball of Hawkin's Zouaves, the Ninth New York Infantry, a regiment organized by famed bibliophile Rush C. Hawkins. Kimball, drunk, drew his sword and refused to let Corcoran pass without the proper password. Corcoran (said by his admirers to have been sober on this occasion) determined to carry out his orders, drew his revolver, and killed Colonel Kimball.[9] For the men of the Ninth New York, there was no doubt about the guilty party. "Lt. Col. K shot by the son of a bitch," wrote the regimental diarist.[10] Whatever the relative guilt or innocence of the two men, Corcoran's reputation suffered a major blow, and his influence declined sharply thereafter.

Eight months later Corcoran himself died in a freak accident in which alcohol again played a role. On 22 December Thomas Meagher paid a visit on his old companion in arms, and on the spur of the moment Corcoran decided to join Meagher on a ride to the railroad station where Meagher boarded a train to Washington. Other officers on the jaunt suggested that Corcoran ride Meagher's big, grey horse back to camp, and Corcoran went along with the idea, even though the horse had a reputation as an unruly beast. It had been an evening of conviviality, and the general cantered on ahead of the others. A short time later the Irish-Americans came upon Corcoran senseless at the bottom of a gully; he had been thrown, and the big horse had fallen on top of him. Corcoran never regained consciousness. Meagher himself felt at least partially responsible for the accident, as his stricken features revealed when he returned to the camp and accompanied the body to Washington.[11] Corcoran's death reminded the nation briefly of his existence, and there was a flurry of retrospective adulation and ethnic praise in the press; but by then Corcoran's position in the Irish-American scene had long been overshadowed by his friend and competitor, the owner of the spirited mount responsible for the general's untimely death, Thomas Francis Meagher.

When Colonel Corcoran went off to a confederate prison after First Bull Run, the old Sixty-ninth New York State Militia was mustered out of federal service. Meagher, who had recruited a company of zouaves for Corcoran's regiment, returned to New York and threw himself into the work of raising a whole brigade of Irish volunteers. The debacle at Bull Run diminished Irish enthusiasm for the war, while Corcoran's absence left wide open the question of leadership of the Irish community. Meagher's chief competitor was Robert Nugent, who had been lieutenant colonel of the Sixty-ninth and thus had strong tradition behind him in the race for primacy of place in the fall of 1861. Meagher's advantages included an unexcelled talent for self-aggrandizement, fierce ambition, and unmatched skill as an orator accompanied by the energy and willingness to travel the ethnic political circuit in pursuit of the twin goals of an Irish brigade and a general's commission for himself. Meagher's oratory played up Irish nationalism, hatred of England, and the need for Irish-Americans to exploit the war for political advantage. From his office in New York (where he used stationery emblazoned with Irish symbols and the title of "Acting Brigadier General"), Meagher of the Sword rejuvenated patriotic fervor, signed up recruits, and spoke to Irish audiences from New York to Boston. In February 1862 Nugent won the coveted post as colonel of the new three-year Sixty-ninth New York Regiment, but Meagher captured the title of brigadier general and command of the Irish Brigade.[12]

Meagher's drive to command the Irish Brigade was a classic example of ethnic politics in action. He wooed and won the public support of the powerful Archbishop John Hughes of New York. Hughes gave his public blessing to the enterprise, but privately he opposed it. Writing to Secretary of State William Seward, Hughes argued that ethnic identifications for regiments and brigades would foment trouble and division, and that the best policy for the Union forces was one of neutral numbers for unit identification. Meagher persuaded New York's governor E. D. Morgan to grant official state backing for the idea of an Irish Brigade, and, while the Irish Brigade was still only an idea, urged officials in other states to support the brigade with companies and regiments raised for the purpose. Irish recruiters in those states used the idea of such a brigade along with the mythic heroism of prisoner-of-war Corcoran to drum up support for their own efforts. Shortly after his return to New York, Meagher wrote a lurid, emotional account of the record of the Sixty-ninth New York Regiment during its three-month service. Published by the *Irish-American* newspaper, the pamphlet repeated every stereotype, every cliché, about the Irish soldier.[13] In an obvious appeal for both recruits and community support, Meagher portrayed the Irish soldier as one victimized by the larger society, better than non-Irish soldiers, and a fighting man whose bravery stemmed from his ethnic heritage. In what would be a familiar theme in Civil War literature, the young officer told his readers that Irish soldiers were superior to "American" soldiers, and that if things went wrong, the fault lay with the government and anti-Irish prejudice.

Thanks to the machinations of Meagher and his supporters, Irish nationalism and Irish politicians from New York played a significant role in the formation of Irish regiments in other states. A veritable "Irish Mafia" spread out from New York and won commissions in Irish regiments raised in New England, Pennsylvania, and the Midwest. For a time Meagher entertained hopes of a whole division of Irish regiments, with himself as its major general, but Washington authorities squelched that ambition.[14] In the event, by February 1862 Brigadier General Meagher commanded a brigade composed of the Sixty-ninth New York Infantry, along with two other New York regiments—the Sixty-third and Eighty-eighth. The Twenty-eighth

Massachusetts Infantry completed the brigade. All of these regiments marched off to war behind a green flag and heard as much rhetoric excoriating the English as they heard promoting the Union.

Meagher of the Sword was an impressive military figure. Erect in posture, he had a ruddy complexion and piercing blue eyes; a large frame and natural eloquence gave him a powerful presence, as born to command. Even as a captain in the New York Sixty-ninth Militia he indulged a fancy for ornate uniforms with enough gold trim and special badges to bedazzle visitors to his tent and those civilians who saw him galloping around the streets of Washington.[15] A popular speaker, he inspired his own men as well as diners at political banquets with a rhetoric emphasizing the martial traits of the Irish, their loyalties, their Catholicism, and the exploits of Irish soldiers on seventeenth- and eighteenth-century battlefields. Even his most ardent admirers, however, admitted that he had a serious weakness. Both boredom and a natural conviviality encouraged him to drink to excess. Like so many of his compatriots, Meagher regularly abused alcohol; this habit ultimately contributed to his undoing. Still, the new brigadier had a genuine concern for the welfare of his men. He fought Washington authorities to keep priests in his regiments as chaplains, encouraged regular religious services, and attended mass faithfully himself. He fought boredom with regular entertainments, from band music to horse races, from whiskey and beer rations to lavish parties on holidays, especially St. Patrick's Day.

Of the three original New York regiments merged into the Irish Brigade, the Eighty-eighth New York Infantry, "Mrs. Meagher's Own," was most closely associated with General Meagher. Commanded first by Col. Henry M. Baker, the Eighty-eighth enjoyed the sponsorship of the influential *Irish-American,* and that newspaper carried regular reports on the activities both of the regiment and the brigade. An officer of the regiment, Irish-born James B. Turner, wrote for the *Irish-American* under a variety of pseudonymns. Turner served as one of Meagher's aides and shared the general's tent, a combination of circumstances that gave him a unique opportunity to record the life and times of the Irish Brigade.

After early duty in a three-month regiment from New Jersey (Turner was from Trenton), he won a commission in the New York Eighty-eighth, began his duties for Meagher in early 1862, and had nothing but praise for the Irish leader.[16] In common with most Union officers, Captain Turner gave keen attention to his own career prospects and recognized that success and advancement for Meagher improved his chances for promotion. While never stinting in his admiration for Meagher in his private correspondence, he was ready to leave the general's staff if those prospects dimmed. Turner's letters to his family show life in the Eighty-eighth New York very much like that found in any Union regiment: long periods of boredom, a preoccupation with food and the presence or absence of comfort, tensions between officers and men, complaints about Washington, and a fierce patriotism that kept the soldiers going when the bureaucracy or the enemy made life uncomfortable. That the regiment was in the famed Irish Brigade was of small import.

Columns written for the *Irish-American* furnish a striking contrast. There, all was Irishness, ethnicity, and politics. (Turner earned five dollars a week for his writing for the *Irish-American,* and newspaper influence lay behind his appointment.) Readers of the Turner columns got a steady diet of Irish nationalism, reports of celebrations and honors accorded the brigade and Meagher, complaints about Great Britain and prejudice in Washington against the Irish, praise of the Irish contribution to the war effort, and rather vague accounts of military action involving the brigade. Turner's private view of the war was almost indistinguishable from that of any Union officer; his public perspective was that of the ardent Irish nationalist who saw the military experience as one to be used afterwards for Irish independence.[17]

In one respect the New York Eighty-eighth differed from the typical ethnic or nonethnic regiment. There is little evidence of the internal bickering and regimental politics so common in most regiments.

Meagher's Irish Brigade participated in several skirmishes and battles in 1862 and 1863, but two battles dominate the unit's history—Antietam and Fredericksburg. Assigned to Israel Richardson's First Division for the Peninsular Campaign, Meagher and his troops got their first real taste of battle at Antietam. From the beginning there was no doubt about the courage, devotion, and willingness to die for the Union on the part of the Irish soldiers. From the beginning, there was doubt and controversy about the behavior of General Meagher.

As early as First Bull Run, when he was captain of a zouave company in Corcoran's Sixty-ninth New York, Meagher's courage was questioned. *London Times* correspondent William Russell claimed that he saw Meagher running "across country" away from the battle, and that as he passed he exclaimed that the Confederates had "established their claim to be a belligerent power." Russell's charges—and his anti-Irish sentiments were common knowledge—aroused a storm of charge and countercharge in Washington and New York newspapers. Irate Irish soldiers threatened bodily harm to the *Times* scrivener, but the episode passed with honor satisfied all around. More serious, in terms of later developments, was the charge by correspondent Henry Villard, then working for the *Cincinnati Commercial,* that when he saw Meagher before the battle started the captain was drunk.[18] But Villard, like many other German immigrants, regarded the soldiers of the New York Irish regiments as riffraff.

It was at Antietam, the "landscape turned red," that the Irish Brigade won national recognition for its bravery and fearsome casualties. On 17

September 1862, the bloodiest single day in American military history, Meagher's Irish Brigade, in the center of the Union lines as a part of Richardson's Division, made its renowned assault at Bloody Lane. Two of Meagher's regiments, the Sixty-third and Sixty-ninth New York, suffered 60 percent casualties attacking the Sunken Road while the other troop units endured losses only slightly less horrendous. General George B. McClellan's personal account of the battle heaped praise on the Irish Brigade, but oddly enough dismissed Meagher himself with a brief reference to the Irish leader's fall from his horse. In his official report of the brigade at Antietam, Meagher described the acknowledged bravery of his men, told of the terrible noise and confusion, and said that he himself suffered injury while at the head of his troops when thrown from his horse and had to be carried from the field. Colonel John Burke of the Sixty-third New York took over command of the Irish Brigade and led the survivors away from Bloody Lane.[19]

Rumor quickly spread around the Army of the Potomac, however, that Meagher was drunk at Antietam and fell intoxicated from his horse. Spluttering with outrage, correspondent Whitelaw Reid of the *Cincinnati Gazette* denounced General Meagher's behavior:

> The General in question . . . was not in the charge at all! — did not lead or follow it! He was too drunk to keep the saddle, fell from his horse . . . several times, was once assisted to remount by Gen. Kimball of Indiana, almost immediately fell off again, was too stupidly drunk to answer the simplest question Gen. Kimball put to him about the disposition of his brigade, and was finally taken up on a stretcher, covered with a cloth, and carried off the field — the bearers circulating the story as they went that Gen. Meagher was dangerously wounded.

Col. Davis Hunter Strother, of McClellan's headquarters staff, recorded in his diary that Meagher was drunk and fell from his horse, while Union Gen. Robert Cox recalled years later the Meagher was commonly reported drunk at Antietam.[20]

Whatever the truth of the matter (and Reid is convincing in his detail), the news of Antietam sent shockwaves through the Irish-American community, especially in New York, which was home to so many members of the Irish Brigade. The *Irish-American* reported Meagher of the Sword suffering a temporary paralysis from his fall but out of danger. The paper also carried a standard Civil War account of an Irish soldier dying to save the green flag. Responding to the dismay among its readers about the scale of bloodshed at Antietam, the paper printed a reminder from correspondent Turner that the Irish fought in a noble cause. Irish enlistments in New York dropped dramatically after Antietam. So few volunteered that at least one state official informed Governor Morgan that a secret organization was at work to stop Irish enlistments.[21]

Meagher's spirits soon revived, helped along by the addition of another regiment to the Irish Brigade—the 116th Pennsylvania Infantry, an Irish unit commanded by St. Clair A. Mulholland. In early October the general paid his first visit to the camp of the Pennsylvanians. It was an occasion designed to impress the newcomers. Meagher and his staff officers, all wearing dress uniforms aglitter with nonregulation gold, swept into the camp with a flourish and inspected the ranks of soldiers. Afterwards, his voice lubricated a bit with the whiskey deemed appropriate for such occasions in an Irish regiment, Meagher dazzled the regimental officers with his poetic language and gracious manner.[22] He was back in stride.

On 13 December 1862 the Irish Brigade battered itself to pieces against the celebrated Stone Wall on Marye's Heights at Fredericksburg. In the early weeks of excitement following the rebel seizure of Fort Sumter in April 1861, many an Irish spokesman in the North had urged Irish-Americans to remain aloof from the sectional war. Civil War, they said, would simply pit Irishman against Irishman. They were right in their prediction. Confederate soldiers hunkered behind the Stone Wall awaiting the Union attack were also Irish. As soldiers of the Irish Brigade worked their way up the Heights, rebel defenders spotted sprigs of greenery in their caps. "Oh, God, what a pity!" one of them called. "Here comes Meagher's fellows."[23]

Once again, the role played by Meagher himself remains obscured by the noise, smoke, and confusion of the battlefield. There is no doubt about the behavior of the Irish soldiers; they fought ferociously, tenaciously, and futilely in a doomed effort to seize the Heights. The brigade never recovered from the slaughter of that December day.

And what of Meagher? His official report of the Battle of Fredericksburg glowed with words of praise for his men and officers. He repeatedly cited the exploits of his old rival, Robert Nugent. He recorded the work of the Twenty-eighth Massachusetts Infantry, assigned the place of honor in the center of the line because it had the only green flag in the brigade that day. After all this he turned to his own activities:

> I myself ordered the advance, encouraged the line and urged it on. Owing, however, to an ulcer in the knee-joint, which I had concealed and borne up against for days, I was compelled, with a view of being of any further service to the brigade that day, to return over the muddy slope and ploughed field to get to my horse, which had been left in charge of an orderly, along with the other horses of the brigade, Brig.-Gen. Hancock having advised us all to dismount and act on foot during the assault. . . . Passing then through crowds of slain and wounded, all befouled with blood and mud in which they had been struck down, and recrossing the mill-race, which I did with the assistance of two wounded soldiers, I reached the head of the street, from which, as I have already stated, the brigade debouched, and there took my horse.[24]

Correspondent Henry Villard, who later found Meagher and some of his men gathered next to a hospital behind the lines, reached a more critical conclusion about Meagher at Fredericksburg:

> His retreat across the river without orders was nothing but a piece of arrant cowardice, for which, however, he never received punishment on account of his popularity among the Irish.[25]

Staunch Meagher supporters always attributed charges of his alleged cowardice at Fredericksburg to anti-Irish prejudice. Critics contended that at Fredericksburg, as at Antietam, Meagher fled the scene rather than face shot and shell with his men.

Correspondent James B. Turner and the editors of the *Irish-American,* in the aftermath of the carnage at the Stone Wall, voiced the anguish and outrage of the Irish-American community. Of the 1300 members of the Irish Brigade at Fredericksburg, 545 were killed, wounded or missing in action. The slaughter of Irish soldiers led the *Irish-American* to question the circumstances of their sacrifice. The hero of the battle for the newspaper was not Meagher, but Maj. William H. Horgan, who died as he led troopers of the Eight-eighth New York to within a few paces of the Stone Wall.[26] *Harper's* magazine, for whom Meagher had been a favorite, was silent on the subject of his conduct at Fredericksburg.

Meagher, even if he lost his aplomb on the field, quickly recovered it. Two days after the battle, while the dead lay still unburied in the frozen fields, he staged a huge party to celebrate the arrival of new green silk flags for his regiments. Invited guests ate and drank at a lavish spread. It was, in the words of one commentator, "like the feast of a Gaelic chieftain."[27] Incoming cannon balls and wrathful messages from Union headquarters brought the banquet to a premature end.

Meagher continued to command the tattered remnants of the Irish Brigade until after the Battle of Chancellorsville, when he resigned on the grounds that what was left of the brigade did not merit a general's authority. He continued to pester the War Department for another commission, and those requests were long ignored. After Corcoran's death, Meagher got an ignominious command of convalescent units. He was relieved of this last post after being found drunk. Bathos continued to mark his final days. There were dark hints that Washington gave him his last army assignment on the condition that he give public support to the war and to the administration in particular. He was the only prominent Irish-American to support Lincoln in the 1864 election, and for this he was denounced by some members of the Catholic hierarchy as a "Red Republican." For his part, Meagher roundly criticized the Catholic churchmen and wrote letters to Irish newspapers vigorously supporting the Union cause, letters that were reprinted for circulation in the United States as part of the "Loyalty Tract" series. In 1867, while holding a modest position in Montana after the war, Meagher drowned in a fall from a river boat, under circumstances that raised once again the question of alcohol abuse.[28]

From the time of Corcoran's capture during First Bull Run until the Battle of Fredericksburg, General Meagher was the most prominent Irish-American military figure in the North. He and his Irish Brigade personified the Irish regiments fighting in Union forces. In his early vacillation about the proper position for an Irish immigrant to take in the Civil War and in his subsequent enthusiastic support of the Union, he typified most Irishmen living in the North. His astute manipulation of political machinery to advance both his personal career and that of his fellow Irish was quite in the mainstream of Irish-American politics. Even in his prime, when his popularity was vast, other Union officers—including the Irish—tended to see him as exploiting Irish nationalism and ethnicity for personal advantage. Until Fredericksburg the common soldier continued to admire Meagher of the Sword and to enjoy his grand gestures and melodramatic oratory. His most telling epitaph, written before his death, came in a letter home written by soldier Maurice Woulfe to his family in Ireland:

> I was speaking to a sergeant here that served under Meagher. He told me that he was a gentleman and a soldier, but that he wanted to gain so much praise he would not spare his men.[29]

Woulfe went on to say that it took more replacements to keep Meagher's brigade replenished than it did the whole Eleventh Army Corps.

After Meagher left the Irish Brigade, its command fell to Col. Patrick Kelly who was killed at Petersburg. Two other commanders, Richard Byrne and Thomas Smyth, also died. Whatever the doubts and suspicions hovering about the name of its founder, none attaches to the honor of the brigade itself.

New York produced other Irish regiments in addition to those of the Irish Brigade and the Corcoran Legion. Known as the "Irish Rifles," the Thirty-seventh New York Infantry was a descendant of an old state militia unit, the Seventy-Fifth Rifles. Mustered in for two years in early June 1861 under the command of Col. John H. McCunn, the Thirty-seventh included two companies of American-born men along with a majority of Irish-born soldiers. Several prominent Irish-American political figures helped organize the unit; these included Judges Charles P. Daly, Lewis P. Woodruff, and James Moncrief. Equipped with its green silk flag, the Thirty-seventh went off to Washington where it remained in reserve during First Bull Run. Before it ended its two-year history, however, the Thirty-seventh New York compiled a fine record and won distinction in such battles as Fair Oaks, Malvern Hill, Chantilly, Fredericksburg, and Chancellorsville. No hint of misbehavior touched the Thirty-seventh, except for the almost universal complaints related to whiskey. As the chaplain once remarked in a diary entry, "Pay Day, and of course drinking. Such a picture of hell I had never seen." With all due respect to the sensitivities of the Thirty-seventh's chaplain, what he observed was not unlike scenes to be seen in other Irish regiments. Indeed, the history of the Thirty-seventh New York "Irish Rifles" is a paradigm of Union army regiments, from its organization by well-known local and state political figures to its record of service on the battlefield. While it lacked the notoriety attached to the regiments of the Irish Brigade, it was typical of those regiments forming the backbone of the federal forces. It is distinguished from nonethnic regiments primarily by the green flag it flew and the Irish names on its company rosters.[30]

Not every effort to organize an Irish regiment in New York was a success story. Colonel James Kerrigan and the Twenty-fifth New York was a case in point. Formed in the summer of 1861, by December of that same year the regiment was in a state of chaos. Colonel Kerrigan was on trial by a court-martial for disgraceful conduct and general incompetence. As the trial proceeded and evidence of the activities of the officers surfaced in testimony, the officers began to resign. Before long only two remained. The regiment was disbanded.[31]

After Fredericksburg the recruitment of Irish volunteers was increasingly difficult. The Emancipation Proclamation, which went into effect in January 1863, affronted many Irish Democrats, who felt betrayed by the very government they supported. The draft riots in the summer of 1863, worse in New York City than anywhere else, marked a climax of Irish alienation from the Union war effort. There would be no more Irish regiments from the Empire State.

In 1861 passenger train service between Boston and New York was frequent and efficient, if a bit dirty and uncomfortable. Mail between the two cities was delivered within a day or two of being posted. Close personal ties existed between leaders of the Irish communities in the two cities. Vigorous political-military entrepreneurs like Thomas Francis Meagher, facing lively competition in New York for recruits and commissions, regarded Irish communities in other cities as opportunities for exploitation. Given these circumstances and the early publicity accorded the exploits of Michael Corcoran and his Irish regiment in New York City, it was almost inevitable that New York influence was a significant factor in the formation of Irish regiments in Massachusetts.

Boston was the home of the *Pilot,* the most influential Catholic newspaper in the United States. Its owner-editor was Patrick Donahoe, an Irish immigrant who used the *Pilot* to combat nativism and promote a siege mentality among his readers. Those readers viewed the *Pilot* as the

"Irishman's Bible," and Donahoe himself bore the nickname of the "Apostle of the Irish." During the spring of 1861 Donahoe waffled on the question of where the Irish should stand on the growing rift between North and South. Fort Sumter settled the question for him, and he threw his considerable prestige simultaneously on the side of the Union and on the formation of an Irish regiment in Massachusetts.[32]

Boston was also the location of a large Irish ghetto, an influential bloc of votes for the Democratic party. Growing numbers of Irishmen entered the business and professional classes, and Irish politicians exercised increasing power. Members of that ethnic society hoarded bitter memories of the Know-Nothing years of the previous decade and saw themselves as victims of WASP prejudice and discrimination. For its part, the non-Irish population of the city viewed the Irish as clannish, suspicious, coarse, and prone to violence, strong, drink, and poverty. These political facts and social attitudes figured prominently in the Bay State's response to Lincoln's call for troops to suppress the rebellion.

Massachusetts fielded two Irish regiments. Both, from their origin to their discharge, mirrored the political and social realities and trends within the state and in the nation. Both had histories that were a microcosm of ethnic America in the 1860s. Both tell a story whose elements of tragedy, comic-opera buffoonery, and heroism, not to mention cupidity and generosity, were together the tribulation and glory of American democracy.

During the first confused weeks of April and early May 1861, Massachusetts received permission to raise six regiments. Responding to the offers and appeals of Thomas Cass, Patrick Donahoe, and other Irish spokesmen, Governor Andrew decreed that one of those six regiments would be Irish. Temporary units (including two potential Irish groups) already existed by then, and one of them included Irish hopefuls from New York. The governor had to choose which of the two groups would absorb the other, and he selected the one led by Cass. It fell to the state's adjutant general, William Schouler, to carry the news to the losers, and he confronted angry and rebellious Irishmen. Some of them agreed to throw their lot in the with the Cass regiment, but others angrily left Boston and went to New York to try their fortune in Irish units there.[33] And so the state's first Irish regiment, even in its infancy the focus of contention and politicking, took the designation of the Ninth Massachusetts Infantry and began its organization and training on Long Island, Boston Harbor.

Before long disquieting reports arrived on the governor's desk about the activities at Fort Warren, the training camp of the Irish regiment on Long Island. Colonel Cass kept up a steady stream of complaints about lack of proper equipment and support, but even freshman Governor Andrew knew not to take such complaints seriously; they were standard procedure for *any* regiment.[34] To look into Fort Warren affairs, the governor dispatched a special representative, George D. Welles. Welles, a trusted Boston Brahmin and Harvard Law School graduate, already had some knowledge of military matters through his position as the lieutenant colonel of the First Massachusetts Infantry, a state militia unit.

George Welles was appalled by what he found. In a lengthy, confidential report to Governor Andrew he claimed that some officers of the Irish regiment would disgrace Massachusetts. The volunteer committee supporting the regiment tried to weed out the worst misfits, he acknowledged, but too many of the officers were ignorant, vicious, and vile. And it was not just the officers. The enlisted men were the lowest element of the population, "the sweepings of our jails," and such men were actually electing their own officers! The common soldiers tippled with their officers, he charged, had no respect for them, and cared nothing for authority. Sending such a unit away from Massachusetts, Welles believed, risked a fearful disgrace and calamity for the state. As an example of the terrible behavior he observed, Welles cited a sentry spotted patrolling his post with bare feet and a pipe in his mouth. Colonel Welles thought the regiment should be disbanded. As an alternative, he recommended the appointment of a new set of officers.[35]

The Welles report may have been the overreaction of a cultured but prejudiced upper-class Bostonian to lower-class immigrants. But Andrew also received a similar report from B. S. Treanor, the Irish editor of the *Irish Patriot*. Treanor portrayed the regiment's officers as inept bullies, drunkards, poorly educated, incompetent, and—worst of all—at least one was an abolitionist. Treanor found the regiment's second-in-command, Lt. Col. Cromwell G. Rowell, thoroughly beyond his depth, and he urged Andrew to replace him with an Irishman of culture or with an American gentlemen. Rowell himself, on the other hand, complained to the governor that, as a non-Irish Catholic, he suffered religious and ethnic prejudice. Beyond that, he claimed that Cass was a tyrant, he and the chaplain were drunkards, and that Father Scully collected money for his own use. There were complaints from other interested parties, and it is difficult to avoid the conclusion—especially in the context of subsequent developments—that the Ninth Massachusetts did indeed have more than its share of problems.[36]

Governor Andrew faced a delicate political problem. Any sweeping reform of the Cass regiment risked a confrontation with the Catholic hierarchy and the Irish voters. Inaction might result at worst in a debacle when the regiment entered active service, and at best an embarrassment to the state. Andrew chose a policy of inaction, and let events take their course.

In late June 1861, escorted by eight hundred well-wishers in formal attire, the Ninth Massachusetts Infantry paraded through the streets of Boston, while Gilmore's Band played Irish airs. Down Beacon Street to the common the men marched, to find tables laden with cold meats, cake, and coffee. Refreshed, the men of the Irish Ninth boarded steamers and headed for Washington.[37]

Trouble and turmoil continued to plague the regiment after it set up camp at the Seventh Street Park in Washington. Two soldiers suffered gunshot wounds, Colonel Cass was injured by an unruly horse, and Lt. Michael H. McNamara was court-martialed on a variety of charges, including assault. George Welles, still making confidential reports on the regiment, found the Boston Irish up to their old tricks in Washington. "All those Irishmen keep poultry," he fumed. "As I write a hen and chickens are picking about *in my tent,* and geese and ducks are quacking all around me." Colonel Cass himself found his men a continuing trial and tribulation. Constant bickering, continuous politicking, and chronic complaints made his life miserable. "If ever a man had a hard row to hoe in this world," he wailed to the governor's adjutant, "I am that man, with incompetent Officers, different peculiarities, vices, attachments." Irish regiment soldiers quarreled and maneuvered like ward politicians. Irishmen might present a united front to the rest of the world, but they engaged in continuous squabbles among themselves. Despite their lavish praise of Irish culture and nationalism, Irish officers and men sought opportunities for advancement in any direction. Despite their complaints about Protestant prejudice, they practiced religious bigotry against Protestants in turn. Men of the Ninth took for granted a casual prejudice against Jews and held strong racist feelings about blacks.[38]

Some men regarded Cass as a tyrant and bigot. The evidence is conflicting; he had his defenders as well as his detractors. There can be little doubt about his patriotism and his courage. He was mortally wounded while leading his regiment at the Battle of Malvern Hill in July 1862. His death precipitated an unseemly struggle for succession within the regiment.

Ordinarily, with the death or resignation of a commanding officer, leadership descended to the second in command. At the time of Cass's death, the lieutenant colonel of the Ninth Infantry was Patrick R. Guiney. Born in Ireland, Guiney joined the regiment as a captain in June 1861, advanced to major in October, and by January 1862 was lieutenant colonel. Governor Andrew barely got the word about Cass's death, however, before he received a petition signed by eleven officers protesting the promotion of Guiney. The petition denounced Guiney as a shirker, more interested in self-glorification than the needs of the regiment.[39]

A monumental donnybrook followed. In the following weeks the chaplain (who took Guiney's side), Maj. Gen. Fitz-John Porter, and several different officers hurled charges and countercharges against each other. From his office in Boston the governor followed the affair, stuck with tradition and Guiney, and gave Guiney command of the Ninth regiment.

The altercation, however, left the regiment badly divided, and Colonel

Guiney was convinced that he dealt with a cabal of malcontented and incompetent officers. He was helpless to do anything about it because they had too much political influence. And as casualties mounted and numbers in the ranks dwindled, concern for ethnic purity gave way to requests for warm bodies needed to keep the regiment up to strength. One factor behind the regiment's personnel problem was the increasing number of desertions. As they increased, Guiney tried to remedy the situation with more severe punishments, which in turn hurt morale and encouraged desertion. Word of the harsh discipline got back to Boston and Guiney had to defend his practices. "I made up my mind long ago," he wrote to Col. James McQuade in the midst of the troubles, "that Irish soldiers cannot be governed by a military dove, with the rank of colonel. They need to be handled as severely as justice will permit, when they do wrong."[40]

Guiney continued to command the Ninth Massachusetts Infantry until he was wounded in May 1864 during the Battle of the Wilderness. Mustered out the next month, he received the brevet rank of brigadier general. The regiment itself left federal service at the same time. The record of the first Irish regiment from Massachusetts was a proud one. During its three years of service the regiment fought at Malvern Hill, Hanover Court House, Gaines Mills, Chancellorsville, and the Wilderness. Of the 1700 officers and men who served, 152 were killed in action and 105 died of wounds or disease. In June 1861, when the Ninth Infantry had left Boston, a citizen was heard to say, "There goes a load of Irish rubbish out of the city." The enthusiastic welcome given the survivors three years later was a more accurate reflection of public opinion in Boston.[41]

Massachusetts contributed a second Irish unit to the Union, and its career was even more colorful and controversial than the first. Pressures to recruit it began in the late summer of 1861. B. S. Treanor and Patrick Donahoe took advantage of the notoriety of New York's Colonel Corcoran to call for a second Irish regiment. Treanor sent Governor Andrew a collection of New York newspaper clippings that extolled Corcoran's virtues and urged him to recruit another Irish unit. He also sent Andrew a letter from Thomas Francis Meagher, a letter in which Meagher asked Treanor's help in raising a regiment for the proposed Irish Brigade. As part of his drive for the Irish Brigade, Meagher cast his net far and wide. On 23 September he went to Boston and addressed a capacity crowd in the Boston Music Hall. While a huge overflow of people milled in the streets outside the hall, Meagher made use of all his oratorical skills, whipping up a frenzy of ethnic and patriotic emotion. When he ended with, "Then up, Irishmen! up! Take the sword in hand! Down to the banks of the Potomac!" The cheering crowd was ready to go. Legend had it that the famous Music Hall speech led to the creation of the second Irish regiment. In reality, the very day Meagher arrived in Boston a letter from the governor's office was already on the way to appropriate authorities with a request for another Irish regiment.[42]

Irish political leaders were already maneuvering for the leadership of such a regiment. Donahoe pushed the candidacy of Francis Parker. New Yorkers urged Andrew to staff the regiment with Irishmen from New York and to assign the unit to Meagher's Irish Brigade. Treanor belittled the Donahoe faction and claimed he had twenty-five Irish nationalists ready to go. He would soon submit the name of a real Irish gentleman as colonel.[43] As the pressures on Andrew mounted, and the rivalry between the local and New York factions intensified, the governor produced another political master stroke; he announced plans for *two* new Irish regiments. One would go to General Butler's "New England Force," and the other would be assigned to the Irish Brigade. That would satisfy everyone.

Life, alas, is seldom so neatly arranged. Donahoe's candidate, Francis Parker, did not win control of either regiment. Parker had agreed to have his name put forward initially under the assumption that the Irish regiment would be given American officers, and when he learned that he had been turned down he was irate. Andrew soothed his feelings by giving him the command of another regiment, the Thirty-second Massachusetts Infantry, an all-American regiment. New Yorkers made a clean sweep of the leadership of the two new regiments. Those New Yorkers were as interested in striking a blow at England as they were in fighting the South. The first of the new regiments, the Twenty-eighth Massachusetts Infantry, went to William Montieth. The second, the Twenty-ninth Massachusetts Infantry, was awarded to an officer of the New York Sixty-ninth, Thomas J. Murphy, who had helped Meagher promote the idea of a Massachusetts regiment for the Irish Brigade. Another disappointed office seeker backed by Donahoe, W. W. Bullock, got as his consolation prize the post of lieutenant colonel in the Thirtieth Massachusetts Infantry. Andrew allowed Donahoe to nominate candidates for the lower-ranking officers. With the preliminary political battle out of the way, the two regiments went into camp, the Twenty-eighth at Camp Cameron and the Twenty-ninth at Framingham.[44]

Recruiting was painfully slow as disorder and trouble prevailed at both camps. When word reached the governor of problems with the new units, he sent Adjutant General Schouler on an inspection trip. Schouler's findings made sorry reading. When he arrived at the camp of the Twenty-ninth he found its commander absent. Moreover, that commander was *not* Thomas J. Murphy at all, but Mathew Murphy, still another Murphy from the Sixty-ninth New York Infantry. (The authorization letter to General Butler simply specified a Murphy — no first name. Mathew Murphy was a member of the Fenian Government Council, along with Corcoran.) It was just as well that this Murphy was usually absent. The regiment's quartermaster in frank language informed Schouler that Mathew Murphy was a "fair example of a New York blower." "He is seldom at the camp," the quartermaster continued. "The men are sorry when he comes and glad when he goes."[45] This Murphy, Schouler concluded, was not the man to lead a Massachusetts regiment. Neither was Murphy the man to stand for criticism. When he threatened to return to New York, Andrew wished him Godspeed.

Things looked a little better at the camp of the Twenty-eighth. Montieth appeared to have matters under control, although there were not enough recruits to form a regiment. But Murphy, instead of leaving directly for New York, went to the camp of the Twenty-eight and urged the men to abandon the regiment. Many promptly deserted. Governor Andrew thereupon acted on Schouler's advice and merged the two units into a single regiment, the Twenty-eighth under Montieth, and requested additional men form the New England headquarters to bring the outfit up to minimum strength. Perhaps blissfully unaware of events in Boston, Meagher meanwhile addressed a request to Governor Andrew for a cavalry squadron for the Irish Brigade. His main argument was that Massachusetts men wanted to serve in the Irish Brigade anyway, and Andrew might as well get credit for their enlistment for his own state. Ever the opportunist, Meagher also hedged his bets with the brigade by arranging for an appointment to command a company in Montieth's regiment, but had no need to take the post since the brigade project was successful.[46]

Patronage requests for the Irish regiments continued to pour in, even as the merger got underway. Orestes Brownson begged a spot for his son, while the indefatigable B. S. Treanor asked for the post of quartermaster (a job with significant economic opportunities in any regiment) in the Twenty-ninth Massachusetts. Andrew turned Treanor down. On the other hand, the governor discovered one soldier in the Twenty-eighth anxious to get out. Dr. B. F. Allen, who had been enticed into the regiment by an eager recruiting officer with the help of whiskey and a promise that the regiment was really composed of Americans, wanted to go home, not to war. Andrew ordered the man discharged.[47]

Schouler's confidence in Montieth was misplaced. From the time the Twenty-eighth left Massachusetts for the South in early 1862, the regiment suffered internal dissension and poor leadership. Part of the difficulty was a continuing conflict between the New Yorkers and those from Massachusetts. "A New York influence seems to pervade the Regt.," complained one officer, "and anything but Massachusetts interests were thought of." Montieth himself drank to excess and violated so many regulations he was court-martialed and dismissed from the service. Although the Twenty-eighth was known as the "Faugh a Ballagh! (Clear the Road)" regiment, and it was touted as 100 percent Irish, it was not; many of the problems plaguing the unit stemmed from the stresses and strains between the Irish and American soldiers. As one officer put it, "An American is entirely out of place in an *Irish* Regiment, and they make things hard as possible for me." While Montieth was still on trial, Brig. Gen. Isaac Stevens tried to persuade Governor Andrew to appoint his son to lead the Twenty-eighth, arguing that an American was needed to command an Irish regiment properly. When Montieth was dismissed, however, Andrew named Lt. Col. Maclelland Moore as his replacement. Then Moore resigned, unable to cope with the feuding officers. Donahoe despaired of the regiment's future, and he pressed Andrew to forget ethnicity and simply appoint a good man to lead the Twenty-eighth.[48]

Once again Andrew demonstrated his astuteness as a politician. Ignoring all the advice pouring into his office about whom to appoint colonel of the second Irish regiment, he reached outside Massachusetts and picked 2d Lt. Richard Byrnes, a professional soldier in the U.S. Fifth Cavalry, to help the Twenty-eighth in its time of crisis. Most of the officers of the regiment protested the appointment, but Andrew stood firm. It was a good appointment.

Byrnes found his new command sadly reduced in numbers (it was a hard-fighting regiment) and he began his program of renewal with a request for new recruits. What he wanted was able-bodied men; ethnicity no longer mattered. He got the regiment back in to shape and led it until he took a mortal wound himself at Cold Harbor in June 1864. During that period he also served briefly as the leader of the Irish Brigade.

Indeed, despite all of its political troubles, the Twenty-eighth Massachusetts Infantry compiled a distinguished record as a fighting unit. From its first combat in South Carolina in February 1862 until a tattered group of two officers and twenty-two men returned to Boston in December 1864, the Twenty-eighth fought on some of the bloodiest battlefields of the Civil War. Second Bull Run, Antietam, Chancellorsville, Cold Harbor, Gettysburg, and New Market are just some of the names in its history. Of the 1856 men who served in the regiment, 161 were killed in action and 203 died of wounds or disease.[49]

No ethnic regiment in the Civil War had a monopoly on the kind of chronic trouble experienced by the Twenty-eighth Massachusetts Infantry. Shoddy equipment, the curse of bureaucratic slowness and error, profane and incompetent officers — all of these things existed in every kind of military organization.[50] The particular curse of the Twenty-eighth Massachusetts and so many other Irish regiments was the intrusion of ethnic Irish politics into regimental affairs. The rough-and-tumble nature of big-city political quarrels and the complications of Fenianism and Irish nationalism took their toll. There was an element of tragedy. Competence and military skills were never the first priority in the selection of regimental officers. Irish units carried the heavy burden of interstate Fenian politics and the determination of men like Donahoe and Treanor to impose *their* cronies on Irish regiments. Men in the ranks paid the price. It was the price demanded by a people's army, an army created by established machinery in state and local governments. Just as Irishness (or "racial" characteristics in nineteenth-century terminology) did not explain the valor displayed by the typical Irish outfit, neither did Irishness explain the persistent disturbances. The regiments participated in the religious, political, social, and economic struggles of the larger society.

On 30 May 1885 an imposing stone monument was dedicated in Chicago's Calvary Cemetery to one of the city's renowned military heroes. Carved into the stone, along with the name, rank, and vital statistics, was a phrase: "Lay Me Down and Save the Flag." So many Civil War soldiers allegedly uttered those words, that a cynic might challenge their authenticity. This is the monument, however, of Col. James A. Mulligan, born in the United States but as fiery an Irish nationalist as Thomas Francis Meagher, and a man whose flamboyant manner and addiction to flowery language made more plausible the possibility that he did indeed call out those words to his men. Mulligan was the center of events in Illinois with striking parallels to those in Massachusetts.

Irishmen in Illinois responded promptly to the call for volunteers. Their political leaders pushed hard for commissions for worthy Irish voters. Some were not above a bit of ethnic blackmail. Irish-American Charles D. B. O'Ryan, a Chicago physician, frustrated in his desire to form his own Irish regiment, accused Governor Yates of being anti-Irish.

> You have been suspected of harboring unfavorable feelings toward the Irish [he wrote]. Appoint me to a high military post and that will gratify the Irish of Chicago. Your refusal to do this would have unfortunate consequences and would revive Know-Nothing sentiments.[51]

An indignant Yates instructed his secretary to tell the "rampant Dr" that he had never been a Know-Nothing, and that the doctor could have an appointment as a regimental surgeon only if a regiment elected him.

In the early days of the war, however, the existing militia units and existing militia leaders stimulated the state's first concrete reaction to the call for volunteers. James A. Mulligan, prominent in both Irish-American society and in Democratic politics, along with several other Irish-American leaders, promoted the idea of an all-Irish regiment. Recruiting posters plastered the city, offices opened, and business was brisk. Within a week twelve hundred men signed up. Events moved so fast, however, that the Illinois quota was already filled by then, and extraordinary effort was required for the Mulligan project to succeed. He visited Sen. Stephen A. Douglas, then on his deathbed, and got a personal letter to President Lincoln urging the acceptance of Mulligan's Irish outfit. Mulligan took the letter to Washington, got the regiment accepted outside the state's quota, and won election as its colonel.[52] It was unfortunate, given the popular image of the Irish as hard drinkers, that the Mulligan regiment, designated the Twenty-third Illinois Infantry, was first organized at the Kanes Brewery in Chicago. As the headquarters of the Twenty-third, it had the name of "Fontenoy Barracks."

Popularly known as the "Irish Brigade," the Twenty-third Illinois Infantry was deliberately patterned after Corcoran's "Fighting Irish" regiment, the Sixty-ninth New York. The use of the "brigade" title for a regiment reflected both Mulligan's ambitions and his romantic notions about the "Wild Geese" Irishmen who fought in European armies. He was an avid reader of military history, especially the history of wars involving Irish volunteers and mercenaries. His private and public language made frequent reference to fabled Irish heroes and feats of arms. Mulligan stood well over six feet, wore a large mustache, and stimulated affection and loyalty among those who knew him. He decorated his uniform with badges of Irish symbolism and frequently wore a green shirt to advertise his commitment to Ireland. He was, in a word, a professional Irishman.

After a brief period of training in Chicago (General Grant noted sourly in his memoirs that Mulligan did not train long enough to learn his craft), the Twenty-third Illinois Infantry went to St. Louis and then on to Jefferson City, Missouri, where its assignment was guarding the state legislature. On 31 August 1861 Mulligan led his men to Lexington and to lasting fame. With his command enlarged by the addition of Home Guard units, he fortified the city and awaited an attack by the forces of Confederate Sterling Price. Fresh from his costly victory at Wilson's Creek, Price on 12 October laid siege to the outnumbered Union troops. The spirited defense by Mulligan's men (at one point Mulligan challenged Price to a personal duel) won the admiration of the whole North, and when the Irish-American colonel led his men out to surrender on 20 October, the Battle of Lexington already had legendary status.[53] While all of his men returned home, Mulligan refused to give his parole and remained Price's prisoner.

Mulligan in captivity, like Corcoran following Bull Run, became a national hero. After some weeks, an exchange was arranged; Confederate Gen. Daniel Frost (captured earlier in St. Louis by Lyons) went south and Mulligan went north. Chicago gave its favorite son a tumultuous welcome. A special train met him in Joliet, and the reception committee escorted him into the city where bonfires and delirious crowds, bands and fireworks, booming cannon, and a mass procession to the Tremont Hotel evidenced the city's esteem.[54] Since the Twenty-third Illinois Infantry no longer existed (it was disbanded officially with the capture of all its officers), Mulligan's first task was the creation of a new Irish Brigade.

With the special permission of General McClellan, Mulligan announced the formation of a new Twenty-third Illinois Infantry, also to be known as the Irish Brigade. Phoenix-like it arose from the remnants of the old outfit. Like most Irish-American entrepreneurs, Mulligan sought new recruits by appealing to Irish nationalism, the glories of early Irish heroes, and the fame of Corcoran and the Sixty-ninth New York "Fighting Irish." Recruiting posters used his own famous name in huge letters. His regimental stationery featured the name LEXINGTON over an Irish harp, along with the motto "Remember Lexington and Fontenoy." The new green flag, by special action of Congress, carried the name of Lexington emblazoned on it. Even though volunteers flocked to that flag, there was a delay in moving to active service because of some difficulties arranging an exchange for the whole regiment with the Confederate authorities. Mulligan used that delay to go on the lecture circuit. He visited churches, orphanages, and other institutions in midwestern cities, talking about the Battle of Lexington. The lecture portrayed his Irish soldiers as happy, singing, carefree warriors, facing death with a song on their lips. The city council of New York presented him with a proclamation inscribed on parchment. Irishmen in other regiments pleaded with him for positions in the new Irish Brigade, often claiming to be the victims of religious and racial bigotry where they were.[55]

Weeks dragged into months, and all the new Irish Brigade did was guard prisoners at Camp Douglas near Chicago. Finally, in June 1862 the regiment went to Harper's Ferry. For the next two years the Twenty-third Illinois engaged in guard duty and antiguerrilla operations in western Virginia.[56] Mulligan chafed at these assignments because he believed opportunities for glory were passing him by. He wanted to be in the center of operations and felt that Lincoln and the War Department did not pursue an energetic strategy that could win the war. In April 1864 the regiment was furloughed home and Mulligan and most of his soldiers reenlisted as a veteran regiment. Then the period of relative inaction ended. The Irish Brigade now found itself in the thick of action. It fought at Kernstown, Cedar Creek, Winchester, Fishers Hill, and the ragged remnants of the Brigade fought at Petersburg. Colonel Mulligan did not make it to the final muster out in July 1865; he suffered a mortal wound at Kernstown on 24 July 1864, and died an enemy prisoner. Mrs. Mulligan fetched his body back to Chicago where it received an elaborate funeral. It was not the end Mulligan had envisioned for himself in April 1861, but it was an end entirely befitting his romantic image of the Irish warrior.

James Mulligan made one serious error of judgment in the early months of his military career. In September 1861, before the fame of Lexington, Lincoln offered him a star—an appointment as a brigadier. He declined, saying that he wanted to stay with his regiment. His refusal seems out of keeping with his great ambition, but it was not. Mulligan dreamed of a real Irish brigade, one composed of all the Irish regiments of the Midwest, with himself as commanding general. From the very beginning of the war, his ambition was nourished by friends and acquaintances. He had reason to believe that there was an adequate political base for such an enterprise, and that it was a matter of time before it materialized.[57] A constant theme in his diary is his burning ambition for promotion. In October 1862 while he was in Washington awaiting an assignment, he mused about the prospects of organizing all the western Irish regiments into a single Irish Brigade:

> I think there is an opening for a splendid march for the western Irishman. I'd like to make it at the head of a true Irish Brigade. I wait. I am patient.

As the days passed his dreams continued. He told himself he would work like a titan to make such a brigade work. But as time went on and no promotion occurred he turned bitter. He blamed the absence of a star on anti-Irish prejudice in Washington. His morale dropped even lower with the issuance of the Emancipation Proclamation. He was outraged that Lincoln "freed the niggers." He now saw the war as nothing but killing white brothers to save the blacks.[58] Like most of the Irish in America, Mulligan was strongly prejudiced against Negroes.

Ethnicity was extremely important to Mulligan. His Irishness was not a pose. His diary and his private correspondence make this explicit. He was well-read and literate; his official correspondence was direct, organized, clear, and revealed a sense of humor. It ignored ethnic references, which were kept for more appropriate forums. Like Meagher and Corcoran, he was determinedly Irish. Except for Irish nationalism, ethnicity meant little to the men in the ranks of the Twenty-third Illinois. Their daily concerns were similar to those of the men in any regiment.[59]

Mulligan's Irish Brigade, like comparable units in other states, with the passage of time was increasingly embroiled in internecine politics. In Mulligan's case, this usually involved the quarrels of the Fenians. Some Fenians derided him as the "Knight of the Green Shirt," perhaps because of his public pose that he was not a Fenian. Like Meagher, Mulligan tried to keep one foot in the Fenian camp and one outside it. He donated money to the famous Fenian Fair in Chicago in 1864, and even wrote a letter of support, all the time convincing the church hierarchy that he was not a Fenian. Most of the officers in his regiment were Fenians, and significant numbers of the soldiers in most of the Irish regiment were also members. For them, of course, ethnicity was extremely important, and perhaps more important than their ties to America.[60]

Illinois contributed a second Irish regiment, and one whose career remarkably parallels that of the second Massachusetts regiment. This was the Ninetieth Illinois Infantry, the "Irish Legion."

A drive to organize a second Irish regiment began in the late summer of 1862. James B. Bradwell, a powerful figure in Chicago's Republican party, promoted the name of Mexican War veteran William Snowhook as the colonel of the Irish Legion. Another Chicago politician, Joseph Knox, who was a personal friend of Illinois Adj. Gen. Allen Fuller, also supported Snowhook, as did Dr. Charles D. B. O'Ryan, the rampant Irishman who had military ambitions of his own. Snowhook in addition enjoyed the favor of John G. Haines, another influential Chicago politico, but Haines later shifted his support to a rival. Snowhook was a Democrat. Born in Ireland in 1804, he emigrated to the United States as a child, and by the 1830s was in Chicago working as a contractor on the Illinois-Michigan Canal. In 1846 he became Chicago's first Collector of Customs. Snowhook worked diligently with other Chicago Democrats and Catholics to recruit troops in the Civil War, but his wife was a Protestant, making the church hierarchy wary of him.[61]

Chicago's vicar general, and the acting bishop of the Chicago diocese, Father Dennis Dunne headed a well-orchestrated rival campaign for control of the Irish Legion. Governor Yates, as usual, was caught in the middle. For a short time there was hope of a third Irish unit, but those hopes faded as recruiting efforts failed to turn up even enough men for one full regiment. Father Dunne was extremely anxious to have an all-Irish, all-Catholic regiment, one that was in the spirit of the "Fighting Irish" New York outfit led by Michael Corcoran, and to ensure this he wanted the Irish Legion commanded by an officer from the Forty-second New York Infantry. His candidate, in opposition to Snowhook, was Captain Timothy O'Meara, the personal choice of Corcoran. A sly, if not underhanded, stratagem won the day for Father Dunne.

Father Dunne's followers arranged a regimental election on short notice while Snowhook was away from the camp. Since the outfit was still seriously understrength, Snowhook was earlier assured that no such election would be held until more men enrolled. The very day of the election, Snowhook received a brief note announcing the election. Men in the regiment were told that if they did not vote for O'Meara the regiment would not get a priest for a chaplain. When the votes were counted (by Dunne's supporters) the vote was unanimous for O'Meara. When Snowhook heard what happened, he was enraged and made a last effort to thwart Father Dunne. He hastily wrote to Yates and suggested that the governor still had a chance to amend the scandalous situation and do so in a way to benefit the regiment. Appoint me colonel, he suggested, make O'Meara the lieutenant colonel, and then rid the regiment of its narrow religious bias by opening the ranks to other recruits. That would broaden support and fill up the companies. Yates, probably impressed by the many big guns on Dunne's side, rejected that plan and named O'Meara colonel of the Irish Legion. In late November, when the Ninetieth Illinois Infantry left Chicago for the front, it was still seriously understrength.[62]

O'Meara's troubles did not end when he got his commission; they were just beginning. He was in almost constant conflict with dissident officers who engaged in a persistent campaign to undermine his position. O'Meara suffered persistent accusations and personal abuse. He was accused of being a drunkard and unfit for duty, of having favorites and mishandling regimental affairs. There were chronic quarrels over appointments. O'Meara believed that he was surrounded by incompetent, negligent underlings, and he faced a steady problem with desertions.[63]

O'Meara was killed at Missionary Ridge. The soldiers of the Irish Legion, despite the bickering and backbiting among their officers and between the officers and politicians at home, were a credit to the army. They earned praise for fighting in their bare feet at Jackson, Mississippi, went through the Atlanta campaign and the March to the Sea, and witnessed the burning of Columbia. As happened so often in the Civil War, the ordinary soldiers of the Irish Legion fought bravely and well despite the political antics of their officers.

Indiana was a bit late in the creation of an Irish regiment, but it made up for its tardiness with the acrimony of its procedure. Governor Oliver Morton grappled with a sharply divided people in April 1861. Indiana Democrats (and most of the state's Irish were Democrats) opposed the use of force against the South, and Morton used all of his forceful personality and formidable powers of persuasion to create a warlike spirit in the Hoosier State. When, several months after the war began, a group of Hoosier Irish-Americans requested permission to raise an Irish regiment, Morton gave his assent.[64]

Governor Morton took a major political risk when he approved an Irish regiment. To direct the state's first Irish regiment the backers proposed the name of John C. Walker. Walker, born in 1828 in Shelbyville, was not a native Irishman, but he was a long-time Democratic politician and had long opposed the use of force against the South. Morton was not known for a sense of humor, especially in politics, but even he recognized the irony in the situation. Moreover, he no sooner got the Walker recommendation than he received expressions of violent opposition to it from loyal Union men who doubted Walker's devotion to the Union cause.[65] Morton, determined at that point to make the war effort bipartisan, authorized Walker to raise the Irish regiment. He soon regretted it.

Walker went to work with great energy to attract volunteers. He had little difficulty getting men into his camp in Indianapolis, but as new recruits arrived the earlier arrivals lost interest and slipped away. Thus, in contrast to the situation in most northern states, the first Irish regiment in Indiana had trouble finding enough men willing to cast their lot with an ethnic unit. Weeks passed and the enterprise continued to languish; not enough men remained in camp to permit an official mustering in by federal authorities. Finally, in December 1861 the first Indiana Irish regiment was mustered into service as the Thirty-fifth Indiana Infantry. On December 13, led by a green flag bearing a harp and shamrock, the Thirty-fifth Indiana Infantry left Indianapolis. Even as it left, the outfit was torn with internal dissent. Not every soldier was Irish, and Governor Morton received a petition from non-Irish troopers objecting to regimental procedures that favored the Irish.[66]

Meanwhile, another petition arrived on Morton's desk, this one asking for a second Irish regiment. The appeal carried the name of Bernard F. Mullen. Morton made his second mistake; he granted Mullen the authority to raise state's second Irish regiment.[67]

Mullen plunged into his task with enthusiasm. His detailed, printed circular gave pride of place to Irish ethnicity and relied heavily on appeals to the fame of New York's Sixty-ninth Infantry, as well as to the fresh publicity associated with Colonel Mulligan in neighboring Illinois.[68] Part of Mullen's solicitation was the argument that Irishmen should forgive the slights and insults they suffered from Americans in the past and rally to the common cause.

Mullen's entreaty to Indiana Irishmen got little response. The war was going poorly for the North, the Irish population base in Indiana was modest, Irish recruiting in neighboring states attracted many Irish Hoosiers, and he competed with the lure, weak as it was, of Walker's first Irish regiment. Mullen got the name of the Sixty-first Indiana Infantry as his unit designation, but a number did not a regiment make. By late November 1861 he had a small number of men in uniform at headquarters in Madison, Indiana, and a few skeleton companies had duty guarding Confederate prisoners.[69]

Walker's disputes with his own men worsened. Even before the departure from Indianapolis, the Thirty-fifth's officers were in a rebellious mood. When Walker brought charges of intoxication and negligence against his lieutenant colonel, some of his officers drew up a strong protest to the governor. The gist of the protest was that Walker and his political cronies, the so-called "La Porte clique," were conspiring to replace good Irishmen with Americans and replace Catholics with Protestants. In the Thirty-fifth Indiana Infantry, politics and religion *did* mix, and it was an explosive mixture. Colonel Walker had other serious problems. Charges of financial irregularities surfaced, and he defended himself against those while coping with the dissident officers. In desperation he asked Governor Morton to appoint a personal friend, Capt. John C. Hughes, to the post of lieutenant colonel in the Thirty-fifth. Morton refused. Instead, in an action that smacked of typical state political patronage, he awarded the position to Maj. John Balfe, whom he regarded as a "worthy and competent officer."[70] This infuriated Walker, who saw the governor's move as a flagrant violation of political-military tradition and courtesy. The plot thickened. Still another petition came to the governor from officers of the Thirty-fifth Indiana; they claimed the Balfe was unfit for the appointment.[71] So far as the Indiana Irish regiment was concerned, Morton was in a no-win situation.

Meanwhile, back at the camp of the struggling Sixty-first Regiment, Mullen got on with a plan that offered a ray of hope to the beleaguered governor. The plan was a common one in Civil War armies. Mullen proposed to Morton that he merge the two regiments, which would make one regiment of decent size, and to demonstrate his own willingness to sacrifice in the cause, he offered to take a demotion to lieutenant colonel in the combined organization. Both because of the modest size of the two regiments and the chronic troubles of Thirty-fifth, the War Department in Washington was thinking along the same line. On 5 February 1862 the first of a series of orders on the same theme called for the merger of the first and second Irish regiments from Indiana.[72] A fight for control of the merged units began.

Walker fought Mullen and Mullen fought Walker in classic political style. The two men used newspapers friendly to their respective sides to carry their story to the people of Indiana. Walker refused to obey Morton's order to merge the regiments, claiming that it was an illegal order. Mullen led his skeletal Sixty-first Regiment to the camp of the Thirty-fifth in Shelbyville. Morton appealed to Secretary of War Stanton, who prudently did nothing. Morton then turned to Major General Halleck, who ordered Walker's removal.[73] The battle continued, now with Walker loyalists against the Mullen supporters within the merged regiment (which retained the designation of the Thirty-fifth Indiana Infantry). Mullen was commissioned colonel of the Thirty-fifth Indiana Infantry in August 1862, but it was another year before the last members of the Walker party were forced out of the regiment. Walker lost the battle, but not the war. He got revenge against Governor Morton. In 1863 Walker ran on an anti-Morton platform in a campaign for the office of Agent of the State. He won, and immediately involved Morton in a complicated legal contest over payment of the state debt. The state legislature, dominated by Democrats, refused to appropriate the needed funds. Walker hoped to force Morton to call a special session of the legislature, but Morton managed to get money from a New York bank and the federal government to stave off this challenge to his position. The language used by the two sides of this partisan hassle was abusive and personal. The question of control of the Indiana Irish regiment was incidental to the Republican-Democratic struggle for control of state government.

The new colonel of the reorganized Thirty-fifth Indiana Infantry kept busy with his own affairs. There was the usual patronage to dispense, which meant confrontations with the Walker clique. There were supporters to satisfy. A large number of his soldiers quietly disappeared as Walker loyalists simply voted with their feet. Mullen found an excuse for those members of the old Sixty-first Indiana Infantry who slipped away; the reputation of the Thirty-fifth up to this point was so bad that they did not want to be associated with it. He tried to stem the hemorrhage of manpower by severely punishing deserters, but his Draconian measures brought protests he had to explain to Morton.[74] And there was a larger war to fight.

Indiana's Irish regiment, in action against the rebels, demonstrated a dash, courage, and effectiveness that belied the confusion of its origin and the politics of its officers and the state's political parties. If there is a mystery at the heart of the record of this and so many other regiments, it is how several hundred men could fight so hard and well and sacrifice so much, in the context of petty competition, personal ambition, and ethnic rhetoric so removed from the reality of war. Writ large in the history of the Thirty-fifth Indiana Infantry are such names as Perryville, Stones River, Chickamauga, Atlanta, and Franklin. The regiment suffered heavy casualties. Mullen himself was wounded at Stones River, and spent much of his remaining time in rank back home in Indiana.[75]

Casualties left the Thirty-fifth Indiana with the problem faced by every Civil War regiment—replenishing the ranks. Mullen tried for a time to maintain the ethnic identity of the Thirty-fifth. In early 1864 he proposed a scheme for transferring several hundred Irishmen from other regiments to his, but nothing came of it. He made personal appeals to the governor, reminding him that when the Thirty-fifth fought, it was described as an *Irish* regiment; if described as an Irish *regiment,* it needed Irishmen in its ranks. He also proposed that the entire regiment be sent home to recruit—a not uncommon practice. Finally, he sent the regiment's chaplain, Father Peter Paul Cooney, back to Indiana to search for Irish recruits. This latter plan involved having Cooney visit Irish priests around the state to get Irishmen who might either be drafted or enlist as substitutes for draftees. None of these projects was successful. In the end, as was the case with other ethnic regiments, saving the regiment took priority over ethnicity. Mullen's successor in late 1864 pleaded for any kind of draftee to fill the ranks.[76]

Father Cooney gave the regiment much of its Irish color and character. Born in Ireland in 1822, he came to America as a child. He attended Notre Dame University, St. Charles's College in Maryland and St. Mary's Theological Seminary in Baltimore. He became a priest in 1859 and volunteered to be a chaplain when the war began. He took readily to the life of a chaplain, and for a time hoped for promotion to the post of brigade chaplain, but that promotion never materialized. Cooney spent almost four years with Indiana's Irish regiment, the longest period of service by a Catholic chaplain during the Civil War. He was popular with the men, served bravely under fire when caring for the wounded, and acted as an informal financial agent for the enlisted men. In this latter capacity he eventually became a sharp critic of Mullen. For the most part Cooney remained aloof from the internal and external politics of the regiment until near the end of Mullen's tenure.[77] Cooney enjoyed army life and believed that his Irish soldiers were better practicing Catholics in uniform than out of it. At the same time, he urged his younger brother to avoid the military and pay a substitute if necessary to avoid conscription. Priests like Cooney were undoubtedly an asset to Irish regiments; in Indiana as in other states the prospect of having a priest for regimental chaplain helped recruit the Catholic volunteer.

Mullen was an ardent Fenian, and he used the regiment as a base for Fenian activities. One of his patronage appointments in the Thirty-fifth Indiana Infantry was his nephew, Hugh D. Gallagher. Gallagher began military service as a sergeant in the Thirteenth Indiana Infantry, was promoted to second lieutenant, and then joined the state's Irish regiment as a first lieutenant in June 1863. Gallagher was Mullen's contact while the colonel was away from the regiment. From his home in Madison, Indiana, Colonel Mullen instructed Gallagher to "Keep up the Fenian organization by all means!" Mullen attended the famous Fenian Fair in Chicago in 1864 and reported the affair a real triumph. "It was a brilliant success," he wrote to his nephew, "not only from a pecuniary point of view but in every other particular." While he was in Chicago, Mullen met with representatives of the Fenians from Ireland, as well as colonels of other Irish regiments, who were also active members. His activities with the secret society involved him at the state level in Indiana, too, and he attended an Indiana Fenian conference in Indianapolis shortly after the Chicago meeting. The end of the war did not end his Fenian connection. Mullen became secretary of war for the Irish Republic of New York, and not until the comic opera invasion of Canada by the Fenians in 1866 ended in fiasco did he return to the mundane business of earning a living in Indiana.[78]

Lieutenant Gallagher himself was a Fenian, and his diary contains a record of attendance at Fenian social functions. He saw the organization primarily in those terms, however, and his ethnicity, in contrast to his uncle's meant little to him. His concerns were those of any other young officer in a Union regiment.

Mullen tried to exploit his regimental connection for personal gain. In the spring of 1864 he ordered two hundred engravings from a publisher and asked his nephew to open a subscription for them in the regiment and collect the money from the men. Then, after his resignation, Mullen apparently concocted a scheme to earn commissions by handling the bounty money paid to men of the Irish regiment. Father Cooney, once his good friend, launched a harsh attack on the ex-colonel over this business.[79]

Colonel Mullen of the Thirty-fifth Indiana Infantry is a virtual caricature of the professional ethnic. A feisty Fenian, his loyalties were divided between Irish nationalism and America. As an army officer, he was more at home in bare-knuckle state politics than in the routine of administering regimental affairs. Like his compatriots elsewhere, he cynically exploited the notoriety of the first Irish heroes to advance his own ambitions. It must be remembered, on the other hand, that he shed his blood on a Civil War battlefield. Every ethnic military leader took that risk. The partisan politics swirling around the Thirty-fifth Indiana Infantry differed from similar regiments in other states only in the violence of the language and the tenacity of the personal animosities.

Spring Grove Cemetery in Cincinnati is an extraordinary institution. As much park as burial ground, its hundreds of landscaped acres are a mecca for students of horticulture and sculpture. Within the grounds are the graves of fifteen Civil War generals, along with those of twenty-two others with a brevet rank of general. Today's visitor passes by the carriage house at the main entrance, goes beneath an underpass, and emerges to see the first prominent stone memorial—a broken column, symbolic of a life cut short. This is the memorial for William Haines Lytle, the commander of Ohio's only Irish regiment. Lytle, in bronze and on horseback, graces the side of the memorial base. The inscription summarizes Lytle's battle record. There is no hint anywhere on the structure that the Tenth Ohio Infantry was an Irish regiment.

Soon after the attack on Fort Sumter, while Ohio's Germans started the formation of several German regiments, a brief announcement appeared in Cincinnati newspapers. Major Joseph W. Burke, who left his native Ireland after the abortive rising of 1848 and who had a military education in Europe, proposed to raise a regiment of light infantry to be called the "Montgomery Guards." Within a month the regiment was full, but Burke retained the rank of major, and the commanding officer was a native American instead of an Irish Catholic. That American was William Haines Lytle, a prominent member of the Cincinnati bar and a well-known figure in local and state Democratic politics. Lytle had seen service in the Mexican War, but the switch from Burke to Lytle was like that from Willich to McCook. The representative of a distinguished local family had a name more likely to attract both state support and federal acceptance of a regiment, when competition for acceptance was so fierce in the early days of the war. From the beginning, then, the Irishness of the regiment was always somewhat diluted. When the city's bar association presented Lytle with a sword, his acceptance speech contained no hint of ethnic character for his outfit. When Judge Storer in May 1861 gave the regiment its flag, his speech, to what was still called the Montgomery Guards, referred to Irish, German, and American members of the regiment. On the other hand, when Lytle accepted the flag, he ended his talk with "Faugh a Ballagh," and he used the same Gaelic phrase to name his horse. The Tenth Ohio Infantry was an Irish unit, but that fact simply did not dominate everything about the life of the regiment.[80]

Lytle, who was Episcopalian, unmarried, and a minor poet, was a Douglas Democrat and a moderate on the question of slavery. After Fort Sumter, however, he gave himself unstintingly in the Union cause. His biographer suggests that he deliberately courted death in the war, and he found her.[81]

Ohio's Irish regiment saw its first combat soon after it left home. At Carnifax Ferry, (West) Virginia, on 10 September 1861, Colonel Lytle led the Tenth Ohio into action and a musket ball passed through his leg and killed his horse.[82] The wounded officer went home for recuperation and Maj. Joseph Burke took the command. Thereafter, Lytle's life and that of the Irish regiment went their separate ways. Lytle was wounded again at Perryville in October 1862. The next month he was promoted to brigadier and commanded a brigade in the Army of the Ohio. While leading a charge on the second day of the Battle of Chickamauga in September 1863, General Lytle took his third and fatal wound; he died the next day. Although his body was buried on the battlefield, it was exhumed the next month and returned to Cincinnati and to an elaborate burial ceremony at the Spring Grove Cemetery.

Mustered in as the "Montgomery Guards," the Tenth Ohio Infantry became simply the "Montgomery Regiment" before it took its final nickname of the "Bloody Tinth." That name hinted at both its battle record and its ethnic origin. It may also suggest still another characteristic—the regiment's reputation for drinking. General Jacob Cox, who had fond memories of the "Bloody Tinth," recalled that while the Tenth Ohio was in its training camp near Cincinnati, the guard house often held Irish members of the regiment who drank too much while visiting their friends in the city and then returned to camp roaring drunk. While such behavior was common enough, more serious was a near riot involving the men of the Irish regiment and the Thirteenth Ohio Infantry. Irishmen from the Tenth, who felt that they had been treated shabbily by the neighboring Thirteenth, decided to attack their neighbor's camp. Cox had to call out his brigade and ward off the fight. By the time Cox arrived on the scene, Lytle had the situation under control. On a later occasion, in April 1862, the Third Ohio happened to bivouac for the night near a distillery and found their neighbors were men of the Irish regiment. Soldiers of the latter unit, according to a member of the Third Ohio, got wildly drunk. The behavior of the "Bloody Tinth" strengthened the image of the Irish as hard drinkers.[83]

Far more significant in the history of the Ohio Irish regiment was the absence of strong political involvement by partisan groups in its formation and in its operations. Lytle, and later Burke, had reputations as good leaders, and the Tenth Ohio was not wracked with the kind of internal struggles so typical of other ethnic regiments. None of the eulogies at Lytle's funeral mentioned the ethnic character of his first command. By early 1862 the recruiting literature for the Tenth Ohio made no mention of ethnicity, but instead stressed the name of Lytle as the founder and the availability of bonus money. As was the case with other ethnic regiments, the focus on Irishness faded with time.

In New Haven, Thomas W. Cahill was the logical person to propose the creation of an Irish regiment for Connecticut, and when he did, Governor William A. Buckingham approved. When the state issued a call in July 1861 for four three-year regiments, one of those, the Ninth Connecticut Infantry, was to be Irish and led by New Haven businessman, political activist, and militia veteran, Thomas Cahill. Like James Mulligan in Illinois, Cahill was born in the United States but was an ardent Irish nationalist nonetheless. In a city and state with strong memories of Know-Nothingism, it was not surprising that from its origin the regiment complained of prejudicial treatment by state officials, of being handicapped by lack of equipment and poor quality uniforms. The state repealed the old Know-Nothing laws about aliens and militia units two months before the recruitment of the Ninth. The Ninth Connecticut Infantry recruited as an Irish regiment, and its posters announced that all the regimental officers were to be Irish. Many, but not all, of the officers were Irish, and when Cahill got his commission as colonel in early September he commanded a regiment whose members included an admixture of Americans and Germans in the ranks.[84]

Connecticut's one Irish regiment (a move to form a second failed) showed the influence of the New York community. Uniforms were patterned after those worn by the soldiers of Meagher's Irish Brigade: blue trousers with a green stripe, black top hats graced by green tassels, and green silk scarves at the waist. The names of Corcoran and Meagher were used to draw interest to the unit. The Ninth Infantry resolved the conflict often found in the choice of a regimental flag by choosing a flag that was blue on one side with the state seal, and green on the other with a gold Irish harp.

To the non-Irish people of New Haven, the Irish immigrants living in the city were people of violent temperament and addicted to whiskey. The behavior of the Irish regiment seemed to justify such feelings. The men chose "Bloody Ninth" as their nickname, and genial Colonel Cahill chose not to impose strict discipline on them. The outfit quickly gained the reputation of being unruly, undisciplined, and an affliction for the city police. When the soldiers boarded a train for Lowell, the panic-stricken citizens of the city hired five hundred special police to protect them from the invading Irish. The extra police were not needed (the Twenty-sixth Massachusetts Infantry escorted the Ninth Connecticut to its new quarters), but the exuberant troops did damage the train that took them to Massachusetts. New Haven gave a collective sigh of relief when the Irish regiment left.

There is a bizarre aspect to the history of the Ninth Connecticut. Assigned to Benjamin Butler's New England Division, the unit went to New Orleans in the spring of 1862. From there, in June, the Ninth Connecticut joined the ill-fated project of digging a canal through the peninsula opposite Vicksburg. Weeks of back-breaking labor in swamps and heat, coupled with poor food and a shortage of medical supplies, left the men prey to disease. In July alone the regiment lost 153 men to malaria and other diseases. Before the Civil War it was a commonplace in the South, especially in Louisiana, for slave owners to hire Irish laborers for the hardest kind of labor; it was cheaper to pay wages to immigrant workers than it was to risk valuable slaves for some tasks. Now, in the summer of 1862, Irish soldiers from New England engaged in the worst kind of pick-and-shovel work as their contribution to the Union war effort. It was both an irony of history, and in terms of casualties the worst disaster of the war for the regiment. The very next month, August 1862, the regiment went south and helped defend Baton Rouge against Confederate attack. The pestiferous New Haven Irishmen, whose departure from Connecticut was welcomed by many of their fellow New Englanders, did some of the hardest and least glamorous work of the war in an area that lacked the public attention given to other theaters.

In Pennsylvania the New York connection was quite direct. At the outbreak of the war, a three-month regiment of militia, the Twenty-fourth Pennsylvania Infantry, was recruited for the most part among the Irish population of Philadelphia. The unit saw little action and was mustered out in August. It became the seed, however, of the Sixty-ninth Pennsylvania Infantry. This regiment deliberately copied the number of Corcoran's Sixty-ninth New York Infantry, and regarded itself as the Pennsylvania equivalent of the "Fighting Irish" regiment. Joshua T. Owen, who led the Sixty-ninth at the beginning, was Welsh, not Irish, but he enjoyed excellent relations with his own men and with other Irish regiments. In November 1862 Owen became a brigadier, and his successor as leader of the Sixty-ninth, Dennis O'Kane, was a native of Ireland. The Sixty-ninth Pennsylvania, like the Sixty-ninth New York under the command of Robert Nugent, had a long and distinguished history. It fought at Yorktown, Fair Oaks, Malvern Hill, Antietam, Fredericksburg, Chancellorsville, Gettysburg, the Wilderness campaign, and Petersburg, serving with distinction until it was mustered out in July 1865 as a veteran regiment.[85] Colonel O'Kane was killed in action at Gettysburg, and remnants of the regiment thereafter were led by Lt. Col. William Davis.

Pennsylvania's second Irish regiment reveals most strongly the influence of the New Yorkers. In early June 1862 Dennis Heenan, a distinguished Irish resident of Philadelphia and the lieutenant colonel of the old 24th militia unit, got permission from Gov. Andrew Curtin to raise an Irish regiment. Heenan sought recruits in Philadelphia and nearby counties. Raising a second Irish regiment proved a painfully slow process, an experience duplicated several times over in other cities. Designated the 116th Pennsylvania Infantry, the unit took the cumbersome name of the "Brian Boru United Irish Legion." In August a meeting of Philadelphia's Irish-American community heard such local dignitaries as William Dowling give stirring appeals for volunteers, with references both to historic Irish heroes and the "gallant Meagher" who fought "before Richmond."[86] Even as the Philadelphia Irish met to stir up enthusiasm for their new regiment, the series of battles known as Second Bull Run was underway. Equally important from one perspective, was the announcement of the exchange of Col. Michael Corcoran, who had been in captivity since First Bull Run.

The Philadelphia city council sent a telegram of congratulations to Corcoran, along with an invitation to come to the city as an honored guest. Corcoran promptly added the city to his list of engagements, and Philadelphia, with funds appropriated in anticipation of the event months before, prepared a grand reception for the new brigadier general.

General Corcoran arrived in the City of Brotherly Love the evening of 21 August and went immediately to the Continental Hotel. There he heard a serenade of Irish songs by Fenians, after which he and his companion, a lieutenant of the Sixty-ninth New York, retired to rest in anticipation of the next day's exhausting schedule.

A formal reception the next morning occurred at Independence Hall. There was a full panoply of attendants, welcoming speeches, a few remarks by Corcoran in which he referred to the Civil War as a "holy war," and in which he noted that he frequently read the Philadelphia newspapers while he was in the Confederate prison. Colonel Heenan led Corcoran's escort around the city. That evening there was a banquet, with a speech by Mayor Henry (who made no mention of the Irish nature of the proceedings), and a brief response by the general. Then the main event of the visit: Corcoran returned to his hotel where, in the square outside, he made a powerful speech to the thousands of Philadelphia Irishmen gathered to hear him and cheer him.

Corcoran's speech was a real stem-winder and similar to those he made in other cities at this time. Some of his points are worth noting. He announced his support for the Lincoln administration—*for the time being*—with the implication that Washington had to do right by the Irish if it wanted continued support from them. He asserted his determination to raise an Irish Brigade and made the usual comments about the superior fighting qualities of the Irish. Support the war now, he urged his listeners, and then after the war the nation will owe a debt to us and we can have the "kind of politics we want." For the moment, he said, "We must go to the rescue of the white people of the South."[87] Corcoran then turned his attention to the Fenians, announced his own long-time membership in the society, and reminded his audience that a major purpose behind Irish military service now was the opportunity to use that experience later against England. Local Irish leaders repeated the same theme after Corcoran finished, and the New Yorker's rousing visit ended. There was a spurt in enlistments following the Corcoran visitation, but before the 116th could fully exploit the situation it was called to Washington in the panic following the events of Second Bull Run. It was a sadly understrength "Brian Boru United Irish Legion" that enjoyed a sedate departure from Philadelphia and took a train to Washington. Colonel Heenan led the unit, while his second-in-command was Irish-born St. Clair Mulholland.

The 116th Pennsylvania Infantry was assigned to Meagher's Irish brigade. So hurried was the departure, the regimental colors did not reach the troops until they camped at Harper's Ferry. Unlike most Irish regiments, the 116th did not carry a green Irish flag; next to the stars and stripes the regiment flew a state flag—the usual practice of Civil War outfits. Most volunteers in the 116th were not Irish-born, and the Irish-Americans in the ranks barely outnumbered the Americans, Germans, and others who shared the fate of the Irish Brigade. The 116th fought with the brigade at Fredericksburg, and as Mulholland described the terrible scene in front of the Stone Wall, the rows of dead and wounded were a cosmopolitan mix of Irish, American, French, and Italian ancestry.[88] With the other units of the Irish Brigade, the 116th suffered severely at Fredericksburg. Colonel Heenan was wounded and Mulholland took command, after which he also was hit. So many soldiers of the 116th became casualties that the regiment was reduced to a battalion, and Mulholland, recovered, was reduced in rank to a major. With this new designation the Philadelphia unit fought on with the Irish Brigade until the battle at Williams' Farm in late June 1864. By then all that was left of the Irish Brigade itself was led by a captain. Mulholland, wounded again in the Wilderness, went into politics after the war and was elected chief of police of the city of Philadelphia. A genuine war hero, Mulholland's postwar career was a virtual model for an Irish-American politician, and his postwar honors included brevet promotions to brigadier and major general, as well as the award of the Medal of Honor in 1895 for his bravery at Chancellorsville. If an Irish regiment fits the stereotype found in the postwar literature, it is the 116th Pennsylvania.

There were a few other Irish regiments, none of which gained the kind of fame or notoriety associated with those already discussed. Late in 1861, John L. Doran of Milwaukee raised the Seventeenth Wisconsin Infantry, sometimes called the "Irish Brigade" and sometimes called the "Irish Regiment." In its early days the Wisconsin outfit endured the Chinese curse; it lived in interesting times. There was considerable confusion surrounding the recruiting process, and when the regiment prepared to move to Camp Randall in Madison, its companies included the "Mulligan Guards" and the "Corcoran Guards," as well as the "Peep O'Day Boys." After a brief stay in Madison, the Seventeenth Wisconsin received orders to entrain for St. Louis. Claiming that they had not been paid, men of the "Irish Regiment" refused their orders, roamed ominously about the streets of the state capital with weapons in hand, and not until troops from Chicago and Milwaukee reached the city to restore order did local citizens breathe easily.[89] There is doubt, however, about whether the Seventeenth Wisconsin Infantry was an Irish unit. Its ranks included many, perhaps a plurality, of Americans, French (one whole company was French), and Indians. At least one recent student asserts that the regiment was not Irish, and surviving evidence from the soldiers themselves suggests that this organization was not an ethnic regiment.[90]

Similar doubts exist about the Fifteenth Maine Infantry. Raised in late 1861 and early 1862 by John McClusky and Isaac Dyer, the "Old Fifteenth" did carry a state flag with a harp and shamrock on one side and did listen to typical Irish oratory at its flag presentation ceremony, but historians of the regiment make no claim that it was Irish.[91] Lonn lists the Seventh Missouri Infantry as an Irish regiment, but if it had an Irish hue at the beginning of the war, it lost that ethnic character in the months that followed.

As a part of their struggle to establish a foothold in American society, seize the commanding heights in urban political battles, and give themselves a power-broker role in national politics, Irish-Americans in the years following the Civil War created a vast hagiographical and filiopietistic literature. It is full of internal contradictions, distortions, falsehoods, boastful exaggerations, and is today a unique chapter in the book of American folklore. Stories of the ethnic regiments that comprise a major part of the literature have as one unfortunate consequence the demeaning and stereotyping of the Irish soldier who fought for the Union. Professional ethnics who manipulated Irish sentiment for their own political ambitions have much to account for, as do subsequent writers who contributed so heavily to the misinformation on the subject.

Daniel O'Connell, one of the folk heroes of the Fenians and a man whose name was regularly cited on both sides of the Atlantic as a symbol of Irish nationalism, held views that were anathema both to most Irish-Americans and to Union patriots. O'Connell was a fiery abolitionist, a matter of chronic disagreement amongst his supporters in Ireland. O'Connell cared not a fig for American independence, but rather saw the United States as simply a political pawn to be used in negotiations with England. Indeed, he placed a higher priority on the interests of England than those of the United States.[92] Irish-American orators who called upon the name of O'Connell, and soldiers who named their companies after O'Connell, used a symbol that at best was a two-edged sword, and at worst one that stood for the destruction of America's national interests.[93]

Irish writers, intent upon the task of creating a mythology, described Irishmen flocking across the Atlantic to enlist in Union regiments in order to free the slaves. This is, of course, poppycock, since the vast majority of Irish emigrants were propelled by economic motives primarily, but the Irish in America were notorious racists whose enthusiasm for the war declined sharply after the Emancipation Proclamation. Irishmen tended to link abolitionists with antiforeign and anti-Catholic elements in America.[94] Just as Irish-American politicians sought to use and shape Irish sentiments toward their goals, so did Democratic and Republican politicians who were not Irish do the same. Irish immigrants and descendants of immigrants together made up a large population regularly exploited by a variety of people who cynically used Irish nationalism and the theme of the Irish-as-victim to get support for other ends. Fenians did it, Peace Democrats did it, political hacks did it, and ambitious careerists did it. Time and again the Irish became the tools of men who deliberately encouraged ethnicity because it served their purposes and not necessarily the purposes of those who were their pawns.

The constant theme of this kind of literature is that all Irishmen are alike. In the Civil War they all fought courageously for the Union; they won the war for the North, and any evidence to the contrary is conveniently ignored.[95] All too often, the accounts of the men in the ethnic regiments add still another unfortunate element—support for the image of the Irishman as a happy-go-lucky, even simple-minded, fellow who saw the war as a lark and who drank whiskey as a part of his jolly nature. Such images are insulting, unhistorical, and a disservice to the memory of the soldiers who fought with the Irish Brigade and the other Irish regiments in Union brigades and divisions. Irish soldiers dying before the Stone Wall at Fredericksburg did not sacrifice their lives for Irish independence; for the most part they fought for the same reasons their compatriots fought — to support their friends and comrades and to preserve the Union.

In his testimony before the Committee on the Conduct of the War, Gen. Fitz-John Porter faced the direct question: "Do you suffer from drinking in your division?" His carefully hedged answer was:

> Not much. We have some men who will have their frolics. We have a great many Irishmen, to whom a frolic is as necessary about once a month as a dinner is; but I have no trouble at all with them.[96]

Porter's answer reflects both image and reality. Irish regiments did have a serious alcohol abuse problem. While this was chronic in Civil War units of all kinds, it was a particularly acute problem for the Irish regiments. Irish recruits carried into military life the customs of civilian life, and since the ethnic regiments had the greatest concentrations of the Irish, they displayed the most obvious evidence of alcohol abuse.

Few Union regiments were models of discipline. Irish regiments had a reputation for more rowdiness and disobedience of orders than most. When George Welles of Boston expressed indignation at the casual behavior and appearance of Irish soldiers, his comments need not be taken seriously. When Irish members of the Fire Zouaves in New York City regularly left the camp at night, and when seventy-five at once got drunk and were dismissed from the ranks, that is more significant.[97] Irish colonels themselves recognized that their charges required especially tough handling. The tradition of street fighting in Irish communities carried over into rowdy behavior in Irish regiments.

Irish regiments shared some characteristics with their German counterparts. As the war continued the regiments and their colonels lost ethnic enthusiasm, and survival replaced ethnic purity as the top priority. Both kinds of regiments owed their origins to the enterprise of ethnic political leaders in cities with large concentrations of their immigrants. Both, especially in the early months of their existence reflected the bare-knuckle politics of ethnic America. In both groups ethnicity was much more important to the leadership than it was to the rank and file soldier.

In two important respects the Irish regiments differed from all the other ethnic organizations. First, there was the pervasive influence and rhetoric of the Fenians. The most famous military leaders, men like Corcoran, Meagher, McIvor, Nugent, and the like, were Fenians, and they did their best to make the ethnic regiments Fenian bastions. They worked diligently to associate the ethnic regiments with Irish nationalism and to persuade the larger society that Irish-Americans fought both for the Union and for Irish independence. Despite the postwar insistence on the part of the hagiographers, nationalists in Ireland did not support the Union. Irish na-

tionalist opinion became increasingly pro-Confederate as the war continued. After the Civil War ended over 150 ex-Union and Confederate Irish
officers went to Ireland and waged a spectacularly unsuccessful rebellion
against English rule.[98] It was the leadership of the Irish ethnic regiments
that played most heavily on a sentimental attachment to the Old World.
Their speeches and their symbols—the green flags, the green shirts, the
badges, the songs—tried desperately to give top priority to Old Country
imagery.

> The land which had failed them became enveloped, through the en-
> chantment of distance, with the mists of loveliness that softened the
> lines of grim reality, and a sentimental Ireland of green fields, silver
> lakes, pink dawns, and cloud-billowed skies . . . established itself in
> emigrant folklore.[99]

These words of George Potter, made in reference to Irish-Americans in
general, are directly applicable to Irish regiment leadership.

The second striking difference of the Irish regiments lay in their relationship with the Irish Catholic Church. Irish priests like Father Cooney
were a fundamental element of the Irish regiments. They were promoters;
alongside the professional politicians they participated in both the internal
and external regimental politics, they provided invaluable emotional and
spiritual support of the soldiers, and they were the strongest link between
the soldiers and their families. They also encouraged those soldiers to think
of themselves as different from American soldiers. The Irish regiments were
a natural continuation of the long tradition of Irish Catholic leadership
that the interests of the Irish were best served by ghettoization. The Irish
regiment was simply the military version of the Boston or New York neighborhood parish.

When the ordinary soldier in the ranks of an Irish regiment committed
his private thoughts to his diary or wrote letters to friends and family, his
beliefs, interests, and hopes were largely indistinguishable from those of the
Germans, Americans, and others. He wanted to survive the war, he wanted
to help save the Union, and he hoped to better himself after the war. His
concerns were remote from the florid language of the Corcorans and the
Meaghers. Most Irish-Americans, after all, enlisted in nonethnic regiments.
Most Irish-Americans were committed to America and to themselves, not
to historic and Old World quarrels and the furtherance of political careers
for professional ethnics.

THOMAS FRANCIS MEAGHER. Perhaps the best-known and certainly most ambitious of ethnic leaders was the Irish rebel exile Thomas Francis Meagher. *(Library of Congress)*

JAMES A. MULLIGAN. Although born in the United States, Colonel James A. Mulligan was a fiery Irish nationalist. He commanded the Twenty-third Illinois Infantry, known as "Mulligan's Brigade." *(Chicago Historical Society)*

OFFICERS OF THE SIXTY-NINTH NEW YORK INFANTRY. Colonel Michael Corcoran, replete with sash and Irish badge, stands alone with a foot resting near the cannon's muzzle. *(Library of Congress)*

OFFICERS OF THE SIXTY-NINTH NEW YORK INFANTRY. A green Irish flag stands furled at the center of the group portrait. *(Library of Congress)*

TWO COMPANIES of the well-equipped German Eighth New York Infantry.
*(Library of Congress)*

HANS CHRISTIAN HEG [*left*]. Heg, the Norwegian colonel of the Scandinavian regiment, the Fifteenth Wisconsin Infantry, was killed at Chickamauga. *(Norwegian-American Historical Association)*

DANIEL CAMERON [*below left*]. Colonel Daniel Cameron promoted the organization of the Sixty-fifth Illinois Infantry as the "Scotch Regiment," but it quickly lost any clear ethnic identity. *(Illinois State Historical Library)*

GÉZA MIHALOTZY [*below*]. As a non-German in the German Twenty-fourth Illinois Infantry, Hungarian refugee Géza Mihalotzy acquired an education in inter-ethnic rivalries within an ethnic regiment. *(Illinois State Historical Library)*

**WILLIAM HAINES LYTLE** [*above left*].
Lytle commanded the Irish Tenth Ohio Infantry
and then won a promotion to brigadier general
before his death at Chickamauga. *(Library of Congress)*

**AUGUSTUS WILLICH** [*above*]. Colonel of
the German Thirty-second Indiana Infantry
before his promotion to brigadier general,
Augustus Willich was the most admired ethnic
officer in the Union forces. *(State Library of Ohio)*

**JULIUS RAITH** [*left*]. Colonel of the German
Forty-third Illinois Infantry, Raith was killed at
the Battle of Shiloh. *(Illinois State Historical Library)*

**AUGUSTUS MOOR.**
Colonel of the German
Twenty-eighth Ohio Infantry before his promotion
to brigadier general, Moor
also served in the Seminole
War and the Mexican War.
*(Library of Congress)*

BLENKER'S BRIGADE HEADQUARTERS. Gloved hand on his belt, General
Louis Blenker (as he faces the camera) stands near the center of his large coterie
of officers and hangers-on. Prince Salm-Salm, both hands on his sword hilt,
stands at Blenker's right. *(Library of Congress)*

# CHAPTER 7

# The Others

We swear by our ancestors in yon heathen land,
  We swear by the graves of our bravest and dearest
Our Wallace and Bruce and the love of that brither band,
To stan' or to fa' by thee when danger's nearest,
    Follow thee! Follow thee! Scotchmen will follow thee,
    *Banner of liberty,* all the world over!

—"The Banner of Liberty," by an anonymous lady of Washington

N the heart of Scotland's capital city of Edinburgh, just at the foot of Calton Hill on Waterloo Place, lies the Old Burial Ground. This ancient cemetery is a veritable necropolis. Ruined tombs, roofless and open to the sky, line the dead streets like little houses. Chapters from Edinburgh's history can be read from inscriptions. Here is the marker for an eighteenth-century merchant. There is the elaborate, circular memorial to David Hume, who died in 1776. All of these monuments are encrusted with age, blackened with many generations of coal smoke. There is a single exception to this picturesque but dreary landscape. Standing tall atop a shiny and polished marble foundation is a life-size bronze of Abraham Lincoln; on one side of the foundation is another bronze figure, a freed slave, raising his hand in gratitude toward Lincoln. This is Edinburgh's remembrance of the American Civil War and a tribute to Scottish-American soldiers who served in the Union forces. It is the burial ground for several Scots who fought in Union regiments.

When the war began Scotsmen in New York already had a militia organization known as the "Highlanders." During the first call for volunteers after the attack on Fort Sumter, the Highlanders were unable to attract many recruits, and so the organization remained behind trying to fill its ranks while larger outfits went off to Washington. Samuel M. Elliot took the lead in turning the militia unit into a regiment of three-month volunteers. Recruiting was done without regard for ethnic purity (despite considerable ethnic hoopla in the process), and so from the very beginning the ethnic nature of the regiment was compromised. Since most Scottish immi-

*161*

grants were probably Lowlanders, a sense of ethnic identity was not strong among the Scots in America and the appeal of a Highlander regiment was not potent.[1]

Given the designation of the Seventy-ninth New York Infantry, the regiment gradually attracted more Scots, Americans, and—surprisingly enough given the enmity between the two ethnic groups—increasing numbers of Irish-Americans. The number assigned the regiment was significant; a Seventy-ninth Regiment of Scots in the British Army fought at Waterloo and was decimated as it stood its ground against French attacks. Part of the ethnic coloration of the New York Seventy-ninth was the use of tartan trousers as a part of the undress uniform and the wearing of kilts for a dress uniform. Less than a third of the men, however, actually acquired kilts. By the end of May the Seventy-ninth had more than eight hundred men enrolled, and 30 May it set off for Washington. It was in the early days of June that the Highlanders enjoyed their greatest ethnic puffery.

As the Seventy-ninth prepared to leave New York, it received a flag bearing a thistle, listened to speeches lauding the glories of Scottish soldiers on historic battlefields, and enjoyed a parade down Broadway—a parade complete with pipers playing the pibroch. In a moment of puckish humor the *New York Times* complained that so many Scottish females in the city were involved in the departure of the Highlanders that a decent bowl of Scotch broth was not to be had anywhere.[2] As the men departed, they were escorted by members of the Caledonian Society. All in all, it was a scene reminiscent of the leave-taking of Corcoran's "Fighting Irish."

On its way to Washington, the Seventy-ninth paraded through Baltimore. There, thousands of cheering spectators noted with disappointment that only a small minority of the troops actually wore the kilt. It was 2:30 A.M. 4 June when the weary soldiers arrived in Washington and went into camp on the Georgetown campus near the Sixty-ninth New York Infantry. Officers wearing the kilt soon added to the colorful scenes on capital streets, and the regiment was treated to a round of entertainment and favorable publicity. President Lincoln visited the camp, and that visit was followed by one from Secretary of War Simon Cameron. Secretary Cameron joined with Lieutenant Colonel Elliott in promoting the name of James Cameron as colonel of the regiment. James Cameron, Simon's brother, was born in Pennsylvania in 1801, served in the Mexican War, and led a militia unit in Pennsylvania before he moved to New York. Already retired when the war erupted, Cameron had been a businessman and a lawyer, and, when chosen colonel of the Highlanders, fit the common pattern of regimental leaders as emerging from persons prominent in the world of business or the professions before taking charge of a regiment.[3]

Elliott left the regiment shortly after Cameron took over. Now the "Cameron Highlanders," the Seventy-ninth New York officers delighted in the hospitality offered by Washington's Caledonian Club; the men paraded to martial Scotch music (their band lacked pipers, which Elliott promised to look for when he left Washington), and there was a banquet provided by the St. Andrew's Society. The unpleasantness of war seemed rather remote in the middle of a Washington summer. Men could still cheer, as they did during Colonel Cameron's speech at the St. Andrew's Society banquet, when they heard that most of the Scots fighting in the Seventy-ninth at Waterloo died rather than retreat. Reality intruded soon after the regiment marched away from Washington to the beginning of the Bull Run campaign.

Kilts were popular on New York and Washington streets, but they were the object of ridicule from other soldiers in the field. Only one die-hard captain retained the kilt after the first days, and he finally gave it up at Centreville the day before the regiment saw its first combat. On 21 July at Henry House Hill the Cameron Highlanders charged repeatedly against Confederate troops led by Beauregard. They suffered heavy losses; only two other regiments that day lost more men. Colonel Cameron himself died as he led an attack on the rebel lines.[4] When the Seventy-ninth New York finally broke and ran, its place was taken by the Sixty-ninth New York Infantry under Colonel Corcoran. That was Corcoran's day to become a prisoner of war.

It was a sullen and angry body of men that returned to camp near Washington. Like other three-month regiments, the Seventy-ninth after Bull Run complained that it had been deceived about its length of service. It grumbled about not being paid. The unrest reached a climax on 14 August.

A correspondent of the *Philadelphia Press* visiting the camp of the Cameron Highlanders on 7 August found many of the men drunk. The reporter claimed that large quantities of whiskey were secreted about the camp, and the men suffered low morale. Then, on the morning of 14 August the regiment got orders to march into Virginia. The Highlanders mutinied. Colonel Isaac Stevens, given charge of the Seventy-ninth after the death of Cameron, lost control of the men. General McClellan ordered the provost general to restore discipline. Provost General Andrew Porter used a battalion of U.S. regulars, two companies of cavalry, and a battery of artillery to do the job. With loaded weapons, they surrounded the mutineers. Ordered now to fall in, the sober members of the Seventy-ninth obeyed. Those too drunk to submit were hustled immediately to the guard house.[5] Disarmed and standing in formation, the men of the Seventy-ninth listened to a lecture on their behavior. Ringleaders of the mutiny were placed under arrest. The regimental colors, a very precious symbol for any Civil War regiment, were seized. Ordered now to march into Virginia, the men obeyed.

While other Civil War regiments mutinied, none received the notoriety gained by the Highlanders in August 1861. The episode illustrates the risks involved by publicity-seeking ethnic leaders. When things went well, the ethnic group relished the limelight. When unpleasantness occurred, the same public spotlight illuminated the group and Scottish-Americans endured the embarrassment. Some very familiar factors encouraged mutiny in the Cameron Highlanders, and ethnicity had little if anything to do with it. The soldiers expected that after Bull Run they would get some time at home before the regiment went on further duty, and this was denied. Some 140 men had already deserted the unit by 14 August, and those remaining on duty felt shabbily treated. And there was alcohol, so often the source of trouble in Civil War affairs.

While all ethnic regiments tended to lose their ethnic character in time, the transition for the New York Seventy-ninth was rapid. As Ella Lonn notes, the "infiltration" of the Irish in the companies of the Highlanders began from the very start, and before long they outnumbered Scots in most companies. Americans and members of other groups also joined, and the result was a regiment whose membership lost its distinctive ethnic character. Within a month after its mutiny the Seventy-ninth New York Infantry saw its colors restored. On Monday, 16 September 1861, in an elaborate, formal ceremony on the brigade parade ground, the Third Vermont Infantry, which had custody of the Seventy-ninth Infantry's flag, turned it over to the Highlanders.[6] To the thunder of a salvo from 32 pounders, the New Yorkers took possession of their flag, and under it in subsequent years fashioned a record worthy of the recruiting rhetoric.

Daniel Cameron, Jr., one of the publishers of the *Chicago Times,* tried to raise a Scotch regiment in that city. In his favor was the tradition of the "Highland Guards," a Scottish militia company that existed before the war, his own prominent position, and the presence in Chicago of both a Caledonian Club (a social and cultural organization that maintained a library of books on Scotland) and a St. Andrew's Society (a charitable society for Scots). Against this was a fundamental fact of life as revealed in the 1860 census; only 1641 Scots lived in Chicago. Even allowing for Scots elsewhere in the state and in neighboring states, the pool of potential volunteers was small.

Cameron proposed a Scotch regiment for Illinois in mid-December 1861 and opened a recruiting office on Washington Street in downtown Chicago. From the very beginning Cameron hedged his bet with appeals to the general population as well as to Scots. While recruiting literature identified the proposed outfit as the "Scotch Regiment," it also stressed several other alleged advantages, such as modern weapons, sutler profits returned to the men, a "distinctive costume," and a hundred-dollar bounty. Governor Yates gave prompt permission to Cameron, the proposed unit got the designation of the Sixty-fifth Illinois Infantry, and there was a deadline. Acting Colonel Cameron had sixty days to fill his companies.[7]

Recruiting was distressingly slow. Even when men signed up, they often disappeared, either legally or illegally. Weeks passed, and the Sixty-fifth Illinois Infantry attracted too few volunteers to go into active service. By late March, Cameron moved to improve his status in Springfield by offering the post of major to Adjutant General Fuller's brother, at the request of Governor Yates. Finally, in May 1862 enough volunteers signed up to give Cameron the minimum number required for acceptance by Washington. Serving under the motto, "Nemo Me Impune Lacessit" (No one attacks me with impunity), the soldiers endured dull and unpleasant routine duty at Camp Douglas, duty that meant they had little opportunity for training. Then Cameron got orders to move his unit to the eastern theater of operations, to Martinsburg, Virginia, where training continued.[8]

In September the Sixty-fifth Illinois Infantry, along with the other Union forces in Martinsburg, retreated before Confederate forces toward Harper's Ferry, and there, on 12 September, it came under the command of the ill-fated Col. D. S. Miles. When Miles surrendered the Harper's Ferry garrison on 15 September, the brief career of the Sixty-fifth Illinois Infantry halted as the men stacked their arms and returned to Chicago under parole.[9] There followed a most frustrating time for the regiment. It remained inactive at Camp Douglas, because under parole status it could not return to active duty until an exchange occurred with a Confederate regiment. Colonel Cameron found the wait onerous. Recruiters from other regiments raided the Sixty-fifth, and his midwesterners got along poorly with the eastern troops in the camp. Not until April 1863 did the regiment return to active duty.

The "Scotch Regiment" of Illinois never really attained the status of an ethnic regiment. Its initial appeal was a mixed one, and when recruiting lagged the ranks gradually filled with nonethnics. During the long weeks of early 1862 as the unit struggled for life, even the piper despaired and left the Sixty-fifth Infantry to join the band of another regiment. Musician James Scholes was a piper without pipes, and he saw no chance that he would ever get them.[10] Despite the efforts of Cameron and his fellow Scots of Chicago, neither the size of the ethnic population nor the strength of ethnic feelings allowed the state to produce a real Scottish regiment.

Two separate efforts failed to produce French regiments in New York. A small French militia organization, the "Guards Lafayette," already existed in the city when the war began. Known officially as the Fifty-fifth New York Volunteers, the unit was too small for federal muster. A well-know immigrant member of New York society, Philippe Regis de Trobriand, was elected colonel of the Fifty-fifth during the summer of 1861, and he became an American citizen at about the same time. As the companies filled in, the original French character of the Fifty-fifth New York Infantry gradually faded. One company was almost entirely German, while another was Irish, and still another American. Governor Morgan had a high opinion of de Trobriand, and the Frenchman's subsequent record justified it. With Morgan's backing, the Fifty-fifth New York went into federal service in August 1861, and the ranks were already quite mixed by then. The ever-inquisitive Ferri Pisani visited the training camp on Staten Island and found the French soldiers there had a lighthearted view of their role.[11] They made fun of everything, he reported, and their zouave uniforms seemed more suitable for a masquerade than making war. Colonel Trobriand regarded his French soldiers as less disciplined than the Americans; their vanity had to be massaged to get good results. Lonn's analysis of the Fifty-fifth New York concludes that the regiment was a medley of several different nationalities, with no French majority.

If the Fifty-fifth New York Infantry never quite succeeded in establishing its French credentials, the Fifty-third New York Infantry in its origin seemed purely French. In August 1861, the same month in which the Fifty-fifth went into federal service, Lionel Jobert D'Epineuil, a recent immigrant from France, got permission to organize a French regiment. D'Epineuil represented himself as a veteran of the French army, convinced the War Department that he had seventeen years of experience, and quickly gave his recruits the trappings of a French zouave outfit. Soldiers in what became the Fifty-third New York Infantry wore hooded cloaks, a red fez, gaiters, baggy trousers, and a blue sash. The career of the regiment was a comedy of errors. Colonel D'Epineuil was an incompetent fraud who had no military experience. Brawling and an absence of discipline characterized the men. D'Epineuil had a quarrel with his lieutenant colonel and at one point actually tried to ambush him and assassinate him. The plot failed. The colonel put his wife in a uniform and kept her in camp with him. By early 1862 D'Epineuil faced a wide variety of charges and was scheduled for court martial. The trial never occurred. In February 1862 federal authorities ordered the break up of the regiment and the men (only a small fraction of whom were actually French) mustered out in March. New York thereafter pretended that the Fifty-third New York Infantry of D'Epineuil never really existed.[12]

Interethnic rivalry stimulated the formation of a Scandinavian regiment in Wisconsin. When Governor Randall in August 1861 announced plans for the creation of a German regiment, Norwegian-American politicians hurriedly gathered in Madison to plan an appropriate reaction. With their customary suspicion of the Germans, they feared such an organization offered their rivals a potential political advantage. On 25 September 1861 they sent a petition to the governor requesting permission to raise a Scandinavian regiment and asked the governor to name Hans Christian Heg as its colonel. Small companies of Norwegians and Swedes were already drilling in several communities in Wisconsin and Illinois, and Governor Randall gave a prompt affirmative response. Heg was, of course, the obvious choice. Already the most prominent Norwegian-American politician in the state, his wide contacts in the midwestern ethnic community and his language skills, along with his administrative experience as a state official, made Heg the ideal person for the job.[13]

Working closely with other Norwegian-American leaders, Heg took the lead in recruiting what became the Fifteenth Wisconsin Infantry. He followed what was virtually a standard procedure by the fall of 1861. Letters went out to significant individuals in several states. Heg prepared an article for the immigrant newspaper, _Emigranten,_ and both the _Emigranten_ and the _Faedrelandet_ urged their readers to promote the idea.[14] He also visited Scandinavian towns in Wisconsin and neighboring states, and the message everywhere was the same. Norwegians, Swedes, and Danes should join the Scandinavian regiment because it offered advantages lacking in regular units. Young men who either spoke no English or whose English was poor could have the great comfort of being in a company where their language was used. Their officers would be fellow Scandinavians. Swedes and Norwegians owed a debt to their adopted homeland, and that debt was paid most visibly to the rest of society in an all-Scandinavian outfit. As with all other ethnic groups, appeals included references to the glorious military exploits of ancestors who fought on European battlefields. There was also an explicit warning that if Scandinavians failed to volunteer for military service, then Germans and Americans would doubt their loyalty and courage.

Heg's own motives were complex but clearly stated in letters to his wife and his friends. He was still a young man and still had political ambitions. Civil War veterans would dominate state and national politics after the war; a grateful state and nation would remember with special fondness those men who enlisted early in the war and risked their lives to save the Union. As he put it in a letter to his wife:

> I think you may feel glad now that I went the time I did. It will be some credit to a man to have gone early. There will not be much credit for a man to enlist, or go in when he is obliged to do so. . . . I have some experience now, that entitles me to a position &c. . . . I have a claim now.[15]

Equally strong was his sense of duty. He owed his state and nation whatever service he could give. As an individual and as a Norwegian he felt that he must demonstrate his courage to others, let the world know that Heg and the Norwegians were not slackers. Finally, he hated slavery, and so he saw the Union cause as a moral crusade.

When the 900 recruits for the Fifteenth Wisconsin Infantry gathered at Camp Randall in Madison, some 90 percent of the men were Norwegians, and the rest were Swedes, Danes, and a sprinkling of Germans and Americans. Heg discovered that he actually enjoyed the life of a regimental commander. The pay was excellent, he had a personal servant, there was a sense of excitement much of the time, the food was good, and he was doing something for his country. Except for missing his family, he was happier than ever before in his life.[16] Heg was a competent officer, and if he tended to brag, it was justified. Ethnicity for Heg was completely political. His personal relations with family and friends ignored ethnic expression, and in his official capacity as regimental commander he was all business—except for a rare and affectionate reference to his Norwegian soldiers. On the political level things were different. There his ethnic status was important, and there he pinned his postwar ambitions.

Those ambitions never materialized. Wisconsin's Scandinavian regiment saw long and hard service. It fought in over twenty battles, including Perryville, Murfreesboro, Chickamauga, Missionary Ridge, and the Atlanta campaign. A third of the men were killed or died of disease. Colonel Heg received a mortal wound at Chickamauga on 19 September 1863 and died the next day. Heg bears comparison with Willich. He was capable, courageous, and always interested in the care of his men. Although clearly ambitious, he was also something of an idealist and certainly devoted to the cause of the Union and his adopted country. If his character had a dark side, it was his casual racism so far as Negroes were concerned. Even though he was an abolitionist, he regarded colored people as inferiors. Heg never wore his ethnicity on his sleeve; it was not the central focus of his life. He wrote regular and anonymous articles for a Madison newspaper about the exploits of the Fifteenth Wisconsin Infantry, and while he praised his men he never identified the regiment as an ethnic unit. It was a *Wisconsin* regiment in those columns.

For most Scandinavians, the ethnic connection was simply not a central focus of their lives. The majority of Norwegian volunteers joined regular units, not the Fifteenth Wisconsin Infantry. The small number of Swedes in the South fought for the Confederacy as the much larger number in the North fought for the Union. Even the men in the Scandinavian regiment paid little attention to matters ethnic. Dr. Stephen O. Himoe, the regimental surgeon, was born in Norway, but his letters to his wife while he served in the Fifteenth Wisconsin are void of ethnic references. Surviving collections of letters written by men in the regiment, whether written in Norwegian or English, reveal the universal interests of Civil War soldiers—

food, family, friends, death, boredom, the routines of army life—and virtually nothing of ethnicity.[17] Effusive accounts of Scandinavians in the Civil War written by later generations fall into the typical pattern of hagiography and filiopietism. One reads about the descendants of Gustavus Adolphus and the Vikings rushing to defend the honor of their Old Country and maintain the military traditions of heroic ancestors. The reality, as found in the record of the Scandinavian regiment, is more prosaic and much more human. The regiment itself was born in ethnic political rivalries, but the soldiers who fought in it and sacrificed their lives in it are largely indistinguishable from their native American comrades.

Out of the extraordinarily polyglot population of New York City in 1861 emerged the most singular ethnic regiment of the Civil War, led by one of the most unsavory soldiers of fortune attracted to the North by the flames of war. Every large-scale war excites the cupidity or adventurous nature of certain men. There are idealists who choose one side or the other to fight for a just cause. A professional soldier in one army may see another nation's war as a golden opportunity for valuable battlefield experience. Unemployed soldiers look for a paying job in expanding armies. Bored dilettantes pursue adventure in foreign uniforms. Then there are opportunists who stir the cauldron of war in search of anything that might turn up, anything with a prospect of personal advantage. New York, both because of its size and shipping ties with the rest of the world and because of the diversity of its population, drew more of these men than any other city. One of them became the colonel of the Thirty-ninth New York Infantry.

Optimistic promoters went after every identifiable ethnic group. The most grandiose schemes envisioned brigades and the modest aimed at companies. There was a Polish Legion, most of whose members were not Polish. An attempt to build a Dutch company came to nothing. Hungarian Legions and Spanish Legions ended as companies. There was even a kind of generic "First Foreign Rifles," which tried an appeal to any non-American. "Colonel" L. W. Tinelli began work on an Italian regiment, to be called the "Garibaldi Guard."[18] When news of this reached the *New York Herald* it jocularly reported that it would include all the organ-grinders in the city. Organ-grinders or no, none of these various groups by itself could produce a regiment, and Tinelli lost his bid to form a Garibaldi Guard.

By the end of April 1861 a hodgepodge of Hungarian, Spanish, Italian, French, and German recruits coalesced into a wildly international "Garibaldi Guard," and coping with this bewildering mixture of people was Frederic George D'Utassy. Any effort to identify D'Utassy ends in frustration. General McClellan later described D'Utassy as Hungarian, a former rider in the Franconi Circus whose real name was Strasser. McClellan also claimed that the New York regiment actually was a motley collection of

Algerian Zouaves, Cossacks, Sepoys, Croats, beer-guzzling Bavarians, English army deserters, Eskimoes, Swiss, and warriors from the mythical army of the Grand Duchess of Gerolstein. For good measure, McClellan added former members of the French Foreign Legion and "zephyrs" to his list. Wilhelm Kaufmann rejected McClellan's description of the regiment; he argued that the Garibaldi Guard consisted of three German companies and a Swiss company—all good soldiers—and the remaining six companies were a collection of Sicilian robbers and murderers. Lonn simply refers to D'Utassy as a former Hungarian officer. Henry Villard, no admirer of the man, scathingly described the leader of the Garibaldi Guard as "D'Utassy, the romantic assumed name of a Hungarian Jew with a German patronymic. . . . D'Utassy was nothing but a swaggering pretender." The New York Historical Society, on the other hand, identifies him as a former language professor (who taught French and German as well as Italian) at Dalhousie College in Nova Scotia. Margaret Leech accurately depicts the man as an adventurer who once was a dancing master. Others saw him as a transplanted romantic Hungarian nobleman. It is possible that *all* of these descriptions are accurate. They are in the spirit of the story D'Utassy himself told *London Times* correspondent William Russell in the Willard Hotel in Washington in December.[19]

At any rate, in May 1861 the Garibaldi Guard, the Thirty-ninth New York Infantry, succeeded in filling up ten companies. As originally formed, these included three companies of Germans, three of Hungarians, and one each of Spanish, Swiss, Italian, and French volunteers. Colonel D'Utassy and his adjutant coped with correspondence and other paper work in six languages—Hungarian, Spanish, German, Italian, French, and English. Some of the officers wrote in a language other than their native tongue, and the resulting handwriting and spelling had attributes of a secret code. Like the talking dog, the remarkable thing about the regiment was not that it worked poorly, but that it worked at all. In keeping with the regular procedure in such matters, the Guard had a formal flag presentation ceremony on 23 May 1861. Three different flags were presented, and three different speeches and acceptances given. Mrs. A. H. Stephens offered first an American flag, on which was inscribed "Garibaldi Guard." Mrs. Stephens then, in a remarkable choice of words, said, "I present to your gallant Regiment, this your native flag . . . ," and handed it over to D'Utassy. The second flag was a green, red, and white Hungarian flag, which bore the motto, "Venecere aut morire" (Conquer or Die). That flag came from the daughter of D'Utassy's powerful patron, excongressman Moses H. Grinnell. Finally there was a replica of the flag of Garibaldi himself, a tricolor standard inscribed "Dio E Popolo" (God and the People). Lieutenant Colonel Alexander Repetti responded in Italian when he accepted this last regimental color, and when he asked the rows of Germans, Hungarians, Spaniards, Swiss, and Italians to swear defense of the sacred banner, there was a great affirmative cry. At the end of the ceremony the band played the *Marseillaise!*[20]

Two other points add to the bizarre nature of a Garibaldi Guard in the Union army. First, there was a "Garibaldi Legion" in the Confederate army, something that those Italians who later bragged about the contributions their compatriots made to the northern victory were wont to overlook. Secondly, Garibaldi himself was a notorious anti-Catholic, a fact that the *Boston Pilot* called to Lincoln's attention when there was talk of giving the aging revolutionary a command in the Union army.[21] It is not the function of symbols to be rational.

Within a week after the flag ceremony, the Thirty-ninth New York Infantry set up camp just outside the nation's capital. Washington was astonished at this apparition in its midst. The uniforms alone caught even the most jaded eye. The men wore chasseur jackets, the baggy pants and leggings of the zouaves, red shirts, a large, feathered "Alps hunter" hat, and they bore side arms. An ordinary regiment had a drum corps; the Garibaldi Guard had a forty-man bugle corps. What really set Washington tongues wagging, however, was the sight of *vivandiére* marching along with each company. These young ladies wore a costume similar to that of the soldiers, and they certainly added an exotic note to an American outfit. Early newspaper reports had the *vivandiére* wives of men in the ranks, but at least two of them turned out to be runaways from Jersey City.[22] Most regiments had one major (unless the surgeon also held that rank); the Thirty-ninth New York had two. George Waring occupied the field staff position, while the original founder of the Garibaldi Guard, L. W. Tenelli, had a special position as a commissary major. Described as "mercurial," "temperamental," and "theatrical," Colonel D'Utassy sported his own highly individual uniform. With his staff following behind him, D'Utassy competed with Louis Blenker as the most spectacular sight on Washington streets. With all this, it was the behavior of the regiment rather than its appearance that kept it in the public eye.

There were the usual shenanigans, the things that happened in even the best-regulated military organizations. The very day after the Guards arrived a soldier from another New York regiment shot a trooper of the Thirty-ninth, who lost his leg in consequence. In another shooting incident the wound was fortunately slight. Within two days members of the regiment were involved in a drunken brawl, and when two soldiers fell into the hands of the police the Garibaldians emptied their barracks and rushed to the scene, where officers managed to restore order.[23] Out of the ordinary was the mass insubordination in the regiment immediately following its arrival at Camp Grinnell.

Men of the Thirty-ninth New York Infantry prided themselves as expert riflemen. Upon the arrival in Washington, they were issued muskets. The French and Spanish companies blamed what happened next on the Germans. "Mutinous" German noncommissioned officers persuaded the Spanish soldiers to reject the muskets. German soldiers hooted and hissed at the French, who, in some confusion, stacked their muskets against a wall. Whereupon the Germans attempted to seize the weapons and the French officers organized resistance. About a hundred soldiers from the regiment left Camp Grinnell and headed toward the city; they seized people they encountered along the way to prevent advance word from reaching the city. Military authorities called out troops to round up the mutineers. By the time order was restored, considerable doubt existed both in New York and Washington about D'Utassy's ability to control his men.[24]

The colonel's troubles continued. Hostility and competition marked the relations between the officers of the different ethnic groups. Some officers refused to obey orders transmitted to them through the adjutant. Seven of the ten companies, including all three Hungarian units, drew up petitions requesting D'Utassy's resignation. His friends in New York urged him to resign. General Joseph Mansfield, commander of the Department of Washington, believed the Garibaldi Guards should be disbanded. Colonel D'Utassy weathered the crisis, however, and by July the Thirty-ninth New York was part of Blenker's brigade.

One crisis gave way to another and then still another. Several officers resigned, sometimes complaining of ethnic prejudice. Rumors reached New York that D'Utassy bilked the government of money by charging for 900 rations when there were only 700 men in the regiment. War Department officials, increasingly unhappy with Union officers unable to speak or write English, began to apply pressure on leaders of ethnic regiments to rely solely on English. That gave D'Utassy a real headache. As one of his captains put it:

> While having to make out the pay list and having no man who kan write English I must have Bader and Willing to do it Sir if I had only one man to do it I would do it. . . .[25]

In the midst of his other troubles, D'Utassy encountered another mutiny, this time more serious than the first. A center of opposition to the colonel was a Captain Takatah, who led one of the Hungarian companies. Takatah tried to circulate a petition demanding D'Utassy's resignation, and when he failed to get permission to do this, his company and the Italian company refused to drill. When ordered to surrender his sword, Takatah not only declined to do so but told his own men to load their weapons and resist his arrest. His company complied. Captain Takatah then marched his company across the famous long bridge into Washington and they settled into a camp on public property nearby. In a word, an armed rogue company was loose in the nation's capital. General Mansfield dispatched a squadron of cavalry and a company of federal infantry to arrest the Hungarians, who were imprisoned in the Treasury building. The affair strengthened Mansfield's opinion that D'Utassy could not control his regiment. When disorders continued to be reported from Camp Grinnell, a peremptory order went to D'Utassy: "Unless the firing and depradations of the regt. cease, it will be discharged from U.S. service and your command destroyed."[26] Gilbert and Sullivan might easily have composed a masterpiece with a plot focused on the fiction of D'Utassy as an innocent, the center around which chaos grew, and then, at the end of Act One, fate intervenes: First Bull Run. Takatah's insurrection was 8 July, and the Army's warning telegram carried the date of 17 July; the troop movements leading to the Battle of Bull Run were already underway. As a part of Blenker's brigade, the Garibaldians stood in reserve that fateful Sunday. The immediate threat to the regiment's existence passed.

Act Two of the Gilbert and Sullivan opera bouffe opens with the Garibaldi Guard back in camp, where D'Utassy learns that the members of his financial support committee in New York mishandled regimental funds. Whenever the outer world intruded upon the life of the regiment, it meant trouble and conflict. To this D'Utassy added his own difficulties. During the year after First Bull Run, the Garibaldi Guard encountered the drive by the federal government to introduce minimal standards of competency among regimental officers through an examination system. On the one hand, that gave the colonel a weapon to use against disputacious officers. On the other hand, incompetents had their political patrons and protectors who demanded that the colonel find loopholes in the testing system. A never-ending problem was that of the conflicts and fights between the ethnic groups, especially the Germans and Irish. Drinking was the usual culprit in the latter instance. In February 1862 General Blenker arrested D'Utassy and charged him with neglect of duty because Garibaldians plundered homes in the neighborhood of their camp. D'Utassy retaliated with articles criticizing Blenker in German newspapers, and that compounded his difficulties with the German general. When the Garibaldians returned to fighting the war instead of themselves and their neighbors, they were surrounded and captured at Harper's Ferry in September 1862 (along with the Sixty-fifth Illinois and the rest of the federal garrison). D'Utassy gained some notoriety later with the revelation that he requested permission to "cut his way out" of the Harper's Ferry trap before the surrender. After this, events took a serious turn, and the Gilbert and Sullivan view of the colonel's career collapses.[27]

In December 1862 an assistant secretary of war gave to a departmental investigator a claim for $3000 submitted by D'Utassy. This was money collected on the basis of expenses incurred on official business for the

Garibaldi Guard. Investigator Olcott reported: "I found it to be a total fraud, the very signatures upon the subvouchers being forged."²⁸ D'Utassy was arrested again, court-martialed, found guilty, and sent to prison. On 29 May 1863 he was officially cashiered from the service.

In little more than a month later, the Thirty-ninth New York Infantry fought at Gettysburg under a new commander, and their regiment went on to fight at Petersburg. Before mustering out, the outfit lost 274 of its number to disease and battlefield casualties.

The Garibaldi Guard was unique among the war's ethnic regiments. It belonged to no single group, and so no ethnic community claimed it as its own. It had no sharp identity, as did an Irish or German unit. In the years following the war, no political interest group raised the banner of the Thirty-ninth, although Italian and Hungarian writers occasionally referred to their segments of the regiment. During its first two years the regiment illustrated within its own ranks, and in the encounters it had with other ethnic units, the tensions and hostilities that often erupted between different immigrant communities. D'Utassy's exploitation of the role of professional ethnic perfectly reveals the dangers of abuse inherent in that system. Six languages, five ethnic groups, at least as many different religious loyalties, and heavy propagandizing based upon what people failed to recognize were Old World rivalries, all made for a volatile and unstable mixture. The Thirty-ninth New York Infantry was a cockpit of nineteenth-century ethnic America.

> Old England sends a Rifle Corps
> to dear New England greeting,
> And will, if wanted, send still more,
> At every future meeting;
> For, though this ain't our native land,
> It still is very handy,
> As riflemen, to lend a hand,
> To Yankee Doodle Dandy.
> — To be sung to the tune of "Yankee Doodle"

When the *Boston Transcript* published the song from which the above lines are excerpted in April 1861, there was more than a little irony of history present. The city of the Boston Tea Party, just a century after the Treaty of Paris that ended the Seven Years' War and gave Britain a globe-girdling empire, now observed an effort by English residents to raise a company of volunteers to fight for the Union. Ultimately, however, ethnicity is defined by the individual. You think of yourself as an ethnic, or you do not. English-Americans, relative to their numbers in the population, contributed more manpower to Union forces than any other group. There was no English regiment. Although many Canadians fought for the North, there was no Canadian regiment. Even most Germans and most Irish joined regular regiments. For most volunteers, *every other factor* — geography, personal friendships, occupation, class, nonethnic politics, and ambition — outweighed ethnicity. The English and Canadians did not identify themselves as ethnics.

Long forgotten in both the popular imagination and the scholarly literature are the many men of foreign birth who joined Union regiments, and, just like their countless American counterparts, fought their war under an American flag and most likely under a state flag. Leonard D. H. Currie offers a case in point. Currie, whose name is not mentioned in Ella Lonn's encyclopedic account of foreigners in the Union army, was a British officer travelling in the United States in 1861. He sold his commission in the British army and sought and won from New York's Governor Morgan a commission to head an American regiment. America's war was his opportunity. Currie took charge of the 133rd New York Infantry. This regiment, called the "Second Metropolitan Guard," was recruited under the sponsorship of New York's metropolitan police. The three-year regiment served its entire period of duty (September 1862 to June 1865) under Colonel Currie. The colonel had his quota of problems. He was accused, and found innocent, of everything from murder to corruption. Currie was ambitious; he simply did not pursue that ambition through ethnic politics. The regiment, born in the most complex mix of people in the country, held a focus on an occupation, not an ethnic community. Its soldiers today are not celebrated as saving the Union in the name of Old World glory.[29]

The Currie story was repeated many times over. Richard Owen, famous as a geologist in his own right as well as being the son of Robert Owen, was born in England, and as colonel of the 60th Indiana Infantry his ethnic origin was was immaterial. William H. Boyd, in the publishing business in Philadelphia at the outbreak of the war, was Canadian by birth; Boyd became colonel of the 21st Pennsylvania Cavalry and indistinguishable from American-born counterparts. George A. Cobham, born in England, was colonel of the 111th Pennsylvania Infantry, and was "American in thought and feeling," in the words of that state's Civil War chronicler.[30] William G. Murray, born in Ireland, was killed in action at Winchester in March 1862, as colonel of the 84th Pennsylvania Infantry. Since he led an American regiment and made no effort to participate in nationalist activities, Murray is absent from the usual lists of ethnic heroes. These men were the "invisible ethnics."

# Song and Story

All wars are boyish, and are fought by boys. . . .

— WALT WHITMAN, "The March into Virginia"

ILLIAM H. McNEILL, writing in *The Pursuit of Power,* identifies a profound ambivalence in warfare. There is in the experience
of war some of the highest expressions of social solidarity, heroism, self-sacrifice, and demonstrations of instinctive human behavior. But war also means suffering, destruction, and brutality on a scale
repugnant to human sensibilities.[1] McNeill makes clear the connection between certain forms of martial display, such as drill and parade, and the
maintenance of discipline and group cohesion and morale. There was a
very practical reason for introducing the raw recruit in the Civil War regiment to his new status as a soldier by company and regimental drill. Both
military and civilian populations developed, from the very beginning of the
war, several kinds of ceremonies and pageantry whose purpose was to tie
the citizen soldier to his society and promote individual and group morale.
The color and excitement of the ceremonies, along with the patriotic rhetoric associated with them, helped to hide or postpone the grim reality of the
battlefield and at the same time justify the sacrifice of blood and treasure
the nation made.

Every Union regiment went through standard rites of passage soon
after its organization. Among the most colorful, formal, and impressive
occasions were the flag presentation ceremony and the official departure
for the seat of war. United States flags and regimental colors repose today
in silent and dusty rows in museums across the North. Those swaths of
bright, decorated silk once embodied the passionate loyalties of men and
units and were valuable trophies of battle. Carrying those colors was a
dangerous honor. Presenting them to a regiment was commonly the charge
of the wife or daughter of a political figure associated with the regiment.
Every regiment received a United States flag. Regular regiments carried a

state flag. Ethnic outfits got the most exotic banners, which used a variety of devices to recall Old World traditions or aspirations.

Indiana's Irish regiment, the Thirty-fifth Infantry, marched beneath a green silk banner on which there was a sunburst, harp, cross, and anchor in gold. In addition there was an eagle holding a shield and arrows, and a wreath of silver shamrocks surrounded all. One observer, carried away by the sight of the regiment marching off with its Irish colors, compared the scene to the "wonderful figure of Nebuchadnezzar's dream."[2] The sunburst, harp, and shamrock appeared on most Irish flags, with a variety of written messages. The Ninth Massachusetts Infantry flag included the words:

> The Sons By Adoption;
> Thy firm Supporters and Defenders
> From
> Duty, Affection and Choice[3]

Silken standards borne by ethnic regiments stressed the dual loyalties of the men. The greater emotional appeal went to the glories of the Old Country.

Ceremonial rhetoric repeated the theme. Flag presentations occurred either on the evening before a departure or on the day itself. Gifts of swords, pistols, badges, sashes, and other symbolic presents added to the solemnity and importance of the occasion. Such gifts could have considerable intrinsic value as well as emotional worth. A typical sequence of events were those associated with the Twentieth New York Infantry, a German outfit known as the "United Turner Rifles," commanded by Col. Max Weber, a veteran of the Revolution of 1848.

On the evening of 30 May 1861, Colonel Weber was the guest of honor at a meeting of the German Liederkranz (choral society) of New York. He accepted a gilt cartouche and a sword belt. Frederick Kapp, president of the society, gave the principal address of the evening. Kapp's speech stressed the dual obligations of the German soldier in America; he fought for his adopted country but also fought for German honor and to show that Germans defended liberty everywhere. Like other ethnic leaders, Kapp on such occasions made use of his public forum to call attention to what Germans were doing.[4]

Two weeks later, on 13 June the United Turner Rifles received its flags and left New York. The whole day was, in the words of the *New York Times,* a German pageant for the city. All of the German social and cultural organizations took part. In his enthusiasm, the *Times* reporter compared the German soldiers to ancient Greeks:

> Those who have not forgotten their Homer will remember that in the second book of the "Iliad" the poet relates that when Grecian warriors disembarked from their ships, they amused themselves with quoits and other athletic games upon the beach. . . . The Turners are experts in all

that the old Greeks regarded as desirable in physical education. They can climb like cats, bound like deer, fight like men, and run a-foot like Indians.[5]

The Twentieth New York Infantry formed at Forty-second Street and Second Avenue, while an escort waited for it at Union Square. The escort outnumbered the soldiers; it included men from several different choral and Turner associations, as well as German firemen and bandsmen. The huge procession made its way to City Hall, where the flag presentation ceremony occurred.

In the absence of Mrs. Charles E. Strong, who was originally scheduled to make the presentation, the Honorable Samuel B. Ruggles did the honors. Several flags went into the hands of the United Turners. Ruggles's long address played heavily on the ethnic theme. From the steps of City Hall marched "Germans of former ages" who battled the slave-holding despots of Rome, in Ruggles's words, and he hailed the representatives before him from the land of poetry and song who came to America seeking freedom. And so on. The speaker assured his listeners that, coming as they did from a land cursed with disunity, they would struggle for unity in America. And that was just for the American flag portion of the affair. Another flag—black, red, and yellow for Germany—was handed over, as was a guide flag bearing the motto "Bahn frei" (Clear the Way). All of its flags in hand, the Twentieth New York Infantry then marched through the Bowery and Canal Street to the docks at North Moore Street, where it boarded the steamer *Alabama* for a voyage to Fortress Monroe. It was a ceremony repeated hundreds of times throughout the North. The colors and symbols on the flags and the content of the dignitary's speech varied according to the ethnic background of the assembled soldiers.

Music and song were important elements in the lives of both soldiers and civilians and were part of official ceremony and leisure alike. Songwriters and publishers quickly seized upon the popular adulation accorded individual regiments and officers, and their products were a rich mixture of hero worship, satire, criticism, patriotism, and humor.

When an ethnic regiment figured prominently in military action, a poetic or musical tribute followed promptly. The Tenth Ohio Infantry, the Irish outfit led by Colonel Lytle, fought in the Battle of Carnifax Ferry in September 1861, its first significant combat. Within weeks, a lengthy poem by Sophia H. Brown appeared in the *Cincinnati Gazette*. In part, Mrs. Brown wrote:

> From the old down-trodden nations,
>     Fighting nobly in the van,
> Marching 'neath our eagle banner,
>     Battling for the rights of man.

> On the banks of the Gauley river,
>     Many a son of Erin died,
> Many a brave and loyal German
>     Fought Columbia's sons beside.
> Honor to the Tenth Ohio,
>     Who the brunt of the battle brav'd;
> Henceforth let it be remembered,
>     Erin's sons the banner sav'd![6]

This kind of folk poetry pervaded the columns of Civil War newspapers. It gave the people at home a way to share vicariously in news from the battlefield and gave civilian and soldier a sentimental tie. The theme here was a simple one, that of the ethnic soldiers fighting alongside the American, with a place of honor (a "save the flag" episode) accorded the Irish.

Lytle's battlefield death found a quick poetic memorial in newspaper columns, and the anonymous author ended his effusion with these lines:

> A Nation mourns her favorite son;
>     His laurels green shall ever wave,
> And Erin's tears shall wet the sod,
>     Where Lytle fills a soldier's grave.[7]

In this example, as in many others, the event stimulated community boosterism as well as a reminder of the ethnic contribution.

Innumerable anecdotes, most no doubt apochryphal, recorded the refusal of soldiers in Confederate regiments to fire upon the Stars and Stripes. (Southerners told similar stories from the opposite perspective.) One such episode allegedly occurred during the Battle of Winchester in May 1862, and this one had an ethnic flavor, as an anonymous poet noted:

> The Irish boys are bold and brave,
>     The Irish boys are true;
> They love the dear old stars and stripes,
>     The spangled field of blue.
> 'Tis Mulligan can tell the tale
>     Of how they fought that day,
> When with the foe at Lexington
>     They met in bloody fray.
> Fast whizzed the shot and murderous shell,
>     The bullets fell like rain;
> But dauntless stood his brave brigade —
>     The heroes of the plain.
> . . . . . . . . . . . . . . . . . . . . . . . . . . . . . . . . .
> Oh! honor to the Irish boys,
>     And cheers of three times three;
> Old Ireland is with our side —
>     I wish that *she* were free.
> . . . . . . . . . . . . . . . . . . . . . . . . . . . . . . . . .

> Oh! brave were those who nobly fought;
>     But braver still the band
> Who, forced by the rebels in their ranks,
>     United, made their stand.
> They saw the old and honored flag
>     Borne out upon the air,
> And not a gun was raised against
>     Its floating folds so fair!
> Ah! Lexington and Springfield boast
>     Their heroes true and grand;
> But Winchester shall stir men's hearts
>     Throughout Columbia's land.[8]

Along with reporting the Winchester episode, the poet reminded his readers of the much celebrated Irish Brigade of Colonel Mulligan, and repeated the familiar and entirely erroneous argument that an Irishman fighting for the South did so under duress.

The reality was that Irishmen fought as enthusiastically for the South as for the North. Southern poets eulogized an Irish Brigade fighting for the Confederacy:

> The Irish green shall again be seen
>     As our Irish fathers bore it,
> A burning wind from the south behind,
>     And the Yankee route before it!
> O'Neill's red hand shall purge the land—
>     Rain fire on men and cattle,
> Till the Lincoln snakes in their cold lakes
>     Plunge from the blaze of battle![9]

The quality of the poetry in the South was at least as bad as that in the North, but the sentiments were the same.

When the Garibaldi Guard had its flag presentation ceremony, the ethnic mixture in its ranks gave its commemorator a real challenge, but author Frank Norton rose to the occasion:

> Forward, men, and meet the foe—
>     You strike for your chosen land;
> Let the tramp, tramp of your marching feet
>     Be the guide to your steady hand.
> Remember how your sires have fought—
>     Remember your wrongs of old—
> And fight for right and justice
>     Till your heart's red blood runs cold.
> Ye come from many a far off clime;
>     And speak in many a tongue,
> But freedom's song will reach the heart
>     In whatever language sung.

. . . . . . . . . . . . . . . . . . . . . . . . . . . . . . . . . .
     Your native lands shall glow with pride
         From Hungary's wide plains
     To Italy's blood-crimsoned fields,
         Your deeds shall cleanse their stains;
     And every man who falls shall leave
         Above the grassy sod
     The name of one who fought and died,
         For Freedom and his God.[10]

Frank Norton's song for the Garibaldi Guard was a kind of perverse masterpiece of the genre. It identified generic wrongs in the Old Country, offered obeisance to an all-purpose deity, and assumed that each of the half-dozen ethnic groups in the regiment had a similar set of martial ancestors. It ignored the probability that those ancestors fought *against* each other on European battlefields.

Dialect — genuine or fake — and brogue were common features of song and poetry associated with the ethnic regiments. Such techniques added both color and an element of incomprehension when the brogue got thick. While recruiting was underway in New York for a Scotch regiment, an example of this appeared in a New York newspaper:

     Come, muster, my bonnie brave Scots,
         An' muster your clans one an' a',
     Nor heed who else lags, so the free Thistle wags,
         When Treason drives Right to the wa';
     For Freedom, for Union, an' Law,
         We'll do a' that true men may dare;
     An' come weal or come scaithe, for these to the death —
         The Seventy-Ninth will be there!
     Come, stir, then, a' trim for the work;
         Come, Borderer, Lowlander, Celt,
     An' wi' firelock in hand, our tartan-clan band
         Will soon mak the auld grit be felt.
     . . . . . . . . . . . . . . . . . . . . . . . . . . . . . . . . . . . . . . . . . . . . . . .
     Then heeze out the pipes wi' a cheer,
         An' up wi' some heart-thrillin' strain,
     To mind us the field is where Scots never yield,
         While ae chance to win may remain.
     Syne shout, lads, the auld battle-cry —
         "Saint Andrew!" — an' let them beware
     When doure Southern knaves wad mak North-folk their slaves —
         The Seventy-ninth will be there![11]

Nothing published by nonethnics intended to belittle or stereotype the ethnics was as broad and crude as materials published by and for the ethnic market itself. In other words, clichés to which ethnics objected when the source was a native American, were simply good fun when they told them on themselves. The Boston firm of Horace Partridge, for example, published a parody of "When this Cruel War is Over," which in part read:

Och, Biddy dear, do you remember,
　　Whin we last did meet,
'T'was at Paddy Murphy's party,
　　Down in Baxter Street;
And there all the boys did envy me,
　　And girls envy'd you —
Whin they saw my great big bounty,
　　In greenbacks, all new.
. . . . . . . . . . . . . . . . . . . . . . . . . . . . . . . .
Next day I shoulder'd my ould musket,
　　Braver thin ould Mars,
And with spirits light and airy,
　　Marched off to the wars.
But now me drame of glory's over,
　　I am homesick I fear,
I'd give this world for a substitute,
　　To take my place here.
Och, weepin' Biddy darlin',
　　For the paymaster's tin;
Whin this cruel war is over,
　　Praying for a good horn of gin.[12]

No other regiment or individual drew the musical and poetic attention given to Corcoran and the Sixty-ninth New York Infantry. It began immediately after Sumter as the regiment started its initial three months of federal service. An anonymous song writer in Brooklyn composed a "New War Song of the Sixty-ninth Regiment," which recited the recent adventures of the militia organization:

Come all you Irish hayroes, where iver that you be,
I pray yees pay 'tintion and listen on to me;
Concerning of the Prince of Wales, when he landed on New York shore
The Sixty Ninth wud not turn out, they had done nothing more.
Their Colonel was court-marshalled, as you may understand,
He was deemed a traitor, to his adopted land,
He will show them, they're Irishmen, he made them this reply
'Tis for the stars and stripes, he willingly will die.
. . . . . . . . . . . . . . . . . . . . . . . . . . . . . . . . . . . . . . . . . . . . . . . . . . . . . . . . . . . . . . .
Now to conclude and finish, as I've no more to say,
May the Lord assist their arms, let every Christian pray;
So we know they've done their duty, which no man can deny
As brave as their ancestors, on the plans of Fontenoy.

　　*Chorus:* With my hum be boo boo boo, what shall we do

> Our sweethearts for to plaze
> And the Union for to save,
> For the 69th is bravest of the brave.[13]

With the defeat of the Sixty-ninth New York at Bull Run and Corcoran's capture and imprisonment, there was an outpouring of song and verse from the regiment's supporters. On 29 August 1861 at Jones' Wood there was a benefit for the widows and orphans of Bull Run casualties; an "Irishman" composed words and music telling Corcoran's story:

> Bear aloft that Flag, boys, Erin's glorious green,
> Foremost in the fight, boys be our "Sun-burst" seen;
> Onward with that uncrown's harp to "victory or death"
> The word—"Remember Limerick and Britain's broken faith."
> Forward now, to aid me in my need,
> By your arms your chief would fain be freed;
> I went into this struggle with my heart and soul,
> And though my jailors gave it me, I would not take parole.[14]

Recruiting started immediately for a new Irish regiment to replace the original militia unit with a three-year regiment. In song and verse the familiar appeals went out:

> Hurroo for the Union! me boys,
> And divil take all who would bother it!
> Secession's a nagur so black,
> The divil himself ought to father it.
> Hurroo for the bould 69th!
> That's presintly bound to go in again;
> 'Tis Corcoran will lead 'em, d'ye mind:
> And I will go with them, says McFinnigan.[15]

> Hail to the men now in triumph returning,
> Black with the battle-smoke, radiant with fame!
> Ireland is proud, and America is grateful,
> The heart of each Irish girl bounds at their name,
> "Caed millea failtha," men!
> Out on the air again—
> Rings the clear sound of the Irish hurrah,
> As up from the surging crowd,
> Bursts the shout, deep and lod,
> Long live the Sixty-ninth! Erin go Bragh![16]

The name of Thomas Francis Meagher soon joined that of Corcoran, as Meagher of the Sword promoted the idea of an Irish Brigade.

> You gallant sons of Erin's Isle, attend to what I say:
> A brother, driven to exile, is up alive to-day.
> He is of the good Hibernian blood that never frets nor fears,
> He has arrayed a new brigade of Irish volunteers.

. . . . . . . . . . . . . . . . . . . . . . . . . . . . . . . . . . . . . . . . . . . . . . . . . . . .

> Long life to Colonel Meagher, he is a man of birth and fame
> And, while our Union does exist, applauded be his name!
> Our land once more to peace restored, and brighter prospects near,
> We will not lack to welcome back the Irish Volunteers.[17]

No practice or phrase infuriated the Irish more than the one familiar in the decade before the war, "No Irish Need Apply." Men organizing Irish regiments often referred to this hated custom when they urged Irishmen to fight for the Union to persuade Americans to stop such discrimination. John F. Poole, who composed both German and Irish dialect songs, wrote for the Irish stage personality, Tony Pastor, a lyric that combined an appeal to the military heroes and loathing for discrimination:

> Ould Ireland on the battle-field a lasting fame has made:
> We all have heard of Meagher's men, and Corcoran's brigade;
> Though fools may flout and bigots rave, and fanatics may cry,
> Yet when they want good fighting men, the Irish may apply,
> And when for freedom and the right they raise the battle-cry,
> Then the Rebel ranks begin to think no Irish need apply.[18]

Pastor was said to have enjoyed great success with this Poole song, whose lyrics are a classic statement of the Irishman-as-victim perspective, and of the assumption that the Irish fought only for the Union and in spite of the bigotry they encountered in their adopted country.

Poole composed another popular ethnic hit in dialect, this time for performer H. W. Egan. He seized upon the notoriety of the "I fights mit Sigel" poem and phrase, and wrote "I'm Going To Fight Mit Sigel." Its words, a travesty of German-American speech, reeked with contempt for the Germans, and were sung to the tune of "The Girl I Left Behind Me."

> I've come shust now to tells you how
>   I goes mit regimentals.
> To SCHLAUCH dem voes of Liberty,
>   Like dem old Continentals,
> Vot fights mit England, long ago,
>   To save de Yankee Eagle;
> Un now I gets mine sojer clothes,
>   I'm going to fight mit Sigel.
> Ven I comes from de Deutsche Countree
>   I vorks some dimes at baking;
> Den I keeps a lager bier saloon,
>   Un den I goes shoe-making. . . . [19]

Other stanzas told of the German soldier's plan to put his wife in trousers and get her into the army and of his concern that if he joined the army he would get no more beer. There was a nasty tone to some of this material and the humor wore thin. After the draft began, one of the pop-

ular ditties of the day was "How Are You Conscripts?" whose last stanza
ran:

> Shoulder arms, now Conscripts!
> Blackguards, what's your name?
> Terence Darby — Blood an' ouns!
> How Paddy jumps for fame!
> Frenchmen, Scotchmen, all press forward!
> O mien got! here Mynheer comes.
> Blow the bugle, split the trumpet,
> Shout Hosannas! pelt the drums![20]

In the perception of some native Americans, the foreign born exploited
their status to evade military service.

Two themes found throughout Irish song and verse of this genre,
which are largely absent from that of the other ethnic literature, are the
pervasive Irish nationalism and a strident racism. In a play on words, poet
"F. D. B." expressed the dual motivation of some Irish-Americans in "The
Two Unions":

> When concord and peace to this land are restored,
> And the Union's established forever,
> Brave sons of Hibernia, oh, sheath not the sword; —
> You will then have a Union *to sever.*
> The flags of two nations appear on the field; —
> You have vowed to defend them forever;
> Your duty to one, is the Union to shield; —
> To the other, the Union *to sever!*
> . . . . . . . . . . . . . . . . . . . . . . . . . . . . . . . . . . . . . . . . . .
>
> On Erin's green soil (and on Erin's alone)
> You can purchase your freedom forever,
> When, join'd with your patriot brothers at home,
> The foul union of tyrants you sever.[21]

Far more serious than this kind of vague romanticism for the Irish in
America was their frequent demonstration of bigotry toward blacks.
Charles Graham Halpine, who was born in Ireland in 1829 and joined the
Sixty-ninth New York Infantry in April 1861 as a private, later became an
officer on the staff of Maj. Gen. David Hunter. It was General Hunter in
1862 who organized the first regiment of Negroes mustered into federal
service. Halpine's reaction to this challenged the feelings of Irish-Americans. Halpine, under the name of "Private Miles O'Reilly," wrote regular
pieces for the *New York Herald;* his essays and poems usually poked fun at
both the Irish and Americans, but this time his response had a bite. It was a
poem entitled, "Paddy On Sambo As A Soldier."

> Some tell us 'tis a burning shame
>   To make the naygurs fight,
> An' that the thrade of bein' kilt
>   Belongs but to the white;
> But as for me, upon my sowl!
>   So liberal are we here,
> I'll let Sambo be murdered in place of myself
>   On every day of the year, boys,
>   And every hour of the day,
> The right to be kilt I'll divide wid him,
>   An' divil a word I'll say.
> . . . . . . . . . . . . . . . . . . . . . . . . . . . . . . . . . . .
>
> The men who object to Sambo
>   Should take his place and fight;
> And it's better to have a naygur's hue
>   Than a liver that's wake and white.[22]

Lincoln's Emancipation Proclamation and congressional action on the creation of black regiments provoked the most virulent racist reaction from Irish-Americans. Written to be sung to the tune of "Wait for the Wagon," was the poem, "I Am Fighting For The Nigger":

> I calculate of niggers we soon shall have our fill,
> With Abe's proclamation and the nigger army bill.
> Who would not be a soldier for the Union to fight?
> For, Abe's made the nigger the equal of the white.
> *Chorus:* Go in for the nigger,
>           The woolly-headed nigger,
>           And cream colored moke.[23]

Subsequent stanzas of this song contained a litany of complaints, from bad food in the army and being led to slaughter, to high taxes and poor treatment of soldiers' wives. These sentiments were not limited to the Irish, but they were most prominent among them.

Humor was the saving grace of men and women living through the Civil War—as it is any war. Lincoln himself relied on the safety valve of humor to keep his sanity and cope with the horrors and trivia of office. Newspapers and magazines made regular use of comic essays, witty "fillers," jokes, and cartoons to relieve the tensions of a wartime society. Much of the humor was ethnic. Americans made good-natured and acid comments about the foreigners, the foreigners did the same for Americans, and ethnics made fun of themselves. Like fine wine, humor does not travel well. The past is a distant country, and what brought guffaws to the citizen of 1861 can wring a groan or embarrassed giggle today. Even so, the use of drollery or satire in the Civil War years gives us one more glimpse into the lives of the ethnic soldiers and their society.

Typical of the stories told about the soldiers in Irish regiments was the following:

Two gallant sons of Erin, being just discharged from the service, were rejoicing over the event with a "wee taste of the cratur," when one, who felt all the glory of his own noble race, suddenly raised his glass above and said, "Arrah, Mike, here's to the gallant ould Sixty-ninth: *The last in the field and the first to leave!*" "Tut, Tut, man," said Mike, "you don't mean that." "Don't mane it, is it?" "Then what do I mean?" "You mane," said Mike, and he raised his glass high and looked lovingly at it, "Here's to the gallant ould Sixty-ninth—*equal to none!*" And so they drank.[24]

Often repeated was some variation of the story about the Irish soldier who apparently performed an incredible deed of heroism, but who modestly admitted afterwards that he was only rescuing his whiskey flask from the enemy.

Florid oratory and elaborate ethnic symbolism associated with public ceremonies in ethnic regiments ultimately tickled the funny bone of the ethnics themselves. When New York dignitaries presented flags to the reorganized Sixty-ninth New York Infantry in November 1861, the event, even when reported seriously, came close to travesty. Handing over the Irish flag, Judge C. P. Daly let loose on the crowd a prototypical oration:

This green flag, with its ancient harp, its burst of sunlight, and its motto from Ossian in the Irish tongue, recalls through the long lapse of many centuries, the period when Ireland was a nation, and conveys more eloquently than by words how her nationality was lost through the practical working of the doctrine of secession for which the rebellious States of the South have taken up arms.[25]

The judge continued with the obligatory reference to Brian Boroimhe, to Fontenoy, Cremona, and Ramilles, to every Irishman or alleged Irishman who had anything to do with early American history, to the long history of perfidious Albion, to the exploits of Irish arms at even obscure battles related to equally obscure and confused causes, and to the racial characteristics of the Irish, which included cheerfulness, bravery, daring impetuosity, endurance, and obedience.

It was Charles Halpine's "Private O'Reilly" who finally reacted to such rhetorical excesses in a minor masterpiece of parody. O'Reilly, like the other prisoners of the Sixty-ninth New York after Bull Run, returned to New York and a celebratory banquet at the famous Delmonico's restaurant. Private O'Reilly (as he reported it for the *New York Herald*) was awestruck by the total Irishness of the affair:

The dining hall was of itself a picture, so well had the artistic effects of colors in glasses, gold and silver ware, dazzling exotics, quivering jelly palaces, and crusted battlements of charlotte russe—been studied. Where the walls were not flashing mirrors, they were covered with banners of every nationality and hue—great interest being excited by the shot and shell torn banner of the Sixty-ninth New York Volunteers, which Colonel Robert Nugent, who was present, kindly volunteered for the occasion. . . . An Irish harper, with an Irish wolfhound at his feet and an Irish harp in his hand—for the archaeological correctness of which Judge Charles P. Daly offered to give his erudite and incontrovertible certificate.[26]

O'Reilly recorded the names of all the distinguished guests, including Thomas Francis Meagher, Marcy Tweed, and a veritable host of Irish judges, lawyers, and priests. It was singularly appropriate, O'Reilly opined, that an American (A. V. Stout) presided over "an Irish demonstration for an Irish object . . . to illustrate an Irish sentiment." Meagher's reputation caught O'Reilly's sharp eye. Meagher's words, marveled the reporter, "are not less trenchant than his sword, whose genius to describe can only be surpassed by the heroism of an action which has become a part of our proudest history." Mr. Stout, who was a New York banker, told the indignant celebrants that English depositors withdrew all their money from his bank because of his notorious association with the Irish. One of the innumerable speakers during the meal, according to the scribbling private, recited a bit of poetry.

> To the flag we are pledged, all its foes we abhor,
> And we ain't for the nigger, but are for the war.

Finally, as the banquet disintegrated in drunken disorder, a rumor spread through the hall that members of the organizing committee had sold O'Reilly as a substitute.[27]

Always on hand for important ethnic occasions, Private O'Reilly accompanied Meagher to the White House when that worthy met President Lincoln. It was another grand occasion. Those present heard Meagher proclaim:

> In the golden hours of sunrise, under the silver watches of the stars, through many a damp dark night on picket duty, or in the red flame and heady fury of the battle, the thought that lay next to the heart of the Irish soldier—only dividing its glow with that of the revered relic from the altar, which piety and affection had annexed, as an amulet against harm around his neck—was the thought that he was there earning a title, which hereafter no foul tongue or niggard heart would dare dispute, to the full equality and fraternity of an American citizen.

For his contribution to the solemnity of the happening, Private O'Reilly insulted the British ambassador and sang an off-color song, whose concluding stanza was:

> There's somethin' quare in Irish air
> And a diet of pitaties,
> That makes us all so prone to fall
> To whiskey and the ladies.

Before leaving the White House, O'Reilly managed to offend all the leading members of the Lincoln administration and told Lincoln that he must give Meagher two stars because he was an Irishman.[28]

The slapstick figure of Private O'Reilly harbored a serious purpose. As a journalist Halpine witnessed at first hand the seamy side of ethnic politics in New York, and he wanted to encourage reform. He saw all too clearly that the publicity surrounding ethnic political-military heroes was simply a veneer for corruption as usual. Halpine proposed in his usual satirical manner that efficiency in city government would be improved if all the corrupt politicians formed a single large organization, the "Joint Stock Consolidated Grand Junction Lobby League," which could then steal the wealth of the city at an accelerated pace. Halpine saw through the posturing of the Meaghers and Corcorans, and his mocking portrayal of the rituals accompanying the ethnic regiments and their leaders was a harbinger of the much more famous Mr. Dooley, Peter Finley Dunne's Irish saloon keeper of the next generation.

Of all the various manifestations of ethnicity, the one that most captured the public consciousness and prompted public participation was St. Patrick's Day. While the day involved some pious gestures, most of the activity was secular, and it centered on Irish nationalism and parties. In cities and army posts 17 March during the war became a day devoted to parades, games, drinking, banquets, and general merriment. Irish hospitality was generous and it was a day when Irish regiments enjoyed public adulation. Revels on 17 March also publicized the problems within the Irish community and gave Fenians a chance to display their influence and tout their cause.

Parades in major cities were a regular feature of St. Patrick's Day even before the war, and the first wartime celebration of the day saw major recognition awarded the Irish regiments. Colonel Mulligan and his "Irish Brigade" left their duties at Camp Douglas to join the parade in Chicago. Members of many benevolent and religious organizations marched down Michigan Avenue with the Twenty-third Illinois Infantry, along with several brass bands. That evening hundreds of Irishmen and their guests consumed a banquet of oysters, fish, and cakes and drank numerous toasts at the Tremont Hotel for the benefit of the suffering poor in Ireland. A similar observance occurred in New York. There the Sixty-ninth New York Infantry paraded in new uniforms, whose cost was borne by the city council. Brass bands played Irish tunes for the marchers and spectators, and the many parading organizations included the Thomas Francis Meagher Club. Artillery salutes added to the excitement, and the day's climax came with a banquet at the Metropolitan Hotel, where the speakers included the Tammany Hall politician, Richard O'Gorman. O'Gorman was with Meagher at the Rising in 1848, and the revolutionary, like Meagher, supported the Fenians but found it politically expedient not to be a member of that organization. New Yorkers, like citizens in Chicago, cheered the St. Patrick's Day marchers and waved American flags in sympathy and thanks for the Irish soldiers fighting in Union ranks.[29]

Inspired by the performance of the Irish regiments at Antietam in late 1862, the St. Patrick's Day festivities of 1863 were a memorable climax to this ethnic ritual. It rained on the parade in Chicago, but the rain and mud failed to dampen the spirits of the marchers and watchers. Long lines of many different charitable groups filed through Chicago streets, along with banner-waving enthusiasts from Catholic temperance societies. Troops from Camp Douglas (the Twenty-third regiment was not available) as well as members of the Horse Shoers Society contributed to the procession. Once again several hundred celebrants gathered at the Tremont House for a banquet. Colonel Daniel Cameron was among the honored guests, and those present joined in thirteen toasts to everyone from St. Patrick himself to the members of the bar association. The influence of the temperance societies did not penetrate the Tremont House.[30]

New Yorkers enjoyed fine weather for their events. Street peddlers hawked paper Irish flags for one cent each, and downtown New York seemed filled with men wearing green vests or green coats and green-stripped trousers. Thanks to the cooperation of the secretary of the navy, a gunboat named the *Shamrock* was launched that morning. Mary Bryant, the daughter of William Cullen Bryant, christened the vessel, which the navy planned to man with an all-Irish crew. Mayor George Opdyke and other city officials reviewed the parade of Irish clubs, societies, and soldiers—a portion of the Sixty-ninth Infantry was on hand, as well as a carriage full of officers from the Irish Brigade. Temperance societies, longshoremen, political clubs, bands, and enthusiastic citizens paraded through the streets. The Sixty-ninth Infantry sponsored a ball that evening, but the main event was a banquet at Delmonico's once again, where speakers took note of the propensity of Irish-Americans to hold political office, and where distinguished lawyer James T. Brady (born in America but with an Irish mother, and a friend of the Fenians) told the cheering diners that St. Patrick's Day was the one day in the year when he could brag about being Irish without being regarded as a demagogue. The *New York Times* devoted most of its front page the next day to a description of events on 17 March, and appropriately enough its editorial comments on the day itself were followed by a "Requiem for the Dead of the Irish Brigade," by John Savage, a prominent Fenian. Parades occurred in cities throughout the East and Midwest. In Brooklyn, marching cadets carried a banner with the message, "All Right—Dad's Sober!" Many of the marchers in Jersey City were school children; the city's patron saint was St. Patrick.[31]

It was in the Army of the Potomac, however, where St. Patrick's Day enjoyed its most ostentatious commemoration. By 1863 the day was practically a holiday for the Union forces. Days of preparation went into very elaborate parties and games. "Last Tuesday," wrote Lieutenant Winterbotham of Corcoran's Legion to his parents from the Legion's headquarters in Virginia, "was a great day in the Brigade, 'St. Patrick's' and you must know that it is an Irishman's second Fourth of July." The Irish camp, he continued, was elaborately decorated with evergreen boughs and banners painted by an artist of the 155th New York Infantry. There was a formal review of the troops that afternoon. Winterbotham was actually quite restrained in his account. It was a day of exuberant gaiety in the Army of the Potomac. General Hooker and his staff were guests at horse races and a feast at the Irish Brigade. Meagher, decked out in a crimson coat as master of the hounds, was master of ceremonies. The 9th Massachusetts Infantry held an open house for the 62d Pennsylvania; there were barrels of beer to drink and a fifteen-day pass atop a greased pole. At the horse races two horses and a soldier were killed. There were foot races, and poetry recitations, huge bowls of a potent punch as well as ample supplies of whiskey. Fenian circles entertained guests from other regiments, and everyone was an honorary Irishman for the day. In an afterthought, Winterbotham told his parents that while the Army of the Potomac celebrated St. Patrick's Day, "the Cavalry were having quite a fight with the Enemy. . . . " That fight was the encounter between Union and Confederate cavalry at Kelly's Ford, an all-day battle involving some three thousand troopers and over two hundred casualties.[32]

By 1864 some of the good feeling disappeared from the St. Patrick's Day events. It was not simply that Chicago streets were a sea of mud. Included in the procession were four companies of Fenians, led by "Colonel" Michael Scanlan, a journalist who was the "center" of the Fenian circle there. Fenians introduced a strident and divisive note to ethnic public pageantry. The Chicago bishop was then engaged in a feud with the Fenians (the Roman hierarchy opposed the Fenians because they were a secret society and because they advocated revolution) and that soured things in the Windy City.[33] Still, the parade included the "Irish Brigade" from Wisconsin (the Seventeenth Wisconsin Infantry) and the usual collection of benevolent and temperance societies, along with other Fenian groups. The postparade banquet was held in the hall of the Fenian Brotherhood. The Fenians now were a conspicuous if not a dominating presence.

New York in 1864 had another large turnout for the parade and the parties. The *Times* estimated 20,000 marchers.[34] One disappointment of the day was the cancellation of the announced commissioning of the *Shamrock*. The navy, in the year since the ship was launched, was unable to complete its Irish crew. It was the last big St. Patrick's Day for the Army of the Potomac, and the last time ladies were on hand for the parties. The Army ordered them away the next day.

There were still big parades in 1865 — and even good weather in Chicago — but no more ethnic regiments marched in the processions. Church dignitaries played a reduced role. Temperance and abstinence societies took a more conspicuous place. The war was winding down, and recruiting of all kinds was slow. What was left of the Ninth Connecticut Infantry (it was down to battalion size) was in Savannah, Georgia, on 17 March, and it borrowed a green flag from a local Confederate Irish militia unit to carry in its modest parade.[35] The days of gala ethnic regimental celebrations were long past.

**79TH NEW YORK "SCOTCH" INFANTRY.** An important Civil War ritual was the formal dress parade of the departing regiment. Here the Seventy-ninth New York Infantry, the city's "Scotch" regiment, leaves for "the seat of war" in its distinctive uniforms. *(Harper's Weekly)*

**GARIBALDI GUARD.** The polyglot Thirty-ninth New York Infantry, known as the "Garibaldi Guard," incorporated members of at least five ethnic groups. Following one of the regimental flags, with its "Deo E Popolo" motto, the regiment files past President Lincoln in a July Fourth ceremony. *(Library of Congress)*

**COLONEL D'UTASSY.** Diminutive, colorful, and corrupt, F. G. D'Utassy led the Garibaldi Guard until his creative accounting of regimental funds sent him to prison. *(Library of Congress)*

ST. PATRICK'S DAY, ARMY OF THE POTOMAC. Everyone became an honorary Irishman on St. Patrick's Day, and horse racing was a central feature of the holiday in the Army of the Potomac. *(Library of Congress)*

A SOUTHERN VIEW OF GERMAN SOLDIERS. Adalbert J. Volck, known as "Vlad," was the most famous of Confederate cartoonists. Here he caricatures pillaging German soldiers in the tradition of Jacques Callot's "The Miseries and Disasters of War" of the seventeenth century. *(Library of Congress)*

DEATH OF COLONEL HEG. A familiar part of Civil War iconography was the lithograph of the heroic leader killed at the head of his charging regiment. Colonel Hans Christian Heg of the Fifteenth Wisconsin Infantry, the Scandinavian regiment, died a genuine hero's death at the Battle of Chickamauga. *(State Historical Society of Wisconsin)*

GENERAL MEAGHER AT FAIR OAKS. Posed by the artist next to the famous green "harp" flag of the Sixty-ninth New York Infantry, Thomas Francis Meagher urges on his Irish soldiers at the Battle of Fair Oaks. *(Library of Congress)*

SUNDAY MASS IN THE CAMP OF THE SIXTY-NINTH. The Catholic priest as regimental chaplain was a potent recruiting device for Irish regiments. Colonel Michael Corcoran of the Irish Sixty-ninth New York Infantry, arms folded, stands next to the officiating chaplain. *(Library of Congress)*

DIVINE SERVICE BY REV. P. P. COONEY. "Chaplain General" of Indiana troops, Father P. P. Cooney, chaplain of the Irish Thirty-fifth Indiana Infantry, is portrayed in a lithograph of an Easter Sunday mass. *(Indiana Historical Society)*

## Wollt Ihr
# Frieden oder Krieg?
## Die Chicago Platform.

„Beschlossen, Daß diese Versammlung ausdrücklich die Meinung des amerikanischen Volkes dahin ausspricht, daß, nach vierjährigen verfehlten Versuchen die Union durch das Experiment der Kriegführung wieder herzustellen, Gerechtigkeit, Menschlichkeit, Freiheit und öffentliche Wohlfahrt die unmittelbare Einstellung aller Feindseligkeiten verlangen, um sodann durch eine letzte Convention aller Staaten, oder durch andere friedliche Mittel, in dem möglichst schnellsten Zeitraume, die Wiederherstellung des Friedens auf der Grundlage der „föderalen Union" zu bewirken."

### Die Chicago Candidaten.
#### M'Clellan.

„Solch eine Rebellion läßt sich aus keinen sittlichen Gründen rechtfertigen und uns bleibt nur die Wahl, dieselbe entweder zu unterdrücken, oder unsre eigene Nationalität zu zerstören. Soll man in spätern Zeitaltern sagen dürfen, daß uns die Kraft mangelte, das begonnene Werk zu vollenden? Daß wir, nach dem freiwilligen Opfer so vieler edlen Kämpfer, verzagten und es unterließen, auszuhalten bis das Vaterland gerettet war."

**Westpoint Oration, den 15. Juni 1862.**

„Ich könnte keinem der tapfern Kameraden der Armee und Flotte, welche so viele blutige Schlachten geschlagen, ins Gesicht schauen und ihnen verkünden, daß alle ihre Mühen und die Aufopferung so vieler erschlagenen und verwundeten Brüder vergeblich gewesen."

**Annahme-Schreiben vom 8. Septbr. 1864.**

#### Pendleton.

„Nun, mein Herr, wo ist die Waffengewalt, welche einen Staat zwingen kann zu thun, was er zu thun eingewilligt hat? Welche Waffengewalt kann einen Staat zwingen, abzulassen von Ausführung dessen, was seine Regierung, unterstützt von der Stimme des Volkes zu thun entschlossen ist? Das ganze System eines Zwanges ist unausführbar. Es widerspricht durchaus dem Geiste des Menschen und dem der Constitution.

Mögen die secedirenden Staaten in Frieden von uns scheiden! Mögen sie sich ihr eigenes Reich und ihre eigene Regierung bilden, und ihr ferneres Schicksal lenken nach Maaßgabe derjenigen Weisheit, die Gott ihnen gegeben."

**Congreß-Rede vom 18. Januar 1860.**

### Demokraten! Könnt Ihr aufrichtig die Frage beantworten: Ob Ihr Eure Stimmen abgebt für
## Krieg oder Frieden, für Union oder Trennung!

Gedruckt bei King und Baird, No 607 Sansomstraße, Philadelphia.

WOLLT IHR FRIEDEN ODER KRIEG? "Do you want peace or war?" Both major political parties appealed to ethnic voters. This 1864 poster is aimed at German-American Democrats. *(Illinois State Historical Library)*

PICKETS OF THE SIXTY-NINTH PENNSYLVANIA INFANTRY. An 1863 sketch of the Irish Sixty-ninth Pennsylvania Infantry suggests that in the field there was little to distinguish the ethnic regiment from its American counterpart. *(Library of Congress)*

**MILITARY REGISTER.**
After the war the memorial lithograph was a popular souvenir for veteran soldiers. This example is of a company in the Irish Twenty-third Illinois Infantry. The iconography used was the same for ethnic and nonethnic regiments. *(Illinois State Historical Library)*

**ENLISTING IRISH AND GERMAN IMMIGRANTS.** Union recruiters enticed immigrants literally right off the docks at New York's Castle Garden, a practice that led to Confederate charges that the Union employed foreign mercenaries. *(Library of Congress)*

**IRISH BRIGADE DEAD AT ANTIETAM.** A Matthew Brady photograph of dead soldiers of the Irish Brigade on the field at Antietam. *(Library of Congress)*

# The Ethnic Factor

I want to be a kurnel,
 With orfissers tu stand;
A kommishun in my poket,
 A sord within my hand.
I'm tired ov staing raound hear,
 Ambishun fills my brest —
O! I long fur a kemmishun,
 And I'd be a kurnel best!

My bussum's daily burnin
 With pattriottick zeel,
No wurds my thorts kan utter,
 Nor tell harf what I feel!
Wood I kood jine aour army,
 Tu meat the rebbel foe;
O! I long tu be a kernel —
 Deer Guvernur, let me go!

—"The Song of the Aspiring Man," *Harper's Weekly,* 13 December 1862

UNE 1861: Three hundred Germans, accompanied by a brass band, rioted and pillaged in the streets of Milwaukee. They cursed the mayor and police chief, stoned these and other city leaders, and looted several commercial buildings. When the Montgomery Guards, an Irish militia company, confronted the mob, stones and epithets drove them away. Fearful of the uncontrolled violence, Mayor James S. Brown began to swear in citizen volunteers as a posse. Responding to ringing fire bells, two engine companies drove to the scene. Another company of city militia, the Milwaukee Zouaves, guarded the firemen while they fought the fires. The mayor telegraphed an appeal to the state capital in Madison for four additional companies of soldiers. The Zouaves managed to wrest a cannon away from the hands of the rampaging Germans. By nightfall, two companies of troops from Racine and two from Madison patrolled city streets, and German leaders met in a saloon in the Ninth Ward to debate their next move. Local newspapers, in subsequent days, deplored the ethnic conflict, and the episode ended with no more rioting.[1]

This was Milwaukee, one of the most thoroughly German of American cities, and certainly the city where Germans felt most at home and very much a part of the local power structure. Was this a "race riot," an outbreak of hostilities between an ethnic minority and the Anglo establishment, or between two different ethnic groups (the Montgomery Guards, hooted at by the Germans, were Irish)? Not really. While the event acquired a certain ethnic coloration, its origin and development had little if anything to do with the ethnic composition of the mob. This was a protest against certain city banks by depositors living in German neighborhoods, who were stirred up by fiery speakers assailing the "monied interests" and the aristocracy. Marxist historians looking for evidence of class conflict might well seize upon the June rioting in Milwaukee as an illustration of the endless class struggle. Psychohistorians could examine the legitimate grievances of the bank customers, ponder their rage at being swindled and then pandered to by civic leaders like banker Alexander Mitchell, and decide that this event should be understood in terms of mob psychology. Ignoring the significance of the location and time of the episode, German-American scholars might argue that the riots were one more example of the long history of prejudice and oppression Germans suffered at the hands of the Anglo-American majority. We each go to the magic mirror of the past and find reflected in it what we want to see.

This was June 1861, but the riot had little to do with the Civil War. The timing was largely fortuitous. Not all of the violence of the Civil War years was an outgrowth of the war.

In St. Louis one month earlier, German soldiers marching along city streets heard shouts of "Damn the Dutch" from churlish secessionists. Those jeers and taunts were universally seen as anti-German prejudice.[2] The stones and insults hurled in St. Louis, however, represented political feelings much more directly than ethnic prejudice. Germans wearing Confederate uniforms prompted cheers from southerners, and those wearing blue uniforms in northern streets heard approving shouts.

John England, a soldier in "Hawkin's Zouaves" (the Ninth New York Infantry) and an Irish-American from New York, reacted vehemently to the news of the draft riots in New York in July 1863. There was no doubt in his mind that the cause of the violence was the three-hundred-dollar exemption clause in the conscription law. The riotous Irishmen in New York, he thought, justly opposed an immoral law that favored the rich at the expense of the poor. England longed for an America free of discrimination between rich and poor—but not an America free of discrimination toward the black. He rejoiced at the news of a white mob beating and killing Negroes and hoped the treatment would be repeated at frequent intervals.[3] He denounced critics of the rioters, especially Horace Greeley and William Cullen Bryant, as anti-Irish bigots. Vandals and protestors rampaging through the streets of New York and other northern cities in July 1863 provided evidence of class conflict, race hatred, opposition to the Lincoln administration, frustration at the conduct of the war, excitement of crowd behavior, and thousands of individual motives. It is reductionist to see them in simple ethnic terms. Any ethnic activity of consequence involved more than ethnicity.

On both a casual and profound level racism and nativism pervaded the thinking of most people of the Civil War generation. The racism was not simply white versus black; it included the assumption that all ethnic groups had distinct characteristics, and the label of "race" applied to Germans, Scots, French, English, Irish, and all other peoples. Americans were regarded as different. While they had their own traits, they were not seen as a "race" in the same sense as peoples of the Old World. This use of race was common in other countries as well as the United States. Germans in Germany as well as Germans in America used the term about themselves as well as other peoples. The Irish in Ireland did it as well as the Irish in America. And so it was with all peoples. It was simply one of those things taken for granted, a given. The same attitude and the same phrases occurred in everyday conversation, in scholarly literature, and in political debate. It was not something that separated liberal from conservative, or North from South, or one ethnic group from another.

More than a decade after the war ended, when former Union general John Cochrane published his memoirs, he parroted the language and attitudes common in America during the war years. Cochrane, born in New York of Irish descent, was a congressman before the war and was the colonel of an American regiment before he became a brigadier. He was a candidate for vice-president on the Frémont ticket, and after the war he was a major figure in Tammany Hall politics and a popular man on the lecture circuit. In a word, he was what the late twentieth century described as an "establishment" personage. General Cochrane recalled the "native" soldier in the Union forces as typically a conscript rather than a volunteer, lacking in zeal and fire, but with a determination to see things through to the end. Immigrant soldiers, in Cochrane's recollection, held flaming partisan views, had dash and spirit, volunteered eagerly, and had real martial ardor.[4] Germans were phlegmatic, Celts impulsive, Germans grave, and Celts gay. The foreigners were the better soldiers because their natural traits were superior to those of the Americans.

Many people firmly believed, despite all the evidence to the contrary, that immigrants instinctively supported the Union, and given the chance, deserted the South and sought their compatriots in northern regiments. Innumerable anecdotes testified to this practice. General Horace Porter, for example, told a story about a Confederate soldier in the Fort Pulaski garrison who succumbed to the allure of German songs and the German language emanating from the lines of the Forty-sixth New York Infantry (the Frémont Rifles) and escaped from the fort to betray his comrades to the New York Germans.[5] Such tales overlook the substantial amount of desertion in both armies involving all kinds of soldiers.

People attributed to ethnicity whatever qualities they wanted to advance their particular cause. Massachusetts educator Charles Brooks in early 1865 encouraged a scheme of compulsory, standard national education. One reason we needed such a plan, he argued, was that immigrants held ideas and views contrary to those of native Americans. He even raised the spectre of a plot by other countries to ship enough people here to overwhelm Americans through sheer numbers and then take over the country. The way to cope with this danger, he insisted, was educating young foreigners in American ways.[6] Where Cochrane found foreigners superior, Brooks found them dangerously different.

As an Irish-American, Cochrane regarded Germans as phlegmatic. Edward Buegger, a Swiss immigrant who served in the Ninth Wisconsin Infantry, identified himself as a German serving in a German regiment and bestowed quite different characteristics on his comrades. They were congenitally jolly and gay — the very properties Cochrane ascribed to the Celts.[7]

Ancient Greeks thought of themselves as being different from everybody else. While that difference was fundamentally a matter of language, it included an element of superiority. Greeks were free men, and their minds were rational, properties not shared by barbarians. Hebrews recognized sharp distinctions between Jews and non-Jews. Members of North American tribes assumed that they were fully human, and others were not. The perception that the stranger, the foreigner, is both different and inferior, is a regular part of the human condition.

Edward C. Hubbard, sergeant-major of the Thirteenth Illinois Infantry, noticed neither jollity nor dash when soldiers of the Seventh Missouri Infantry (the Missouri Irish Brigade) set up camp near his outfit. "It is said," he wrote to a friend, "that there are 800 men, and the first day they came here there were 900 fights." This kind of casual slur recorded not a quantitative analysis of the appearance of the Irish soldiers, but an automatic and expected social response to a given situation. It had less bite and insult to it than many a geographic anecdote, when persons from one state or region spoke disparagingly of those from a different location. Much more insulting was Hubbard's later reaction to German soldiers. "Americans can curse the day," he wailed, "that a dutchman joined her army. They rob and steal from every sutler all, all they have, to the last ounce." And two months later his rage grew:

> Everyone in the whole command had hoped that those *animals,* the G-d-d-d-d dutch would go in one direction, and the white men in another.

> I used to think any white man was better than a negro, but I had rather sleep or eat with a negro than a dutchman.[8]

Whatever the nature of Hubbard's experience with his German allies, his sharp words described a highly emotional situation. There was at least a touch of intended humor toward the Irish, but the Irish spoke English and many Germans did not; that made them much more alien.

John Winterbotham, who helped organize a company for an Irish regiment (the 155th New York Infantry), lived for years in the awkward daily situation of an American in an Irish regiment, as an officer over Irish enlisted men. This left him with mixed emotions. There was a sense of superiority toward them, a compound of an officer with some education dealing with uneducated or poorly educated men, coupled with the ethnic difference. He told his family about payday in his regiment:

> The paymaster arrived with a supply of greenbacks receiving his usual joyous welcome at the hands of the officers and men of the Irish Legion. Many a poor fellow exalted in the thought of how much good his $26 would do his Bridget, his Mary or his Biddy at home in New York and how as one remarked he would send it by "telegraph" per Adams Express, while others wished for a good drink "on the head of it."

His stance combined a sense of class superiority with an ethnic put-down, but the latter involved affectionate good humor with the insult. He regularly praised his men, but he was consistently critical of his fellow officers, especially Col. Hugh Flood, whom he described as a fool and rascal, with nary a hint of good nature or humor in his words. Colonel Flood, claimed Winterbotham, was a "cunning Irishman" who acquired high office by intrigue, and who, along with his friends, stole regimental funds. Young Winterbotham's righteous indignation, however, stemmed less from ethnic animosity and moral disgust than it did from frustrated ambition. He waged an unsucessful campaign to get the post of major in the 155th New York Infantry. Ethnic relationships always involved nonethnic elements.[9]

Disputes between ethnics and Americans, as often as not, emerged from their different backgrounds and perceptions rather than from xenophobia or innate distrust. Hugh B. Ewing of Ohio, the son of a United States senator and secretary of the treasury, came from a privileged American family whose members were staunch patriots. Hugh attended West Point but failed to graduate, and when the war began in 1861 he enlisted promptly in an Ohio regiment. First a major in the Thirtieth Ohio Infantry, he rose to colonel and by 1863 was a brigadier. Hugh Ewing was an ambitious, literate, and intelligent American officer, one who felt a sense of responsibility for the men of his command and who combined West Point experience with the Civil War system of officer election. In his autobiography Ewing described an encounter he had with Col. Augustus Moor. Moor, a fellow Ohioan was also a German, born in the Old Country and educated in the Prussian military tradition. Moor led the Twenty-eighth Ohio Infantry and later commanded a brigade. One day in 1862 Colonel Moor, angered when an enlisted man in Ewing's regiment failed to get out of his way with alacrity when ordered to do so, struck the man with his sword. When Ewing heard what happened, he rode to Moor's headquarters to demand an apology:

> He was at table [Ewing recalled] with his Staff and Colonels, drinking Ohio wine from long-necked bottles, and smoking, and presented quite an old-time German scene. I told him I would not tolerate the German custom of treating common soldiers, if applied to my men, by any officer. . . . I preserved discipline by taking care of my troops, collectively and individually.[10]

Moor promptly apologized for the incident. Ewing admired the drill and discipline of the German regiments, but he promoted a different environment in his own regiment, one better suited to Americans, in his judgment. The episode illustrated not nativism but a typical example of an officer preserving his turf and at the same time recognizing the validity of the German military tradition for other units.

Americans serving in ethnic regiments often complained that they felt out of place and mistreated. Their unhappiness was not simply the result of ethnic prejudice. It included such other factors as religious beliefs (a Protestant in an Irish Catholic unit), partisan politics (a Republican surrounded by Democrats), rigid and formal discipline (the Prussian martinet as colonel), personal ambition (the valid assumption that the majority favored its own kind in the matter of promotions), and the middle-class prejudice against working-class drinking habits.[11]

Ethnic soldiers shared all of these attitudes and experiences in what amounted to a mirror image of the American perspective. A German soldier, stinging from a rebuke by an American officer, readily rationalized his feelings by assigning blame—not to any failure of his own—but to anti-German prejudice. An Irish officer, frustrated in his drive for promotion, sought transfer to an Irish regiment to escape what he perceived as anti-Irish prejudice. A semiliterate German private, with no understanding of English, complained of his treatment at the hands of American officers, and attributed it not to his own status, but to prejudice on the part of those officers. A German sergeant, grieving at the casualties suffered by his comrades, charged his "Yankee" officer with not caring what happened to "Dutch" soldiers. While American soldiers worried about Fenian plots and favoritism, Irishmen in American regiments fumed over alleged conniving by Masons to care for their own and discriminate against Catholics. That prejudice and favoritism existed was beyond doubt. It was equally certain that individuals rationalized their condition by ignoring other factors and laying all blame at the door of prejudice. Favoritism and unfair influence took many forms in the Civil War regiment, and its most frequent manifestation was political, not ethnic.[12]

A German soldier, bitterly grumbling about his lot, was likely in the next breath to brag about how much better life in the American army was to life in a German regiment. Here the pay was much better, the discipline lax, relations with officers more relaxed, the food more plentiful, and the leisure time abundant. The Irish soldier fretting about the possibility of a Protestant chaplain, wanted a competent regimental surgeon, with skill paramount over religion. All soldiers believed that other regiments got better treatment than theirs; the ethnics attributed the difference to ethnic prejudice. The strength of this feeling of biased treatment shows in the low rate of reenlistment in veteran regiments by ethnics.[13]

In the early months of the war while he was observing developments throughout the northern states, Ferri Pisani made a stop in St. Louis, the scene of the dramatic confrontation between German regiments and Confederate sympathizers. What he saw and heard shocked the sophisticated European visitor. General Frémont assigned two officers to escort Prince Napoleon's party around the city. Both officers were foreign born and German speaking. One was a Swiss, Col. Francis J. Joliat of the Fifteenth Missouri Infantry; the other was a German, Col. Peter Osterhaus of the Twelfth Missouri Infantry.

What the party and its guides saw and heard were German officers loudly denouncing American soldiers. "Yankees" were insulted and demeaned, dismissed as incompetent and dependent upon the skills of Germans to fight their war for them. Ferri Pisani thought it odd that foreigners enjoying the trust, pay, and hospitality of America should be so vehement in their criticisms.

> If we were to judge the United States by the talk heard about the St. Louis headquarters [he wrote] one could easily believe that the heirs of Washington, Jefferson, Franklin, and Jackson have become a people of selfish and cowardly *nouveaux riches,* whose only social mission is to pay the brave children of the German fatherland to defend them, their institutions—of which they are unworthy—and the great principles of freedom.[14]

German officers expressed contempt and hostility toward the U.S. regulars as well as the state volunteers, and even West Pointers bore their scorn. A special target of derision was Col. Charles F. Smith, an officer greatly admired by Grant and one who later earned a reputation as one of the best officers in the Union army. Joliat and Osterhaus were chagrined that their foreign guests heard these imprecations. Such remarks, however, were common currency in the Civil War; native Americans did not hold a monopoly on xenophobia.

Ethnic soldiers reserved their sharpest barbs for fellow ethnics. Within the ethnic regiments, where Old Country emotions ran strong, traditional hostilities surfaced as part of the intellectual baggage that crossed the Atlantic. Scandinavians in Europe held little affection for Germans; serving with Germans in an American war did not change their minds. To some naive American officials, all Europeans were alike, and there was a tendency to fill in the ranks of ethnic regiments by throwing in a company or two of a different nationality. When Hecker's second German regiment (the Eighty-second Illinois Infantry) proved slow to fill, the adjutant general added a Scandinavian company. Fireworks erupted immediately. Captain Ivar A. Weid of the Scandinavians telegraphed an objection from Chicago. It is a mistake to put my company into Hecker's regiment, he told Adjutant General Fuller. "Germans and Scandinavians never agree. They are natural enemies."[15] The other officers and men of the company shared Captain Weid's opinion. As another Scandinavian officer put it:

> The facts are simply this: there have for many centuries existed a great national Enmity between the Scandinavian and German nations, which feeling of national hatered is daily exhibited in this country, as much as it is in Europe.

Save us from Hecker, pleaded the descendants of Vikings. We want to be commanded by an American, they told the authorities. As their final argument, they insisted that few of their number knew any German, but at least some knew English.[16] Even the much admired Hans Heg of Wisconsin voiced criticism of Germans. (One of the motives of Wisconsin Scandinavians in forming their regiment was to counter the earlier similar moves by the Germans.) After his regiment went into the field, Heg told his wife, "I want to see them drive some of the Germans into the Army from around Waterford."[17]

Tension and mutual contempt often characterized relations between Germans and Hungarians. The history of the Garibaldi Guard dramatized this. The Twenty-fourth Illinois Infantry, while largely German, had some Hungarians among its members. Surgeon William Wagner, who kept state authorities abreast of regimental news, bristled on the subject of Hungarians. Hungarian Captain Kovats, he wrote to Adjutant General Fuller, is ignorant and has "undue Hungarian pride." Kovats regularly spoke contemptuously toward Germans, and Wagner urged Fuller to deny promotion to the Hungarian.[18] "Deserving Germans" should get such promotions. For good measure, Wagner lashed out at the Slavs in the regiment, a group he described as intriguers. Only the Germans, of course, were good fighters.

Like other ethnics, the Germans objected to outsider criticism aimed at one of their own, but there was vigorous censure of Germans by Germans themselves. John T. Buegel, whose initial enlistment in a St. Louis German regiment occurred in part because of his desire to hit out at the city's Anglo-Saxons, had little use for Franz Sigel. He thought the general was too ambitious, and he felt the same way about Frémont, despite the adulation usually heaped on him by Germans. Buegel had a keen eye for humbug, and when a Lieutenant Colonel Bischoff joined Buegel's German regiment, the St. Louis soldier quickly concluded that the newcomer was a phoney. Among his many faults, Bischoff curried favor with the Americans. Buegel rejoiced when Bischoff ended the disruption he caused within the regiment by dying.[19]

No critic of the Germans was more strident than the German journalist, Karl Heinzen. In the pages of the *Pionier* Heinzen ridiculed claims that Germans were the best soldiers in the Union forces and poked fun at the elaborate ceremonies surrounding regimental flag presentations and departures. It was Heinzen, not Americans, who tried to drive General Blenker out of the army, and he published strong critisms of Sigel and other German officers. But when Americans found fault with the behavior of German troops at Chancellorsville, Heinzen closed ranks with fellow Germans and defended those troops against this revival of nativism. Like other educated German immigrants, Heinzen regarded German culture as superior to that of America, and belittled the notion that Germans should create a hybrid German-American culture. At the same time he recognized that German snobbery and the flouting of strongly held American beliefs by the Germans encouraged xenophobia. By the end of the Civil War Heinzen was objecting to continued large-scale immigration, and he particularly objected to the admission of "raw and uncouth" Irish Catholics.[20]

Irish and German soldiers occasionally found each other continuing in uniform the brawls they had in city streets as civilians. The legendary Irish propensity for violence was eclectic; it was directed at other ethnics as well as themselves and Americans. In his column for the *Irish American,* James Turner expressed the resentment his Irish readers held toward the Jews. In lurid language he referred to Jews as the "pestiferous and poisonous purveyors of armies." The Irishman instinctively knows, he wrote, that with no remorse a Jew would "filch the last copper from the hands of improvident youth, from the imbecile." Jews lie, plunder, and carry the mark of an enraged God, he argued and concluded with the traditional charge that Jews were Christ-killer. Themselves the victims of bias and prejudice, Irish-Americans held fast to as many warped opinions as any of their countrymen.[21]

Ethnic soldiers told the same kinds of jokes on each other and their fellow ethnics as Americans told on them. Their state loyalties or socioeconomic status likely outweighed any attachment to ethnic group.[22] Overwhelmingly their personal interests coincided with those of American soldiers. And in most circumstances, different ethnic soldiers got along well with each other and with native Americans.

In mixed regiments, those with an American majority or plurality and with a mixture of ethnic minorities, problems of bias and prejudice were minimal and relations between the various groups good. Such a regiment was the Nineteenth Illinois Infantry. In addition to native Americans, its membership included men from Germany, Ireland, and England. When it was organized, the outfit had a choice between U.S. Grant and John Basil Turchin for its colonel. Perhaps bedazzled by the glamour of a former member of Russia's Imperial Guard and the awe in which foreign officers were held in the early days of the war, the men chose Turchin. The new colonel, who was a railroad employee when the war began, had some experience in the Crimean War and got a thorough military education in Russia. Under Turchin's leadership the Nineteenth Illinois (a Zouave unit) quickly acquired a reputation for precision in drill and high morale. Traditional state politics, not ethnic politics, mark the history of the regiment; a variety of Illinois politicians made the usual interference in its affairs, and Turchin himself was interested in his personal career, not in promoting an ethnic cause. When the officers of the Nineteenth Illinois pursued their career ambitions, they did it without recourse to ethnic politics. When trouble and internal dissension plagued the unit, it carried no ethnic overtones. Germans comprised the largest ethnic group, but neither they nor the Irish left a record of ethnic conflict or prejudice. The combat record of the regiment was commendable; its reputation for poor discipline had nothing to do ethnicity.[23] The troubles Turchin encountered with state and federal officials were not an outgrowth of his ethnicity. This is not to say that all was sweetness and light in a mixed regiment, but rather that away from the artificial atmosphere in the ethnic unit, the universal conditions of soldiers in wartime took precedence over ethnic relationships.

"In the end," concluded T. Harry Williams, "much of the effectiveness of a Civil War army came down to the personal qualities of its colonels."[24] The citizen army created by the North included about 1600 regiments commanded by civilians, not professional soldiers. In the early days of the war, most of those colonels (and the other field officers) attained their positions by the vote of those regiments; a few were appointed by governors without an election. The guiding spirit of a regiment, in Williams's words, was its colonel. He educated himself and his subordinates, attended to the most elementary details of military life (made certain that basic hygiene was enforced and that firearm discipline was kept), walked a fine line between discipline and popularity, and frequently served as a father figure for frightened youngsters away from home for the first time. A colonel with a colorful personality or with a prominent position in civilian life personified a regiment; his name attracted recruits and newspapers gave state and national recognition to many of those names. Colonels and other officers dealt with soldiers who were really civilians temporarily in uniform; virtually all were volunteers. The best colonels were shrewd judges of men, balanced authority with at least the appearance of democracy, displayed courage in crisis, and used caution when advisable. They learned how to work with and use the state and national bureaucracy to exploit the system to maintain and promote their units, and to get financial and moral support from the folks back home. The qualities of a good colonel were those of a good politician. The system encouraged men to carry over into military life any practices and techniques that worked well for them in civilian politics.

Professional ethnic politicians turned into professional ethnic colonels—and even generals. As politicians, professional ethnics denied themselves the prospect of national power and set boundaries to their statewide influence for the advantage of a safe but limited power base. Professional ethnic politicians exercised a role as power brokers; they bargained with traditional leaders to win personal advantage and gains for their voting bloc. Their claims and their abilities to manipulate significant numbers of votes won limited and sometimes prominent success, at the cost of always playing a subordinate and never a dominant role in party affairs. It was a system that encouraged and often rewarded short-term advances while it made unattainable longer-term and more substantial benefits.

Professional ethnic politicians by 1861 carved out an important niche in American politics. Their rhetoric focused the consciousness of members of ethnic groups and provided an identity that otherwise might fade away.[25] Social psychologist Kurt Lewis argued that there was a tendency for ethnic political leaders in American to be "marginal to their own groups" and, under the guise of group loyalty, be fundamentally eager to leave the group. Thomas Meagher typified this role. Meagher's rhetoric passionately cultivated group identity and pride. He deliberately turned upside down the language of prejudice and glorified a kind of reverse prejudice. He created an image of the Irishman as a natural fighter, a nationalist, an exile from a glorious green island, a brave and superior being. This was in Meagher's world, a "pardonable prejudice."[26] The assumption behind the "pardonable prejudice" was the virtue of an exclusive political and military world, inhabited by fortunate and superior Irishmen, dedicated to the promotion of Irish legend, Irish nationalism, ethnic pride, and the careers of the leaders. Underprivileged groups (which the Irish were in 1861 in America), according to Lewis, tended to select leaders relatively acceptable to the larger society; Meagher, Corcoran, Cass, Mulligan, and the other ethnic regiment leaders certainly supported that generalization.

Meagher's willingness, indeed enthusiasm, for abandoning the Democratic party and supporting the Lincoln administration in 1864 to advance his personal career adds further support for the Lewis profile. All professional ethnic colonels willingly abandoned the principle of ethnic purity for their regiments for the sake of preserving and advancing their own status.

When they entered the military, professional ethnic leaders carried with them the successful tactic of making claims on the government for themselves in the name of an ethnic presence or quota. A striking difference between the Irish, German, Scottish, or other ethnic group leader following the professional ethnic route and others was his insistence that the government owed him an appointment, advancement, and recognition, not on the basis of ability or achievement, but because he was a symbol. Thus Meagher went to Lincoln and demanded support because Irish-Americans deserved it, not because Meagher deserved it.[27] Meagher and Mulligan distanced themselves publicly from the Fenians to burnish their image with the larger society. Ethnic colonels and generals and their home-base supporters practiced the kind of quota politics familiar to city and state party organizations. The greater their success, the stronger the resistance in Washington, and the greater the skepticism with which nonethnic officers regarded their ethnic counterparts.

The successes of the Corcorans and Blenkers attracted to the field the real tricksters like Lionel D'Epineuil. War and uncommonly rapid growth were a golden opportunity for fraud; the only difference between D'Epineuil and the native confidence man was his skill at exploiting the system of ethnic politics. When his natural ineptness led to chaos and disaster for the Fifty-third New York Infantry, the critical function of the Civil War colonel was evident. General McClellan ordered the dissolution of "D'Epineuil's Zouaves" with a single telling sentence:

> This reg't was mustered out of the service because it was found to be in a demoralized condition and according to the Inspection Report it became so through the inefficiency of the Colonel.[28]

As a recent immigrant, just an adventurer after fame and fortune in a foreign war, D'Epineuil had no political base in New York. When his time of troubles came, he had no support group, no powerful patron to rescue him or provide alternative employment. It was the same with D'Utassy. Other inept, corrupt, or lackluster colonels (it was the same with nonethnics) could count on rescue. There could be a transfer to a post that carried no real responsibility, a resignation and then appointment to a patronage job, or removal to a remote location. There was even the ultimate sinecure — an order to go home and await further orders, all the while remaining in rank and on the payroll.

When appointments and promotions occurred primarily for ethnic political reasons, the results tended to be unfavorable.[29] When Archbishop

John Hughes urged Seward to make Corcoran a general solely on the grounds that it would placate the Irish community, he knowingly participated in a process that endangered the lives of soldiers by placing them in the hands of poor leaders. The same risk occurred, of course, when the ardent abolitionist, staunch Republican, or War Democrat got a commission because of his symbolic importance. And as Ezra J. Warner concluded, the risk of appointing a Meagher was less than the risk of alienating a large immigrant community by not making the appointment.

Franz Sigel, who began his military career for the Union as the colonel of a German regiment in St. Louis, followed a course thereafter.that clearly illustrated the Lewis analysis. Despite his European background, Sigel's leadership of an ethnic regiment was quite undistinguished. What he did have was a strong political base in the German community. When efforts to get an immediate promotion for him failed to get a prompt response in Washington, cries of ethnic prejudice came from his claque. By August 1861, thanks in part to such ethnic agitation, he was promoted. General Halleck had no confidence in Sigel's abilities and tried to shunt him off to a post where he could do little harm. Sigel threatened to resign, and the resultant political fire storm in the German community brought a new command and still another promotion for Sigel. There is no doubt that Sigel's advancement was nothing more than Washington's gesture toward the Germans to assure their continued advocacy of the Union cause. Sigel was inept and a constant trial for the administration and the military, but his political popularity protected him from dismissal. What he could not win on the battlefield, he won through canny politics. "His first priority," asserted Murray M. Horowitz, "was consistently that of cultivating his German-American consituency as a means of furthering his own political fortunes."[30] When Lincoln made Alexander Schimmelfennig a general, he had doubts about the man's competency. He accepted the risk on the ground that Schimmelfennig's name was so obviously German that it would insure the favor of German voters. German, Irish, and Scandinavian men enlisting in ethnic regiments were witting or unwitting supporting actors in a complex political drama. The plot centered on status.

Sociologist Daniel Bell, in a penetrating analysis of the behavior of ethnic groups, argued that ethnicity is a means to an end: "In the competition for the values of the society to be realized politically, ethnicity can become a means of claiming place or advantage."[31] Ethnic politicians practice status politics. Officers in ethnic regiments practiced the same status politics.

Cynthia H. Enloe, in her pioneering work *Ethnic Soldiers: State Security in Divided Societies,* argued that *any* civil war must be viewed from the perspective of the military-ethnic connection.[32] According to Enloe, authority figures within a given community gather recruits in much the same way they mobilize voters. To that extent, the operations of ethnic leaders and followers in the American Civil War fit her model. But Enloe, who drew most of her evidence from Asian and African experience, saw the ethnic group or groups largely in terms of a security threat to the nation and a management problem for those controlling the society. When she turned her attention to the American Civil War, she devoted most of her attention to blacks, and the reluctance of the North to use black soldiers and the fear in the South over such use. At least to a degree, her view of blacks in the Civil War supported the record of ethnic troops in other societies and other times.

Enloe went astray when she examined the history of immigrants in the North. "State security planners" she argued, treated recent immigrants as though they were outside the nation-state political system in the early part of the war, as they did blacks. Exactly the reverse happened. Immigrants in the North participated in main-stream politics, both at the national and state levels. And far from regarding immigrants as a threat to national security, state and federal authorities from the very beginning of the war eagerly recruited ethnics, both as individuals in regular regiments and in accepting the ethnic regiments for military service. (Much the same thing can be said of the South, where immigrants proved loyal to their region.) In sharp and happy contrast to most of the rest of the world and perhaps most of history as well, the United States had nothing to fear from ethnic units. No security threat at all, ethnic Americans in 1861 added their strength to that of native-born citizens.

Strong opinions about the past reveal efforts to manipulate the future. In the words of the Commissar in George Orwell's *1984,* he who controls the past controls the future. In today's climate of opinion, any efforts to create an ethnic unit in the armed forces would elicit cries of prejudice and segregation. No Irish-American or German-American would countenance such action. Today's Irish-American or German-American is not the same as his Civil War ancestor, but ethnic politicians and historians continue to use a moralistic and filiopietistic view of the past to wring concessions or power from society for members of their groups. Thomas Sowell, in *Ethnic America,* concluded that the failure to apply ordinary standards of critical scholarship to the history of ethnic groups concealed the truth.[33] The ultimate victims of that failure are the ethnics themselves. If they accept a morality play with themselves as victims and everyone else as exploiters as a substitute for critical historical analysis, they will never understand the complex factors that produced the present society and their status in it. Today's Irish-American would find repugnant the personal behavior of his nineteenth-century ancestors. Today's German-American must remain perplexed about how his status differs from earlier generations, unless he studies conflict *within* the German-American community as well as relationships between Germans and non-Germans.

# "What Then Is the American, This New Man?"

The Mansion of History, which has always been located
directly in the forum of the community, has many rooms.
Some of the shops on the ground floor of the Mansion,
selling goods on the busy thoroughfare, are the equivalent
of the penny arcade. The mythmakers, using the materials
of history for non-historical purposes, call out their wares,
while hawkers push shoddy fakes hastily produced without
fear and without research.

—CARL G. GUSTAVSON, *The Mansion of History*

HE past is infinitely various," notes Oxford University historian
Michael Howard, "an inexhaustible storehouse of events from
which we can prove anything or its contrary." History is what the
historian writes, he continues, and everything we believe about
the present depends upon what we believe about the past. This gives the
historian the opportunity of helping to shape the future, but it also imposes
the obligation of constant vigilance against present-mindedness. From
World War I to the Vietnam War, historians all too often tailored their
scholarship to fit contemporary prejudice.[1] Some historians, determined to
reform what they regarded as a fatally flawed society, deliberately abandoned the ideal of objectivity and shaped the past into a cudgel with which
to pummel the present.[2] To be sure, all historians are to some extent
mythmakers. In a democratic society, the challenge is to create a myth as
close as possible to reality and also retain intellectual integrity. Efforts to
create a usable past should include the conservation of those values in
Western society that permit and encourage the freedom to research and
publish an unlimited variety of myths.

One person's myth is another's reality.[3] One of the more persistent and
commonly accepted American myths pervades ethnic history. More often
than not, writers of the history of any ethnic group divide the total population into members of their group and everybody else. Everybody else then
automatically becomes "the Americans." This approach virtually guaran-

tees an image in which a small minority confronts an overwhelming majority. The history of the ethnic regiments challenges such images; it contends that the majority is mythical, that it really consists of many other minorities, and that one key to understanding America is found in a candid examination of those intergroup relationships. That history also asserts America is more than a collection of groups; it is a collection of ideals. For most members of ethnic groups the ideals are more important than group membership.

The facts of history are both essential and trivial. There can be no history without verifiable facts, but the art of the historian consists in arranging facts into a credible pattern. Facts cannot speak for themselves, and when the historian speaks for them, he gropes for a pattern that others will recognize as a shared truth, a truth with survival value. Without such shared truths, no society can long preserve itself. William H. McNeill in his 1985 presidential address to the American Historical Association declared, "Historians are . . . under perpetual temptation to conform to expectation by portraying the people they write about as they wish to be."[4] An even stronger temptation for some historians is to regard themselves as the possessor of divine knowledge, the ultimate and ugly truth about America. What the true believer—to use Eric Hoffer's phrase—lacks is a sense of humor and a sense of humility. Ethnicity and nativism are highly charged subjects. Ethnic historiography, for the most part, perfectly illustrates McNeill's dictum. Its practitioners seldom resist the temptation he identifies. Ethnic history gains maturity only to the extent it applies to itself the standards of evidence and critical analysis found in other fields.

Recent years witnessed the development of two conflicting schools of thought about American culture. One school rests on the assumption that the contemporary era is characterized by the nationalization and homogenization of American society. The other emphasizes the powerful forces of disunity, of class differences, of the persistence of racial, ethnic, religious, and gender conflicts. Fixing personal loyalties is one of the most critical decisions made by each individual. Each person has many choices. "Historians," avers William McNeill, "by helping to define 'us' and 'them,' play a considerable part in focusing love and hate, the two principal cements of collective behavior known to humanity." Americans, like all of humanity, share a common past as well as a past of individual and group differences. Caught in the maelstrom of the Civil War, ethnic Americans for the most part rejected those mythmakers who would exploit the American agony to promote personal ambition and increase centrifugal forces. The evidence of the ethnic regiments is that most foreign-born Americans of the Civil War generation made their individual choices on the side of common ideals, in favor of the myth of the shared community.[5]

In the spring of 1861, amid all the excitement and fervor accompanying the outbreak of the war, the St. Louis *Westliche Post* eloquently urged German-Americans to make personal choices supporting the image of a free America. What was at hand, proclaimed the newspaper, was nothing less than the second American Revolution.[6] This revolution, more important than the first, was the reaffirmation of the American ideal. It announced to the world a renewed commitment to America as the haven for the oppressed and the poor, of America as a "pillar of fire" lighting the way to a homeland for the wretched of the earth. This mythic republic, this inspiration for peoples in other lands, demanded the support of decent people so that it might continue to inspire future generations of mankind. Young Henry Kircher, who quite literally sacrificed an arm and a leg to fight for the Union in a German regiment, lacked the lofty rhetoric of the *Post,* but he and the other Belleville Germans shared that newspaper's devotion to the ideal of America.[7]

Just as the recent past observed the evolution of two opposing interpretations of the meaning of American culture, it also marked the development of two opposing views of how to make ethnic history a part of a usable past for Americans. One view, largely confined to traditional scholars and academic historians, is that ethnic history is similar to any other field of history; it is simply a framework or perspective used to illuminate the past.[8] The investigator works, not to add luster and glory to a given minority or to determine the extent of guilt present in the rest of society, but rather to add to our understanding of the nature and behavior of all Americans by viewing the past through the prism of ethnicity. The present study stands unabashedly in that school.

The opposing view regards ethnic history as a means of correcting perceived injustices and of promoting a sense of self-worth on the part of individual members of ethnic groups. Politicians employ this kind of ethnicity with laws mandating the teaching of the "contributions" of selected ethnic groups in the public schools. This approach to ethnic studies can reach the absurd length of textbook selection committees in major cities counting paragraphs of narrative and numbers of illustrations in an effort to insure that every selected group has its share of space.

In the pursuit of the laudable goal of promoting a sense of pride among school children, teachers are encouraged or even required to provide materials designed to give a positive image for the ethnic child. One measure of success for this approach is seen in the testimony of a young girl:

> I am proud that my parents are Spanish immigrants. We are descended from a people that have a rich and civilized culture. Spain once ruled a great empire and was the world's foremost nation.[9]

One child's positive image, alas, can be another's Black Legend. Which Spain produces the appropriate image? Is it the Spain of the Inquisition, or of the conquest of Mexico and Peru, or of the bloody suppression of revolt in the Netherlands? Would the son or daughter of a Dutch immigrant or a Mexican immigrant share the positive image of Spain?

There are risks in the "contributions" approach to ethnic studies. There was no "Scotch-Irish" regiment in the Union forces. Some scholars deny that such an ethnic group exists, but ethnic identity is to some extent a matter of self-selection, and many people are confident that there was a "Scotch-Irish" contribution to American history.[10] A generation ago it was a part of the conventional wisdom that the "Scotch-Irish" played a major role in subduing the wild frontier. High school textbooks lauded the ferocity of Scotch-Irish Indian fighters. Now that Indians, or Native Americans, demand and receive a revised version of the chapter of American history, the Scotch-Irish Indian fighter claims are strangely muted.

There is another problem in the "contributions" version of ethnic history, a problem precisely defined by Louis L. Gerson:

> As proof of immigrant contributions to America, ethnic leaders are quick to compile long rosters of prominent immigrants who have made illustrious names for themselves. Seldom do they acknowledge the fact that these people in whose glory they bask would have had little if any chance to discover their potential, their worth, and their genius in the country of their origin. It was in America that they were able to cultivate and achieve their greatness—and when they did so, they did so as Americans.[11]

None of the ethnic regiment leaders enjoyed success in Europe, although a few earned a certain notoriety. It was the war that made Louis Blenker famous. It was American ethnic politics that gave stature to Franz Sigel. Michael Corcoran would have lived and died in obscurity in Ireland; it was the American context that made him a folk hero. Lists of great immigrants in reality are a tribute to American society.

Iowa produced no Irish or German regiment. Early in the war a determined effort to recruit an Irish regiment ended in failure and left a heritage of frayed tempers and political animosities. Not only was the population base for such a regiment inadequate, but many Iowa Irishmen (along with Germans and Scandinavians) joined ethnic regiments recruited in neighboring states. It was something of a blow to state pride—in the view of some Iowans—that no ethnic regiment came out of their state. Ironically enough, New York, which produced more ethnic regiments than any other state in the Union, was the only state to field an *American* regiment, a unit whose claim to fame was that all of its members were native-born Americans.

In 1861 and 1862 ethnic regiment recruiters employed ethnic history in ways remarkably similar to those used today. Irish, German, French, and

Scandinavian recruiters painted glowing pictures of a Golden Age in the past of a given culture in the Old World. That Golden Age was a moment frozen in time, a mythic moment populated by great heroes, men whose exploits were to serve as models for Civil War soldiers; recruits were urged to shine in the reflected glory of the remote ethnic hero. The Golden Age had no problems of its own; it was a Camelot. This vision of the past — still too much used today — was utterly ahistorical. It contradicted a basic tenet of history, that of change as a constant.[12] One can forgive military recruiters for a lack of historical sophistication. It is less easy to forgive such lapses on the part of professional scholars today.

Historians like to think that their discipline embodies some socially redeeming virtues. They frequently justify a place for history in school and university programs with arguments that its study inculcates certain values. One major and traditional justification for history is that it combats parochialism; it provides perspectives of time and place absent from other disciplines. History, according to its professional defenders, offers invaluable vicarious experience, the collective record of all mankind. It is just this perspective of time and place that is conspicuously absent from much ethnic history.

Donald L. Horowitz, professor of law and public policy at Duke University, recently produced a monumental analysis of the role of ethnic groups that furnishes exactly the perspective of time and place needed for deep understanding of the subject.[13] His vast and authoritative *Ethnic Groups in Conflict* places all students of the topic in his debt. Horowitz gives detailed and chilling descriptions of ethnic conflicts in Asia, the Middle East, Africa, and the Caribbean. Ethnic hostilities are endemic in many parts of the world: large-scale rioting in India, genocide in Burundi, civil war in Uganda, endless slaughter in Lebanon, coups in Nigeria, terror and violence in Sri Lanka, massive killings in Indonesia, bombings in Spain — the nature and scale of the discord and its persistence over time eventually numb the mind. At the same time, it is salutary reading for the student of ethnic relations in the United States.

Nativist dismay in New England over the existence of ethnic military units in the 1850s is almost laughable when compared with the bloody struggles for control of the armies in several African nations. The formation of ethnic regiments in the Union armies in 1861 did not signal the start of murderous fighting for control of the military machine. It was instead evidence of ethnic loyalty to the Washington government and to the state governments in the North. The quarrels and squabbles between and within ethnic groups, related to those regiments, were fought usually in the political arena and rarely in the streets. The Massachusetts Irish and the Missouri Germans used existing and thoroughly understood democratic institutions to achieve their goals and make their contributions to the common cause.

The record of the ethnic regiments is a testament to a singularly resilient political and social system for the midnineteenth century. Far from exacerbating national disunity—what one should expect from the record of ethnic relations in most of the world—the ethnic regiments were proof that in the United States an ethnic identity could actually strengthen the nation and promote democracy, not automatically threaten both. Nativism and interethnic rivalries, before and during the Civil War, as important as they seem from a parochial perspective, pale in importance when placed alongside the conflicts recorded by Professor Horowitz. That is one message found in the history of the ethnic regiments.

There is another and less pleasant message, one almost completely lost in the mists of hagiography and filiopietism. Oftentimes members of the two largest ethnic groups, the Germans and the Irish, had to be wooed hard to win their support for the Union.[14] Feelings were touchy. After the first rush of patriotic enlistments, loyalty to the Union could not be taken for granted. State and federal authorities as well as ethnic leaders realized that immigrant ardor for the Union had to be nurtured, and that a perceived insult to a popular figure, like Frémont, turned off enlistments in a given group. The creation of ethnic regiments, even though demanded by ethnic political leaders, repelled immigrants who believed that the exploitation of immigrants was often the work of fellow ethnics instead of native Americans.[15] Ethnic political and military leaders were frequently as biased and prejudiced toward native Americans as the latter were toward immigrants.

Hugh Judson Kilpatrick, an Irish-American officer from New Jersey, was a West Point graduate who acquired the nickname of "Kill Cavalry" because of his consistently poor judgment on the battlefield. Described by Sherman as a "hell of a damned fool" and by others as a man of notorious immorality and rapacity, Kilpatrick was a thoroughly political general in a thoroughly political army.[16] His postwar memoirs are a classic example of mythologizing ethnic Civil War history. In the years following the war, Kilpatrick gave a standard speech to scores of audiences on the Irish lecture circuit, and as many as three thousand people at a time cheered his quaint version of the war. Kilpatrick's legendary Irishman was one with a congenital love of liberty who leaped to the defense of the Union no matter where he lived. It was the struggle for freedom in the Emerald Isle that forged the character of the Irish soldier. His Irish heroes reaffirmed on American battlefields the valor shown at famed Fontenoy. The general's stock phrases and anecdotes, repeated over the years, simply confirmed for his listeners an image long promoted by ethnic politicians.[17]

That quixotic view, which was the core of the argument used by recruiters for Irish regiments, never disappeared. Strongly reinforced in the years after the war, it continued generation after generation down to the present.[18] Only the Irish continuously strengthened and renewed their Civil

War fantasies. The Germans, Scandinavians, and Scots, while occasionally reminding themselves and America of their version of Civil War history, felt no need for the constant and shrill claims of the Irish. The difference stemmed from the kind of ethnic politics practiced by Irish politicians, plus the continuation of Irish nationalism.

America's Civil War produced different consequences for Germans than for the Irish. The war ended the division between the "Grays" and "Greens" (the pre-1848 and post-1848 immigrants), and terminated what was already the waning influence of German nationalism in the immigrant community. Within a few short years after the war Carl Schurz wrote of the triumph of the melting pot for America's Germans. Schurz urged Germans to turn their backs on European nostalgia and commit themselves totally to their new homeland. Most did, and World War I finished what remained of German-American political influence and consciousness.[19]

The careers of Carl Schurz and Thomas Francis Meagher provide a striking contrast in ethnic political leadership of the Civil War generation. Both men owed much of their influence to their eloquence in speech and in print. Both established a political base within an ethnic community, and both threw themselves enthusiastically into the creation of ethnic regiments when the war began. And there the similarities end and the differences emerge. Schurz was always a nationalist and an abolitionist; he built his career outside the ethnic fold as well as within it. He never wavered, despite his heated defense of German-American interests, in his belief that Germans must commit their loyalties entirely to their new homeland. After the war, Schurz was not simply one more ethnic politician; he had a national following that crossed ethnic and nonethnic lines. Meagher never took that step, although he made a few quite unsuccessful efforts to do so. The pattern he set in the early days of the Sixty-ninth New York Infantry and through the heady years of the Irish Brigade remained fixed for the rest of his brief life. Where Schurz directed his listeners and readers toward national issues, Meagher never threw off his narrow Irish nationalism, and his temperament forever involved him in bitter personal and factional disputes within the ethnic bloc. While both men pursued personal ambition, that of Meagher was so blatant and so exploitive of others that ultimately his claque forgot him. He constantly courted fame and notoriety so that he could use it to promote himself. As a captain in Corcoran's Sixty-ninth New York and as the promoter making deals for the leadership of the Irish Brigade, Meagher of the Sword always saw the American system as one in which fame was a commodity used for political barter. He lived on his name, used the ethnic regiments as chessmen in his play for influence, and died in obscurity without ever understanding the need for substance and solid achievement on which to lay the foundation of a national political success.[20]

Civil War ethnic regiments have been seen as a moment frozen in time, and ethnic tradition preserves that moment as though it were a permanent reality. Heady rhetoric from the early days of the war took on a life of its own. Fixed in a kind of folk memory is a story of all foreigners flocking to recruiting offices to defend the Union. Newspaper accounts of April 1861, stories of Hungarians, Italians, Germans, Irishmen, and others joyously forming ethnic regiments, persisted as though carved in stone; historians who normally cast a critical eye at sources and were careful to note change over time, lost those analytical habits when dealing with this subject.[21]

Identifying and explaining change over time, as well as illuminating the complexities of human affairs, are crucial elements of historical analysis. The record of the ethnic regiments sheds light on the changing role of America's ethnics during the Civil War and sharpens our understanding of the intricate nature of that role.

With ethnics, as with the larger population, the first rush of enthusiasm for the war soon dwindled. By the winter of 1861–1862, bounties replaced patriotism as a major inducement. While the War Department initially welcomed foreigners into the military with open arms, the notorious "General Order No. 45" of 19 July 1861 hinted at second thoughts on the matter. That order caused consternation in ethnic communities and slowed recruitment in ethnic regiments. "In the future," stated General Order No. 45, "no volunteer will be mustered into the service who is unable to speak the English language."[22] So vehement was the opposition to this policy, however, that the War Department quickly backed off and "clarified" its position with a new order stating that the English language requirement did not apply to companies and regiments composed of foreigners. That change encouraged the recruitment of a second round of ethnic regiments in late 1861.[23] When states instituted their first draft laws, the most riotous opposition to those laws came from localities with heavy concentrations of foreign-born residents. In Wisconsin there was an antidraft parade in Milwaukee and serious rioting in neighboring counties with many German inhabitants.[24] Increasing numbers of aliens claimed exemption from the draft, renounced their intention of becoming citizens, and many fled to Canada to escape military service.

A closer look at those draft riots in Wisconsin reveals far more than simple opposition to military service. First, there was interethnic rivalry. Fighting between Germans and Irishmen was far from unknown in the area, and many of the rioters were Luxembourgers, who were mostly Roman Catholic, while many of the rioting Germans were Protestants. The two groups disliked each other. Both were suspicious of the government, and as Democrats they regarded the draft as a Republican plot. The two draft commissioners appointed for Milwaukee were both Protestants and Masons, and when they exempted several fellow Masons from the draft they added to the hostility toward the law and the war. When the violence began members of the mob seized whiskey, and so alcohol encouraged the spread of fighting and destruction.[25] An explosive mixture of religious conflict, ethnic tensions, partisan politics, and class rivalries (the law allowed the rich to buy substitutes) lay behind the rioting.

When the Seventeenth Wisconsin Infantry rioted in the presence of the governor, it did so not because many of the soldiers were Irish but because the regiment had not been paid. When soldiers of the Sixth Wisconsin Infantry angrily destroyed their mess hall, they did so not because they were German and Irish but because the food was miserable. On the other hand, when troops from an Irish regiment enthusiastically quashed a disturbance in Heg's Scandinavian outfit, and when American soldiers of the Ninety-first Illinois Infantry savagely attacked the men of Hecker's Eighty-second Illinois Infantry in Camp Butler, ethnic rivalries and nativism were clearly a factor.[26] Any episode of violent, disorderly behavior on the part of Civil War soldiers must be scrutinized carefully before assigning an explanatory label to it. Early in the war, for example, Governor Andrew of Massachusetts received a confidential report (with instructions to burn it after reading, which the governor happily failed to carry out) about the outrageous conduct of one of the state's regiments:

> Col. Cowdin's Regiment is going to ruin and unless something is done it will bring disgrace upon our state. On their way [to Washington] the men fired their muskets out of the windows of their cars, killed hogs and endangered life. Here they were distinguished by their unruly conduct, and at their encampment they were turbulent and unruly. Cowdin has no control over his men and no sense of his position. He is an honest, good-hearted man but utterly unfit for his place.[27]

Such a report about an Irish or German regiment was commonplace, but this one referred to the First Massachusetts Infantry, a distinguished militia unit, and Colonel Cowdin went on to earn promotion to the rank of brigadier and to noteworthy service on many battlefields. Riotous and disorderly behavior was not an exclusive ethnic trait.

Draft riots, especially the massive disturbances in the summer of 1863, convinced the casual observer that evasion of conscription was especially keen among the foreign born. In their efforts to rationalize the prominence of German and Irish participation in those riots, ethnic historians resorted to tortured casuistry to shift the blame elsewhere. Descendants of those rioters should feel neither guilt nor pride. Draft evasion was equally popular among ethnics and nonethnics. Native-born evaders tended to use legal means, and the foreign-born used illegal means of evasion.[28]

"What then is the American, this new man?" When Crèvecoeur asked the question in 1782 in *Letters from an American Farmer,* he began an inquiry that has continued to the present. He raised the issue as a friendly foreigner, a naturalized American citizen who later returned to his native France. His all-too-familiar question continues to nag and interest Americans; few persons today recall the answer he himself provided:

> He is either an European, or the descendant of an European; hence that strange mixture of blood, which you will find in no other country. I could point out to you a man, whose grandfather was an Englishman, whose wife was Dutch, whose son married a French woman, and whose present four sons have now wives of four different nations. *He* is an American, who, leaving behind him all his ancient prejudices and manners, receives new ones from the new mode of life he has embraced, the new government he obeys, and the new rank he holds. He becomes an American by being received in the broad lap of our great *Alma Mater.*
>
> Here individuals of all nations are melted into new race of men, whose labours and posterity will one day cause great change in the world.[29]

As eloquent as his answer was, it was unsatisfactory then and remains so today. Unsatisfactory because it ignores Africans, Orientals, and Native Americans, and still other peoples whose presence added to the incredibly rich mixture of the American population. Unsatisfactory, too, because it said that the American left behind all of his ancient prejudices and manners. Americans did no such thing, no more than did immigrants from any origin arriving at whatever destination. The prejudices of the homeland are a part of the intellectual baggage, and the manners and customs of the Old Country accompany the migrant to the new.

What Crèvecoeur asserted was the idea of the melting pot, the notion that the new nation, acting as a crucible, melted down the cultures of other nations and forged them into something new and unique, an American culture. Crèvecoeur was also an idealist. He believed that immigrants to America took as their motto, "Where my bread is earned, there is my country." Some did, and others did not. Finally, Crèvecoeur asked another rhetorical question: "What attachment can a poor European immigrant have for a country where he had nothing?" He neglected the power of romantic imagination and the lure of another old saw, "Absence makes the heart grow fonder."

After his Civil War experiences, Carl Schurz accepted without reservation the melting pot process. Any effort to preserve a hybrid German culture in America he thought doomed to disappointment, and such a hybrid was inferior to either the culture of Germany or America. And so, as strong as was his love for German culture, he advised German-Americans to adopt American culture. By 1914 the idea of the melting pot took its most popular form in the play with that title by Israel Zangwill. Melting pot theory, however, scarcely reached full development before it came under fire. By the 1920s scholars in the fields of history and the social sciences approached the immigrant experience from the perspective of the "contributions" of specific ethnic groups; the popular and scholarly writing urged readers to acknowledge the unique and valuable efforts heroic individuals and hardworking groups contributed to the total American experience.

This viewpoint reflected not only a new interest in "history from below," an effort to write the history of the common people rather than elites, but it also emerged from a growing feeling that the melting pot was in reality "forced Anglo conformity." There was no "new man" in this construct; rather, newcomers were formed by economic, social, and political pressures, as well as violence, to abandon their Old World heritage and become little Englishmen. The forced Anglo conformity model was used to explain nativism, discrimination, exploitation, and a wide variety of other social ills.

By the 1960s, when many Americans questioned everything about themselves and their country's past and did so in the context of the civil rights movement and the Vietnam War, the forced Anglo conformity model became sacred writ and a vigorous corollary known as the "rise of the New Ethnics" took the nation's intellectuals and politicians by storm. The old melting pot melted away. It was roundly denounced as a fraud and a failure, a thinly disguised weapon of the Establishment to keep the downtrodden downtrodden and keep the elite in power.

Accompanying the renewal of interest in ethnicity was an interest in class. One pioneer in the subject, sociologist Milton M. Gordon, argued that ethnicity was extremely hardy, that American social institutions powerfully reinforced it, and that membership in an ethnic group filled some potent need for the individual. Gordon believed that this need for ethnic identity had its origin in a mystery, some essential trait of human nature.[30] He also believed that for most aspects of cultural behavior, class was more important than ethnicity, but that ethnicity remained important for Americans in their primary relations with others, and that it would continue to do so for the foreseeable future. Gordon concluded that America was a "multiple melting pot," a society with strong drives for assimilation but not strong enough to eliminate ethnicity. His term for American society was "structural pluralism."

One book more than any other made the debate a matter of public interest and more than academics scoring debating points on each other. That was *Beyond the Melting Pot,* coauthored by Nathan Glazer and Daniel Patrick Moynihan. The melting pot never happened, Glazer and Moynihan declared, and ethnicity and race remained critical factors in American politics. Moreover, they found that in the United States there is no "American" identity; the individual saw himself as an ethnic, a member of a religious group, or a resident with some kind of regional identity. This absence of a clear American archetype troubled many critics. As Glazer put it, if ethnic activism consumed the energies and attention of the ordinary citizen, there would be nothing left to devote to those broader memberships and functions that bind a people together in a democratic society. As the years passed Glazer expressed growing concern about the institutionalization of ethnicity in America, with a political system of rewards and punishments built into laws, laws which classified people on the basis of presumed ethnic status. He warned the United States and Western Europe that the pattern of ethnic conflicts and even wars in other parts of the world might portend the future in the West. Classification by ethnic group violated the American tradition of individualism, and the tradition of judging a person by what he or she did, according to Glazer and others disturbed by the extension of ethnic quotas into the worlds of work and education.[31]

As obituaries for the melting pot proliferated, and acknowledgments of American society as composed of competing ethnic groups became a cottage industry, the worries and criticisms of the Glazers were drowned in praise for pluralism. Champions of the New Ethnicity looked upon pluralism and found it good. Ethnicity was the central theme of all of American history, ran the new consensus. Pluralism, not assimilation, was the reality of America. The good news was that ethnic conflict prevented class conflict, was more tolerant than assimilation, and created a richer more diverse culture. The bad news was that ethnic conflict, like racism, would forever be part of the American scene. The peak (or nadir) of the literature on the New Ethnicity came in the early seventies with the publication of Michael Novak's *The Rise of the Unmeltable Ethnics*. In this extraordinary book, whose very title read like a mixed metaphor, Novak managed to conflate religion and ethnicity, ignore centuries of religious conflict by assuming that all Catholics were alike, and find something nice to say about Al Capone. His book raised the temperature of the national debate on the subject, and the careful and generous reader found that he blamed the New Ethnicity on a national loss of confidence in Anglo-Saxon and WASP leadership brought on by the Vietnam War, trouble in the cities, and a long history of anti-Catholic attitudes and behavior on the part of Protestants. Whatever the lapses of reason, logic, and common sense—to say nothing of history—in the Novak perspective, his version of flourishing ethnicity and growing ethnic power politics (copied from the tactics of blacks and civil-rights activists) encouraged the states and the federal government to legislate ethnic studies, establish ethnic quotas in colleges and professional schools, and finance endless conferences, studies, research, and pageantry, all to the greater glory of selected ethnic groups. The major political parties, perhaps recalling the vigor with which Carl Schurz pursued ethnic voters in 1860, went after ethnic bloc votes with a vengeance.[32]

Even as the New Ethnicity triumphed, its very successes and excesses prompted opposition. Here and there a still, small voice raised a challenge. Unlike the Glazers and Gordons, who accepted the myth or failure of the melting pot but worried about the consequences of pluralism, these critics questioned the fundamental premises of that pluralism.

Sociologist Stephen Steinberg examined all the paths of ethnic conflict and discovered they began and ended in the same place. Ethnic conflict and all the debate about the role of ethnics in society came out of the class struggle. Class difference, he asserted, in opposition to the basic assumption of the New Ethnicity, was far more important than ethnic difference.[33] For Steinberg, ethnicity was little more than a myth, an illusion designed to shield us from the grim realities of life. Unlike Gordon, who thought ethnicity was a rather mysterious trait deeply embedded in human nature, Steinberg regarded ethnic conflict as simply evidence of class conflict.

Howard F. Stein applied the techniques of psychohistory to ethnicity and produced a devastating critique.[34] The sectarians of ethnic power, according to Stein, used ethnic power arguments as a way to compete for scarce resources, such as jobs, housing, and education. To do this, they promoted a myth of a noble past in the Old Country, a myth that involved the rejection of an American identity and the invention of an "idealized pre-immigrant feudal identity." The sense of individualism gave way to a sense of collective identity, a new reality. In this view Americanization or assimilation became a crime because it destroyed the identity of its passive, innocent victim. Anglo conformity, charged Stein, is the language of the New Ethnics turned into ethnic conformity; proponents of the New Ethnicity used the power of government to ensure that potential ethnics turn into ethnics. The New Ethnics in Stein's analysis rewrote history so that Americans would grant reparations to alleged victims of injustice or the descendants of those victims. The New Ethnics wanted society's rewards to go to persons, not for what they did, but for what they were. By careful selection of a "frozen time" past, the New Ethnics created a Golden Age past, one that had no reality for today's ethnic American, other than its symbolism. Ethnicity, in the Stein analysis, was a search for status, a way of escaping unpleasant reality, and a way of avoiding an unpleasant future by a return to childhood. For Stein, America had its own, readily identifiable culture and one that over several centuries proved enormously attractive to scores of millions of immigrants. The New Ethnics denied that culture, feared the growing influence of blacks and Jews, were uneasy about an uncertain future growing out of a rapidly changing society, and sought comfort and escape by submerging their own personality in that of an artificial group.

University of Michigan historian John Higham used the tools of traditional historical analysis to reach conclusions similar to those of Stein. With tongue in cheek, he denied the failure of the melting pot; assimilation really worked, but not in the traditional sense. What it did was melt disparate individuals and small groups into larger, made-in-America groups. All the descendants of slaves, whose ancestral roots go back to a wide variety of ethnic and tribal clusters in Africa, meld into a new classification of "African." Sicilians, Neapolitans, Tuscans, and other newcomers, whatever their former sense of identity and loyalty, in America turned into Italian-Americans. Saxons, Bavarians, Hanovarians, and Prussians, achieved in the American context what they failed to achieve in Europe, a national identity! The nineteenth-century peasant migrated to America with no feeling of national identity, and then, sometimes bewilderingly, acquired it here unless he simply merged into the American culture. In a similar fashion, the omnipresent WASPs were an abstraction, a symbolic group whose members not only had no sense of ethnic relationship but whose roots were as distinctive and separate as those of other immigrants. Much of the opposition and hostility encountered in America by new arrivals, what is usually seen as nativism, in reality came from other immigrants.

Ethnic leaders, in Higham's view, faced insoluble problems and paradoxes. Their goals conflicted, and if they attained one they might well lose another. To begin with, they had to identify their group, a task that was not always easy in the absence of any legal or generally accepted cultural definition. (This was not as serious a problem for the Irish as for other groups, but even in this instance the Irish Protestant, the Anglo-Irishman, or the Scotch-Irish might have little in common with the stereotyped Catholic Irishman.) Leaders faced the additional problem of conflicting and shifting loyalties among their followers. Ethnicity was self-defined, and the individual had economic, class, religious, and other interests competing with ethnic interests. If a leader preached accommodation he risked the loss of the true believers; if he led protest, he risked the dropping away of the timid, the conservative, and those whose goals were acceptance and not confrontation. Assimilation was a minefield for the leader. Without assimilation, the immigrant remained forever a stranger; with it, he lost the identity created and sought by the leadership.

Higham identified the Civil War as a watershed in ethnic history, especially for the Irish. Nativism and the Know-Nothing movement faded away with the war. The slaughter of Irishmen at Fredericksburg, Higham argued, was directly related to the disappearance of the nativist Order of United Americans. Other nativist groups, such as the American Party and the Sons of America, vanished as hundreds of thousands of alien soldiers served in Union forces. Finally, like Stein and Gordon, Higham detected an element of mystery and irrationality at the heart of American ethnicity.[35]

The history of the Civil War ethnic regiments bears directly on the continuing national debate on the nature of ethnicity in American life. It demolishes some stereotypes and challenges several axioms often presented as self-evident truths.

Critics of the melting pot theory regard ethnic identity as a primordial trait, as a basic, innate part of the personality brought from the Old World; they think of ethnicity as a given, something internal that resists change. The origin and development of ethnic regiments refutes this notion. Ethnic regiments were political creations; they grew out of the mid–nineteenth-century political situation in America. The vast majority of immigrants came to America because they did not like their lives in the countries where they were born.[36] Even the Irish, whose nationalism set them apart from other immigrant groups, overwhelmingly chose to come to America to better themselves; only a few came as involuntary exiles. Immigrants left behind societies where their prospects were poor, where they lacked status and power, and came to the United States where many as individuals acquired both status and power, and where the immigrants as groups gained political power. Ironically, it was in America that some of those immigrants developed an affection for and an awareness of the Old Country, an awareness and affection probably not felt when they lived there. Just as the growing numbers of ethnic voters translated into political power in municipal and state elections and thus benefitting ethnic politicians, those same numbers lay behind the formation of the highly visible ethnic regiments. Exiled rebels from Hungary, Ireland, and Germany did not come to America because they were successful revolutionaries; they came here because they failed in Europe. Most German and Irish immigrants were not disgruntled nationalists; they sought economic opportunity, not the greater glory of the Old Country.

Both the formation and the subsequent evolution of the ethnic regiments show that the typical immigrant held stronger loyalties than ethnicity. Most volunteers avoided the ethnic regiments, and those who did seek one out gradually lost enthusiasm for it. All such regiments suffered a gradual loss of ethnic identity and composition. The pull of neighborhood, state, personal friendship, occupation, and even alternative myth proved stronger than ethnicity. Urban and regional concentrations lay behind ethnic political power, and those same concentrations lay behind the creation of ethnic regiments. Ethnic recruiters in ethnic neighborhoods using ethnic appeals in the short run attracted some ethnic recruits; over the long run most immigrants rejected such appeals.

Ethnic politicians used the rhetoric of a mythical or legendary past to attract support and promote group identity and unity. That rhetoric would produce disappointing results, however, unless supported with organizational skill, patronage, highly visible benefits for some members of the groups, and a sense that the leaders could manipulate the system to the advantage of the group. Ethnic entrepreneurs promoting ethnic regiments used the same rhetoric and tried to offer similar patronage benefits, but unlike the Boston or Chicago politician, they offered limited patronage over a short period of time; their patronage obviously was a one-time thing. Fiery and sentimental rhetoric offered a postwar goal that, except for the leaders with political ambitions, was not worth the risk of death or injury. There is paradox here. Neighborhood concentrations increased a sense of ethnic identity but undermined the *local* loyalties the German or Italian had in Europe; those concentrations increased ethnic visibility that stimulated nativism, but they also increased power and self-confidence and encouraged eventual assimilation.[37] Ethnic regiments, whose very existence was an affront and challenge to assimilation, made visible the ethnic contribution and loyalty to the Union and helped destroy nativism.

The very formation of ethnic regiments in 1861 and early 1862 lays to rest the myth of ethnic impotence and political powerlessness for that generation of Americans. From San Francisco to Boston, from New Haven to Philadelphia, the Civil War generation of immigrant Americans already exercised potent political power, a power that was growing. As elected officials and as power brokers, as well as in militia units and the regular army, immigrants mastered the system and used it for their benefit. The ethnic influence on politics and foreign affairs, an influence increasingly visible in subsequent generations, was already well-established in 1861. Those ethnic regiments challenge belief in forced Anglo-conformity; the greater popularity of nonethnic regiments for most ethnics affirms the position that most ethnics consciously sought assimilation.[38] Hans Christian Heg, Carl Schurz, Gustave Koerner, Adolphus Engelmann, August Willich, all of these and most other ethnic regiment leaders actively encouraged assimilation. Engelmann regularly encouraged his wife to write to him in English, not German, and urged her to use English, too, in their conversations. He wanted the family to become American. Schurz in the strongest terms advised German-Americans to abandon the notion of a separate culture and assimilate. Heg and other leaders of smaller ethnic communities feared the power of larger ethnic blocs and saw assimilation as a safeguard.

Ethnic identity was a matter of self-selection. This was seen most clearly in immigrants from Eastern Europe. Julian Kuné, George Frederick D'Utassy, Wladimir Krzyzanowski, and Géza Mihalotzy all had to define their ethnic association when they formed or joined ethnic regiments. Austrians like Gotthilf Bourray de Ivernois became "German," as did many Swiss. James Cameron of New York and Daniel Cameron of Chicago worked hard to convince Scottish-Americans that they had a unique ethnic identity, but the vast majority chose to blend into American regiments. Second-generation ethnics like James Mulligan consciously sought the ethnic regiment identification for its political possibilities, not out of some primordial instinct.

Ethnic regiments, both in their internal affairs and in their relations with other regiments and the larger society, provide evidence that rivalries and conflicts *between* the several ethnic communities, rather than between all ethnics and "old stock" Americans, explained much of the conflict in American society in the nineteenth century. Animosities and even riotous behavior between the several nationalities in the Garibaldi Guard, the violent confrontations between Irish and Scandinavian and German soldiers on several occasions, the fear and rivalry between groups as they recruited, and the intense lobbying in Washington and the state capitals, all reflect both the transfer of European traditions to America and the development of new antipathies in the new homeland. It is reductionist to view those conflicts simply growing out of the "exploitation" or "oppression" of newcomers by natives. The process by which the ethnic regiments formed was similar to the long records of conflicts between older and newer immigrants. The Germans and the Irish often competed for the same jobs in eastern and midwestern cities. They competed for political power. They struggled for control of the Catholic church. That kind of conflict of the mid–nineteenth century continued to the end of the century as the Irish fought street battles with Jews and Italians. Hostility between the Irish and Italians was not unlike that between Irishmen and Germans. The Irish opposed Italian unification because that would diminish the power of the papacy.[39] The outrage expressed by the *Boston Pilot* at the thought of a commission in the Union army for Garibaldi, and the use of a name like the Garibaldi Guard for an ethnic regiment, mirror the interethnic and religious antagonisms planted in the American soil. They were not just the invention of prejudiced natives. The attitudes and behavior of the various ethnic groups toward each other cries out for further exploration.[40] Ethnic regimental history shows that the tradition in American historiography of looking for saints and sinners in ethnic and native relations is simplistic and misleading.

Careerism lay at the core of ethnic regiment leadership. For the colonels and other officers, as for the organizers in the civilian population, the military and political career of the individual had top priority. Michael Corcoran was content with his role as an Irish general. His most ardent admirers admitted that he never lived up to his rhetoric or to the expectations of his claque. Once he attained the goal of a general's rank, his military record was singularly free of solid achievement. Thomas Francis Meagher always had his eye on a postwar political career. Those who knew him acknowledged his ambition and his willingness and eagerness to use ethnicity and to risk the lives of his men to win notoriety for himself. His hypocritical stance toward the Fenians and his shift in party allegiance to the support of the Lincoln administration in return for the renewal of a failed military game plan testify to his cynical manipulation of Irish nationalism for the sake of office. Bernard Mullen, Mathew Murphy, and other Fenians combined a determination to carve out a high position for themselves with a desire to exploit America's agony to advance Irish nationalism. Even the most idealistic and high-minded of the ethnic regiment commanders, men like Hans Heg and Augustus Willich, placed the promotion of their personal careers above other choices. At the other extreme, genuine rogues like D'Utassy and D'Epineuil differed from other bent Union officers only in their exploitation of the ethnic card for their corrupt purposes. Frederick Hecker, Louis Blenker, and the Prince Salm-Salm had utterly contrasting styles, but each persistently and unerringly promoted himself, making every possible use of America's political machinery in the process. All of these men knew that their course was risky; some paid with their lives the cost of admission to the game. With a few exceptions, these men were also American patriots and staunch nationalists. Thomas Cass, William Lytle, Alexander Schimmelfennig, and men from the ranks like Henry Kircher, whatever their civilian careers and however they exploited their military service for postwar politics, *fought* for the Union. Careerism was not their sole motive.

Ethnic regimental histories reveal the keen political rivalries *within* the larger ethnic communities. Those relationships were at least as bitter and destructive as anything between ethnic and nonethnics. When Meagher, Nugent, and Corcoran campaigned for the top spot in Irish regimental circles, their actions belied the language of ethnic solidarity. Friedrich Hecker learned from personal experience how vicious German-American politics could be. The cat-and-dog fighting between William Snowhook and Father Dunne in Chicago to dominate the second Illinois Irish regiment portrays the extreme nature of intraethnic political contests. Ethnic versus American challenges were not as intemperate as the literal name-calling and figurative hair-pulling that characterized the battles swirling around the Indiana Irish regiment and the two Massachusetts Irish regiments. Any portrayal of nineteenth-century American society solely as a clash between native and immigrants gravely distorts a more complex reality.

In most respects the ethnic regiment experience buttresses the scholarship of John Higham, Oscar Handlin, and others whose recent work rejects the simplistic accounts of moralists and reformers who divide the American people into two groups, old stock natives and foreigners, and tell a story of one group regularly and successfully victimizing the other. On two points, the annals of the ethnic regiments go beyond traditional scholarship. First, the formation of those regiments demonstrates the failure of nativism in the fifties. Under whatever name, nativism had little impact on American politics. Far from representing a potent force, the Know-Nothings in their various guises were a failed minority. They achieved none of their goals at the national level and in state governments they were an embarrassment. In a few states xenophobic laws placed temporary handicaps on some aliens, but the overwhelming presence of foreigners in the peacetime army, the prominence of alien militia units in many states, the persistence of unofficial organizations even in the two states that banned alien military companies, and the instant acceptance of ethnic regiments at the outset of the Civil War show the essential impotence of nativist sentiment, despite all the attention paid to its spokesmen. "Military organizations," asserts Peter Karsten, "reflect the societies they serve." The ethnic and nonethnic regiments of the Civil War strongly support his argument. Both evidence the rejection of nativism by most Americans.[41]

Secondly, the history of the ethnic regiments reveals the growing political power of ethnic leaders and voting blocs in the years preceding the war. When state quotas filled in the early days of the war, ethnic clout got regiments accepted beyond those quotas. Governors reluctant to field regiments of foreigners discovered they dare not oppose their formation. At the city and state levels ethnic politics already held a balance-of-power position by 1861. State officials and city leaders recognized the authority and influence of the German vote, the Irish vote, and even the Scandinavian vote. From California to Connecticut, immigrant Americans in 1861 held elected and appointed positions that ranged from United States senator to local school board member, from state governor to commander of the state militia, from prison commissioner to the Congress of the United States. This is a remarkable achievement for a nation just two generations removed from its own independence. It is all the more remarkable when one considers the *voluntary* role played by the foreign born in the American military. This was not the result of press gangs, or the lure of refuge in a foreign legion, or (despite the cries of the Confederates) the hiring of foreign mercenaries. Most immigrant volunteers shared the motives of the native born, and those who chose the distinctive ethnic outfits in the early days of the war dramatized the status of those communities.

When Robert E. Lee's tired and beaten troops stacked their arms in that famous "stillness at Appomattox," and the victorious men in blue paraded in the Grand Review before returning home, and the nation stirred itself to count the cost of four years of war and struggle with the problems of peace, diligent bureaucrats in every state capital and in Washington sifted through mountains of regimental rosters, correspondence, telegrams, published orders, and other materials to write it all down. Archivists ordered and shelved mounds of paper treasure, the raw materials from which annalists and pension claimants would draw sustenance. Every state in the years following the war, conscious that the Civil War was America's national tragedy and triumph and aware of the supreme importance of the war in the lives of the Civil War generation, published detailed official reports of its men in uniform. Stored now in their dusty rows on library shelves, these reports preserve the names of every regiment, every company, every individual. The battles, the boredom, the casualties, the sick, and the deserters—they are all still present. As one turns the pages, brittle now and yellow with age, softened at the edges where generations of Americans fingered them as they searched for evidence about the role of their ancestors, the supreme importance of the *record* to the Civil War generation becomes evident. The thousands of tightly printed pages with their tables and lists, the endless rows of file folders with their rosters and letters, the faded and furled regimental flags, the carefully preserved pocket diaries and boxes of souvenir medals and minie balls, all bespeak a desperate need to preserve a collective memory. Each new generation of Americans after 1865 goes to that record and searches for meaning.

When historians question the past and search through the records for answers, their questions necessarily reflect contemporary concerns. For the past to have meaning it must relate to the present. Before they can write a sensible narrative, historians must locate a mainstream in society; as they do this they consciously or unconsciously divide the country's population into "insiders" and "outsiders."[42] This division involves more than finding a center; it includes assumptions about the distribution of power and rewards and about victims and exploiters. It arranges people into *the* majority and minorities. Majority persons are the insiders, the minorities are outsiders and the victims. It is part of the function of the outsider to be a victim— and a hero. He is never a villain. He tends to be self-defined, and the historian accepts that definition without question. American historians display a curious blind spot in their critical analysis of the past and present. They are quick to ascribe selfishness and ulterior motives to insiders, to the elite of the insiders. That criticism and skepticism vanish with the appearance in the narrative of the outsider. In American history the ethnic, the immigrant or his descendant, is the classic outsider. In ethnic studies criticism is less welcome than in any other area of scholarly analysis.

Bishop John Hughes of New York learned early in his career that the tradition of outsiderhood had important uses. A powerful figure himself, he never passed up an opportunity to depict his Irish Catholic flock as victims and outsiders. He developed a vested interest in building an image of America as a Protestant country hostile to Irish Catholics, whose only hope for survival then was to draw the wagons into a circle and fight off the attackers. Promoters of Irish, German, and other ethnic regiments used the same imagery. Regimental commanders had to be seen as larger than life, pure, selfless, and heroic. Meagher and Corcoran were military heroes before they ever heard a shot fired in anger. But outsiders, like insiders, have selfish interests; they can victimize as well as insiders. The outsider tradition is as American as apple pie. It must be seen, however, for what it often is, as a vehicle for shining in reflected glory. Ironically enough, the Know-Nothings regarded themselves and tried to present themselves as outsiders, the victims of a new and alien majority. To be an outsider is not an assurance of being either a victim or a promoter of justice. There must come a time when historians discuss immigration and ethnicity in the same critical manner used for other aspects of American life. They must look at the record and not simply accept without question what each groups says about itself.

Standing on a pedestal in a park or square in hundreds of northern towns is a statue of a Civil War soldier. These statues memorialize a generic warrior, an anonymous patriot, *the* soldier, not a Scot, or Swede, or German, or Irishman, but a Union volunteer. The men in the ethnic regiments as well as native regiments are in those memorials. The best-kept secret of the ethnic regiments is how truly American they were.

# Notes

## 1. PROLOGUE

1. Carl Schurz to Mrs. Schurz, 5 Oct. 1854, in Joseph Schafer, ed. and trans., *Intimate Letters of Carl Schurz, 1841–1869* (Madison: State Historical Society of Wisconsin, 1928), 134–37. Schurz also describes this visit in his *Reminiscences*, 2 vols. (New York: McClure, 1907), 2:42.

2. Earl J. Hess, Jr., ed., *A German in the Yankee Fatherland: The Civil War Letters of Henry A. Kircher* (Kent, Ohio: Kent State Univ. Press, 1983), 1–2.

3. Georg von Bosse, *Das Deutsche Element in den Vereinigten Staaten* (Stuttgart: Chr. Belsesche Verlagsbuchhandlung, 1908), 261–62; Alice Reynolds, "Friedrich Hecker," *American-German Review* (Apr. 1946), 4–7; Joseph G. Rosengarten, *The German Soldier in the Wars of the United States* (Philadelphia: J. B. Lippincott, 1886), 129–30.

4. *Dictionary of American Biography*, 1935 ed., s.v. "Carl Schurz." Hereafter cited as the *DAB*.

5. Charles D. Stewart, "A Bachelor General," *Wisconsin Magazine of History*, 17(1933):131–54; Loyd D. Easton, *Hegel's First American Followers* (Athens, Ohio: Ohio Univ. Press, 1966), 167–75.

6. Schurz to Mrs. Schurz, 22 Sept. 1954, in Schafer, *Letters*, 124.

7. Peter M. Harshman, "A Community Portrait: Over-the-Rhine, 1860," *Cincinnati Historical Society Bulletin* 40(Spring 1982):63–71. Even as Willich arrived, however, the Cincinnati German population dwindled in relative importance. By 1860 even the Over-the-Rhine wards were no longer predominantly German.

8. Easton, *Hegel's Followers*, 29–30; *DAB*, s.v., "Johann Bernhard Stallo."

9. Howard Elkinton, "George Engelmann: Greatly Interested in Plants," *American-German Review* (Aug. 1946), 16–21. George Engelmann was a distinguished amateur botanist; the Engelmann spruce was named in his honor.

10. Oswald Garrison Villard, "Theodor Hilgard, 'Latin Peasant,'" *St. Louis Post-Dispatch*, 5 Oct. 1941; Howard Elkinton, "Ferdinand Jacob Lindheimer: Botanist in Early Texas," *American-German Review* (Dec. 1945), 17–20; B. A. Beinlich, "The Latin Immigration in Illinois," *Transactions of the Illinois State Historical Society* (Springfield: State Historical Library, 1910), 208–14.

11. Schurz, *Reminiscences* 2:18–19. The reference to non-Germans as "Irish" is significant in terms of ethnic relations in the United States.

12. *DAB*, s.v., "Friedrich Kapp."

13. Rudolph A. Hofmeister, *The Germans of Chicago* (Champaign, Ill.: Stipes, 1976), 229–33.

14. *DAB*, s.v., "Gustave Philipp Körner."

15. John Moses, *Illinois: Historical and Statistical*, 2 vols. (Chicago: Fergus, 1892), 2:636–37; John H. Krenkel, ed., *Richard Yates, Civil War Governor* (Danville, Ill.: Interstate, 1966), 235. Hoffman was known as the "Little Dutchman," and one of his jobs was the translation of German materials for Yates.

16. Alfred G. Raphelson, "Alexander Schimmelfennig: A German-American Campaigner in the Civil War," *Pennsylvania Magazine of History and Biography* 87(Apr. 1963):156–81.

17. L. B. Bennett and William M. Haigh, *History of the Thirty-Sixth Regiment Illinois Volunteers* (Aurora, Ill.: Knickerbocker and Holder, 1876), 12–16.

18. Harshman, "A Community Portrait," offers evidence that native Americans, not German-Americans, were more upwardly mobile in the 1850s.

19. Wolfgang Kollmann and Peter Marschalck, "German Emigration to the United States," trans. Thomas C. Childs, *Perspectives in American History* 7(1973):499–554.

20. Desmond Ryan, *The Fenian Chief: A Biography of James Stephens* (Coral Gables, Fla.: Univ. of Miami Press, 1967), 110–53.

21. Stephens quotes the letter of 26 Jan. 1859 in his diary. A photocopy of the diary is in the New York Public Library, 9–10.

22. William Corby, *Memoirs of Chaplain Life: Three Years Chaplain in the Famous "Irish Brigade," Army of the Potomac* (Notre Dame, Ind.: Scholastic Press, 1894), 28.

23. Paul Jones, *The Irish Brigade* (New York: Robert B. Lucas, 1969); Christian D. Stevens, *Meagher of the Sword* (New York: Dodd, Mead, 1967); Robert G. Athearn, *Thomas Francis Meagher: An Irish Revolutionary in America* (Boulder: Univ. of Colorado Press, 1949). Athearn's biography is the only scholarly account of Meagher's life.

24. W. F. Lyons, *Brigadier-General Thomas Francis Meagher: His Political and Military Career* (New York: D. and J. Sadler, 1870), 15–16.

25. "Colonel Corcoran," *Harper's Weekly,* 10 Aug. 1861, 509. It was not uncommon for Irish nationalists to find employment in the British army.

26. "Colonel Mulligan," *Harper's Weekly,* 19 Oct. 1861, 658.

27. "An Irish Catholic Patriot," *Chicago New World,* 29 Nov. 1902, a clipping in the Records of the Executive Committee of the Irish Brigade, James A. Mulligan Papers, Chicago Historical Society. Hereafter cited as the Mulligan Papers, CHS.

28. [Father T. J. Butler] to Mulligan, 17 Feb. 1864, Mulligan Papers, CHS. Italics in the original. A *ten*-foot pole was another matter, as shown below.

29. Jennie Devin Kelly to Mulligan, 15 Feb. 1864, Mulligan Papers, CHS. Italics in the original. To avoid pedantry and textual interruptions, *sic* is not used in quotations from manuscript sources.

30. "Col. Thomas Cass," *Boston Pilot,* 27 July 1861.

31. Daniel G. Macnamara, *The History of the Ninth Regiment Massachusetts Volunteer-Infantry* (Boston: E. B. Stillings, 1899), 2–3.

32. Know-Nothingism in Boston was neither simple antiforeign prejudice nor as pervasive as it is commonly depicted. The Know-Nothing election victories, for example, were in part a revolt of party members against professional politicians and of countrymen against the city. See Roger Lane, *Policing the City: Boston, 1822–1885* (1967; reprint, New York: Atheneum, 1971), 92–93, 196. See also Michael F. Holt, "The Politics of Impatience: The Origins of Know Nothingism," *Journal of American History* 60 (Sept. 1973):309–31. Holt makes it quite clear that Know-Nothingism was far more than xenophobia.

33. Thomas Hamilton Murray, *History of the Ninth Regiment, Connecticut Volunteer Infantry* (New Haven, Conn.: Price, Lee, and Adkins, 1903), 322–23.

## 2. ETHNIC POLITICS

1. William Andrew Allen to his wife, 5 July 1860, William Anderson Allen Papers, Illinois State Historical Library, Springfield.

2. *Historical Statistics of the United States: Colonial Times to 1957* (Washington, D.C.: U.S. Bureau of the Census, 1960), 7, 56. Such population statistics, and those cited in other sources, should be regarded as rough approximations. Before the twentieth century, the federal government recorded land arrivals (from Mexico and Canada) only on a haphazard and irregular basis.

3. Thomas Walker Page, "The Distribution of Immigrants in the United States Before 1870," *Journal of Political Economy* 20(July 1912):676–94, 679–80.

4. Holt, "The Politics of Impatience," 309–31; Ray Allen Billington, *The Protestant Crusade, 1800–1860* (1938; reprint, Gloucester, Mass.: Peter Smith, 1963), 407–10; Thomas Walker Page, "Some Economic Aspects of Immigration Before 1870: Part I," *Journal of Political Economy* 20(Dec. 1912):1011–28.

5. Frederick Luebke, ed., *Ethnic Voters and the Election of Lincoln* (Lincoln: Univ. of Nebraska Press, 1971); Schurz to Gottfried Kinkel, 15 Feb. 1858, in *Speeches, Correspondence and Political Papers of Carl Schurz*, 6 vols., ed. Frederick Bancroft (New York: G. P. Putnam, 1913), 1:34, and Schurz to Abraham Lincoln, 22 May 1860, 1:116–18.

6. Joseph Schafer, "Who Elected Lincoln?" *American Historical Review* 47(Oct. 1941):51–63; Robert P. Swierenga, "The Ethnic Voter and the First Lincoln Election," *Civil War History* 11(Mar. 1965):27–43.

7. Oliver MacDonagh, "The Irish Famine Emigration to the United States," *Perspectives in American History* 10(1976):444.

8. Paul Kleppner, *The Cross of Culture: A Social Analysis of Midwestern Politics, 1850–1900* (New York: Free Press, 1970), 18–69; Benjamin J. Blied, *Catholics and the Civil War* (Milwaukee: The Author, 1945), 18–69.

9. Bayard Still, *Milwaukee: The History of a City* (1948; reprint, Madison: State Historical Society of Wisconsin, 1965), 111–12.

10. Kathleen Neils Conzen, *Immigrant Milwaukee, 1836–1860* (Cambridge: Harvard Univ. Press, 1976), 6. The Irish of San Francisco have a history quite different from that of the Irish of eastern and midwestern cities, and more like that of the Milwaukee Germans. See R. A. Burchell, *The San Francisco Irish* (Berkeley: Univ. of California Press, 1980).

11. Conzen, *Immigrant Milwaukee*, 196–210.

12. Ibid., 216.

13. Ernest Brunchen, "The Political Activity of Wisconsin Germans," *Proceedings of the Wisconsin State Historical Society* (1901), 197.

14. Ibid., 196.

15. Ibid., 204. Regional differences carried over from Germany meant more to many Germans than American issues.

16. Sister M. Justille McDonald, *History of the Irish in Wisconsin in the Nineteenth Century* (Washington, D.C.: Catholic Univ. of America Press, 1954), 127–28.

17. Ibid., 134.

18. "Hans Christian Heg," WPA Writers' Project Biography, typescript in the Wisconsin State Historical Society, Madison; Theodore C. Blegen, *Norwegian Immigration to America* (Northfield, Minn.: Norwegian-American Historical Association, 1931), 349–77.

19. Robert C. Nesbit, *Wisconsin: A History* (Madison; Univ. of Wisconsin Press, 1973), 242–62.

20. Schurz to Mrs. Schurz, 10 Feb. 1861, in Bancroft, *Schurz Speeches and Papers* 1:175–80.

21. Noah Brooks, *Washington in Lincoln's Time* (New York: Century, 1895), 19–20.

22. Sidney David Brumner, *Political History of New York State during the Civil War* (1910; reprint, New York: AMS Press, 1967), 27–28; Alexander B. Callow, Jr., *The Tweed Ring* (New York: Oxford Univ. Press, 1966), 18.

23. Albon P. Man, Jr., "The Irish in New York in the Early Eighteen Sixties," *Irish Historical Studies* 7(Sept. 1950):94; Leonard Tabachnik, "Political Patronage and Ethnic Groups: Foreign-born in the United States Customhouse Service, 1821–1861," *Civil War History* 17(Sept. 1971):222–31.

24. Joseph P. O'Grady, *How the Irish Became Americans* (New York: Twayne, 1973), 44–45.

25. R. Laurence Moore, "Insiders and Outsiders in American Historical Narrative and American History," *American Historical Review* 87(Apr. 1982):390–412; Man, "New York Irish," 99–100.

26. Ibid., 71.

27. Brumner, *New York Political History*, 326.

28. Lincoln to Gustave Koerner, 25 July 1858, in Roy P. Basler, ed., *Collected Works of Abraham Lincoln*, 8 vols. (Rutgers: Rutgers Univ. Press, 1955), 5:534; Lincoln to Norman B. Judd, 20 Oct. 1858, in *Lincoln*, ed. Basler, 5:330. A doggery was a low-class saloon.

29. Arthur C. Cole, *The Era of the Civil War*, vol. 3 of the *Centennial History of Illinois* (Springfield: Illinois Centennial Commission, 1919), 16, 341–43.

30. Hofmeister, *Chicago Germans*, 87.

31. Schurz to J. F. Potter, 17 Mar. 1860, in Bancroft, *Schurz Speeches and Papers* 1:107; James Albert Woodburn, "Party Politics in Indiana during the Civil War," *Annual Report of the American Historical Association* 1(1902):223–52.

32. Emma Lou Thornbrough, *Indiana in the Civil War Era* (Indianapolis: Indiana Historical Bureau and the Indiana Historical Society, 1965).

33. *Boston Pilot,* 19 Jan. 1861; Francis R. Walsh, "Who Spoke for Boston's Irish? The Boston *Pilot* in the Nineteenth Century," *Journal of Ethnic Studies* 10(Fall 1982):21–36; *Boston Pilot,* 2 Feb. 1861.

34. Dale Baum, "The 'Irish Vote' and Party Politics in Massachusetts, 1860–1876," *Civil War History* 26(June 1980):120.

35. John Niven, *Connecticut for the Union* (New Haven: Yale Univ. Press, 1965), 13, 9.

36. Rollin G. Osterweis, *Three Centuries of New Haven, 1638–1938* (New Haven: Yale Univ. Press, 1953), 286–87.

37. Ibid., 10.

38. J. Thomas Scharf and Thompson Westcott, *History of Philadelphia, 1609–1884,* 3 vols. (Philadelphia: L. H. Everts, 1884), 1:717–19.

39. Ibid., 1:731.

40. Louis Leonard Tucker, *Cincinnati During the Civil War* (Columbus: Ohio State Univ. Press, 1962), 4–5. When Wendell Phillips tried to give an abolitionist speech there as late as 1862 he had to flee the city to save his life.

41. *Cincinnati Daily Commercial,* 13 Feb. 1861.

42. Walter Harrington Ryle, *Missouri: Union or Secession* (Nashville: George Peabody College for Teachers, 1931), 6–7; Robert J. Rombauer, *The Union Cause in St. Louis in 1861* (St. Louis: Nixon-Jones, 1909), 127.

43. "Doom of Slavery," in Bancroft, *Schurz Speeches and Papers* 1:156, 159.

44. Ryle, *Missouri,* 205–6.

## 3. "THE WAR IS COMMENCED"

1. Edith Ellen Ware, *Political Opinion in Massachusetts during the Civil War and Reconstruction* (New York: Columbia Univ., 1916), 43–47; Scharf and Westcott, *History of Philadelphia* 1:746.

2. Samuel P. Bates, *Martial Deeds of Pennsylvania* (Philadelphia: T. H. Davis, 1875), 74.

3. Lawrence A. Gobright, *Recollections of Men and Things at Washington* (Washington, D.C.: W. H. and O. H. Morrison, 1869), 286.

4. Holmes to John Lathrop Motley, 16 Feb. 1861, quoted in Ware, *Massachusetts Political Opinion,* 47.

5. J. F. Hauser to Governor Randall, 26 Dec. 1860. Governor Alexander W. Randall Letter Book, Wisconsin State Historical Society, Madison. Hereafter cited as Randall Papers, WSHS; *Milwaukee Daily Sentinel,* 5 Feb. 1861.

6. Niven, *Connecticut for the Union,* 42.

7. W. A. Swanberg, *First Blood: The Story of Fort Sumter* (New York: Charles Scribner, 1957), 298 (there is some dispute about who fired that first shot); Samuel P. Bates, *History of Pennsylvania Volunteers, 1861–65,* 2 vols. (Harrisburg, Pa.: B. Singerly, 1869), 1:33.

8. Osterweis, *New Haven,* 319.

9. *Cincinnati Daily Enquirer,* 19 Apr. 1861, 21 Apr. 1861; Frederick Phisterer, *New York in the War of the Rebellion* 6 vols. (Albany: F. R. Lyon, 1912), 1:20; Frank Moore, ed., *The Rebellion Record* 12 vols. (New York: G. P. Putnam, 1862), 1:83–119; Brumner, *New York Political History,* 144–46; Justin Winsor, ed., *Memorial History of Boston,* 4 vols. (Boston: Ticknor, 1881), 1:314; *Cincinnati Daily Gazette,* 22 Apr. 1861; James L. Bowen, *Massachusetts in the War* (Springfield: Bowen, 1893), 16; Scharf and Westcott, *Philadelphia History* 1:762–64.

10. James Barnett, "Augustus Willich, Soldier Extraordinary," *Cincinnati Historical Society Bulletin* 20(Jan. 1962):60; Easton, *Hegel's Followers,* 59; Orville James Victor, *Incidents and Anecdotes of the War* (New York: J. D. Torrey, [1862]), 14; Charles M. Knapp, *New Jersey Politics during the Period of the Civil War and Reconstruction* (Geneva, N.Y.: W. F.

Humphrey, 1924), 54–55; *Milwaukee Daily Sentinel,* 16 Apr. 1861. According to Knapp, there were still eighteen slaves in New Jersey in 1860.

11. George H. Walther to Governor Randall, 16 Apr. 1861, Randall Papers, WSHS. Similar letters are in the files of the Ohio governor. See the William Dennison, Jr., Collection, Ohio Historical Society, Columbus. Hereafter cited as the Dennison Papers, OHS.

12. *Cincinnati Daily Gazette,* 23 Apr. 1861 – in this instance, the unfortunate victim was actually trying to enlist in a local militia unit; N. Daniels to Governor Randall, 16 Apr. 1861, Randall Papers, WSHS.

13. Joseph George, Jr., "Philadelphia's *Catholic Herald:* The Civil War Years," *Pennsylvania Magazine of History and Biography* 103(Apr. 1979):196–221.

14. *Boston Pilot,* 12 Jan. 1861.

15. Craig Lee Kautz, "Fodder for Cannon: Immigrant Perceptions of the Civil War," (Ph.D. diss., University of Nebraska, 1976), 46–47; Frank L. Klement, *Wisconsin and the Civil War* (Madison: State Historical Society of Wisconsin, 1963), 35.

16. Francis Grierson, *The Valley of Shadows* (New York: John Lane, 1913), 254–55, 257.

17. Walter D. Kamphoefer, "St. Louis Germans and the Republican Party, 1848–1860," *Mid-America* 57(Apr. 1975):69–88.

18. Harvey Saalberg, "The *Westliche Post* of St. Louis: Daily Newspaper for German-Americans, 1857–1938," (Ph.D. diss., University of Missouri, 1967), 62–72; Arthur Roy Kirkpatrick, "Missouri on the Eve of Civil War," *Missouri Historical Review* 55 (Oct. 1960):99–105; Thomas J. McCormack, ed., *Memoirs of Gustave Koerner* 2 vols. (Cedar Rapids, Iowa: Torch Press, 1909), 2:131–32. Audrey Louise Olson, "St. Louis Germans, 1850–1920: The Nature of an Immigrant Community and Its Relation to the Assimilation Process," (Ph.D. diss., University of Kansas, 1970), points out quite correctly that there was no monolithic German community in St. Louis. Most German immigrants sought homes near their jobs. There were several different German areas, with the Germans settling down along the lines of provincial origin in Europe. Unlike Milwaukee, St. Louis as a city was not "Germanized." Still, to the non-German, "all Germans were alike."

19. Charles Daniel Drake, "Autobiography," State Historical Society of Missouri, Columbia; Arthur Roy Kirkpatrick, "Missouri in the Early Months of the Civil War," *Missouri Historical Review* 55 (Apr. 1955): 235–66; James W. Covington, "The Camp Jackson Affair," *Missouri Historical Review* 55 (Dec. 1960):197–212; Charles D. Drake, *Camp Jackson: Its History and Significance* (St. Louis: Missouri Democrat, 1863), 1–19; Wiley Britton, *The Civil War on the Border* 2 vols. (New York: G. P. Putnam, 1899); Alexander C. Niven, "The Role of German Volunteers in St. Louis, 1861," *American-German Review* (Feb.-Mar. 1962):29–30; Galusha Anderson, *The Story of a Border City during the Civil War* (Boston: Little, Brown, 1908), 16–85; *Cincinnati Daily Gazette,* 13 May 1861; Frederick F. Schrader, *The German in the Making of America* (Boston: Stratford, 1924), 203–6; Arthur B. Faust, *The German Element in the United States* 2 vols. (New York: Steuben Society of America, 1927), 1:531–35; *Cincinnati Daily-Express* 23 Apr.–14 May 1861; Ryles, *Missouri: Union or Secession.*

20. Drake, *Camp Jackson,* 9.

21. Ella Lonn, *Foreigners in the Union Army and Navy* (1951; reprint, New York: Greenwood Press, 1969), 295.

22. Robert C. Nesbit, *Wisconsin: A History* (Madison: Univ. of Wisconsin Press, 1973), 255.

23. Peter Karsten, *Soldiers and Society: The Effects of Military Service and War on American Life* (Westport, Conn.: Greenwood Press, 1978), 7.

24. William B. Skelton, "Officers and Politicians: The Origin of Army Politics in the United States before the Civil War," in *The Military in American,* ed. Peter Karsten (New York: Free Press, 1980), 89–110.

25. Conzen, *Immigrant Milwaukee,* 288.

26. Eugene C. Murdock, *One Million Men: The Civil War Draft in the North* (Madison: State Historical Society of Wisconsin, 1971), 306; Scharf and Westcott, *History of Philadelphia* 1:755; Lonn, *Foreigners in the Union Army,* 184–85.

27. Stephen Z. Starr, "The Grand Old Regiment," *Wisconsin Magazine of History* 48(Autumn 1964):21–31; Fred Albert Shannon, *The Organization and Administration of the Union Army* (1928; reprint, Gloucester, Mass.: Peter Smith, 1965), 39–41.

28. Camille Ferri Pisani, *Prince Napoleon in America: 1861: Letters from His Aide-De-Camp,* trans. Georges J. Joyoux (Port Washington, N.Y.: Kennikat Press, 1973), 72–73. First published in 1862 under the title *Lettres sur les Etats-Unis d'Amerique.*

## 4. RECRUITING THE ETHNICS

1. Theodore Calvin Pease and James G. Randall, eds., *The Diary of Orville Hickman Browning,* vol. 20, *Collections of the Illinois State Historical Society* (Springfield: Illinois State Historical Society, 1925), 20:487–88.
2. John A. Callicott to Governor Yates, 3 Aug. 1862, Richard Yates Papers, Illinois State Historical Society, Springfield. Hereafter cited as the Yates Papers, ISHS
3. William Dudley Foulke, *Life of Oliver P. Morton.* 2 vols. (Indianapolis: Bowen-Merrill, 1899), 1:149–50; Woodburn, "Indiana Party Politics," 239.
4. Armin Rappaport, "The Replacement System during the Civil War," *Military Affairs* 20(Summer 1951):95–106; Henry Villard, *Memoirs of Henry Villard,* 2 vols. (Boston: Houghton, Mifflin, 1904), 1:177.
5. Carl Wittke, *Refugees of Revolution, The German Forty-Eighters in America* (Philadelphia: Univ. of Pennsylvania Press, 1952), 235–36; Bancroft, *Schurz Speeches and Papers* 1:180–81; Basler, *Lincoln Works* 4:367–68; Schurz, *Reminiscences* 2:228–37.
6. McCormack, *Koerner Memoirs* 2:206, and 2:184; Koerner to Yates, 3 Sept. 1861 and 9 Sept. 1861, Yates Papers, ISHS.
7. Julian Kuné, *Reminiscences of an Octogenarian Hungarian Exile* (Chicago: The Author, 1911); Hecker to Koerner, 21 May 1861, in McCormack, *Koerner's Memoirs* 2:151; Petition to Governor Yates, 28 June 1861, Yates Papers, ISHS; Lonn, *Union Army Foreigners,* 104–5. Lonn says that Hecker "gracefully accepted" command of the regiment on May 25.
8. A simplified regimental identification is used throughout the remainder of this work. Each regiment is identified by number and state, as Twenty-fourth Illinois Infantry.
9. Yates to Hecker, 16 July 1862, Yates Papers, ISHS.
10. Peter Page to Yates, 4 Dec. 1861, and Yates to Page, 11 Dec. 1861, Yates Papers, ISHS.
11. Easton, *Hegel's American Followers,* 59; Tucker, *Civil War Cincinnati,* 15–16. Frank Blair led the first German regiment organized in St. Louis, and part of the reason for his election was the hope of reducing anti-German prejudice in the larger society.
12. J. A. Swain to Governor Randall, 1 May 1861, Randall Papers, WSHS.
13. *Tracts Issued by the Loyal Publication Society,* 2 vols. (New York: Loyal Publication Society, 1864–65).
14. Quoted in Lonn, *Union Army Foreigners,* 665; Steven Rowan, trans. and ed., *Germans for a Free Missouri: Translations from the St. Louis Radical Press, 1857–1862* (Columbia: Univ. of Missouri Press, 1983).
15. Nels Hokanson, *Swedish Immigrants in Lincoln's Time* (New York: Harper, 1941), 71; broadside, ISHS.
16. *Philadelphia Evening Bulletin,* 22 Aug. 1862.
17. *Cincinnati Daily Enquirer,* 20 Apr. 1861; quoted in Moore, *Rebellion Record* 2:40; *Philadelphia Evening Bulletin,* 14 Aug. 1861.
18. All the speeches are printed in Moore, *Rebellion Record* 1:107ff.
19. Theodore C. Blegen, ed., *The Civil War Letters of Colonel Hans Christian Heg* (Northfield, Minn.: Norwegian-American Historical Association, 1936), 23; Rowan, *Germans for a Free Missouri,* 224–46.
20. Winterbotham to his parents, 16 Aug. 1862, Winterbotham Papers, CHS; Hokanson, *Swedish Immigrants,* 71–72; Wittke, *Refugees,* 232.
21. Princess Felix Salm-Salm, *Ten Years of My Life* (Detroit: Balford, 1877), 51.
22. Broadside, ISHS; Ferri Pisani, *Napoleon in America,* 76.
23. Melanie R. Rosborough, "One Hundred Years Ago: The F. L. Soldier," *South Atlantic Bulletin* 30(Mar. 1965):8–11.
24. Scharff and Westcott, *Philadelphia History* 1:772.
25. See the correspondence involving Blenker, Secretary of War Simon Cameron, and

General McClellan, in *War of the Rebellion: A Compilation of the Official Records of the Union and Confederate Armies* (Washington: U.S. Government Printing Office, 1902), series III, 1:458–59.

26. Robert Ernst, *Immigrant Life in New York City, 1825–1863* (1949; reprint, Port Washington, N.Y.: Ira J. Friedman, 1965), 128. There was a British Drill Club in Boston that organized a volunteer company in 1861, but nothing came of an effort to make it the nucleus of a British regiment. See George G. W. Morgan to Governor Andrew, 19 Oct. 1861, Governor Andrew Collection, Massachusetts Historical Society, Boston. Hereafter cited as the Andrew Collection, MHS.

27. Aram Bakshian, "Foreign Adventurers in the American Revolution," *History Today,* Mar. 1971, 187–97.

28. William Howard Russell, *My Diary North and South* (Boston: T. O. H. P. Burnham, 1863), 580.

29. Joseph Tyler Butts, ed., *A Gallant Captain of the Civil War, Being the Extraordinary Adventures of Frederich Otto Baron Von Fritsch* (New York: F. Tennyson Neely, 1902); Wittke, *Refugees,* 232; Butts, *Gallant Captain,* 12–13.

30. Mabel McIlvaine, ed., *Reminiscences of Chicago During the Civil War* (Chicago: R. R. Donnelley, 1914), 97–150; Griner to his mother, 17 Apr. 1861, quoted in D. H. Woodward, "The Civil War of a Pennsylvania Trooper," *Pennsylvania Magazine of History and Biography* 87(Jan. 1963):40; K. Jack Bauer, ed., *Soldiering: The Civil War Diary of Rice C. Bull, 123rd New York Volunteer Infantry* (San Rafael, Calif.: Presidio Press, 1977), 1–3.

31. Jacob Dolson Cox, "Why the Men of '61 Fought for the Union," *Atlantic Monthly,* Mar. 1892, 382–94.

32. Victor Hicken, *Illinois in the Civil War* (Urbana: Univ. of Illinois Press, 1966), 128–29; Pease and Randall, *Browning Diary* 1:620–21.

33. D. L. Day, *My Diary of the Rambles With the 25th Mass. Volunteer Infantry* (Milford, Mass.: King and Billings, 1884), 5; McIlvaine, *Chicago Reminiscences,* 79–95.

34. Leslie Anders, *The Twenty-First Missouri* (Westport, Conn.: Greenwood Press, 1975), 3–19.

35. Woodward, "Pennsylvania Trooper," 40; G. W. Thompson to Yates, 2 Sept. 1861, Yates Papers, ISHS.

36. Titus Crawshaw to his father, 28 Mar. 1862, in Charlotte Erikson, *Invisible Immigrants: The Adaptation of English and Scottish Immigrants in Nineteenth-Century America* (Coral Gables, Fla.: Univ. of Miami Press, 1972), 351; Lonn, *Union Army Foreigners,* 67–79.

37. Robert C. Goodell and P. A. M. Taylor, "A German Immigrant in the Union: Selected Letters of Valentin Bechler," *Journal of American Studies* 2(Feb. 1971):145–62,161; George Augustus Sala, *My Diary in America in the Midst of War,* 2 vols. (London: Tinsley, 1865), 1:399–402; Man, "New York Irish," 107; Ferri Pisani, *Napoleon in America,* 69–75.

38. Thomas Francis Galway, *The Valiant Hours* (Harrisburg, Pa.: Stackpole, 1961), 1; Comte de Paris, *History of the Civil War in America,* trans. Louis F. Tasistro, 4 vols. (Philadelphia: Jos. H. Coates, 1876–78), 1:173.

39. Quoted in Lonn, *Union Army Foreigners,* 76–77; Man, "New York Irish," 103; P. Casey to James Mulligan, 23 Mar. 1863, James A. Mulligan Papers, CHS.

40. *Mississippi Blätter,* 21 Apr. 1861, in Rowan, *Germans for a Free Missouri,* 182–83.

41. Lonn, *Union Army Foreigners,* 659; Blied, *Catholics in the Civil War,* 39; Man, "New York Irish," 105; Paris, *Civil War in America* 1:177–78.

42. Ella Lonn, *Foreigners in the Confederacy* (1940; reprint, Gloucester, Mass.: Peter Smith, 1965), 96–107; David T. Maul, "Five Butternut Yankees," *Illinois State Historical Society Journal* 56(June 1963):177–92.

43. Hofmeister, *Chicago Germans,* 88.

## 5. THE GERMAN REGIMENTS

1. Kuné to Yates, 26 Aug. 1861, Yates Papers, ISHS.
2. Hecker to Illinois Adj. Gen Thomas Mather, 5 Sept. 1861, Twenty-fourth Illinois Infantry File, Springfield, Illinois State Archives. Hereafter cited as ISA.

3. Hecker to Yates, 22 Sept. 1861, Twenty-fourth Illinois Infantry File, ISA.

4. Mitchel to General Buell, 16 Dec. 1861, Twenty-fourth Illinois Infantry File, ISA.

5. Petition to Colonel Hecker, 31 Oct. 1861, Twenty-fourth Illinois Infantry File, ISA.

6. Copy of War Department Order, 14 Oct. 1861, Twenty-fourth Illinois Infantry File, ISA. McCormack, *Koerner's Memoirs* 2:193; Hecker to Yates, 23 Oct. 1861, Twenty-fourth Illinois Infantry File, ISA.

7. Assistant Adjutant General of the Department of the Cumberland to Mihalotzy, 26 Oct. 1861, Mihalotzy Papers, ISHS; Special Order No. 72, 26 Oct. 1861, Mihalotzy Papers, ISHS.

8. S. M. Wilson to Yates, 31 Oct. 1861, Yates Papers, ISHS; Butz to Yates, 1 Nov. 1861, Yates Papers, ISHS.

9. Butz to Mather, 2 Nov. 1861, and Hecker to Yates, 5 Nov. 1861, Twenty-fourth Illinois Infantry File, ISA.

10. Special Order No. 4, 19 Nov. 1861, Mihalotzy Papers, ISHS; Butz to Adjutant General Fuller, 26 Nov. 1861, Twenty-fourth Infantry File, ISA.

11. Hoffman to Fuller, 30 Nov. and 6 Dec. 1861, Twenty-fourth Illinois Infantry File, ISA.

12. Yates to Cameron, 3 Dec. 1861, Yates Papers, ISHS; Hoffman to [Fuller], 5 Dec. 1861, and Hoffman to Fuller, 6 Dec. 1861, Twenty-fourth Illinois Infantry File, ISA; D. W. Wagner to Fuller, 15 Dec. 1861, Twenty-fourth Illinois Infantry File; Captain A. Mauss to −, n.d., Twenty-fourth Illinois Infantry File, ISA; William Wagner, *History of the 24th Illinois Volunteer Infantry Regiment* (Chicago: *Illinois Staats-Zeitung* [?], 1864/1911), 8–18.

13. Butz to Yates, 27 Jan. 1862, Twenty-fourth Illinois Infantry File, ISA;

14. Hoffman translated the item in a letter to Yates, 6 Feb. 1862, Yates Papers, ISHS. Hoffman himself underlined the section on whiskey.

15. Wagner, *Twenty-fourth Illinois Infantry,* 43.

16. Lonn, *Union Army Foreigners,* 217; Butz to Yates, 27 May 1862, Eighty-second Illinois Infantry File, ISA.

17. Butts, *Gallant Captain,* 50–51; Schurz, *Reminiscences* 3:424.

18. Hecker to Yates, 19 July 1863, Eighty-second Illinois Infantry File, ISA. Even in the Eighty-second Regiment, Hecker's ambitions continued to antagonize his men. One disgruntled enlisted man regularly complained to his parents that Hecker's desire for personal glory endangered the lives of his soldiers. See the Friedrich Kappelman Correspondence, especially the letters of 18 Jan. 1863 and 10 May 1863. Photocopies of these letters can be found in the *Civil War Times Illustrated* Collection, U.S. Army Miilitary Institute, Carlisle Barracks, Pennsylvania, hereafter cited as USAMHI.

19. McCormack, *Koerner's Memoirs* 2:164–94; Raith to Yates, 7 Dec. 1861, Yates Papers, ISHS.

20. Engelmann to his wife, 29 Dec. 1861 and 12 Jan. 1862, Engelmann-Kircher Papers, ISHS. Engelmann wrote in both English and German. I have used the English translations of the German letters made by his son.

21. Engelmann to Koerner, 19 Apr. 1862, and Engelmann to his wife, 29 Mar. 1863, Engelmann-Kircher Papers, ISHS.

22. Bell Irvin Wiley, *The Life of Billy Yank* (Indianapolis: Bobbs-Merrill, 1952), 334–35; "Address," 4 Jan. 1865, Engelmann-Kircher Papers, ISHS; *Report of the Adjutant General of the State of Illinois* (Springfield, Ill.: Phillips, 1901), 3:274–77.

23. William A. Fritsch, *German Settlers and German Settlements in Indiana* (Evansville, Ind.: The Author, 1915), 29–39; Foulke, *Morton* 1:149–50; Logan Esarey, *A History of Indiana,* 2 vols. (Indianapolis: B. F. Bowen, 1918), 2:746; Elfreda Lang, "The Germans of Dubois County, Their Newspapers, Their Politics, and Their Part in the Civil War," *Indiana Magazine of History* 42(Sept. 1946):229–48.

24. Stewart, "Bachelor General," 143–44.

25. James Barnett, "Willich's Thirty-Second Indiana Volunteers," *Cincinnati Historical Society Bulletin* 37(Spring 1979):49–70.

26. [Catherine Merrill], *The Soldiers of Indiana in the War for the Union,* 2 vols. (Indianapolis: Merrill, 1866–1869), 1:230–31.

27. Arville L. Funk, *Hoosiers in the Civil War* (Chicago: Adams, 1967), 172. The "fightingest" label comes from the famous list by William Fox; *Harper's Weekly* 11(Jan. 1862, 28), with a dramatic drawing accompanying the story—*Harper's* made no mention of the ethnic character of the regiment; quoted in Barnett, "Willich's Indiana Volunteers," 67.

28. Carl Schnitz to Adj. Gen. Lazarus Nobel, 11 Nov. 1861, Thirty-second Indiana Infantry File, Indianapolis, Indiana State Archives. Hereafter cited as InSA.

29. Quoted in James Barnett, "The Vilification of Augustus Willich," *Cincinnati Historical Society Bulletin* 24(Jan. 1966):29; Barnett, "Willich Soldier Extraordinary," 70–71.

30. Ibid., 74; Villard, *Memoirs* 2:215.

31. Schnitz to Adjutant General Noble, 11 May 1862, Thirty-second Infantry File, InSA; Kautz, "Cannon Fodder," 76–77; Fritsch, *German Settlers,* 32.

32. Fritsch, *German Settlers,* 34; Michael Frash Diary (photocopy), Oct.-Dec. 1864, Indianapolis, Indiana Historical Society. Hereafter cited as InHS.

33. Lonn, *Union Army Foreigners,* 192.

34. Rosengarten, *German Soldiers,* 114–15, lists seven German regiments for New York. This includes the Fifth New York Militia, the Seventh New York Infantry (Steuben Rangers), the Eighth New York Infantry (First German Rifles), the Twentieth New York Infantry (United Turner Rifles), Twenty-ninth New York Infantry (Astor Rifles), Forty-first New York Infantry (DeKalb Guards), and the Fifty-second New York Infantry (Sigel Rifles). Lonn, *Union Army Foreigners,* 666, includes all of these and adds the Forty-fifth New York Infantry (Platt Deutsch Regiment), the Forty-sixth New York Infantry (Frémont Regiment), the Fifty-fourth New York Infantry (Schwarze Jäger), and the Fourth New York Cavalry (Dickel's Mounted Rifles). Most New York regimental records were destroyed in a fire in Albany.

35. Schurz, *Reminiscences* 2:234.

36. *Washington Daily National Intelligencer,* 29 May 1861; Margaret Leech, *Reveille in Washington, 1860–65* (New York: Harper, 1941), 84–85; Villard, *Memoirs* 1:174.

37. *Washington Evening Star,* 5 June 1861; undated clipping D'Utassy Collection, New York, New York Historical Society. Hereafter cited as NYHS.

38. See Blenker to Cameron, 25 July 1861, Cameron to Curtis, 23 Sept. 1861, and Blenker to McClellan, 27 Aug. 1861, in *War of the Rebellion,* series III, 1:458–59 and 534. In his own official account of the Battle of Bull Run, Blenker made no reference to the ethnic makeup of his command; see his report, *War of the Rebellion,* series III, 2:426–28. In their official reports, commanders seldom made ethnic references.

39. Salm-Salm, *Ten Years,* 22–23; Schurz, *Reminiscences* 2:235; Rosengarten, *German Soldier,* 97; Leech, *Washington Reveille,* 114.

40. *Washington Evening Star,* 2 Oct. 1861.

41. *DAB,* s.v., "Gustav Struve."

42. Wittke, *Refugees,* 233.

43. M. C. Gritzner, *Blenker und Frémont* (Washington, D.C.: n.p., 1862). Constantin Sander, *Der Amerikanische Bürgerkrieg von Seinem Beginn bis zem Schluss des Jahres 1862* (Frankfurt am Main: Druck und Verlag von Wilhelm Küchler, 1863), 61, also insisted that Blenker was a victim of anti-German prejudice. This kind of defense was routine when an ethnic soldier encountered legal problems or political attacks.

44. Carl Wittke, *Against the Current: The Life of Karl Heinzen* (Chicago: Univ. of Chicago Press, 1945), 180.

45. D'Utassy's story is given in Gritzner, *Blenker und Frémont,* 34; Wittke, *Karl Heinzen,* 182–83.

46. Salm-Salm, *Ten Years,* 24; Brooks, *Lincoln's Washington,* 69; Butts, *Gallant Captain,* 114.

47. Salm-Salm, *Ten Years,* 32–34.

48. Ibid., 40–41.

49. "Prince Salm-Salm," *Harper's Weekly,* 9 May 1863, 301; Butts, *Gallant Captain,* 24.

50. See, for example, Dieter Cunz, ed., "Civil War Letters of a German Immigrant," *American-German Review* 11(Oct. 1944):30–33; Col. Georg von Amsberg, Forty-fifth New York, to Sen. Edwin Morgan, n.d., Morgan Papers, Albany, New York State Library. Hereafter cited as NYSL; Eugene A. Kozley, colonel of the Fifty-fourth New York Infantry, to

Governor Morgan, 24 Nov. 1861, Morgan Papers, NYSL; Wladimir Kryzanowski to Governor Morgan, 16 Sept. 1861, CHS.

51. Bosse, *Deutsche Element,* 103, 667–68. No "pure" ethnic regiment existed.

52. Thomas Crofts, ed., *History of the Service of the Third Ohio Veteran Volunteer Cavalry* (Toledo: Stoneman, 1910); Stephen Z. Starr, "The Third Ohio Volunteer Cavalry: A View from the Inside," *Ohio History* 85(Autumn 1976):306–18; John W. Large Papers (photocopies), Columbus, Ohio Historical Society. Hereafter cited as OHS; Robert M. Atkinson Papers, OHS; Joseph A. Saunier, ed., *History of the Forty-Seventh Regiment Ohio Veteran Volunteer Infantry* (Hillsboro, Ohio: Lyle, 1903); Thomas Taylor Collection OHS; Whitelaw Reid, *Ohio in the War,* 2 vols. (Cincinnati: Moore, Wilstach, and Baldwin, 1868), 2:291–95.

53. *Die Neuner: Erstes Deutsches Regiment von Ohio* (Cincinnati: Druck von S. Rosenthal, 1897), 13; James H. Rodabaugh, "The Fighting McCooks," *Civil War History* 3(1957):287–90; Carl Wittke, "The Ninth Ohio Volunteers," *Ohio Archaeological and Historical Quarterly* 35(Apr. 1926):402–17; Reid, *Ohio in the War* 1:876.

54. Quoted in Barnett, "Augustus Willich," 61.

55. James Barnett, "Crime and No Punishment: The Death of Robert L. McCook," *Cincinnati Historical Society Bulletin* 22(1964):29–37.

56. Petitions and other papers in the Ninth Ohio Infantry File, Cincinnati Historical Society (hereafter CiHS), show a remarkably tranquil regiment for most of its history; undated, unidentified newspaper clipping, William Lytle Scrapbook, Lytle Papers, CiHS.

57. "Murder of General Robert L. McCook," *Harper's Weekly,* 23 Aug. 1862, 530; Barnett, "Crime," 29–33.

58. Kaufmann, *Die Deutschen,* 516.

59. Wittke, *Refugees,* 413–14.

60. Special Order No. 265, 10 Aug. 1864, Ninth Ohio Infantry File, CiHS.

61. Brauer to George H. Harris, 22 Oct. 1862, and Brauer to Harris, 1 Dec. 1862, Ninth Ohio Infantry File, CiHS; a different recruiter lodged the same complaint, 14 Nov. 1862, and Ohio's governor, David Tod, informed Kämmerling that the recruiting problems related to entrepreneurs opting for new regiments instead of keeping the old units filled, 23 Oct. 1862, Ninth Ohio Infantry File, CiHS. A diarist in the Forty-first New York Infantry noted in his entries for 23 July 1863 and 26 Nov. 1863 that this German outfit filled its depleted ranks after Gettysburg with several hundred conscripts. See the Charles S. Bornemann Diary, a copy of which is in the Civil War Miscellaneous Collection, USAMHI.

62. Gen. Joshua H. Bates to Dennison, 11 July 1861, Dennison Papers, OHS; Reid, *Ohio in the War* 2:194–96; Godfrey Weitzel, "Biographical Sketch of Augustus Moor," Letter Book 1:746–48, Twenty-eighth Ohio Infantry File, CiHS.

63. *History of the 37th Regiment, O. V. V. I.* (Toledo, Ohio: Montgomery and Vrooman, 1890); General Order No. 10, 3 Feb. 1863, Limberg File, CiHS.

64. Alfred C. Raphelson, "Alexander Schimmelfennig, A German-American Campaigner in the Civil War," *Pennsylvania Magazine of History and Biography* 87(Apr. 1963):156–81.

65. M. Gritzner to E. B. Washburne, 17 Aug. 1861, Yates Papers, ISHS.

66. Raphelson, "Schimmelfennig," 165–66; Schurz, *Reminiscences* 2:351.

67. Frank R. Taylor, *Philadelphia in Civil War, 1861–1865* (Philadelphia: City of Philadelphia, 1913), 98–99; Raphelson, "Schimmelfennig," 165–66.

68. Butts, *Gallant Captain,* 29–30; Lonn, *Union Army Foreigners,* 594–96.

69. Butts, *Gallant Captain,* 29–30.

70. "General Schimmelfennig," *Harper's Weekly,* 7 Oct. 1865, 629.

71. Bates, *Deeds* 2:476–79; Rosengarten, *German Soldier,* 110.

72. Edward J. Longacre, "The Most Inept Regiment of the Civil War," *Civil War Times Illustrated,* Nov.1969, 4–7.

73. Chester Harding, Jr., to Gov. H. R. Gamble, 1 Jan. 1862, in *War of the Rebellion,* series III, 1:794–96; Rombauer, *Union Cause in St. Louis,* 195.

74. James Neal Primm, "Introduction," Rowan, *Germans for a Free Missouri,* 37–41.

75. *New York Times,* 15 June 1861; Primm, "Introduction," 37.

76. John T. Buegel, "Civil War Diary, 1861–64," 1–3, Columbia, Missouri, State Historical Society. I used the English translation by William Bek.

77. Charles A. Raeuber, "A Swiss Regiment in the American Civil War," *Swiss Review of World Affairs* 13(1963):11–14; Saalberg, "Westliche Post," 105; Joseph Conrad to Adj. Gen. John B. Gray, 10 Aug. 1864, and N. D. Randall to Adjutant General Gray, 9 Apr. 1863, Fifteenth Missouri Infantry file, Springfield, Missouri, Adjutant General Records.

78. Lincoln to William T. Sherman, 26 July 1864, in Basley, *Lincoln Works* 7:463; Earl J. Hess, "The 12th Missouri Infantry: A Socio-Military Profile of a Union Regiment," *Missouri Historical Review* 76(Oct. 1981):53–77.

79. Henry Goedeking to Kircher, 8 June 1861, Engelmann-Kircher Papers, ISHS. A selection of Kircher letters, translated into English when the original was in German, is in Hess, *A German in the Yankee Fatherland.*

80. Kircher to his mother, 14 June 1862, Engelmann-Kircher papers, ISHS.

81. In his diary entry for 21 Apr. 1863, for example, he noted that an officer made a speech to the regiment in German; Henry Kircher Diary, Engelmann-Kircher Papers, ISHS; Henry to his father, 30 Jan. 1863, and Kircher to his mother, 3 Jan. 1863, in Hess, *A German in the Yankee Fatherland.* 62, 46.

82. George E. Waring, Jr., *Whip and Spur* (New York: Doubleday and McClure, 1897) — chapter titles in this bizarre book are the names of the colonel's successive personal horses; Rosengarten, *German Soldier,* 94; Gen. Peter J. Osterhaus to Col. William D. Wood, 17 Nov. 1862, Fourth Missouri Cavalry File, Springfield, Missouri, Adjutant General Records.

83. "Proclamation," 20 Aug.1861, Governor's Journal, WHS; Edwin B. Quiner, *The Military History of Wisconsin* (Chicago: Clarke, 1866), 540–47; *Milwaukee Daily Sentinel,* 4 Dec. 1861; J. J. Schlicher, "Bernhard Domschcke," *Wisconsin Magazine of History* 29(1945–46):319–32, 435–56.

84. Lonn, *Union Army Foreigners,* 573–79.

85. Schrader, *Germans in America,* 220–28.

86. Wittke, *Refugees;* Ella Lonn, "The Forty-Eighters in the Civil War," in *The Forty-Eighters: Political Refugees of the German Revolution of 1848,* ed. A. E. Zucker (New York: Columbia Univ. Press, 1950), 204–31. For a more recent assessment, see Köllmann and Marschalck, "German Emigration."

87. Frank P. Robinson, "I Fights Mit Sigel," *Loyalty Tract No. 49* (1864), 8.

88. Schurz to Theodore Petrarch, 12 Oct. 1864, and Schurz to his wife, 8 July 1867, in Schafer, *Schurz Letters,* 310, 382–83.

## 6. THE IRISH REGIMENTS

1. James Bowen to Morgan, 20 Apr. 1861, and Thurlow Weed to Morgan, 20 Apr. 1861, Albany, Morgan Papers, New York State Archives. Hereafter cited as NYA.

2. Patrick O'Flagherty, "The History of the Sixty-Ninth Regiment of the New York State Militia, 1852–1861," (Ph.D. diss., Fordham University, 1963), 230–31; William D'Arcy, *The Fenian Movement in the United States, 1858–1886* (Washington: Catholic Univ. of America Press, 1947), 11, 37. If you *must* join the army, concluded Corcoran's advice, join an Irish regiment.

3. *New York Times,* 24 Apr. 1861; Florence E. Gibson, *The Attitudes of the New York Irish toward State and National Affairs, 1848–1892* (New York: Columbia Univ. Press, 1951), 122–23.

4. *New York Times,* 5 June 1861; *Boston Pilot,* 4 May 1861.

5. "We Will Have the Union Still," undated broadside, CiHS.

6. John Rose Greene Hassard, *Life of the Most Reverend John Hughes* (New York: D. Appleton, 1866), 443; Basler, *Lincoln Works,* 4:419; G. W. Bungary to Morgan, 28 Apr. 1862, and a copy of a letter to James B. Kirker, 11 May 1862, Morgan Papers, NYSL.

7. Winterbotham to his parents, 16 Aug. 1862, Winterbotham Papers, CHS. Other letters in this collection give a valuable portrait of an ambitious aspirant for position in a Civil War regiment.

8. McIvor to Capt. Gray, 9 Dec. 1863, and on the back of a letter, John P. Rogers to McIvor, 15 Aug. 1863, James McIvor Papers, New York, NYHS.

9. John O'Leary, *Recollections of Fenians and Fenianism*, 2 vols. (1896; reprint New York: Barnes and Noble, 1969), 1:212–17. Corcoran gives his version of the episode in a letter to Colonel Hawkins, 17 Apr. 1863, reprinted in the *New York Times*, 22 Apr. 1863.

10. "Official Journal of Hawkins' Zouaves, Ninth N.Y. Vols., 1861–1863," entry for 11 Apr. 1863, New York, NYPL.

11. Caoimhin O'Danachair, "A Soldier's Letters Home, 1863–74," *Irish Sword*, Summer 1957, 64; *New York Times*, 25 Dec. 1863.

12. Athearn, *Meagher;* Jones, *Irish Brigade;* Lyons, *Meagher;* D. P. Conyngham, *The Irish Brigade and Its Campaigns* (New York: William McSorley, 1867). Daniel Devlin and Judge Charles P. Daly played prominent roles in the formation of the brigade. Hernon, in *Celts, Catholics and Copperheads*, says that Meagher got command of the Irish Brigade through political conniving (p. 18).

13. Hughes to Seward, 12 Sept. 1861, in Hassard, *Hughes*, 443–44; Thomas Francis Meagher, *The Last Days of the 69th in Virginia* (New York: Irish-American, n.d.).

14. L[orenzo] Thomas to Meagher, 18 Feb. 1862, in *War of the Rebellion*, series III, 1:895.

15. Leech, *Reveille in Washington*, 85; Lonn, *Union Army Foreigners*, 203; Conyngham, *Irish Brigade*, 75; Corby, *Chaplain Memoirs*, 28.

16. Turner to his parents and sister, 4 Mar. 1862, James B. Turner Papers, Albany, NYSL. Turner's many family letters, done with a literate hand and revealing an astute observer, provide an intimate look at life in an Irish regiment.

17. The Turner Papers include clippings of his *Irish-American* columns.

18. Russell, *Diary*, 511; *Washington Evening Star*, 27 Aug. 1861 and 30 Aug. 1861; Villard, *Memoirs* 1:183–84. Villard had a dislike of Meagher well before Bull Run. He regarded him as a poseur.

19. Stephen W. Sears, *Landscape Turned Red: The Battle of Antietam* (New Haven: Ticknor and Fields, 1983), 242–43; George B. McClellan, *Report on the Organization of the Army of the Potomac* (1864; reprint, Freeport, N.Y.: Books for Libraries, 1970), 382; Francis W. Palfrey, *The Antietam and Fredericksburg* (New York: Charles Scribner, 1889), 101.

20. Quoted in J. Cutler Andrews, *The North Reports the Civil War* (Pittsburgh: Univ. of Pittsburgh Press, 1955), 284; Sears, *Antietam*, 244, 394.

21. Clippings in the James B. Turner Papers, Albany, NYSL; Col. Silas W. Burt to Morrow, 21 Aug. 1862, Edwin D. Morgan Papers, Albany, NYSL.

22. St. Clair A. Mulholland, *The Story of the 116th Regiment, Pennsylvania Infantry* (Philadelphia: F. McManus, Jr., 1899), 32–33.

23. G. F. R. Henderson, *The Civil War: A Soldier's View* (Chicago: Univ. of Chicago Press, 1958), 74.

24. Moore, *Rebellion Record* 6:82.

25. Villard, *Memoirs* 1:371.

26. Paul Jones, "The Irish Brigade at Fredericksburg," *Catholic Digest*, Jan. 1963, 105–10; clippings in the James B. Turner Papers, Albany, NYSL; John D. McCormack, "Never Were Men So Brave," *Civil War Times Illustrated*, Apr. 1969, 36–44.

27. Jones, "Irish Brigade," 109.

28. Joseph M. Hernon, Jr., *Celts, Catholics, and Copperheads: Ireland Views the American Civil War* (Columbus: Ohio State Univ. Press, 1968), 105–6; Meagher to the editor of the *Dublin Irishmen*, 5 Sept. 1863, and to the *Dublin Citizen*, 26 Sept. 1863, in *Loyalty Tract No. 38*, 1–15.

29. Maurice Woulfe to his family, 25 Sept. 1863, in Caoimhin O'Danachair, "A Soldier's Letters Home, 1863–74," *Irish Sword*, Summer 1957, 57. The best account of Meagher's last years is in Athearn, *Meagher.*

30. A. Milburn Petty, "History of the 37th Regiment, New York Volunteers," *American Irish Historical Society Journal* 30(1932):101–24; Phisterer, *New York in the War of the Rebellion* 3:2159; Wittke, *Irish in America*, 137.

31. Gibson, *New York Irish Attitudes*, 128.

32. Walsh, "Boston's Irish" 21–36; *Boston Pilot*, 27 Apr. 1861; *DAB*, s.v. "Patrick Donahoe."

33. William Schouler, *A History of Massachusetts in the Civil War,* 2 vols. (Boston: E. P. Dutton, 1868–1871), 1:210–11.

34. Cass to Andrews, 3 May 1861, and 6 June 1861, in Ninth Massachusetts Infantry File, Boston, Massachusetts State Library. Hereafter cited as MSL.

35. George D. Welles to Andrew, 16 May 1861, marked "confidential," Governor Andrew Collection, Boston, Massachusetts Historical Society. Hereafter cited as Andrew Papers, MHS. In all fairness to Welles, it should be noted that this was a comment often made about Irish regiments everywhere.

36. B. S. Treanor to Andrew, 10 June 1861, Andrew Papers, MHS; Rowell to Andrew, n.d., Andrew Papers, MHS. It is difficult to imagine a more inappropriate first name for an officer in an Irish regiment.

37. *Boston Pilot,* 29 June 1861.

38. *Washington Evening Star,* 20 July 1861; General Order No. 11, Army of the Potomac, 14 Sept. 1861, Ninth Massachusetts Infantry File, MSL; Welles to Andrew, 22 June 1861, Andrew Papers, MHS; Cass to —, 25 Sept. 1861, Ninth Massachusetts Infantry File, MSL; D. Macnamara, *History of the Ninth Massachusetts,* and M. Macnamara, *Irish 9th.*

39. Petition to Andrew, 31 July 1863, Ninth Massachusetts Infantry File, MSL.

40. Guiney to Treanor, 25 Oct. 1862, Ninth Massachusetts Infantry file, MSL; Guiney to McQuade, 5 Apr. 1863, Boston Public Library.

41. Walsh, "Boston's Irish," 29.

42. Treanor to Andrew, 11 Sept. 1861, with Meagher to Treanor, 5 Sept. 1861, in Twenty-eighth Massachusetts Infantry File, MSL; Lyons, *Meagher,* 99–118; A. G. Browne, Jr., to Maj. Gen. Benjamin Butler, 23 Sept. 1861, in *War of the Rebellion,* series III, 1:819.

43. Donahoe to Andrew, 9 Sept. 1861, Andrew Papers, MHS; Treanor to Andrew, n.d., Twenty-eighth Massachusetts Infantry File, MSL.

44. Parker to Andrew, 21 Sept. 1861, Donahoe to Andrew, 23 Sept. 1861, Andrew Papers, MHS; Donahoe to Andrew, 23 Sept. 1861, Bulloch to Andrew, 3 Dec. 1861, Andrew Papers, MHS; A. G. Browne, Jr., to Butler, 23 Sept. 1861, in *War of the Rebellion,* series III, 1:819.

45. Schouler to Andrew, 30 Oct. 1861, Andrew Papers, MHS.

46. Schouler to Lt. Col. Henry Lee, 25 Oct. 1861; Schouler to Andrew, 4 Nov. 1861, and a copy of a letter from Schouler to Gen. George C. Strong, 9 Nov. 1861; Meagher to Andrew, 22 Oct. 1861, Twenty-eighth Massachusetts Infantry File, MSL.

47. Brownson to Andrew, 23 Oct. 1861, Twenty-eighth Massachusetts Infantry File, MSL; Treanor to Andrew, 24 Oct. 1861, Andrew Papers, MHS; Mrs. B. F. Allen to Andrew, 24 July 1862, Twenty-eighth Massachusetts Infantry File, MSL.

48. Capt. John Reily to Andrew, 24 July 1862, Schouler to Andrew, 19 May 1862, Twenty-eighth Massachusetts Infantry File, MSL; Bowen, *Massachusetts in the War,* 419; Benjamin F. Weeks to Lt. Col. Ritchie, 8 Aug. 1862, Stevens to Andrew, 26 July 1862, and 2 Aug. 1862, Donahoe to Andrew, 13 Sept. 1862, Twenty-eighth Massachusetts Infantry File, MSL.

49. Bowen, *Massachusetts in the War,* 434.

50. The letters of George D. Welles in the Andrew Papers, MHS, reveal all of the problems for the First Massachusetts Infantry.

51. O'Ryan to Yates, 28 Dec. 1861, Yates Papers, ISHL.

52. Harold F. Smith, "Mulligan and the Irish Brigade," *Journal of the Illinois State Historical Society* 56(1963):164–76; "Colonel Mulligan," *Harper's Weekly,* 19 Oct. 1861, 658; Thomas M. Eddy, *The Patriotism of Illinois* 2 vols. (Chicago: Clark, 1865), 1:567–79; Lonn, *Union Army Foreigners,* 227–28. There is a file of newspaper clippings on Mulligan at the Chicago Historical Society.

53. James A. Mulligan, "The Siege of Lexington, Mo.," in *Battles and Leaders* 1:307–13. Grant's comment can be found in his *Personal Memoirs* (New York: Charles L. Webster, 1885), 1:258.

54. *Washington Daily National Intelligencer,* 15 Nov. 1861.

55. The parchment is in the James A. Mulligan Papers, Chicago, Chicago Historical Society. Hereafter cited as Mulligan Papers, CHS. The speech is in Moore, *Rebellion Records*

3:439–42. With the Mulligan Papers is his Diary (Oct. 1862–July 1863), an invaluable source of information.

56. *Report of the Adjutant General of the State of Illinois* (Springfield: Phillips, 1900), 2:276–78.

57. Basler, *Lincoln's Works* 4:538; Thomas C. Fitzgibbon to Mulligan, 21 May 1861, and John McDermott to Mulligan, 14 Nov. 1861, Mulligan Papers, CHS.

58. Mulligan Diary, 29 Oct. 1862, 3 Jan. 1863, CHS.

59. See his letters in the Twenty-third Illinois Infantry File, ISA; see Albert V. B. Phillipps Papers, ISHL (Phillipps was a private in Company D., Twenty-third Illinois Infantry); the letters of James H. Nugent in the Mulligan Papers, CHS (Nugent was Mulligan's brother-in-law and a member of the Twenty-third Illinois Infantry); and James M. Doyle, "The Diary of James M. Doyle," *Mid-America* 20(Oct. 1938):273–83 (Doyle was a private in the Twenty-third Illinois Infantry).

60. A Twenty-third Illinois Infantry recruiting officer (signature illegible) to Mulligan, 20 Jan. 1864, Mulligan Papers, CHS; Jennie Devin Kelly to Mulligan, 15 Feb. 1864; J. C. S. Fitzpatrick to Mulligan, 3 Feb. 1864; and Father Butler to Mulligan, 27 Feb. 1864, Mulligan Papers, CHS; D'Arcy, *Fenian Movement,* 61.

61. In the Ninetieth Illinois Infantry File, ISA, see Bradwell to Fuller, 15 Aug. 1862, Haines to Yates, 29 Aug. 1862, Knox to Fuller, 6 Sept. 1862, and O'Ryan to Yates, 25 Aug. 1862. In the Yates Papers, ISHL, see Haines to Yates, 13 Aug. 1862; Newton Batemen, et al., *Historical Encyclopedia of Illinois* (Chicago: Munsell, 1921), 1:490.

62. The episode can be pieced together from the following correspondence: Haines to Yates, 13 and 19 Aug. 1862; O'Ryan to Yates, 25 Aug. 1862, and Dunne to Yates, 10 Sept. 1862, Ninetieth Illinois Infantry File, ISA; Haines to Yates, 9 and 17 Aug. 1862, and P. O'Marsh to William Gooding, 18 Sept. 1862, Yates Papers, ISHL; Snowhook to Francis Hoffman, 23 Sept. 1862, A. H. Van Buren to Snowhook, 23 Sept. 1862, and Dunne to Fuller, 13 Nov. 1862, Ninetieth Illinois Infantry File, ISA. A Chicago alderman, Richmond Sheridan, became the regiment's quartermaster.

63. See the correspondence between O'Meara and his officers, to Fuller, in the Ninetieth Illinois Infantry File, ISA.

64. Petition to Governor Morton, 2 Aug. 1861, Fifteenth Indiana Infantry File, Indianapolis, Indiana State Archives. Hereafter cited as InSA.

65. Andrew Wallace to Morton, 2 Aug. 1861, Thirty-fifth Indiana Infantry File, InSA.

66. Petition to Morton, 4 Nov. 1861, Thirty-fifth Indiana Infantry File, InSA.

67. Petition to Morton, 21 Aug. 1861, Thirty-fifth Indiana Infantry File, InSA.

68. Recruiting Circular, 9 Nov. 1861, Thirty-fifth Indiana Infantry File, InSA.

69. Andrew Mullen, "The Struggle for Command," unpublished essay, Indiananpolis, Indiana Historical Society. Hereafter cited as InHS.

70. Petition to Morton, 13 Feb. 1862, and Walker to Maj. Gen. John Love, 1 Dec. 1861, Thirty-fifth Indiana Infantry File InSA; Foulke, *Life of Morton* 1:262–63; G. R. Tredway, *Democratic Opposition to the Lincoln Administration in Indiana* (Indianapolis: Indiana Historical Bureau, 1973), 160–61. Balfe was, like Mullen, a Fenian. The episode suggests typical Fenian infighting.

71. Petition to Morton, 25 May 1862, Thirty-fifth Indiana Infantry File, InSA. The petition includes a lengthy history of the internecine quarrels of the regiment.

72. Mullen, "Struggle for Command," 1.

73. Tredway, *Democratic Opposition,* 161.

74. J. B. Barrett to Morton, 11 June 1862; Joseph O. Noyes to Adjutant General Nobel, 12 Aug. 1862; Lizzie S. Milliken to Morton, 11 June 1862; Maj. H. N. Conklin to Morton, 4 Dec. 1862; B. F. Mullen to Noble, 10 June 1862; and Mullen to Morton, 27 Nov. 1862, all in the Thirty-fifth Indiana Infantry File, InSA.

75. *Report of the Indiana Adjutant General* 2:352–53.

76. B. F. Mullen to Hugh Gallagher, 16 Apr. 1864, photocopy of the Hugh Gallagher Papers, InHS; Mullen to Morton, 21 Nov. 1863, and August G. Tassin to Noble, 24 Oct. 1864, Thirty-fifth Indiana Infantry File, InSA. The Emancipation Proclamation turned Indiana Irishmen sour on the war. Irish mobs interfered with recruiting in Indianapolis, and one

Irishman was stoned to death when he tried to enlist. See Kautz, "Cannon Fodder," 70.

77. Thomas T. McAvoy, "Peter Paul Cooney, Chaplain of Indiana's Irish Regiment," *Journal of the American-Irish Historical Society* 30(1932):97–102; Thomas T. McAvoy, "The War Letters of Father Peter Paul Cooney of the Congregation of the Holy Cross," *Records of the American Catholic Historical Society of Philadelphia* 44 (Mar., June, and Sept., 1933):47–69, 151–69, 220–37.

78. Mullen to Gallagher, 16 Apr. 1864, Mullen to Gallagher, 10 Apr. 1864, Mullen to Gallagher, 30 Apr. 1864, Gallagher Papers, InHS; Mullen, "Struggle for Command," InHS.

79. Mullen to Gallagher, 24 Apr. 1864, Gallagher Papers, InHS; Cooney to Adjutant General Terrell, 15 Feb. 1865, Thirty-fifth Indiana Infantry File, InSA. Mullen denied that he did anything underhanded in a letter to Gallagher, 20 Feb. 1865, Gallagher Papers, InHS.

80. *Cincinnati Daily Gazette*, 18 Apr. 1861; Lonn, *Union Army Foreigners*, 224–25; unidentified clippings (May 1861) in the Lytle Scrapbook, Lytle Family Papers, Cincinnati, CiHS.

81. Ruth Brill, "Cincinnati's Poet-Warrior: William Haines Lytle," *Historical and Philosophical Society of Ohio Bulletin* 21(July 1963):188–201.

82. William H. Lytle, "Report of the Action at Carnifax Ferry, Virginia," in Moore, *Rebellion Record* 3:41–42.

83. Jacob D. Cox, "War Preparations in the North," in *Battles and Leaders* 1:84–98; John Beatty, *The Citizen-Soldier; or, Memoirs of a Volunteer* (Cincinnati: Wilstach, Baldwin, 1879), 130.

84. Niven, *Connecticut for the Union*, 65–66; Murray, *Ninth Connecticut*.

85. Bates, *Pennsylvania Volunteers* 1:218–19, 548–49, 697–98; Taylor, *Philadelphia in the War*, 87–88.

86. *Philadelphia Daily Evening Bulletin*, 14 Aug. 1862.

87. *Philadelphia Daily Evening Bulletin*, 22 Aug. 1862.

88. Mulholland, *The Story of the 116th Regiment*, 67.

89. *Milwaukee Daily Sentinel*, 16 Nov. 1861; McDonald, *Irish in Wisconsin*, 141; William D. Love, *Wisconsin in the War of the Rebellion* (Chicago: Church and Goodman, 1866), 493–95. Many of the soldiers were drunk.

90. Richard M. Current, "The 'New Ethnicity' and American History: Wisconsin as a Test Case," *History Teacher* 15(Nov. 1981):43–55. The diaries of Orin M. Johnson, Levi H. Nickel, and James B. Fowler, WSHS, all soldiers in the Seventeenth, contain no hint of ethnicity for this regiment.

91. Henry A. Shorey, *The Story of the Maine Fifteenth* (Bridgton, Me.: Press of the Bridgton News, 1890); E. S. Whitman and Charles H. True, *Maine in the War for the Union* (Lewiston, Me.: Nelson Dingley, Jr., 1865), 334–42; *Kennebec Maine Journal*, 28 Feb. 1862.

92. Douglas C. Riach, "Donald O'Connell and American Anti-Slavery," *Irish Historical Studies* 77(Mar. 1976):3–25.

93. Richard J. Purcell, "Ireland and the American Civil War," *Catholic World* 115(1922):72–84.

94. Gibson, *New York Irish*, 142.

95. Edward T. Roberts, *Ireland in America* (New York: G. P. Putnam, 1931), and James Bernard Cullen, *The Story of the Irish in Boston* (Boston: J. B. Cullen, 1889), are classic examples of this literature.

96. *Report of the Joint Committee on the Conduct of the War*, 3 vols. (Washington: U.S. Government Printing Office, 1861), 2:175. Father Corby of the Irish Brigade admitted that alcohol was the special curse of the Irish; see Corby, *Chaplain Memoirs*, 291.

97. Carl Wittke, *We Who Built America* (New York: Prentice-Hall, 1940), 175.

98. Joseph M. Hernon, Jr., "The Irish Nationalists and Southern Secession," *Civil War History* 12(Mar. 1966):43–53. The letters of Sergeant Peter Welsh of the Twenty-eighth Massachusetts Infantry are filled with emotional references to Irish nationalism and religious fervor. See Lawrence Frederick Kole and Margaret Cossé Richard, eds., *Irish Green and Union Blue: The Civil War Letters of Peter Welsh* (New York: Fordham Univ. Press, 1986).

99. George Potter, *To the Golden Door: the Story of the Irish in Ireland and America* (1960; reprint, Westport, Conn.: Greenwood Press, 1973), 510.

## 7. THE OTHERS

1. Lonn, *Union Army Foreigners,* 129–31; Malcolm Gray, "Scottish Emigration: The Social Impact of Agrarian Change in the Rural Lowlands, 1775–1875," *Perspectives in American History* 7(1973):95–175; William Todd, *The Seventy-Ninth Highlanders* (Albany: Press of Brandow, Barton, 1886); Samuel M. Elliott, *The Highland Brigade* (n.d., n.p.).

2. *Washington Daily National Intelligencer,* 31 May 1861; *New York Times,* 3 June 1861.

3. *Washington Evening Star,* 4 June 1861; Leech, *Reveille,* 84; *New York Times,* 12 July 1861; *Washington Daily National Intelligencer,* 5 June 1861.

4. *Battles and Leaders,* 1:185, 190.

5. Moore, *Rebellion Record,* 2:527–28; *Washington Daily National Intelligencer,* 15 Aug. 1861.

6. *Washington Daily National Intelligencer,* 19 Sept. 1861.

7. Cameron to Yates, 16 Dec. 1861, Sixty-fifth Illinois Infantry File, ISA; undated recruiting poster, CHS — bounties, of course, were by then common in most regiments; Yates to Fuller, 31 Dec. 1861, Sixty-fifth Illinois Infantry File, ISA.

8. Cameron to Fuller, 20 Mar. 1862 and 8 Apr. 1862, and Cameron to Fuller, 23 Mar. 1862, Sixty-fifth Illinois Infantry File, ISA.

9. Cameron to Fuller, 10 Nov. 1862, Sixty-fifth Illinois Infantry File, ISA.

10. Mark Bangs to Fuller, 15 Dec. 1862, Sixty-fifth Illinois Infantry File, ISA. Lonn does not list the Sixty-fifth Illinois Infantry as an ethnic regiment. The letters of David C. Bradley, adjutant of the Sixty-fifth Illinois, contain no hint of an ethnic character for the regiment. See the copies of the David C. Bradley Letters, Civil War Miscellaneous Collection, USAMHI.

11. Morgan to William H. Seward, 25 July 1861, NYSA; Ferri Pisani, *Napoleon in America,* 78–79; Regis de Trobriand, *Four Years in the Army of the Potomac* (Boston: Tichnor, 1889).

12. Gerald E. Wheeler and A. Stuart Pitt, "The 53rd New York: A Zoo-Zoo Tale," *New York History* 37(Oct. 1956):414–31. A vivid picture of the chronic bickering and brutal treatment meted out both to officers and enlisted men within this regiment is described in the Charles W. Dustan Diary, a copy of which is in the Harrisburg Civil War Round Table Collection, USAMHI.

13. Blegen, *Heg Letters,* 20–21; Lonn, *Union Army Foreigners,* 136–38.

14. Heg to [J. A.] Johnson, 2 Oct. 1861, Heg Papers, WSHS; Arlow W. Anderson, "Lincoln and the Union: A Study of the Editorials of *Emigranten* and *Faedrelandent,*" *Norwegian-American Studies and Records* 15(1949):85–121.

15. Heg to his wife, 23 July 1862, in Blegen, *Heg Letters,* 108; Anderson, "Lincoln and the Union," 97.

16. Heg to his wife, 23 July 1862, in Blegen, *Heg Letters,* 113.

17. Lester M. Kuhns, "An Army Surgeon's Letters to His Wife," *Proceedings of the Mississippi Valley Historical Association* 7(1914):306–20; Doris Fleming, ed., "Letters From a Canadian Recruit in the Union Army," *Tennessee Historical Quarterly* 16(1957):159–66; Hans Hansen Papers, WSHS; "Narrative of the Lt. Rollin Olson Family Heritage," unpublished essay, WSHS.

18. Howard R. Marraro, "Lincoln's Italian Volunteers From New York," *New York History* 24(Jan. 1943):56–67.

19. Kaufmann, *Die Deutschen in amerikanische Bürgerkreige,* 170; Villard, *Memoirs* 1:174; Frederic George D'Utassy Papers, New York, NYHS; Leech, *Reveille,* 85.

20. *New York Tribune,* 29 May 1861; *Harper's Weekly,* 8 June 1861, 359; unsigned statement, 23 May 1861, D'Utassy Papers, NYHS.

21. *Boston Pilot,* 24 Aug. 1861.

22. *Washington Evening Star,* 30 May 1861 and 5 June 1861; *Washington Daily National Intelligencer,* 31 May 1861; Leech, *Reveille,* 83.

23. *Washington Evening Star,* 1, 3, and 7 June 1861. Later in June a group of drunken New Jersey soldiers demolished a Washington restaurant and injured several customers.

24. Captain of the Spanish Company to D'Utassy, 31 May 1861; Captain Reits to D'Utassy, 31 May 1861; Charles B. Norton to D'Utassy, 11 June 1861; — to D'Utassy, 31 May 1861; undated newspaper clippings; all in the D'Utassy Papers, NYHS.

25. Captain Robitsick to D'Utassy, 4 Aug. 1861, D'Utassy Papers, NYHS.

26. Telegram to D'Utassy from Headquarters of the Army of Northeastern Virginia, 17 July 1861. See also, *Washington Evening Star,* 9 and 10 July 1861; Mahlon D. Sands to D'Utassy, 14 July and 2 Sept. 1861, D'Utassy Papers, NYHS.

27. G. H. Whitney to D'Utassy, 24 Oct. 1861; Elijah Ward to D'Utassy, 10 Jan. 1862; R. C. Shriber to D'Utassy, 6 Feb. 1862; A. P. Zyla to D'Utassy, 26 and 27 Mar. 1862, D'Utassy Papers, NYHS; *New York Tribune,* 5 Apr. 1862; *War of the Rebellion,* series I, 19:545–601 and 12:786–87.

28. Olcott, "The War's Carnival of Fraud," in Alexander K. McClure, *The Annals of the War Written by Leading Participants North and South* (Philadelphia: Times Publishing, 1879), 711.

29. Currie to Morgan, 2 Mar. 1863, Morgan Papers, NYSH; Currie to Adjutant General Hillhouse, 23 Oct. 1862, NYSL; Phisterer, *Rebellion in New York* 4:3559.

30. Bates, *Martial Deeds,* 446–48.

## 8. SONG AND STORY

1. William H. McNeill, *The Pursuit of Power: Technology, Armed Force, and Society, since A. D. 1000* (Chicago: Univ. of Chicago Press, 1982), viii.

2. Mullen to Gallagher, 28 Mar. 1864, Gallagher Papers, InHS.

3. D. Macnamara, *Ninth Massachusetts,* 24.

4. *New York Times,* 1 June 1861.

5. *New York Times,* 14 June 1861. The *Times* reporter was confused about the "quoits" in Book Two of the *Iliad.* A more appropriate reference from Book Two of the *Iliad* for the occasion would have been to "Thersites of the endless speech."

6. Undated (Oct. 1861) clipping, Lytle Papers, CiHS.

7. Undated clipping, Lytle Papers, CiHS.

8. "The Irish Boys," in Moore, *Rebellion Record* 5:2. The poem originally appeared in the *Philadelphia Press.*

9. "Song for the Irish Brigade," *Boston Pilot,* 29 June 1861; reprinted from the *New Orleans True Delta.*

10. *Washington Evening Star,* 30 May 1861.

11. Thomas Frazer, "The Seventy-Ninth," in Moore, *Rebellion Record* 1:122. The song first appeared in the *New York Commercial Advertiser,* 2 May 1861.

12. "When This Cruel War Is Over," Broadside, CiHS.

13. "New War Song of the Sixty-ninth Regiment," Broadside, CiHS.

14. "Corcoran to His Regiment, or, 'I Would Not Take Parole,'" Broadside, CiHS.

15. "O'Toole & McFinnigan On The War," Broadside, CiHS.

16. "Long Live the Sixty-Ninth," Broadside, CiHS.

17. "The Irish Volunteers," Broadside, CiHS.

18. "No Irish Need Apply," Broadside, CiHS.

19. "I'm Going To Fight Mit Sigel," Broadside, CiHS.

20. "How Are You Conscripts?" Broadside, CiHS.

21. "The Two Unions," in Moore, *Rebellion Record* 2:63.

22. Frank Moore, ed. *The Civil War in Song and Story* (1865; reprint, New York: Johnson Reprint, 1970), 269. See also, Charles Graham Halpine, *Life and Adventures, Songs, Services, and Speeches of Private Miles O'Reilly* (New York: Carleton, 1864).

23. "I Am Fighting For the Nigger," Broadside, CiHS.

24. "The Gallant Sixty-ninth," in Moore, *Rebellion Record* 1:391.

25. "Speech of Judge C. P. Daly," in Moore, *Rebellion Record* 1:401–2.

26. Halpine, *O'Reilly,* 75–76.

27. Ibid., 86–87, 92.

28. Ibid., 159, 171–72.

29. *Chicago Tribune,* 18 Mar. 1862; *New York Tribune,* 18 Mar. 1862.

30. *Chicago Tribune,* 18 Mar. 1863.

31. *New York Times,* 18 and 17 Mar. 1863.

32. Winterbotham to his parents, 21 Mar. 1863, Winterbotham Papers, CHS; Bruce Catton, *Bruce Catton's Civil War* (New York: Fairfax, 1984), 297; Galway, *Valiant Hours,* 74–78.

33. *Chicago Tribune,* 18 Mar. 1864.

34. *New York Times,* 18 Mar. 1864.

35. Murray, *Ninth Connecticut,* 203.

## 9. THE ETHNIC FACTOR

1. *Milwaukee Daily Sentinel,* 25 and 29 June 1861; Kautz, "Cannon Fodder," 55–57.

2. Rombauer, *Union Cause in St. Louis,* 233–35.

3. England to Ellen Hargedon, 24 July 1863, John England Papers, NYPL.

4. John Cochrane, *American Civil War: Memoirs of Incidents* (New York: Rogers and Sherwood, 1879), 36–46.

5. Quincy Adams Gillmore, "Siege and Capture of Fort Pulaski," in *Battles and Leaders* 2:1–12.

6. Charles Brooks, "Some Reasons for the Immediate Establishment of a National System of Education for the United States," *Loyalty Tract No. 86* (21 Mar. 1865), 21–22.

7. Edward Ruegger, "Five Weeks of My Army Life," *Wisconsin Magazine of History* 37(1954):163–68.

8. Quoted in Leo M. Kaiser, "Letters from the Front," *Illinois State Historical Society Journal* 56(Summer 1963):150–64.

9. Winterbotham to his family, 22/23 Feb. 1864, and 5 Apr. 1864, Winterbotham Papers, CHS.

10. Hugh Boyle Ewing, "Autobiography of a Tramp," 272; Columbus, Ohio Historical Society.

11. Lizzie S. Mulliken to Governor Morton, 3 Nov. 1862, Thirty-fifth Indiana Infantry File, InSA; Petition to Governor Yates, 4 Aug. 1862, and John W. Watts to J. R. Dubois, 1 Aug. 1862, Yates Papers, ISHS; S. H. Tourtellot to Fuller, 7 Aug. 1862, Twenty-third Illinois Infantry File, ISA.

12. Joseph Conrad, "Diary," Fifteenth Missouri Infantry File, Missouri Adjutant General Archives, Jefferson City; Robert C. Goodell and P. A. M. Taylor, "A German Immigrant in the Union Army: Selected Letters of Valintin Bechler," *Journal of American Studies* 4(Feb. 1971):145–62; Charles Wicksburg to his family, 21 May 1863, in *Civil War Letters of Sergeant Charles Wicksburg* (Milwaukee: Alfred Wicksburg, 1961), 15–16; R. F. Ferrell to James A. Mulligan, 8 Feb. 1863, Mulligan Papers, CHS.

13. August Mersey to Gustav Koerner, 23 June 1861, in Koerner, *Memoirs* 2:152; Adolphus Englemann to his sister, 2 Mar. 1864, Engelmann-Kircher Papers, ISHS. Engelmann said he knew of instances in which Americans suffered the same discrimination.

14. Ferri Pisani, *Napoleon in America,* 252.

15. Weid to Fuller, 13 Sept. 1862, Eighty-second Illinois Infantry File, ISA.

16. Frode Heegaard to Fuller, 13 Sept. 1862, Eighty-second Illinois Infantry File, ISA. See also in the same location, Van H. Higgins to Fuller, 13 Sept. 1862 and John Hillburgh to Governor Yates, 11 Apr. 1863.

17. Heg to Gunild Heg, 18 Aug. 1862, in Blegen, *Heg Letters,* 125.

18. Wagner to Fuller, 26 Nov. 1862, Twenty-fourth Illinois Infantry File, ISA.

19. Buegel, "Diary," Columbia, SHSM.

20. Wittke, *Heinzen,* 180–84, 282–84, 286–87. Heinzen's views on immigration restriction were widely shared among German immigrants. See Frank Freidel, *Francis Lieber* (Baton Rouge: Louisiana State Univ. Press, 1947), 393–94. The Princess Salm-Salm minced no words when it came to the Irish: "The low Irish rabble of New York are the most degraded and brutish set of human beings I know. . . ." She went on to compare the Irish most unfavorably with the Negro. See Salm-Salm, *Ten Years,* 55.

21. *Cincinnati Daily Gazette,* 9 and 10 May 1861; *Irish-American,* 24 Jan. 1862.

22. See, for example, Fred L. Ledergerber to Governor Yates, 19 July 1862, Yates Papers, ISHS.

23. Lonn, *Union Army Foreigners,* 212–23; James Fenton, "Diary," ISHS; correspondence in the Nineteenth Illinois Infantry File, ISA; *Illinois Adjutant General's Report* 1:141–48.

24. T. Harry Williams, "Badger Colonels and the Civil War Officer," *Wisconsin Magazine of History,* 47(Autumn 1963):36.

25. John Higham, "Introduction: The Forms of Ethnic Leadership," in *Ethnic Leadership in America,* ed. John Higham (Baltimore: Johns Hopkins Univ. Press, 1978), 1–13.

26. John Francis Maguire, *The Irish in America* (1868; reprint, New York: Arno Press, 1969), 551–52.

27. Maurice M. Horowitz, "Ethnicity and Command: The Civil War Experience," *Military Affairs* 42(Dec. 1978):182–89.

28. Gerald E. Wheeler, "D'Epineuil's Zouaves," *Civil War History* 2(1956):99.

29. Ezra J. Warner, *Generals in Blue* (Baton Rouge: Louisiana State Univ. Press, 1964), xix.

30. Lonn, *Union Army Foreigners,* 175; Horowitz, "Ethnicity," 185.

31. Daniel Bell, "Ethnicity and Social Change," in *Ethnicity: Theory and Experience,* ed. Nathan Glazer and Daniel Patrick Moyniham (Cambridge: Harvard Univ. Press, 1975), 169.

32. Cynthia H. Enloe, *Ethnic Soldiers: State Security in Divided Societies* (Athens, Ga.: Univ. of Georgia Press, 1980), 28–29, 68–69, and 204.

33. Thomas Sowell, *Ethnic America: A History* (New York: Basic Books, 1981), 296.

## 10. "WHAT THEN IS THE AMERICAN . . ."

1. Michael Howard, "The Lessons of History," *History Teacher,* 15(August 1982):491; Thomas A. Bailey, "The Mythmakers of American History," *Journal of American History* 55(June 1968):5–21.

2. For examples of this literature, see Howard Zinn, *The Politics of History* (Boston: Beacon Press, 1970); John Lukacs, *Historical Consciousness: Or the Remembered Past* (New York: Harper and Row, 1968); and Jean Chesneaux, *Pasts and Futures: Or What Is History For?* (London: Thames and Hudson, 1976). Gordon Leff describes this phenomenon in "From Partisans to Participants," *Encounter,* Apr. 1979, 50–58.

3. James Oliver Robertson, *American Myth, American Reality* (New York: Hill and Wang, 1980) 229–33 345–53.

4. William H. McNeill, "Mythistory, or Truth, Myth, History, and Historians," *American Historical Review* 90(Feb. 1986):1–10.

5. Alan Brinkley, "Writing the History of Contemporary America: Dilemmas and Challenges," *Daedalus* (Summer 1984), 121–41; McNeill, "Mythistory," 7.

6. Rowan, *Germans for a Free Missouri,* 202–3. The *Post* did not use the phrase in the sense popularized by Charles and Mary Beard in their *The Rise of American Civilization.* For the Beards, "The Second American Revolution" was the economic, legal, and demographic triumph of the North over the South.

7. Charles Stierlin to Joseph Kircher, 7 Dec. 1863, in Hess, *A German in the Yankee Fatherland,* 149–50.

8. Moses Rischin, "Foreword," in Frederick C. Luebke, *Bonds of Loyalty: German Americans and World War I* (DeKalb: Northern Illinois Univ. Press, 1974), ix–xi.

9. Philip Rose, *The Neglected Dimension: Ethnicity in American Life* (Notre Dame: Univ. of Notre Dame Press, 1980), 19.

10. Robert Gray, "The Scotch-Irish in American History," *Transactions of the Illinois State Historical Society* (1904):308–13.

11. Louis L. Gerson, *The Hyphenate in Recent American Politics and Diplomacy* (Lawrence: Univ. of Kansas Press, 1964), 235.

12. Carl G. Gustavson, *The Mansion of History* (New York: McGraw-Hill, 1976), 75–79, 179–87.

13. Donald L. Horowitz, *Ethnic Groups in Conflict* (Berkeley: Univ. of California Press, 1985).

14. Hernon, *Celts, Catholics, and Copperheads,* 122.

15. Wittke, *We Who Built America*, xii, 119–23, 144–45.

16. Boatner, *Civil War Dictionary*, 459–60; Warner, *Generals in Blue*, 266–67.

17. Judson Kilpatrick, *The Irish Soldier in the War of the Rebellion* (Deckertown, N. J.: Independent Steam Press, 1880[?]).

18. Maguire, *Irish in America*, 546–51; O'Grady, *How the Irish Became American*, 44–47, 156; Edward F. Roberts, *Ireland in America* (1931; reprint, New York: AMS, 1976), 145.

19. Wittke, *Refugees*, 241; Frederick Luebke, "The Germans," in Higham, *Ethnic Leadership*, 64–90.

20. Athearn, *Meagher*, 168–71.

21. *Washington Daily National Intelligencer* 29 Apr. 1861; Pierce, *Chicago* 2:258; Paul M. Angle, "1861: Chicago Goes to War," *Chicago History* 3(Spring 1961):65–76.

22. "General Orders No. 45," 19 July 1861, War Department, Adjutant General's Office.

23. "General Orders No. 51," 3 Aug. 1861, War Department, Adjutant General's Office; *Washington Evening Star*, 8 Aug. 1861.

24. Still, *Milwaukee*, 159; Klement, *Wisconsin*, 35.

25. *Milwaukee Daily Sentinel*, 10 Sept. 1861; Lawrence H. Larsen, "Draft Riot in Wisconsin, 1861" *Civil War History* 7(Dec. 1961):421–27.

26. Nesbit, *Wisconsin*, 249; Kautz, "Fodder," 148.

27. W. Wilson to Governor Andrew, 27 June 1861, Andrew Papers, MHS.

28. Peter Levine, "Draft Evasion in the North during the Civil War, 1863–1865," *Journal of American History* 67(Mar. 1981):816–34.

29. Quoted in Willard Thorpe, et al., eds., *American Issues*, 2 vols. (Chicago: J. B. Lippincott, 1944), 1:105.

30. Milton M. Gordon, *Assimilation in American Life* (New York: Oxford Univ. Press, 1964), 24–25.

31. Nathan Glazer and Daniel Patrick Moynihan, *Beyond the Melting Pot* (Cambridge: MIT Press, 1970); *Affirmative Discrimination: Ethnic Inequality and Public Policy* (New York: Basic Books, 1978); "The Ethnic Factor," *Encounter*, July 1981, 6–15.

32. James Olson, *The Ethnic Dimension in American History*, 2 vols. (New York: St. Martin's, 1979); Richard Krickus, *Pursuing the American Dream: White Ethnics and the New Populism* (Garden City, N.Y.: Anchor Books, 1976); Michael Novak, *The Rise of the Unmeltable Ethnics* (New York: Macmillan, 1973).

33. Stephen Steinberg, *The Ethnic Myth: Race, Ethnicity and Class in America* (Boston: Beacon Press, 1981), 170.

34. Howard F. Stein, "The White Ethnic Movement, Pan-ism, and the Restoration of Early Symbiosis: The Psychohistory of a Group-fantasy," *Journal of Psychohistory* 6(Winter 1979):319–59.

35. John Higham, "Leadership," in Michael Walzer et al., *The Politics of Ethnicity* (Cambridge: Belknap Press of Harvard Univ. Press, 1982), 70–90; John Higham, *Strangers in the Land: Patterns in American Nativism* (1955; reprint, New York: Atheneum, 1963); "Interpreting America: The Problem of Assimilation in the Nineteenth Century," *Journal of American Ethnic History* (Fall 1981):7–25; "Introduction," in *Ethnic Leadership*, ed. John Higham, 2–11. Support for these interpretations is found in Jonathan D. Sarna, "From Immigrant to Ethnic: Toward a New Theory of 'Ethnicization,'" *Ethnicity*, 5(1978):370–78; Burchell, *San Francisco Irish*, "Preface" and 1–13; Oscar Handlin and Mary F. Handlin, "The New History and the Ethnic Factor in American Life," *Perspectives in American History* 4(1970):5–24. On the point of the Anglo-Saxon as an abstraction, see Forrest McDonald and Ellen Shapiro McDonald, "The Ethnic Origin of the American People, 1790," *William and Mary Quarterly* 37(1980):179–99.

36. Philip Gleason, "Identifying Identity: A Semantic History," *Journal of American History* 69(Mar. 1983):910–31; Charles McC. Mathias, Jr., "Ethnic Groups and Foreign Policy," *Foreign Affairs* 59(Summer 1981):975–98; Kerby A. Miller, "Emigrants and Exiles: Irish Culture and Irish Emigration to North America 1790–1922," *Irish Historical Studies* 22 (Sept. 1980):97–125.

37. Kathleen Neils Conzen, "Immigrants, Immigrant Neighborhoods, and Ethnic Identity: Historical Issues," *Journal of American History* 66(Dec. 1979):603–15.

38. Current, "The 'New Ethnicity,'" 48–50.

39. Ronald H. Bayor, *Neighbors in Conflict: The Irish, Germans, Jews, and Italians of New York City, 1929–1941* (Baltimore: Johns Hopkins Univ. Press, 1978) 1–3. It is remarkable, wrote Thomas Walker Page of the University of Virginia in 1912, that most of the extortion and fraud inflicted on newcomers to America were perpetrated by members of their own race. See Page, "The Distribution of Immigrants in the United States Before 1870," *Journal of Political Economy* 20(July 1912):676–94.

40. Handlin and Handlin, "New History," 18–19.

41. Thomas J. Archdeacon, *Becoming American* (New York: Free Press, 1983), 82; Peter Karsten, *Soldiers and Society: The Effects of Military Service and War on American Life* (Westport, Conn.: Greenwood Press, 1978), 7.

42. H. Laurence Moore, "Insiders and Outsiders in American Historical Narrative and American History," *American Historical Review* 87(Apr. 1982):390–412.

# Selected Bibliography

## I. MANUSCRIPTS

Letters, diaries, telegrams, reports, broadsides, and other unpublished materials are the most important sources. Correspondence filed with individual regimental archives is invaluable. Library and historical society collections include individual items too numerous to list. Items identified with several locations below are those of particular richness and value.

### ILLINOIS

Chicago Historical Society
 Gustav Haller Papers
 Wladimir Kryzanowski Papers
 James A. Mulligan Diary and Papers
 John R. Winterbotham Papers
Springfield, Illinois State Historical Society Library
 Engelmann-Kircher Papers
 Richard Yates Papers
 William Anderson Allen Papers
Springfield, Illinois State Archives
 Nineteenth Illinois Infantry File
 Twenty-third Illinois Infantry File
 Twenty-fourth Illinois Infantry File
 Sixty-fifth Illinois Infantry File
 Eighty-second Illinois Infantry File
 Ninetieth Illinois Infantry File

### INDIANA

Indianapolis, Indiana State Historical Society
 Hugh Gallagher Diary and Papers (microfilm copy)
Indianapolis, Indiana State Archives
 Thirty-second Indiana Infantry File
 Thirty-fifth Indiana Infantry File

### MASSACHUSETTS

Boston, Massachusetts Historical Society
 John Andrew Collection
Boston Public Library
Boston, Massachusetts State Library

Ninth Massachusetts Infantry File
Twenty-eighth Massachusetts Infantry File
Twenty-ninth Massachusetts Infantry File
Letters of John Andrew

MISSOURI

Jefferson City, Missouri Adjutant General's Office
Columbia, State Historical Society of Missouri
    Abiel Leonard Collection
    John Buegel Diary
Columbia, University of Missouri Library
    Alvord Collection

NEW YORK

Albany, New York State Archives
Albany, New York State Library
    Edwin D. Morgan Papers
    Frederick George D'Utassy Letters
    James B. Turner Papers
New York City, New York Historical Society
    Frederick George D'Utassy Papers
    James P. McIvor Papers
New York City, New York Public Library
    John England Papers
    James Stephens Diary (photocopy)

OHIO

Cincinnati Historical Society
    Civil War Broadsides
    Lytle Family Papers
    Ninth Ohio Infantry File
Columbus, Ohio Historical Society
    William Dennison, Jr., Collection
    Hugh Boyle Ewing Papers
    Thomas T. Taylor Collection

PENNSYLVANIA

United States Army Military History Institute, Carlisle Barracks
    Civil War Miscellaneous Collection
    *Civil War Times Illustrated* Collection

WISCONSIN

Madison, State Historical Society
    Governor Alexander W. Randall Letter Book and Journals
    Hans Hansen Papers
    Hans Christian Heg Papers

## II. GOVERNMENT PUBLICATIONS

*Report of the Adjutant General of the State of Illinois*
*Report of the Adjutant General of the State of Indiana*
*Report of the Adjutant General of Ohio*
*Report of the Joint Committee on the Conduct of the War,* 3 vols. Washington: U.S. Government Printing Office, 1863.
Taylor, Frank R. *Philadelphia in the War.* Philadelphia: City of Philadelphia, 1913.
*War of the Rebellion: A Compilation of the Official Records of the Union and Confederate Armies.* Series I, 128 vols. Washington: Government Printing Office, 1902.

## III. BOOKS

Anders, Leslie. *The Twenty-First Missouri.* Westport, Conn.: Greenwood Press, 1975.
Anderson, Galusha. *The Story of a Border City during the Civil War.* Boston: Little, Brown, 1908.
Andreas, A. T. *History of Cook County Illinois.* Chicago: A. T. Andreas, 1884.
Andrews, J. Cutler. *The North Reports the Civil War.* Pittsburgh: Univ. of Pittsburgh Press, 1955.
Archdeacon, Thomas J. *Becoming American.* New York: Free Press, 1983.
Armstrong, John A. *Nations Before Nationalism.* Chapel Hill: Univ. of North Carolina Press, 1982.
Athearn, Robert G. *Thomas Francis Meagher: An Irish Revolutionary in America.* Boulder: Univ. of Colorado Press, 1949.
Babcock, Kendrick Charles. *The Scandinavian Element in the United States.* 1914. Reprint. New York: Arno Press, 1969.
Bailey, George W. *A Private Chapter of the War.* St. Louis: G. I. Jones, 1880.
Bancroft, Frederic, ed. *Speeches, Correspondence and Political Papers of Carl Schurz.* 6 vols. New York: G. P. Putnam, 1913.
Bardeen, Charles W. *A Little Fifer's War Diary.* Syracuse, N.Y.: C. W. Bardeen, 1910.
Barnhart, John. D., and Donald F. Carmony. *Indiana: From Frontier to Industrial Commonwealth.* 3 vols. New York: Lewis Historical, 1954.
Basler, Roy P., ed. *The Collected Works of Abraham Lincoln.* 8 vols. Rutgers, N.J.: Rutgers Univ. Press, 1955.
Bateman, Newton, et al., eds. *Historical Encyclopedia of Illinois.* 2 vols. Chicago: Munsell, 1921.
Bates, Samuel F. *History of Pennsylvania Volunteers, 1861–1865.* 2 vols. Harrisburg, Pa.: B. Singerly, 1869.
———. *Martial Deeds of Pennsylvania.* Philadelphia: T. H. Davis, 1875.
Bauer, K. Jack, ed. *Soldiering: The Civil War Diary of Rice C. Bull, 123rd New York Volunteer Infantry.* San Rafael, Calif.: Presidio Press, 1977.
Bayor, Ronald H. *Neighbors in Conflict: The Irish, Germans, Jews, and Italians of New York City, 1929–1941.* Baltimore: Johns Hopkins Univ. Press, 1978.
Beatty, John. *The Citizen-Soldier: Or, Memoirs of a Volunteer.* Cincinnati: Wilstach, Baldwin, 1879.
Bennett, Lyman G., and William M. Haigh. *History of the Thirty-Sixth Regiment*

*Illinois Volunteers, during the War of the Rebellion.* Aurora, Ill.: Knickerbocker and Holder, 1876.

Bickham, William Denison. *Rosecrans' Campaign With the Fourteenth Army Corps, or the Army of the Cumberland.* Cincinnati: Moore, Wilstach, Keys, 1863.

Billington, Ray Allen. *The Protestant Crusade, 1800–1860.* 1938. Reprint. Gloucester, Mass.: Peter Smith, 1963.

Blegen, Theodore C. *Norwegian Immigration to America.* Northfield, Minn.: Norwegian-American Historical Association, 1931.

_____, ed. *Civil War Letters of Colonel Hans Christian Heg.* Northfield, Minn.: Norwegian-American Historical Association, 1936.

Blied, Benjamin J. *Catholics and the Civil War.* Milwaukee: The Author, 1945.

Bosse, Georg von. *Das Deutsche Element in den Vereinigten Staaten.* Stuttgart: Chr. Belsersche Verlagsbuchhandlung, 1908.

Bowen James L. *Massachusetts in the War.* Springfield, Mass.: Bowen, 1893.

Britton, Wiley. *The Civil War on the Border.* 2 vols. New York: G. P. Putnam, 1899.

Brock, Peter. *Pacifism in the United States From the Colonial Era to the First World War.* Princeton: Princeton Univ. Press, 1968.

Brooks, Noah. *Washington in Lincoln's Time.* New York: Century, 1895.

Brummer, Sidney Davis. *Political History of New York State during the Period of the Civil War.* 1910. Reprint. New York: AMS Press, 1967.

Burchell, R. A. *The San Francisco Irish.* Berkeley: Univ. of California Press, 1980.

Burdette, Robert J. *The Drums of the 47th.* Indianapolis: Bobbs-Merrill, 1914.

Butts, Joseph Tyler, ed. *A Gallant Captain of the Civil War, Being the Extraordinary Adventures of Frederick Otto Baron von Fritsch.* New York: F. Tennyson Neely, 1902.

Callow, Alexander B., Jr. *The Tweed Ring.* New York: Oxford Univ. Press, 1966.

Catton, Bruce. *Bruce Catton's Civil War.* New York: Fairfax, 1984.

Cavanagh, Michael. *Memoirs of Gen. Thomas Francis Meagher.* Worcester, Mass.: Messenger Press, 1892.

*Civil War Letters of Sergeant Charles Wickesberg.* Milwaukee: Alfred Wickesberg, 1961.

Clark, Dennis. *The Irish in Philadelphia.* Philadelphia: Temple Univ. Press, 1973.

Cochrane, John. *American Civil War: Memories of Incidents.* New York: Rogers and Sherwood, 1879.

Cole, Arthur Charles. *The Era of the Civil War, 1848–1870.* Vol. 3. *Centennial History of Illinois.* Springfield: Illinois Centennial Commission, 1919.

Conyngham, D. P. *The Irish Brigade and Its Campaigns.* New York: William McSorley, 1867.

Conzen, Kathleen Neils. *Immigrant Milwaukee, 1836–1860.* Cambridge: Harvard Univ. Press, 1976.

Copp, Elbridge J. *Reminiscences of the War of the Rebellion.* Nashua, N.H.: Telegraph Publishing, 1911.

Copps, Frank J., and Thomas J. Curran, eds. *The Immigrant Experience in America.* Boston: Twayne, 1976.

Corby, William. *Memoirs of Chaplain Life: Three Years Chaplain in the Famous "Irish Brigade," Army of the Potomac.* Notre Dame: Scholastic Press, 1894.

Cort, Charles Edwin. *"Dear Friends": The Civil War Letters and Diary of Charles Edwin Cort.* N.p., 1962.

Crofts, Thomas, ed. *History of the Service of the Third Ohio Veteran Voluntary Cavalry.* Toledo: Stoneman, 1910.

Cullen, James Bernard. *The Story of the Irish in Boston.* Boston: J. B. Cullen, 1889.

D'Arcy, William. *The Fenian Movement in the United States: 1858–1886.* Washington, D.C.: Catholic Univ. of America Press, 1947.

Day, D. L. *My Diary of Rambles With the 25th Mass. Volunteer Infantry.* Milford, Mass.: King and Billings, 1884.

De Forest, John Wilkins. *A Volunteer's Adventures.* New Haven: Yale Univ. Press, 1946.

De Hauranne, Ernest Duvergier. *A Frenchman in Lincoln's America,* trans. Ralph H. Bowen. 2 vols. Chicago: Lakeside Press, 1975.

Dickens, Charles. *American Notes and Pictures From Italy.* 1842. Reprint. London: Oxford Univ. Press, 1957.

Dinnerstein, Leonard, Roger L. Nichols, and David M. Reimers. *Natives and Strangers: Ethnic Groups and the Building of America.* New York: Oxford Univ. Press, 1979.

Drake, Charles D. *Camp Jackson: Its History and Significance.* St. Louis: Missouri Democrat, 1863.

Easton, Loyd D. *Hegel's First American Followers.* Athens, Ohio: Ohio Univ. Press, 1966.

Eby, Cecil D., Jr., ed. *A Virginia Yankee in the Civil War: The Diaries of David Henry Strother.* Chapel Hill: Univ. of North Carolina Press, 1961.

Eddy, Thomas M. *The Patriotism of Illinois.* 2 vols. Chicago: Clark, 1865.

Enloe, Cynthia H. *Ethnic Soldiers: State Security in Divided Societies.* Athens, Ga.: Univ. of Georgia Press, 1980.

Erickson, Charlotte. *Invisible Immigrants: The Adaptation of English and Scottish Immigrants in Nineteenth Century America.* Coral Gables, Fla.: Univ. of Miami Press, 1972.

Ernst, Robert. *Immigrant Life in New York City, 1825–1863.* 1949. Reprint. Port Washington, N.Y.: Ira J. Friedman, 1965.

Esarey, Logan. *A History of Indiana.* 3 vols. Indianapolis: B. F. Bowen, 1918.

Faust, Albert Bernhardt. *The German Element in the United States.* 2 vols. New York. 1909. Reprint. New York: Steuben Society of America, 1927.

Favill, Josiah Marshall. *The Diary of a Young Officer.* Chicago: R. R. Donnelly, 1909.

Ferri Pisani, Camille. *Prince Napoleon in America, 1861: Letters from His Aide-De-Camp,* trans. Georges J. Joyoux. Port Washington, N.Y.: Kennikat Press, 1973. First published in 1862 in Paris under the title *Lettres sur les États-Unis d'Amérique.*

Field, Charles D. *Three Years in the Saddle.* N.p.

Fisher, George Adams. *The Yankee Conscript, or Eighteen Months in Dixie.* Philadelphia: J. W. Daughaday, 1864.

Forney, John W. *Anecdotes of Public Men.* New York: Harper, 1874.

Foulke, William Dudley. *Life of Oliver P. Morton.* 2 vols. Indianapolis: Bowen-Merrill, 1899.

Freidel, Frank. *Francis Lieber: Nineteenth Century Liberal.* Baton Rouge: Louisiana State Univ. Press, 1947.

Fritsch, William A. *German Settlers and German Settlements in Indiana.* Evansville, Ind.: The Author, 1915.

Fry, James Barnet. *Military Miscellanies.* New York: Brentano's, 1889.

Funk, Arville L. *Hoosiers in the Civil War.* Chicago: Adams, 1967.

Galway, Thomas Francis. *The Valiant Hours.* Harrisburg, Pa.: Stackpole, 1961.

Garrathan, Gilbert J. *The Catholic Church in Chicago.* Chicago: Loyola Univ. Press, 1921.

Gates, Theodore B. *The Ulster Guard and the War of the Rebellion.* New York: Benj. H. Tyrrel, 1879.

Gibson, Florence E. *The Attitudes of the New York Irish toward State and National Affairs, 1848–1892.* New York: Columbia Univ. Press, 1951.

Glazer, Nathan, and Daniel Patrick Moynihan. *Beyond the Melting Pot.* 2d ed. Cambridge, Mass.: MIT Press, 1970.

————, eds. *Ethnicity: Theory and Experience.* Cambridge, Mass.: Harvard Univ. Press, 1975.

Gobright, Lawrence A. *Recollections of Men and Things at Washington.* Washington: W. H. and O. H. Morrison, 1869.

Gordon, Milton M. *Assimilation in American Life.* New York: Oxford Univ. Press, 1964.

Goss, Warren Lee. *Recollections of a Private: A Story of the Army of the Potomac.* New York: Thomas Y. Crowell, 1890.

Grant, Ulysses S. *Personal Memoirs.* 2 vols. New York: Charles L. Webster, 1885.

Gray, Wood. *The Hidden Civil War.* New York: Viking, 1942.

Greeley, Andrew M. *Ethnicity, Denomination, and Inequality.* Beverly Hills, Calif.: Sage, 1976.

Grierson, Francis. *The Valley of Shadows.* New York: John Lane, 1913.

Gritzner, M. C. *Blenker und Frémont.* Washington: N.p. 1862.

Gurowski, Adam. *Diary.* 3 vols. Boston: Law and Shepard, 1862.

Halpine, Charles Graham. *The Life and Adventures, Songs, Services, and Speeches of Private Miles O'Reilly.* New York: Carleton, 1864.

Handlin, Oscar. *The Uprooted.* New York: Grosset and Dunlop, 1951.

————. *Boston's Immigrants.* Rev. and enl. ed. New York: Atheneum, 1976.

Hannaford, Ebenezer. *The Story of a Regiment: A History of the Campaigns, and Associations in the Field, of the Sixth Regiment Ohio Volunteer Infantry.* Cincinnati: The Author, 1868.

Hassard, John Rose Greene. *Life of the Most Reverend John Hughes.* New York: D. Appleton, 1866.

Hecker, Friedrich. *Reden und Vorlesungen.* St. Louis: Verlag der C. Mitter'schen Buchhandlung, 1872.

Henderson, G. F. R. *The Civil War: A Soldier's View.* Chicago: Univ. of Chicago Press, 1958.

Hernon, Joseph M., Jr. *Celts, Catholics, and Copperheads: Ireland Views the American Civil War.* Columbus: Ohio State Univ. Press, 1968.

Hertle, Daniel. *Die Deutschen in Nordamerika und Der Freiheitskampf in Missouri.* Chicago: Illinois *Staatszeitung,* 1865.

Hess, Earl J., Jr., ed. *A German in the Yankee Fatherland: The Civil War Letters of Henry A. Kircher.* Kent, Ohio: Kent State Univ. Press, 1983.

Hicken, Victor. *Illinois in the Civil War.* Urbana: Univ. of Illinois Press, 1966.

Higham, John. *Strangers in the Land: Patterns of American Nativism, 1860–1925.* 1955. Reprint. New York: Atheneum, 1963.

Higham, John, ed. *Ethnic Leadership in America.* Baltimore: Johns Hopkins Univ. Press, 1978.

*Historical Memoranda of the 52nd Regiment Illinois Infantry Volunteers.* Elgin, Ill.: Gilbert and Post, 1868.

*History of the 37th Regiment, O. V. V. I.* Toledo, Ohio: Montgomery and Vrooman, 1890.

Hofmeister, Rudolph A. *The Germans of Chicago*. Champaign, Ill.: Stipes, 1976.

Hokanson, Nels. *Swedish Immigrants in Lincoln's Time*. New York: Harper, 1942.

Horowitz, Donald L. *Ethnic Groups in Conflict*. Berkeley: Univ. of California Press, 1985.

Jackson, Harry F., and Thomas F. O'Donnell. *Back Home in Oneida: Hermon Clarke and His Letters*. Syracuse, N.Y.: Syracuse Univ. Press, 1965.

Johnson, Robert U., and Clarence C. Buel, eds. *Battles and Leaders of the Civil War*. 4 vols. New York: Century, 1884–1887.

Jones, Paul. *The Irish Brigade*. Washington: Robert B. Luce, 1969.

Karsten, Peter. *Soldiers and Society: The Effects of Military Service and War on American Life*. Westport, Conn.: Greenwood Press, 1978.

Karsten, Peter, ed. *The Military in America*. New York: Free Press, 1980.

Kaufmann, Wilhelm. *Die Deutschen in amerikanischen Bürgerkrieg*. München und Berlin: R. Oldenbourg, 1911.

Kee, Robert. *Ireland, A History*. Boston: Little, Brown, 1982.

Kilpatrick, Judson. *The Irish Soldier in the War of the Rebellion*. Deckertown, N.J.: Independent Steam Press, 1880[?].

Klement, Frank L. *The Copperheads in the Middle West*. Chicago: Univ. of Chicago Press, 1960.

_____. *Wisconsin and the Civil War*. Madison: State Historical Society of Wisconsin, 1963.

Kleppner, Paul. *The Cross of Culture: A Social Analysis of Midwestern Politics, 1850–1900*. New York: Free Press, 1970.

Knapp, Charles Merriam. *New Jersey Politics during the Period of the Civil War and Reconstruction*. Geneva, N.Y.: W. F. Humphrey, 1924.

Kohl, Lawrence Frederich, and Margaret Cossé Rochards, eds. *Irish Green and Union Blue: The Civil War Letters of Peter Welsh*. New York: Fordham Univ. Press, 1986.

Körner, Gustav. *Das Deutsche Element in dem Vereinten Staaten von Nordamerika*. New York: Steiger, 1884.

Krenkel, John H., ed. *Richard Yates, Civil War Governor*. Danville, Ill.: Interstate, 1966.

Krikus, Richard. *Pursuing the American Dream: White Ethnics and the New Populism*. Garden City, N.Y.: Anchor Books, 1976.

Kuné, Julian. *Reminiscences of an Octogenarian Hungarian Exile*. Chicago: The Author, 1911.

Lane, Roger. *Policing the City: Boston, 1822–1885*. 1967. Reprint. New York: Atheneum, 1971.

Leech, Margaret. *Reveille in Washington, 1860–1865*. New York: Harper, 1941.

Lonn, Ella. *Foreigners in the Confederacy*. 1940. Reprint. Gloucester, Mass.: Peter Smith, 1965.

_____. *Foreigners in the Union Army and Navy*. 1951. Reprint. New York: Greenwood Press, 1969.

Love, William D. *Wisconsin in the War of the Rebellion*. Chicago: Church and Goodman, 1866.

Luebke, Frederick, ed. *Ethnic Voters and the Election of Lincoln*. Lincoln: Univ. of Nebraska Press, 1971.

Lyons, W. F. *Brigadier-General Thomas Francis Meagher: His Political and Military Career*. New York: D. and J. Sadler, 1870.

McClellan, George B. *Report on the Organization and Campaigns of the Army of the Potomac*. 1864. Reprint. Freeport, N.Y.: Books for Libraries, 1970.

McClure, Alexander K. *The Annals of the War Written by Leading Participants North and South.* Philadelphia: Times Publishing, 1879.

McCormack, Thomas J., ed. *Memoirs of Gustave Koerner.* 2 vols. Cedar Rapids, Iowa: Torch Press, 1909.

McDonald, Sister M. Justille. *History of the Irish in Wisconsin in the Nineteenth Century.* Washington: Catholic Univ. of America Press, 1954.

McIlvaine, Mabel. *Reminiscences of Chicago During the Civil War.* Chicago: R. R. Donnelly, 1914.

Macnamara, Daniel George. *The History of the Ninth Regiment Massachusetts Volunteer Infantry.* Boston: E. B. Stillings, 1899.

Macnamara, Michael H. *The Irish Ninth in Bivouac and Battle.* Boston: Lee and Shephard, 1867.

McReynolds, Edwin C. *Missouri: A History of the Crossroads State.* Norman: Univ. of Oklahoma Press, 1962.

Maguire, John Francis. *The Irish in America.* 1868. Reprint. New York: Arno Press, 1969.

Meagher, Thomas Francis. *The Last Days of the 69th in Virginia.* New York: *Irish-American,* n.d.

[Merrill, Catherine]. *The Soldiers of Indiana in the War for the Union.* 2 vols. Indianapolis: Merrill, 1866–1869.

Moore, Frank. *The Civil War in Song and Story.* 1865. Reprint. New York: Johnson Reprint, 1970.

_____, ed. *The Rebellion Record.* 12 vols. New York: G. P. Putnam, 1861–1868.

Morrison, Marion. *A History of the Ninth Regiment Illinois Volunteer Infantry.* Monmouth, Ill.: John C. Clark, 1864.

Moses, John. *Illinois: Historical and Statistical.* 2 vols. Chicago: Fergus, 1892.

Mulholland, St. Clair A. *The Story of the 116th Regiment, Pennsylvania Infantry.* Philadelphia: F. McManus, Jr., 1899.

Murdock, Eugene C. *Patriotism Limited, 1862–1865: The Civil War Draft and the Bounty System.* Kent, Ohio: Kent State Univ. Press, 1967.

_____. *One Million Men: The Civil War Draft in the North.* Madison: State Historical Society of Wisconsin, 1971.

Murray, Thomas Hamilton. *History of the Ninth Regiment, Connecticut Volunteer Infantry, "The Irish Regiment".* New Haven, Conn.: Price, Lee and Adkins, 1903.

Nesbit, Robert G. *Wisconsin: A History.* Madison: Univ. of Wisconsin Press, 1973.

*Die Neuner: Erstes Deutsches Regiment von Ohio.* Cincinnati: Druck von S. Rosenthal, 1897.

Niven, John. *Connecticut for the Union.* New Haven: Yale Univ. Press, 1965.

Novak, Michael. *The Rise of the Unmeltable Ethnics.* New York: Macmillan, 1973.

O'Grady, Joseph P. *How the Irish Became Americans.* New York: Twayne, 1973.

O'Leary, John. *Recollections of Fenians and Fenianism.* 2 vols. 1896. Reprint. New York: Barnes and Noble, 1969.

Olson, James S. *The Ethnic Dimension in American History.* 2 vols. New York: St. Martin's, 1979.

Osterweis, Rollin. *Three Centuries of New Haven, 1638–1938.* New Haven: Yale Univ. Press, 1953.

Palfrey, Francis Winthrop. *The Antietam and Fredericksburg.* New York: Charles Scribner, 1889.

Paris, Comte de. *History of the Civil War in America,* trans. Louis F. Tasistro. 4

vols. Philadelphia: Jos. H. Coates, 1876–1878.

Pease, Theodore Calvin, and James G. Randall, eds. *The Diary of Orville Hickman-Browning.* Vol. 20 of the *Collections of the Illinois State Historical Society.* Springfield: Illinois State Historical Society Library, 1925.

Phisterer, Frederick. *New York in the War of the Rebellion.* 6 vols. Albany, N.Y.: F. R. Lyon, 1912.

Pierce, Bessie Louise. *A History of Chicago.* 3 vols. New York: Alfred A. Knopf, 1940.

Piványi, Eugene. *Hungarians in the American Civil War.* Cleveland, O.: Cleveland Printing House, 1913.

Porter, George H. *Ohio Politics During the Civil War Period.* 1911. Reprint. New York: AMS Press, 1976.

Potter, George. *To the Golden Door: The Story of the Irish in Ireland and America.* 1960. Reprint. Westport, Conn.: Greenwood, 1973.

Quiner, Edwin B. *The Military History of Wisconsin.* Chicago: Clarke, 1866.

Reid, Whitelaw. *Ohio in the War.* 2 vols. Cincinnati: Moore, Wilstach, and Baldwin, 1868.

Richardson, Albert D. *Der Geheime Dienst.* Hartford, Conn.: American, 1865.

Rippley, La Verne, Jr. *The German Americans.* Boston: Twayne, 1976.

Roberts, Edward F. *Ireland in America.* New York: G. P. Putnam, 1931.

Rombauer, Robert J. *The Union Cause in St. Louis in 1861.* St. Louis: Nixon-Jones, 1901.

Roseboom, Eugene H., and Francis P. Weisenburger. *A History of Ohio.* Columbus: Ohio State Archeological and Historical Society, 1953.

Rosen, Philip. *The Neglected Dimension: Ethnicity in American Life.* Notre Dame: Univ. of Notre Dame Press, 1980.

Rosengarten, Joseph G. *The German Soldier in the Wars of the United States.* Philadelphia: J. B. Lippincott, 1886.

Rowan, Steven, trans. and ed. Introduction by James Neal Primm. *Germans for a Free Missouri: Translations from the St. Louis Radical Press, 1857–1862.* Columbia: Univ. of Missouri Press, 1983.

Rusling, James Fowler. *Men and Things I Saw in Civil War Days.* New York: Eaton and Mains, 1899.

Russell, William H. *My Diary North and South.* Boston: T. O. H. P. Burnham, 1863.

Ryan, Desmond. *The Fenian Chief: A Biography of James Stephens.* Coral Gables, Fla.: Univ. of Miami Press, 1967.

Ryle, Walter Harrington. *Missouri: Union or Secession.* Nashville, Tenn.: George Peabody College for Teachers, 1931.

Sala, George Augustus. *My Diary in America in the Midst of War.* 2 vols. London: Tinsley, 1865.

Salm-Salm, Princess Felix. *Ten Years of My Life.* Detroit: Belford, 1877.

Sander, Constantin. *Der Amerikanische Bürgerkrieg von Seinem Beginn vis zum Schluss des Jahres 1862.* Frankfurt am Main: Druck und Verlag von Wilhelm Küchler, 1863.

Saunier, Joseph A., ed. *A History of the Forty-Seventh Regiment Ohio Veteran Volunteer Infantry.* Hillsboro, Ohio: Lyle, 1903.

Schafer, Joseph, trans. and ed. *Intimate Letters of Carl Schurz.* Vol. 30 of the *Collections of the State Historical Society of Wisconsin.* Madison: State Historical Society of Wisconsin, 1928.

Scharf, J. Thomas, and Thompson Westcott. *History of Philadelphia, 1609–1884.* 3 vols. Philadelphia: L. H. Everts, 1884.

Schouler, William. *A History of Massachusetts in the Civil War.* 2 vols. Boston: E. P. Dutton, 1868–1871.

Schrader, Frederick F. *The Germans in the Making of America,* a volume in the Racial Contribution Series of the Knights of Columbus. Boston: Stratford, 1924.

Schrier, Arnold, and Joyce Story, trans. and eds. *A Russian Looks at America: The Journey of Aleksandr Borisovich Lakier in 1857.* Chicago: Univ. of Chicago Press, 1979.

[Schurz, Carl]. *The Reminiscences of Carl Schurz.* 3 vols. New York: McClure, 1907.

Sears, Stephen W. *Landscape Turned Red: The Battle of Antietam.* New Haven: Ticknor and Fields, 1983.

Seller, Maxine. *To Seek America: A History of Ethnic Life in the United States.* N.p.: Jerome S. Ozer, 1977.

Shankman, Arnold M. *The Pennsylvania Antiwar Movement, 1861–1865.* Madison, N.J.: Fairleigh Dickinson Univ. Press, 1980.

Shannon, Fred Albert. *The Organization and Administration of the Union Army, 1861–1865.* 2 vols. 1928. Reprint. Glouchester, Mass.: Peter Smith, 1965.

Shannon, William V. *The American Irish.* New York: Macmillan, 1963.

Shorey, Henry A. *The Story of the Maine Fifteenth.* Bridgton, Me.: Press of the Bridgton News, 1890.

Sowell, Thomas. *Ethnic America: A History.* New York: Basic Books, 1981.

Stampp, Kenneth M. *Indiana Politics During the Civil War.* Indianapolis: Indiana Historical Bureau, 1949.

Steinberg, Stephen. *The Ethnic Myth: Race, Ethnicity, and Class in America.* Boston: Beacon, 1981.

Stevens, Christian D. *Meagher of the Sword.* New York: Dodd, Mead, 1967.

Still, Bayard. *Milwaukee: The History of a City.* 1948. Reprint. Madison: State Historical Society of Wisconsin, 1965.

Swanberg, W. A. *First Blood: The Story of Fort Sumter.* New York: Charles Scribner, 1957.

Taylor, Philip. *The Distant Magnet.* New York: Harper and Row, 1971.

Thornbrough, Emma Lou. *Indiana in the Civil War.* Indianapolis: Indiana Historical Bureau and Indiana Historical Society, 1965.

Todd, William. *The Seventy-Ninth Highlanders.* Albany, N.Y.: Press of Brandow, Barton, 1886.

Tredway, G. R. *Democratic Opposition to the Lincoln Administration in Indiana.* Indianapolis: Indiana Historical Bureau, 1973.

Trefousse, Hans L. *Carl Schurz: A Biography.* Knoxville: Univ. of Tennessee Press, 1982.

Trobriand, Regis de. *Four Years With the Army of the Potomac.* Boston: Tichnor, 1889.

Trollope, Anthony. *North America.* 2 vols. 1862. Reprint. New York: Augustus M. Kelley, 1970.

Trumbull, H. Clay. *The Knightly Soldier: A Biography of Major Henry Ward Camp, Tenth Conn. Vols.* Boston: Nichols and Noyes, 1865.

Tucker, Louis Leonard. *Cincinnati during the Civil War.* Vol. 9. *Publications of the Ohio Civil War Centennial Commission.* Columbus: Ohio State Univ. Press, 1962.

Varnum, Joseph Bradley, Jr. [Viator]. *The Washington Sketch Book*. New York: Mohun, Ebbs and Hough, 1864.

Victor, Orville James. *Incidents and Anecdotes of the War*. New York: J. D. Torrey, 1866.

Villard, Henry. *Memoirs of Henry Villard*. 2 vols. Boston: Houghton, Mifflin, 1904.

Wagner, William. *History of the 24th Illinois Volunteer Infantry Regiment*. Chicago: *Illinois Staats-Zeitung,* 1864.

Walkley, Stephen, comp. *History of the Seventh Connecticut Volunteer Infantry*. N.p.

Walzer, Michael, Edward T. Kantowicz, John Higham, and Mona Harrington. *The Politics of Ethnicity*. Cambridge, Mass.: Belknap Press of Harvard Univ. Press, 1982.

Ware, Edith Ellen. *Political Opinion in Massachusetts during Civil War and Reconstruction*. New York: Columbia Univ., 1916.

Waring, George E., Jr. *Whip and Spur*. New York: Doubleday and McClure, 1897.

Warner, Ezra J. *Generals in Blue*. Baton Rouge, La.: Louisiana State Univ. Press, 1964.

Whitman, William E. S., and Charles H. True. *Maine in the War for the Union*. Lewiston, Me.: Nelson Dingley, Jr., 1865.

Wibberley, Leonard Patrick O'Conner. *The Coming of the Green*. New York: Henry Holt, 1958.

Wiley, Bell Irvin. *The Life of Johnny Reb*. Indianapolis: Bobbs-Merrill, 1943.

_____. *The Life of Billy Yank*. Indianapolis: Bobbs-Merrill, 1952.

Winsor, Justin. *The Memorial History of Boston*. 4 vols. Boston: Ticknor, 1881.

Wittke, Carl. *We Who Built America*. New York: Prentice-Hall, 1940.

_____. *Against the Current: The Life of Karl Heinzen*. Chicago: Univ. of Chicago Press, 1945.

_____. *Refugees of Revolution: The German Forty-eighters in America*. Philadelphia: Univ. of Pennsylvania Press, 1952.

_____. *The Irish in America*. Baton Rouge: Louisiana State Univ. Press, 1956.

Zucker, A. E., ed. *The Forty-Eighters: Political Refugees of the German Revolution of 1848*. New York: Columbia Univ. Press, 1950.

## IV. NEWSPAPERS

*Boston Pilot,* 1861–1865.
*Chicago Tribune,* 1861–1865.
*Cincinnati Daily Enquirer,* 1861–1865.
*Cincinnati Daily Gazette,* 1861–1865.
*Daily Missouri Democrat* (St. Louis), 1861.
*Kennebec (Maine) Journal,* 1861–1865.
*Milwaukee Daily Sentinel,* 1861–1865.
*New York Irish-American,* 1861–1865.
*New York Times,* 1861–1865.
*New York Tribune,* 1861–1865.
*Philadelphia Daily Evening Bulletin,* 1862.
*Washington Daily National Intelligencer,* 1861–1865.
*Washington Evening Star,* 1860–1862.

## V. PERIODICALS

*Harper's Weekly Magazine,* 1860–1865.

Anderson, Arlow W. "Lincoln and the Union: A Study of the Editorials of the *Emigraten* and *Faedrelandet.*" *Norwegian-American Studies and Records* 15(1949):85–121.

Angle, Paul M. "1861: Chicago Goes to War." *Chicago History* 6(Spring 1961):65–76.

Bakshian, Aram. "Foreign Adventurers in the American Revolution." *History Today,* Mar. 1971, 187–97.

Barnett, James. "August Willich, Soldier Extraordinary." *Cincinnati Historical Society Bulletin* 20(Jan. 1962):60–74.

_____. "Crime and No Punishment: The Death of Robert L. McCook." *Cincinnati Historical Society Bulletin* 22(1964):29–37.

_____. "The Vilification of Augustus Willich." *Cincinnati Historical Society Bulletin* 24(Jan. 1966):29–40.

_____. "Willich's Thirty-Second Indiana Volunteers." *Cincinnati Historical Society Bulletin* 37(Spring 1979):49–70.

Barnett, James, ed. "Some Civil War Letters of John Lycurgus Barnett." *Indiana Magazine of History* 37(June 1941):162–73.

Baum, Dale. "The 'Irish Vote' and Party Politics in Massachusetts, 1860–1876." *Civil War History* 26(June 1980):117–41.

Beaudot, William J. K. "A Milwaukee Immigrant In the Civil War." *Milwaukee History* 7(1984):18–28.

Belfiglio, Valentino J. "Italians and the American Civil War." *Italian Americana* 4(Spring-Summer 1978):163–75.

Blegen, Theodore C. "Colonel Hans Christian Heg." *Wisconsin Magazine of History* 4(1920–1921):143–57.

Brill, Ruth. "Cincinnati's 'Poet-Warrior': William Haines Lytle." *Historical and Philosophical Society of Ohio Bulletin* 21(July 1963):188–201.

Burton, William L. "Indiana's Ethnic Regiments." *Journal of Popular Culture* 14(Fall 1980):229–40.

_____. "Title Deed to America: Union Ethnic Regiments in the Civil War." *Proceedings of the American Philosophical Society* 124(Dec. 1980):455–63.

_____. "Irish Regiments in the Union Army: The Massachusetts Experience." *Historical Journal of Massachusetts* 11(June 1983):104–19.

Chrobot, Leonard F. "The New Ethnicity in America: Toward Cultural and Human Resources." *Indiana History Bulletin* 55(May 1978):62–68.

Conzen, Kathleen Neils. "Immigrants, Immigrant Neighborhoods, and Ethnic Identity: Historical Issues." *Journal of American History* 66(Dec. 1979):603–15.

Covington, James W. "The Camp Jackson Affair." *Missouri Historical Review* 55(Dec. 1960):197–212.

Cox, Jacob Dolson. "Why the Men of '61 Fought for the Union." *Atlantic Monthly,* Mar. 1892, 382–94.

Cunz, Dieter, ed. "Civil War Letters of a German Immigrant." *American-German Review* 11(Oct. 1944):30–33.

Current, Richard N. "The 'New Ethnicity' and American History: Wisconsin as a Test Case." *History Teacher* 15(Nov. 1981):43–55.

Delaney, Norman C. "Letters of a Maine Soldier Boy." *Civil War History* 5(1963):45–61.

Dorpalen, Andreas. "The German Element and the Issues of the Civil War." *Mississippi Valley Historical Review* 29(June 1942):55–76.

Doyle, James M. "The Diary of James M. Doyle." *Mid-America* 20(1938):273–83.

Elkinton, Howard. "Ferdinand Jacob Lindheimer: Botanist in Early Texas." *American-German Review* 12(Dec. 1945):17–20.

_____. "George Engelmann: Greatly Interested in Plants." *American-German Review* 13(Aug. 1946):16–21.

Farr, Clifford B. "The Civil War Correspondence of Dr. Thomas S. Kirkbride." *Pennsylvania Magazine of History and Biography* 83(Jan. 1959):74–89.

"A Fat Dutchman's Opinion on the Civil War." *Cincinnati Historical Society Bulletin* 23(1965):188–90.

Fish, Carl. "Back to Peace in 1865." *American Historical Review* 24(Apr. 1919):435–43.

Fleming, Doris, ed. "Letters From a Canadian Recruit in the Union Army." *Tennessee Historical Quarterly* 16(1957):159–66.

George, Joseph, Jr. "Philadelphia *Catholic Herald:* The Civil War Years." *Pennsylvania Magazine of History and Biography* 103(Apr. 1979):196–221.

Glazer, Nathan. "The Ethnic Factor." *Encounter,* July 1981, 6–15.

Gleason, Philip. "Identifying Identity: A Semantic History." *Journal of American History* 69(Mar. 1983):910–31.

Goodell, Robert C., and P. A. M. Taylor. "A German Immigrant in the Union Army: Selected Letters of Valentin Bechler." *Journal of American Studies* 4(Feb. 1971):145–62.

Gray, Malcolm. "Scottish Emigration: The Social Impact of Agrarian Change in the Rural Lowlands, 1775–1875." *Perspectives in American History* 7(1973):95–175.

Handlin, Oscar, and Mary F. Handlin. "The New History and the Ethnic Factor in American Life." *Perspectives in American History* 4(1970):5–24.

Harshman, Peter M. "A Community Portrait: Over-the-Rhine, 1860." *Cincinnati Historical Society Bulletin* 40(Spring 1982):63–72.

Harsted, Peter T. "A Civil War Medical Examiner: The Report of Dr. Horace O. Crane." *Wisconsin Magazine of History* 48(Spring 1965):222–31.

Hernon, Joseph M., Jr. "The Irish Nationalists and Southern Secession." *Civil War History* 12(Mar. 1966):43–53.

Hess, Earl J. "Sigel's Resignation: A Study in German-Americanism and the Civil War." *Civil War History* 26(Mar. 1980):5–17.

_____. "The 12th Missouri Infantry: A Socio-Military Profile of a Union Regiment." *Missouri Historical Review* 76(Oct. 1981):53–77.

Higham, John. "Integrating America: The Problem of Assimilation in the Nineteenth Century." *Journal of American Ethnic History* 1(Fall 1981):7–25.

Holt, Michael F. "The Politics of Impatience: The Origins of Know-Nothingism." *Journal of American History* 60(Sept. 1973):309–31.

Horowitz, Murray M. "Ethnicity and Command: The Civil War Experience." *Military Affairs* 42(Dec. 1978):182–89.

Jones, Paul. "The Irish Brigade at Fredericksburg." *Catholic Digest,* Jan. 1963, 105–10.

Kaiser, Leo F., ed. "Letters from the Front." *Illinois State Historical Journal* 56(Summer 1963):150–64.

Kamphoefner, Walter D. "St. Louis Germans and the Republican Party, 1848–1860." *Mid-America* 57(Apr. 1975):69–88.

Keil, Hartmut, ed. "A German Farmer Views Wisconsin, 1851–1863." *Wisconsin Magazine of History* 62(Winter 1978–1979):128–43.

Kirkpatrick, Arthur Roy. "Missouri on the Eve of the Civil War." *Missouri Historical Review* 55(Oct. 1960):99–108.

———. "Missouri in the Early Months of the Civil War." *Missouri Historical Review* 55(Apr. 1961):235–66.

Köllman, Wolfgang, and Peter Marschalck. "German Emigration to the United States," Trans. Thomas C. Childers. *Perspectives in American History* 7(1973):499–554.

Lang, Elfrieda. "The Germans of Dubois County, Their Newspapers, Their Politics, and Their Part in the Civil War." *Indiana Magazine of History* 47(Sept. 1946):229–48.

Larsen, Lawrence H. "Draft Riot in Wisconsin, 1862." *Civil War History* 7(Dec. 1961):421–27.

Levine, Peter. "Draft Evasion in the North during the Civil War, 1863–1865." *Journal of American History* 67(Mar. 1981):816–34.

Longacre, Edward T. "The Most Inept Regiment of the Civil War," *Civil War Times Illustrated,* Nov. 1969, 4–7.

McAvoy, Thomas T. "Peter Paul Cooney, Chaplain of Indiana's Irish Regiment." *American-Irish Historical Society Journal* 30(1932):97–102.

———, ed. "The War Letters of Father Peter Paul Cooney of the Congregation of the Holy Cross." *Records of American Catholic Historical Society of Philadelphia* 44(1933):47–69, 151–69, 220–37.

McCormack, John F., Jr. "Never Were Men So Brave," *Civil War Times Illustrated,* Apr. 1969, 36–44.

MacDonagh, Oliver. "The Irish Famine Emigration to the United States." *Perspectives in American History* 10(1976):357–446.

McDonald, Forrest, and Ellen Shapiro McDonald. "The Ethnic Origins of the American People, 1790." *William and Mary Quarterly* 37(1980):179–99.

McNeill, William H. "Mythistory, or Truth, Myth, History, and Historians," *American Historical Review* 90(Feb.1986):1–10.

Man, Albon P., Jr. "The Irish in New York in the Early Eighteen Sixties," *Irish Historical Studies* 7(Sept. 1950):87–108.

Marraro, Howard R. "Lincoln's Italian Volunteers from New York." *New York History* 24(Jan. 1943):56–67.

Mathias, Charles M., Jr. "Ethnic Groups and Foreign Policy." *Foreign Affairs* 59(Summer 1981):975–98.

Maul, David T. "Five Butternut Yankees." *Illinois State Historical Society Journal* 56(Summer 1963):177–92.

Miller, Kerby A. "Emigrants and Exiles: Irish Culture and Irish Emigration to North America, 1790–1922." *Irish Historical Studies* 22(Sept. 1980):97–125.

Moore, R. Laurence. "Insiders and Outsiders in American Historical Narrative and American History." *American Historical Review* 87(Apr. 1982):390–412.

Niven, Alexander C. "The Role of the German Volunteers in St. Louis, 1861." *American-German Review* 28(Feb.–Mar. 1962):29–30.

O'Danachair, Caoimhin. "A Soldier's Letters Home, 1863–74." *Irish Sword* 3(Summer 1957):57–64.

Page, Thomas Walker. "The Distribution of Immigrants in the United States Before 1870." *Journal of Political Economy* 20(July 1912):676–94.

———. "Some Economic Aspects of Immigration Before 1870: Part I." *Journal of Political Economy* 20(Dec. 1912):1011–28.

Pessen, Edward. "How Different from Each Other Were the Antebellum North and South?" *American Historical Review* 85(Dec. 1980):1119–49.

_____. "Social Structure and Politics in American History." *American Historical Review* 87(Dec. 1982):1290–1325.

Peterson, Robert L., and John A. Hudson, "Foreign Recruitment for Union Forces." *Civil War History* 7(June 1861):176–89.

Petty, A. Milburn. "History of the 37th Regiment, New York Volunteers." *American Irish Historical Society Journal* 30(1932):101–24.

Purcell, Richard J. "Ireland and the American Civil War." *Catholic World* 115(1922):72–84.

Raeuber, Charles A. "A Swiss Regiment in the American Civil War." *Swiss Review of World Affairs* 13(1963):11–14.

Raphelson, Alfred C. "Alexander Schimmelfennig, a German-American Campaigner in the Civil War." *Pennsylvania Magazine of History and Biography* 87(Apr. 1963):156–81.

Rappaport, Armin. "The Replacement System during the Civil War." *Military Affairs* 15(Summer 1951):95–106.

Reynolds, Alice. "Friedrich Hecker." *American-German Review* 13(Apr. 1946):4–7.

Riach, Douglas C. "Daniel O'Connell and American Anti-slavery." *Irish Historical Studies* 20(Mar. 1976):3–25.

Rodabaugh, James H. "The Fighting McCooks." *Civil War History* 3(1957):287–90.

Rosborough, Melanie R. "One Hundred Years Ago: The F L Soldier." *South Atlantic Bulletin* 30(Mar. 1965):8–11.

Ruegger, Edward. "Five Weeks of My Army Life." *Wisconsin Magazine of History* 37(1954):163–68.

Sarna, Jonathan D. "From Immigrants to Ethnics: Toward a New Theory of 'Ethnicization.'" *Ethnicity* 5(1978):370–78.

Schafer, Joseph. "Who Elected Lincoln?" *American Historical Review* 47(Oct. 1941):51–63.

Schlicher, J. J. "Bernhard Domschke." *Wisconsin Magazine of History* 29(1945–1946):319–32.

Smith, Harold F. "Mulligan and the Irish Brigade." *Journal of the Illinois State Historical Society* 56(Summer 1963):164–76.

Snyder, Charles M. "A Teen-Age G. I. in the Civil War." *New York History* 35(Jan. 1954):14–31.

_____. "Robert Oliver, Jr., and the Oswego County Regiment." *New York History* 38(July 1957):276–93.

Starr, Stephen Z. "The Grand Old Regiment." *Wisconsin Magazine of History* 48(Autumn 1964):21–31.

_____. "The Third Ohio Volunteer Cavalry: A View from the Inside." *Ohio History* 85(Autumn 1976):306–18.

Stein, Howard F. "The White Ethnic Movement, Pan-ism, and the Restoration of Early Symbiosis: The Psychohistory of a Group Fantasy." *Journal of Psychohistory* 6(Winter 1979):319–59.

Stewart, Charles D. "A Bachelor General." *Wisconsin Magazine of History* 17(1933):131–54.

Swierenga, Robert P. "The Ethnic Voter and the First Lincoln Election." *Civil War History* 11(Mar. 1965):27–43.

Sylvester, Lorna Lutes, ed. "The Civil War Letters of Charles Harding Cox." *Indiana Magazine of History* 48(Mar. 1972):24–78.

Tabachnik, Leonard. "Political Patronage and Ethnic Groups: Foreign-born in the United States Customhouse Service, 1821–1861." *Civil War History* 17(Sept. 1971):222–31.

"Transatlantic Fenianism." *Blackwood's Magazine,* May 1867, 590–606.

Walsh, Francis R. "Who Spoke for Boston's Irish?" *Journal of Ethnic Studies* 10(Fall 1982):21–36.

Wheeler, Gerald E. "D'Epineuil's Zouaves." *Civil War History* 2(1956):93–100.

————, and A. Stuart Pitt. "The 53rd New York: A Zoo-Zoo Tale." *New York History* 37(Oct. 1956):414–31.

Williams, T. Harry. "Badger Colonels and the Civil War Officer." *Wisconsin Magazine of History* 47(Autumn 1963):35–46.

Wittke, Carl. "The Ninth Ohio Volunteers." *Ohio Archeological and Historical Quarterly* 35(Apr. 1926):402–17.

Woodward, D. H. "The Civil War of a Pennsylvania Trooper." *Pennsylvania Magazine of History and Biography* 87(Jan. 1963):39–62.

Wright, James E. "The Ethnocultural Model of Voting." *American Behavioral Scientist* 16(May-June 1973):653–74.

Zuckerman, Michael. "Myth and Method: The Current Crisis in American Historical Writing." *History Teacher* 17(Feb. 1984):219–45.

## VI. REPORTS, TRANSACTIONS, PROCEEDINGS, PAPERS

Beinlich, B. A. "The Latin Immigration in Illinois." *Transactions of the Illinois State Historical Society.* Springfield: Illinois State Historical Society, 1910. Pp. 208–14.

Brunchen, Ernest. "The Political Activity of Wisconsin Germans, 1854–60." *Wisconsin State Historical Society Proceedings.* Madison: State Historical Society, 1901. Pp. 190–211.

Burton, William L. "Ethnic Regiments in the Civil War: The Illinois Experience." *Selected Papers in Illinois History.* Springfield: Illinois State Historical Society, 1980. Pp. 31–40.

Gray, Robert A. "The Scotch-Irish in American History." *Transactions of the Illinois State Historical Society.* Springfield: State Historical Library, 1904. Pp. 308–13.

Kuhns, Lester M. "An Army Surgeon's Letters to His Wife." *Proceedings of the Mississippi Valley Historical Association* 7(1914):306–20.

*Tracts Issued by the Loyal Publication Society.* 2 vols. New York: Loyal Publication Society, 1864–65.

Woodburn, James Albert. "Party Politics in Indiana during the Civil War." American Historical Association *Annual Report* 1(1902):223–52.

## VII. UNPUBLISHED MATERIALS AND MISCELLANEOUS

Dayton, Aretas Arnold. "Recruitment and Conscription in Illinois during the Civil War." Ph.D. diss., University of Illinois, 1940.

Drake, Charles D. "Autobiography." Columbia, State Historical Society.

Elliott, Samuel M. *The Highland Brigade.* N.d., n.p. Pamphlet. New York Historical Society.

Ewing, Hugh Boyle. "Autobiography of a Tramp." Columbus, Ohio Historical Society.

Kautz, Craig Lee. "Fodder for Cannon: Immigrant Perceptions of the Civil War." Ph.D. diss., University of Nebraska, 1976.

Mullen, Andrew. "The Struggle for Command." Indianapolis, Indiana Historical Society.

O'Flagherty, Patrick. "The History of the Sixty-Ninth Regiment of the New York State Militia, 1852–1861." Ph.D. diss., Fordham University, 1963.

Olson, Audrey Louise. "St. Louis Germans, 1850–1920: The Nature of an Immigrant Community and Its Relation to the Assimilation Process." Ph.D. diss., University of Kansas, 1970.

Roziene, Frederick A. "Civil War Diary." Photocopy, Western Illinois University Library.

Saalberg, Harvey. "The *Westliche Post* of St. Louis: A Daily Newspaper for German-Americans, 1857–1938." Ph.D. diss., University of Missouri, 1967.

# Index

*Individual regiments are entered in numerical sequence under the heading of the individual state. To find the Ninth Ohio Infantry, for example, look under Ohio regiments, Ninth Infantry.*

Abel, Joseph, 101
*Alabama,* steamer, 178
Allen, B. F., 133
Allen, William A., 15
American Party, 226
*Amistad* trial, 27
Anderson, Robert, 35, 95
Andrew, John Albion: election of, 26; and Massachusetts regiments, 128–134
Angeroth, Charles, 101
Anglo conformity, 223, 225, 228
Annede, Fritz, 109
Antidraft riots: in New York (city), 37, 127; in Wisconsin, 220
Antietam, Battle of, 122–23
Anti-Semitism, 207
*Anzeiger des Westens* (St. Louis), 30, 103
Assimilation, 223–26

Baker, Henry M., 121
Balfe, John, 142
Ballier, John F., 102
Bechler, Valentin, 68
Belleville, Illinois, 3–4, 106–8
Billington, Ray Allen, *Protestant Crusade,* viii
Blair, Francis P., Jr., 31–32, 240n.11; and Camp Jackson Affair, 40–41; and First Missouri Infantry, 103
Blandowski, Constantin; 41–42
Blenker, Louis, 57; background, 8; death, 89; and D'Utassy, 173; and Eighth New York Infantry, 84–86; promotion, 86; and troubles, 86–89
"Blenkered," 111
Bloody Lane, 123
"Bloody Ninth." *See* Connecticut regiments, Ninth Infantry
"Bloody Tenth." *See* Ohio regiments, Tenth Infantry

Boernstein, Henry (Heinrich), 30, 40, 103–4
Bohlen, Bohl, 102
Bohlen, Henry (Heinrich), 99–100, 102
Boston, 12, 25–26, 128. *See also* Massachusetts regiments
*Boston Pilot,* 25–26, 115, 127–28; and abolitionism, 68; opposes Garibaldi Guard, 171; and secession, 37
Boyd, William H., 175
Brady, James T., 23, 190
Brauer, Martin, 97
Brentano, Lorenz, 49
"Brian Boru United Irish Legion." *See* Pennsylvania regiments, 116th Infantry
Bristed, Charles Astor, 51
British Drill Club, 241n.26
Brooks, Charles, 202
Brown, James S., 199
Browning, Orville H., 50
Brownson, Orestes, 133
Bryant, Mary, 190
Bryant, William Cullen, 200
Buegel, John T., 104, 207
Buegger, Edward, 202
Buell, Don Carlos, 73
Bull, Rice C., 60
Bullock, W. W., 132
Bungary, G. W., 116
Burke, John, 123
Burke, Joseph W., 145
Buschbeck, Adolph, 101
Butler, Benjamin, 148
Butler, Charles, 51
Butler, Thaddeus J., 11
Butz, Casper, 24, 49; background, 8; and Hecker regiments, 50, 74–77
Byrne, Richard, 126, 134

Cahill, Thomas W.: background, 13; and Ninth Connecticut Infantry, 147–48

Caledonian Club: Chicago, 164;
    Washington, 163
Caledonian Society, 162
Cameron, Daniel, Jr., 164–65, 190
Cameron, James, 162–63
Cameron, Simon, 73, 113, 162
"Cameron Highlanders." *See* New York
    regiments, Seventy-ninth Infantry
"Cameron Rifles." *See* New York regiments,
    Sixty-eighth Infantry
Camp Jackson Affair (St.Louis), 38–42,
    104
Cass, Thomas: background, 12–13; and
    Ninth Massachusetts Infantry, 128–30
*Catholic Herald* (Philadelphia), 37
Census (1860), 15–16, 236n.2
Chicago, 8, 11, 24. *See also* Illinois
    regiments; St. Patrick's Day
*Chicago Tribune,* 75
Cincinnati, 5, 28–29. *See also* Ohio
    regiments, Ninth Infantry; Ohio
    regiments, Tenth Infantry
Cobham, George A., 175
Cochrane, John, 201–2
Colonels, importance of, 208–9
Columbia Artillery, 12
Columbia Association, 13
Comte de Paris, 70
Connecticut, 26–27; Know-Nothings in, 13.
    *See also* Connecticut regiments; New
    Haven
Connecticut regiments, Ninth Infantry,
    147–48
Conrad, Joseph, 105
Cooney, Peter Paul, 143–45
Corcoran, Michael: background, 10–11;
    death, 119; description, 113–14; and
    Fenians, 113; honored, 183; in
    Philadelphia, 149–50; and Prince of
    Wales Affair, 11, 37; promoted, 116;
    and recruiting, 52–53; and Sixty-ninth
    New York Militia, 10–11, 112–14
"Corcoran Guards," 151
"Corcoran's Irish Legion," 116–17
Cowdin, Robert, 221
Cox, Jacob, 67, 146
Crawshaw, Titus, 68
Crèvecoeur: *Letters from an American
    Farmer,* 221–22
*Criminalzeitung* (New York), 84
Currie, Leonard D. H., 175
Curtin, Andrew G., 33; and Pennsylvania
    regiments, 149

Daly, Charles P., 126, 187

Danes, 167–68
Davis, William, 149
"DeKalb Regiment." *See* New York
    regiments, Forty-first Infantry
Delmonico's, 187
Dennison, William, and Ohio regiments, 97
D'Epineuil, Lionel Jobert, 166, 210
de Trobriand, Philippe Regis, 165–66
*Der Deutsche Pionier* (Boston), 88, 207
d'Ivernois, Gotthilf Bourray, 59–60
Dodge, William E., Jr., 51
Domschcke, Bernard, 109
Donahoe, Patrick, 25, 127–28, 131–32. *See
    also Boston Pilot*
Doran, John L., 151
Douglas, Stephen A., 27, 135
Dowling, William, 149
Drake, Charles D., 41
Duffy, John, 37
Dunne, Dennis, 139
Dunne, Peter Finley, 189
D'Utassy, Frederick George: background,
    59; and Blenker, 89; and Thirty-ninth
    New York Infantry, 169–74
Dyer, Isaac, 151

Egan, H. W., 184
Einstein, Max, 101
Election (1860): in Cincinnati, 29; in
    Illinois, 8, 24; in Indiana, 24–25, 80; in
    Massachusetts, 26; in New York (city),
    23; in Philadelphia, 28; and Schurz, 5
Elliot, Samuel M., 161–63
Emancipation Proclamation, 67, 127; Irish
    reaction to, 152, 186, 248n.76
*Emigranten* (Madison), 20, 167
Engelmann, Adolphus: background, 6; and
    the Forty-third Illinois Infantry, 78–79
Engelmann, Friederich, 6
Engelmann, George, 6, 235n.9
England, John, 200
Enloe, Cynthia H., *Ethnic Soldiers,* 211–12
Ethnic conflict (other countries), vii–viii.
    *See also* Horowitz, Donald L.
Ethnic historiography, 214–16
Ethnic regiment: changes in, 227; defined,
    44
Ewing, Hugh B., 203–4

Farwell, Leonard J., 20
Fenian circles, 70
Fenian Fair (Chicago), 138, 144
Fenians, 9–10, 152–53, 191; in Chicago,
    12; in Indiana, 144; in Massachusetts,

134–35; in New York, 113; in
Philadelphia, 149–50. *See also* St.
Patrick's Day
Ferri Pisani, Camille: describes Union Army
formation, 45; on ethnic prejudice,
205; on recruitment, 55, 68
"Fighting Irish." *See* New York regiments,
Sixty-ninth Infantry
Fire Zouaves, 153
"First Foreign Rifles," 169
First German Regiment of Ohio. *See* Ohio
regiments, Ninth Infantry
"First German Rifles." *See* New York
regiments, Eight Infantry
"First Hecker Jaeger Regiment." *See* Illinois
regiments, Twenty-fourth Infantry
Flood, Hugh, 203
Fort Sumter, 34–35
Forty-Eighters, 3–4, 6–7, 9, 53; in
Cincinnati, 29; in Indiana, 80;
motivation of, 69–70; in St. Louis, 30;
in Wisconsin, 19, 109–10
*Fraedrelandet* (La Crosse, Wis.), 20, 167
Frash, Michael, 83
Fredericksburg, Battle of, 122, 124–25
Free Soilers, 20
Frémont, John C., 73
"Frémont Rifles." *See* New York regiments,
Forty-sixth Infantry
French regiments. *See* New York regiments.
Fifty-third Infantry; New York
regiments, Fifty-fifth Infantry
Fritsch, Frederich Otto, Baron von, 59–60,
91, 100
Frost, Daniel, 136
Fuller, Allen C., 74

Gallagher, Hugh D., 144–45
"Galvanized Yankees," 70
Galway, Thomas Francis, 68
Gamble, Hamilton R., and Missouri
regiments, 103
Gardes Lafourchettes. *See* New York
regiments, Fifty-fifth Infantry
Gardner, Henry J., 12
Garibaldi Guard. *See* New York regiments,
Thirty-ninth Infantry
"Garibaldi Legion," 171
General Order No. 45, 220
German House, 24
Germans, 7–9, 13, 18–20, 37, 39. *See also*
Butz, Casper; Chicago; Cincinnati;
Forty-Eighters; Grays and Greens;
Illinois; Indiana; Kapp, Frederick;
Milwaukee; Philadelphia; Schurz, Carl;
St. Louis

Glazer, Nathan, *Beyond the Melting Pot*,
223–24
Goedeking, Henry, 4, 106
Gordon, Milton M., 223
Grant, Ulysses S, 136, 208
Grays and Greens, 80, 219
Greeley, Horace, 200
Greusel, Nikolas, 9
Grierson, Francis, 38
Griner, Joseph, 60
Griner, Michael, 67
Grinnell, Moses H., 170
Gritzner, M. C., 88
"Guards Lafayette." *See* New York
regiments, Fifty-fifth Militia
Guiney, Patrick R., 130–31
Gurley, John A., 97

Haines, John G., 139
Halleck, Henry Wagner, 142
Halpine, Charles Graham, 185, 187–89
Harding, Chester, Jr., 103
Hartung, Adolph van, 100
Hauser, J. F., 34
Hawkin's Zouaves. *See* New York
regiments, Ninth Infantry
Hecker, Friedrich Karl Franz: background,
3–4; description, 72; enlists, 48; and
Twenty-fourth Illinois Infantry, 70–72;
and Eighty-second Illinois Infantry,
76–77, 242n.18
Heenan, Dennis, 149–50
Heg, Even, 20
Heg, Hans Christian: background, 20–21;
criticizes Germans, 206; death, 168;
and Fifteenth Wisconsin Infantry, 167–
68; and Scandinavians, 54, 68–69
Heinzen, Karl, 88–89, 207
Helmrich, Gustav von, 108
Hesing, Anton C., 49–50
Higham, John, 225–26
"Highlanders." *See* New York regiments,
Seventy-ninth Infantry
Himoe, Stephen, 168–69
Hipp, Charles, 84
Hoburg, Gottlieb, 100
Hoffman, Francis A., 8, 50, 75–76, 235n.15
Horgan, William H., 125
Horowitz, Donald L. *Ethnic Groups in
Conflict*, 217
Hubbard, Edward C., 202–3
Hughes, John J., 116, 142, 211; opposes
ethnic regiments, 120; as "outsider,"
232

Hungarian Legions, 169
Hungarians, 206
Hunter, David, 185

"I Fights Mit Sigel," 111, 184
Illinois, 8; immigrants in, 24
Illinois regiments:
  Ninth Infantry, 106
  Thirteenth Infantry, 202
  Nineteenth Infantry, 208
  Twenty-third Infantry, 55, 133–38
  Twenty-fourth Infantry, 49–50, 71–73,
    76, 206
  Twenty-ninth Infantry, 46–47
  Forty-third Infantry, 77–80
  Sixty-fifth Infantry, 164–65, 250n.10
  Eighty-second Infantry, 76–77, 206, 221
  Ninetieth Infantry, 139–40
  Ninety-first Infantry, 221
*Illinois Staats-Zeitung* (Chicago), 8, 49, 76
Immigrants: major groups, 16–17;
    motivation, 227; in U.S. Army, 43
Indiana, population and politicis, 25
Indiana regiments:
  Thirty-second Infantry, 80–84
  Thirty-fifth Infantry, 140–45, 177
  Sixtieth Infantry, 175
  Sixty-first Infantry, 141–43
*Indianapolis Sentinel,* 47
"Insiders and outsiders," 232
Iowa, 216
Irish, 13, 17–18; in San Francisco, 237n.10.
    *See also* individual cities and states
*Irish American* (New York), 23, 120–23,
    125; anti-Semitism in, 207
Irish Brigade (Confederate), 180
Irish Brigade: Meagher's, 116, 120–27;
    Mulligan's, 136–38
"Irish Legion." *See* Illinois regiments,
    Ninetieth Infantry
Irish nationalism, 9–10, 20, 52–53, 70, 120,
    219. *See also* Fenians
*Irish Patriot* (Boston), 129
"Irish regiment." *See* Wisconsin regiments,
    Seventeenth Infantry
"Irish Rifles." *See* New York regiments,
    Thirty-seventh Infantry

Jackson, Claiborne F., 31–32, 39
Jacobs, Wilhelm, 109
*James Adger,* steamer, 114
Joliat, Francis J., 105, 205

Kämmerling, Gustav, 96–97

Kapp, Friedrich, 23, 50, 53, 100, 177;
    background, 7–8
Kelly, Patrick, 126
Kerrigan, James, 127
Kilpatrick, Hugh Judson, 218
Kimball, Edgar, 119
Kircher, Henry (Heinrick): background, 4;
    and Ninth Illinois Infantry, 106; and
    Twelfth Missouri Infantry, 106–8
Kircher, Joseph, 4
Knobelsdorf, Charles, 49
Know-Nothings, 16; in Connecticut, 26,
    147; failure of, viii, 230–31; in
    Massachusetts, 26, 128, 236n.32; as
    "Outsiders," 233; in Wisconsin, 43
Knox, Joseph, 139
Koerner, Gustave, 4, 8, 48, 52, 74; and the
    Forty-third Illinois Infantry, 77–78
"Koerner Regiment." *See* Illinois regiments,
    Forty-third Infantry
Koltes, John A., 101
Kovats, Captain, 206
Krenz, Conrad, 109
Kuné, Julian, 49; and Twenty-fourth Illinois
    Infantry, 72–73

Laclede Guards, 38
Lane, Harry S., 25
Latin Farmers, 3
Leclerq, Agnes. *See* Salm-Salm, Agnes
Lexington, Battle of, 136
Lieber, Francis, 51
Limberg, George T., 98
Lincoln, Abraham: calls for volunteers, 44;
    and 1860 election, 17, 21, 24, 27, 29; as
    president-elect, 33–34; and Schurz, 4,
    21
*London Daily Telegraph,* 68
Lonn, Ella, *Foreigners in the Union Army
    and Navy,* viii
Louisiana Zouaves, 115
Loyal Publication Society, 51
Loyalty tracts, 126
Lyon, Nathaniel, 40
Lytle, William Haines, 179; and Tenth Ohio
    Infantry, 145–47

McClellan, George G., 123, 163, 169, 210
McClurg, Alexander C., 60
McClusky, John, 151
McCook, Daniel, 94
McCook, John, 94
McCook, Robert L., 50; and Ninth Ohio
    Infantry, 81, 94–96
McCunn, John H., 126

McDowell, Irvin, 115
McIvor, James P., 117–18
McKnight, Charles, 101
McNamara, Michael H., 130
McQuade, James, 131
Maine regiments: Fifteenth Infantry, 151
Mansfield, Joseph, 172–73
Marye's Heights, 124
Massachusetts, 25–26
Massachusetts regiments:
    Ninth Infantry, 128–31, 177
    Eleventh Infantry, 79
    Fifteenth Infantry, 67
    Twenty-sixth Infantry, 148
    Twenty-eighth Infantry, 121, 124, 131–34
    Twenty-ninth Infantry, 132–33
    Thirtieth Infantry, 132
    Thirty-second Infantry, 132
    First Militia, 129, 221
    Fifth Militia, 12
Mather, Thomas, 74
Mattson, Hans, 69
Mauss, August, 75
Meagher, Thomas Francis: background, 9–
    10, 20; death, 126; description, 121; on
    ethnicity, 209–10; honored, 183–84;
    and Irish Brigade, 53, 119–25; and
    Massachusetts regiments, 131, 133;
    satirized, 188
Melting pot, 111, 219, 222–23, 227
Mihalotzy, Géza, 49, 74–76
Miles, D. S., 165
Milwaukee: Germans in, 18–19, 109; and
    Irish regiments, 151; riot in, 199–200
Milwaukee Zouaves, 199
Minnesota, 69
*Mississippi Bl*ätter (St. Louis), 69
Missouri, 30, 103. *See also* St. Louis
Missouri Irish Brigade. *See* Missouri
    regiments, Seventh Infantry
Missouri regiments:
    Fourth Cavalry, 108–109
    First Infantry, 103
    Second Infantry, 103–4
    Third Infantry, 104
    Fifth Infantry, 104
    Seventh Infantry, 151, 202
    Twelfth Infantry, 105–8, 205
    Fifteenth Infantry, 105, 205
Mitchell, Alexander, 200
Mitchell, John, 20
Mitchell, Ormsby M., 73
Moncrief, James, 126
Montgomery Guards, 199
"Montgomery Regiment." *See* Ohio
    regiments, Tenth Infantry
Monteith, William, 132–34

Moor, August, 97–98, 203–4
Moore, Maclelland, 134
Morgan, Edwin D., and New York
    regiments, 59, 112–13, 120, 166
Morton, Oliver P., 25; and Indiana
    regiments, 47, 80, 140–43
Moynihan, Daniel Patrick, *Beyond the
    Melting Pot,* 223–24
Mozart Hall, 21–23
"Mrs. Meagher's Own." *See* New York
    regiments, Eighty-eighth Infantry
Mulholland, St. Clair A., 124, 150–51
Mullen, Bernard F., and Thirty-fifth
    Indiana Infantry, 141–45
Mulligan, James A.: background, 11–13,
    43; death, 137; and Twenty-third
    Illinois Infantry, 135–38
"Mulligan Guards," 151
Mulligan's Brigade. *See* Illinois regiments,
    Twenty-third Infantry
Murphy, Mathew, 132–33
Murphy, Thomas J., 132
Murray, William G., 175

Native American party, 28
Nativism, 201; in Cincinnati, 29; in
    Massachusetts, 12–13; in Philadelphia,
    27–28; in St. Louis, 30–31; in
    Wisconsin, 18–19. *See also* Know-
    Nothings
"Die Neuner." *See* Ohio regiments, Ninth
    Infantry
New England Division, 148
New Ethnics, 224–25
Newhall, George F., 79
New Haven, 27; and Irish regiment, 147–48
New Jersey regiments:
    Third Infantry, 68
    Eighth Infantry, 68
    Twelfth Infantry, 67
New York, German regiments, problems of,
    243n.34
New York (city), 21–23; draft riot in, 200–
    201
*New York Demokrat,* 88
New York regiments:
    Eighth Infantry, 84–92
    Ninth Infantry, 119, 200
    Twentieth Infantry, 177–78
    Twenty-fifth Infantry, 127
    Thirty-seventh Infantry, 126–27
    Thirty-ninth Infantry, 59, 169, 174, 180–
        81
    Forty-first Infantry, 92, 244n.61
    Forty-sixth Infantry, 92, 202
    Fifty-third Infantry, 166, 210

Fifty-fifth Infantry, 68
Sixty-third Infantry, 120, 123
Sixty-eighth Infantry, 59–60
Sixty-ninth Infantry, 119–20, 182–83, 187
Seventy-ninth Infantry, 161–64, 181
Eighty-eighth Infantry, 120–22, 125
123d Infantry, 60
133d Infantry, 175
155th Infantry, 54, 117
170th Infantry, 118
Seventh Militia, 43, 113
Fifty-fifth Militia, 165–66
Sixty-ninth Militia, 11, 112–15
Seventy-fifth Militia, 126
New York Tribune, 88, 116
*Nordlyset* (Muskego, Wis.), 20
Norwegians, 20–21, 167–68
Novak, Michael, *Rise of the Unmeltable
    Ethnics,* 224
Nugent, Marion, 11
Nugent, Robert, 119, 124


O'Brien, Smith, 20
O'Connell, Daniel, 152
O'Gorman, Richard, 189–90
Ohio regiments:
  Third Cavalry, 83
  Third Infantry, 147
  Eighth Infantry, 68
  Ninth Infantry, 50, 56, 80–81, 93–97
  Tenth Infantry 145–47, 178–79
  Thirteenth Infantry, 146
  Twenty-eighth Infantry, 93, 97, 204
  Thirtieth Infantry, 203
  Thirty-seventh Infantry, 93, 98
  Forty-seventh Infantry, 93
  Seventy-fourth Infantry, 93
  106th Infantry, 93
  107th Infantry, 93
  108th Infantry, 93, 98
O'Kane, Dennis, 149
"Old Fifteenth." *See* Maine regiments,
    Fifteeth Infantry
O'Meara, Timothy, 139–40
Opdyke, George, 190
Order of United Americans, 226
O'Ryan, Charles D. B., 135, 139
Osterhaus, Peter J., 30, 105–6, 205
Otto, William H., 80
"Over-the-Rhine," 5, 235n.7
Owen, Joshua T., 148–49
Owen, Richard, 175


Page, John A., 67

Parker, Francis, 132
Pastor, Tony, 184
Partridge, Horace, 182
Patronage, 46–48
Patterson, Robert, 44
"Peep O'Day Boys," 151
Peninsular campaign, 122
Pennsylvania regiments:
  Fifth Cavalry, 103
  Twenty-first Cavalry, 175
  Twenty-seventh Infantry, 101
  Thirty-fifth Infantry, 99
  Sixty-ninth Infantry, 148–49
  Seventy-third Infantry, 101
  Seventy-fourth Infantry, 99
  Seventy-fifth Infantry, 101–2
  Eighty-fourth Infantry, 175
  Ninety-eighth Infantry, 101–3
  111th Infantry, 175
  116th Infantry, 149–51
  Twenty-fourth Militia, 148
Philadelphia, 7, 27–28, 149–50
Phillips, Wendell, 238n.40
Phoenix Brigade, 114
Pluralism, 224
Polish Legion, 169
Poole, John F., 184
Porter, Andrew, 163
Porter, Fitz-John, 130, 153
Porter, Horace, 201–2
Poschner, Frederich, 93
Poull, Jacob, 73
Prentiss, Benjamin M., 73
Price, Sterling, 136
"Private Miles O'Reilly," 185–89


Race, viii
Racism, 52, 201
Raith, Julius, 78
Randall, Alexander W., 36; and Wisconsin
    regiments, 109, 166–67
Reen, Charles, 103
Regiments, organization of, 44, 47–48
Reid, Whitelaw, 123
Repetti, Alexander, 170
*Republikaner* (Cincinnati), 5
Richardson, Israel, 122
Richardson's Division, 123
Rombauer, Theodore, 30
Roosevelt, James A., 51
Rorty, James M., 115
Rowell, Cromwell G., 129
Ruffin, Edmund, 34
Ruggles, Samuel B., 178
Russell, William Howard, 58–59, 122, 170

St. Andrew's Society: in Chicago, 164; in Washington, 163
St. Louis: federal arsenal in, 32, 39–40; Germans in, 30–31, 38–39, 103–4; 239n.18; Irish in, 39. *See also* Camp Jackson Affair
St. Patrick's Day, 189–92
Sala, George Augustus, 68
Salm-Salm, Agnes: background, 89–90; and Eighth New York Infantry, 90–91; on Irish, 252n.20; on recruitment, 54–55
Salm-Salm, Felix zu, 87–91
Salomon, Charles, 109
Salomon, Edward S., 38, 75, 109
Salomon, Fredrich Sigel, 109
"Salomon Guards." *See* Wisconsin regiments, Ninth Infantry
Savage, John, 190
Scandinavian regiments. *See* Wisconsin regiments, Fifteenth Infantry
Scandinavians, 167–69, 206
Scanlan, Michael, 191
Schadt, Otto, 105
Schaefer, Friedrich, 104
Schimmelfennig, Alexander, 56, 60, 211; background, 8; at Gettysburg, 100; and the Seventy-fourth Pennsylvania Infantry, 98–100
Schneider, George, 49–50
Schnitz, Carl, 82–83
Scholes, James, 165
Schouler, William, 128, 132–33
Schurz, Carl: background, 3–5, 7–8, 17, 19, 21, 24; and 1860 election, 30–31; on melting pot, 111, 219, 222; on recruitment, 48; and Schimmelfennig, 99–100; visits Blenker, 85
Schuttner, Nicholas, 40
Scotch-Irish, 216
Scotch regiments. *See* Illinois regiments, Sixty-fifth Infantry; New York regiments, Seventy-ninth Infantry
Scully, Father, 129
Secession, 33–36
"Second Metropolitan Guard." *See* New York regiments, 133d Infantry
"Seventy-fifth Rifles." *See* New York regiments, Thirty-seventh Infantry
Seward, William, 120
*Shamrock,* gunboat, 190–91
Sherman, William T., 83
Shields, James, 70
Shield's Guards, 11
"Sickle's Brigade," 117
Siebuck, I. I., 101
Siebuck, Joseph G., 101

Sigel, Franz: background, 8; and Camp Jackson Affair, 40; and Eighty-second Illinois Infantry, 77; and ethnicity, 211; promotion, 104; and Third Missouri Infantry 104
Smith, Charles F., 205
Smyth, Thomas, 126
Snowhook, William, and the "Irish Legion," 139
Soldiers of fortune, 58–59, 102
Sons of America, 226
Sowell, Thomas, *Ethnic America,* 212
Spanish Legions, 169
"Spinola's Brigade," 117
*Staats Anzeiger* (Springfield, Ill.), 24
Stahel, Julius, 92
Stallo, Johann Bernhard: background, 5–6; and Ninth Ohio Infantry, 80–81; reacts to secession, 36, 50
Stanton, Edwin M., 59, 100, 142
Stein, Howard F., on ethnicity, 225
Steinberg, Stephen, on ethnic conflict, 225
Stephens, Mrs. A. H., 170
Stephens, James, 9–10
"Steuben" artillery, 80
Stevens, Isaac, 134, 163
Stone Wall, 124–25
Strong, Mrs. Charles E., 178
Strother, Davis Hunter, 123
Struve, Gustave, 9; and Eighth New York Infantry, 87–88
Sunken Road, 123
Swedes, 69, 167–68
Swiss, 105
"Swiss Regiment." *See* Missouri regiments, Fifteenth Infantry

Tafel, Gustav, 81
Tammany Hall, 22–23
Thomas, George, 97
*Times* (London). *See* Russell, William Howard
Tinelli, L. W., 169, 171
Treanor, B. S., 129, 131–33
Tremont Hotel, 189–90
Turchin, John Basil, 208
Turner, James B., 121–22, 207
Turners: in Cincinnati, 3, 36, 50; in Indiana, 25; in St. Louis, 30–32, 41
Tweed Ring, 22
Tweed, William Marcy, 22

Union meeting: at Cooper Institute, 23; in New York, 36; in St. Louis, 31

"United Turner Rifles." *See* New York regiments, Twentieth Infantry

Vandor, Joseph, 109
Verandah Hall, 31
Villard, Henry: and Blenker, 85; and D'Utassy, 170; and Meagher, 122, 125
*Vivandiére,* 171
von Gilsa, Leopold, 92
von Rosa, Rudolph, 92
von Tebra, Heinrich, 83

Wagner, William, 75, 206
Walker, John C., 47; and Thirty-fifth Indiana Infantry, 140–42
Wallace, Lew, 81–82
Walter, George H.,36
Wangelin, Hugo von, 105–6, 108
Waring, George E., Jr., 108, 171
Washington, D.C., 85–87, 114–15, 171–72
*Washington Evening Star,* 88
Washington Guards: New Haven, 13; St. Louis, 38
Weber, Max, 177
Weed, Thurlow, 113
Weid, Ivar A., 206
Welles, George D., 129–30
*Westliche Post* (St. Louis), 215
"Wide Awakes," 31–32
"Wild Geese," 136
"Wild Irish Regiment." *See* New York regiments, 155th Infantry
Willard Hotel, 59
Willich, Augustus: background, 5–6;

description, 82; and Thirty-second Indiana Infantry, 80–82; and Ninth Ohio Infantry, 50, 80–81, 94–95; retirement, 84
Wilstach, Charles, 93
Wilstach regiment. *See* Ohio regiments, Forty-seventh Infantry
Winchester, Battle of, 179–80
Winkler, F. C., 109
Winterbotham, John R., 191; and recruiting the Irish, 54, 117, 203
Wisconsin, ethnic politics in, 4, 18–21
*Wisconsin Demokrat* (Milwaukee), 19
Wisconsin regiments:
  Sixth Infantry, 221
  Ninth Infantry, 109, 202
  Fifteenth Infantry, 56, 166–68
  Seventeenth Infantry, 151, 221
  Twenty-sixth Infantry, 109
  Twenty-seventh Infantry, 109
  Thirty-fourth Infantry, 109
  Fifth Militia, 109
  Seventh Militia, 109
Wood, Fernando, 21–22
Woodruff, Lewis P., 126
Woulfe, Maurice, 126

Xenophobia. *See* Know-Nothings; Nativism

Yates, Richard, 8, 40; and Illinois regiments, 46–47, 49, 74, 135, 139–40, 164–65; and Salm-Salm Agnes, 91

Zangwill, Israel, 222